Sir John Macdonell

A Survey of Political Economy

Sir John Macdonell

A Survey of Political Economy

ISBN/EAN: 9783337073312

Printed in Europe, USA, Canada, Australia, Japan

Cover: Foto ©Suzi / pixelio.de

More available books at **www.hansebooks.com**

A SURVEY

OF

POLITICAL ECONOMY

BY

JOHN MACDONELL, M.A.

EDINBURGH

EDMONSTON AND DOUGLAS

1871

ʹ PREFACE.

———◆———

THIS Preface is no piece of formality, seeing I have an apology to make.

Many writers possess some pretext for severely blaming their predecessors, and thereby secure to themselves a hearing. I have no such pretext. The works of John Stuart Mill, greatest of Economists, Adam Smith not excepted, of Chevalier, of Roscher, and of many others who might fitly be named in their company, are, each in his way, admirable; and I here freely acknowledge the very great obligations which I owed to them in preparing this little book.

Many writers are able to boast that they have set forth their science as it will always be. I can make no such boast, for while I write Political Economy changes. My apology for essaying, in these circumstances, such a task as is implied in the title "A Survey of Political Economy," rests on the possibility of this modest work turning attention to others more exhaustive, on the absence of any book conceived on the same plan, and on an intense desire, which is not of yesterday, to see Political Economy divested of many fallacies, not the less false because sometimes harsh and degrading.

The following pages are based on a series of articles which I contributed to the *Scotsman* newspaper.

J. M.

AUGUST 22, 1871.

CONTENTS.

CHAPTER I.

THE subject of this book is Wealth. At the outset it behoves us to take a general survey of the road on which we are to travel. This survey will be to the tyro in Political Economy what a map of the world is to a person who begins the study of geography. From one position the whole world may be viewed as an immense storehouse, which mankind keeps laboriously filling—a domestic establishment with about 1,200,000,000 inmates—a joint-stock company composed of some 200,000,000 shareholders, with an unknown capital. Seen from the point where we now stand, the sum of history is an effort to fill this granary ever fuller, to increase the income of this establishment, and to work to better advantage the race's concession of many millions of square miles. One generation, rude, ignorant, and lazy as only savages are, disappears, having made a scanty addition to the existing stock of wealth. Another comes with more knowledge, and more of the virtues that lead to and foster industry, and departs with the heap of wealth, and knowledge fusible into wealth, much increased. A third, still more industrious or skilled, and labouring, it may be, in the wake of some momentous discovery or invention, such as that of the power-loom or the steam-engine, reaps an unexampled harvest. It may be that there then come thriftless generations, or those addicted to war ; and, fallen on evil days, industry may go backwards. Even arts may perish : the Renaissance was literally the birth of certain arts that had been familiar to antiquity. But, taking stock at long intervals, and eliminating transient refluxes, we shall discern a progress in wealth, slow, local, and unsteady at first, but by and by universal and quickening. What is the result? Marvellous in the extreme. From little things men have attained to great. Only a few thousand years ago all of us seem to have roamed as outdoor paupers

B

over a miserable planet. The effects of primitive man, or, to speak more correctly, of man as primitive as we know him by history or archæology, if put up to auction, would now fetch only a few pounds; to-day the wealth of the race is incalculable.

The outlines of the story of this progress we shall have briefly to relate. As regards the two great divisions of Political Economy—the production and distribution of wealth—the scientific and historical orders of exposition coincide. The one order begins with the simplest modes of producing and distributing wealth, and then passes to the more complex; and it was thus that men proceeded. Each chapter of a work on Political Economy ought, therefore, to be a new chapter, the picture of a new era, in the great industrial history, whose first page tells how man made to himself a rude tool of a gnawed bone or sharp stone, and whose last will tell—who shall say what? Sometimes we may be compelled to deviate from this plan; but these deviations ought to be few.

Into this exposition it will be well to guard against introducing needless hypotheses. Past errors serve as beacons to warn one not to mingle facts and conjectures. It will be well to forbear giving countenance to the too prevalent suspicion that Political Economy is a spurious science, which attempts to arrive at correct theories by a shorter method than examining facts, and through much fluent talk about "the early ages of society," or "primitive man," respecting whom we are in almost total darkness, not clearly knowing whether he was, as Hobbes alleges, perpetually making war, or, as Rousseau alleges, an ignorant and naked, but virtuous, well-bred, and courageous person of limited means and simple tastes, or, as Whately will have him to be, acquainted with some of the arts and a few of the sciences. It would be well for the economist not to go so far back in his survey as primitive times, but only so far as written documents or trustworthy inferences carry him—say, to the state of society pictured to us in the earlier books of the Bible, or in the Homeric poems. And what do we there see? What is the economical condition depicted? Little wealth, and that little obtained by the simplest means. The complexity and vastness of production which we call manufacturing are unknown; save in the case of half-a-dozen articles of food and dress, the

rudiments of it do not appear. Even agriculture is but beginning. Property in land is rudely defined—so rudely that perhaps the only way to obtain a conception of it is to transfer to
land the present comparatively rude and fragmentary notions of
ownership over the sea. Individual ownership is almost unknown ; the *gens*, or rather, perhaps, the family, is the unit,
and the head of the family has, in general, only a life interest
in its property. Of capital there is little. The net income,
if there be any, is insignificant. Exchange is almost unknown.
Every family lives in miserable self-sufficiency. Its wants are
few ; the adjoining forest, river, and plain, satisfy them all.
This state of society—if that can be called a society whose
peculiarity is deplorable absence of intercourse, where kinsmen
are the only *socii*, and which does not rival the complexity of a
hive—has been termed natural economy. The first step out of
it is by an increase of the circulating capital, due, perhaps,
most frequently to the introduction or abundance of slave labour.
With this increase leisure comes to a few, and soon the offspring of leisure—arts, luxury, civilisation. Exchange beginning to spread, especially on frontiers, commerce, internal and
international, a considerable increase in the division of labour,
agriculture no longer entirely rudimentary—these are the accompaniments of the state of society which emerges from that of
natural economy ; they are the characteristics, for example, of
those civilisations which edged the Mediterranean with cities
that dominated over the Old World, and which, being dead,
yet live and rule over us in their literature, and sculpture, and
architecture, and those still older civilisations of India, Peru,
and Mexico, which were vast, one cannot doubt, in their reality,
and which seem still vaster and more imposing, looming as
they do through the magnifying mists of tradition and un-
verified report. To-day, and at no great distance from us, we
come upon this economical *régime*. It is not extinct. Antiquity ends only when men cease to live like the ancients ; so
understanding antiquity, we see ancients near our shores, as we
see savages at our doors. Industrial progress is not an unin-
terrupted advance of all nations marching abreast. Nature has
in truth done to the historian much as she has done to the
geologist. Over the surface of the earth stratum has not been
piled on stratum so that the old deposits are buried deep and
eternally out of knowledge ; but here the oolite comes to the

surface, and here again the coal-measures, and the silurian sandstones and limestones are spread out to view; while by a winding stair, as it were, the geologist descends from the roof of drift to earth's flooring, and is able to read secrets which the miner never could have reached, and which no single convulsion could have laid bare. So is it with the historian. Finding a society similar to one that has perished, he compares his observations with records; he notes what is essential and accidental; one society is used as a key to another; and the living are made the interpreters and resuscitators of the dead. With its different civilisation, its institutions of yesterday and antiquity huddled alongside of each other, the world is thus a great historical museum; and samples of every stage in industry lie on its shelves.

A vast step in industrial progress is the extensive use of tools and machinery. Not that they were ever unknown; man without tools and machines is as purely a creature of abstraction as souls without bodies. By the fact that all mythologies are full of inventors, promoted to the rank of deities—for deification was the reward, patent, or royalty of the ancient inventor—we are reminded of the antiquity of tools; but machines, though known, were rude and rare; and in antiquity slaves held the place which machinery now holds. The use of machines common, it remained only to create various other kinds of fixed capital, to extend credit, to develop foreign trade, to increase production on a large scale, and to carry out complete division of labour, in order to produce the marvellous complexity, vastness, and efficiency of modern industry.

Of all its characteristics, none is more striking than the degree to which community of interest and dependence between people far removed from each other by time and space are created. Each city or country, once isolated as a snail within its shell, is now an organ of a vast body, whose health is dependent on that of every other component. Men are forced to be the helpmates of one another. In the pursuit of riches from pure egoism, you are anxiously labouring for your fellows. No one works alone. To quote Balzac, the untranslatable, "We have *des produits*—we have no longer *œuvres*." No generation has to work for itself alone—each is a partner, and a function is assigned to each. Modern industry, while warring against socialism and communism, seems to have absorbed much of their teaching—men are obliged to be social-istic. Such an event as the American Civil War strikingly illustrates how the threads of material interests are prolonged and interlaced. Primarily affecting only America, that event was felt keenly in Lancashire, among German cotton-spinners, by the Swiss silk-trade, and even by the Silesian tobacco-trade. Each of us has, in consequence of this solidarity, thousands of unknown servants to go his errands, and in distant places fulfil his multifarious desires. However poor and obscure a man may be, he has, and had before his birth, people so numerous and powerful working such work for him as no Cæsar of them all or Charlemagne could have obtained by the aid of thousands of servants. You may be a subordinate; but, however humble you are, thousands, whose names you will never know and who will never know yours, are labouring for you in lands that are to you but shadowy names ; so that, if retinues of servants and far-stretching power, and command over past and distant people, are the attributes of the rich, you, poor though you may count yourself, are among the rich of the earth. However mean may have been your lot, and however bleak the prospect upon which you look out, it will be strange if you die before you consume, in virtue of this solidarity, articles so costly, numer-ous, and difficult of attainment, that, though your strength and your years had been multiplied a thousandfold, you could not have obtained them ; and if length of life be measured by variety of experiences, you will not die till you have many times outlived the oldest of the patriarchs, for you will have crammed into your life the varied experiences of thousands of men earlier born. Thus, in sober truth, each one of us is an heir.

It requires, perhaps, much philosophy and culture to be filled with unaffected wonder at that which we every day behold. In time a crust of commonplace grows over things, a film of indifference forms on our eyes, and we have raptures only for what is remote. Yet I think that the sight of men, acting from motives of selfishness in pursuit of their own aggrandisement, and working out results such as enlightened unselfishness would approve, ought to inspire the most stolid with a little wonder. At the same time, wonder is not the only feeling proper. That somewhat barren species of philosophy which makes constant demands on our amazement is not, after all, the best ; there are higher duties than standing with mouth agape. We have looked at the image and read the superscription on one side; turn now to the obverse of the medal. Poverty a big fact—an immense number of men living without enough to keep them in health; a still greater number toiling like cattle in order to obtain somewhat scanty aliment; a large percentage of children dying from deficient nutriment before the age of ten; many men quitting work long before they have fully repaid the capital expended in rearing them; famine not quite unknown; vast waste and destruction of capital, and an unthrifty distributing organisation; pauperism holding its own.* These are a few of the items which damp somewhat one's admiration of past industrial achievements, and make one think that the work to be done is at least as arduous as that accomplished.

Acquaintance with Political Economy will be sure to help men in some degree to overcome the difficulties that still exist. How general is the ignorance of Political Economy, even among the well educated, every day calls to mind. Nothing more common than to hear men uttering their private vagaries or ideas in the name of science, and declaring that Political Economy teaches such and such, when the truth is that they alone teach it. Mr. Lowe, for example, writes a pamphlet on education, based on the assumption that Political Economy teaches such a law of supply and demand, as no economist ever taught; and he is answered by people who, questioning much of his doctrine, never, or rarely, question this assumption. Or he speaks of the Government monopoly of the telegraphs, and terms this a breach of Political Economy! " Demand and supply," and " the immutable laws" of Political Economy, are perennial fountains of absurdity. How often is *laissez faire*, the modern deification of chance and ignorance, announced as the sum and substance of the teaching of Political Economy! How often is it supposed that this science countenances selfishness and stinginess! And it is not uncommon for people who do a shabby thing to think that Political Economy in some way makes it all right. Bumble, the beadle, who backs up the starving of paupers with a reference to Political Economy, is the type of a class. And yet, the truth is, that there is nothing in the whole science, rightly understood, to forbid the most unsparing generosity, so be it the hand of the giver

* See *Statistical Journal* for March 1866.

is wise as well as liberal; and, in fact, it will appear that economical studies supply new and most powerful inducements to encourage the charitable. Many employers look on Political Economy as an apology for low wages and high profits—an unsubsidised organ for persuading the poor to be content with their lot, however wretched, as fixed for them by eternal and immutable laws; and workmen, even intelligent workmen, mutter that Political Economy is a master's invention to prove that the workman is always in the wrong. A huge delusion all this, for there is nothing which comes more prominently to light in Political Economy than the generally beneficial effect of high wages, provided they be steady; and all intelligent economists will be the first to admit that high profits are not the infallible signs of a desirable state of society, but that permanently high wages almost infallibly are. How common, too, to speak harshly or contemptuously of Political Economy because it tells nothing of things with which it has nothing to do! Mr. Carlyle, in the character of the ideal Prime Minister of England, tells us he has read "barrowfuls" of economical works, but, be it respectfully said, he has read too plainly with little understanding, since he rates them for not giving charts of the universe, or sailing directions for the big-coming eternities. Now, Political Economy has little to say of the universe, and is positively dumb about the immensities and big-coming eternities; and he who is curious about them must knock elsewhere to obtain information. But, if everything need not be in everything,—if every book need not resemble an Eastern bazaar, or a village shop, where all wares are sold,—it is unreasonable to condemn the Science of Wealth because it is not every other science, and to accuse it of cruelty because it may not directly enjoin kindness. Mr. Ruskin, an estimable and unwearied calumniator of this science, launches philippics against the "common economist" who does not mix philanthropy with the science; but the strictures are true only if everybody is bound to treat simultaneously of everything, and if division of labour, which has done so much for handicrafts, is to be abandoned in mental labour. I may notice another charge brought against Political Economy:—It is materialistic in its tendency. This is the charge of ignorance. Political Economy is an emphatic reiteration of the vast things which mind has effected. The triumphs of industry as much as the triumphs of literature and abstract science—a cotton-mill or a well-ordered railway system, as much as the *Iliad* or the *Inferno*—speak to us of the resources of human intellect; and one of the first delusions which I shall try to destroy will be the delusion that mere manual labour has been the most important agent in the production of wealth. But if it be materialistic to devote much attention to wealth, Political Economy is materialistic—wealth is the entire theme. And, grand though contempt for it seems to many who have it, and who dimly realise what it is to be poor, few wise men will join in that contempt; for, until hunger, and thirst, and poverty, and corporeal misery, are put out of the world, and the door closed on these, our primal enemies, wealth, its production, and its distribution, will be, in any wise scheme of things, among the really grandest themes for meditation. Prudence and duty tell each one of us to pursue necessaries in the first place, and superfluities afterwards; and so long as there continues unsatisfied in any great degree an elementary want—such as hunger—the duty which lies to hand is the appeasing of this want. Materialistic though the sentiment sound, it is probably of far greater consequence at the present moment to discover how every family may get meat three times a week, than to solve the problem of the origin of evil—a solution of the problem how evil got here would probably not lessen the amount of it, and might perplex us still more; and a solution of the other problem would infinitesimally diminish the amount of evil. The history of hunger must long be a large segment of the history of the race. So much one may admit without falling into the error of regarding the accumulation of wealth as synonymous with the prosperity of society; for wealth is but a means to an end, and that end the happiness of us all. And should accumulation be due to the fact that men live as dollar-hunters, and should it be accompanied with gross inequalities in the distribution of it, wealth serves only to turn us from and to defeat this end.

I have mentioned the prevalent ignorance of Political Economy. That should suffice to show the need of instruction. But look around, and in the circumstances of our time will be discerned very peculiar reasons for studying it. Industry, once the synonym of peace, is, both here and abroad, a great camp. Almost every trade is either at war or preparing for it; and

much capital, which might have shed abundance, is lost as
entirely as if it had been cast into the sea.   Strikes are common,
and good feeling between employers and employed, once general,
is now almost exceptional.   There is mutiny in the army of
industry.   Its captains have lost command.   To any country
this would be serious, but to this country, which, as we are
warned by the advances made abroad, the tendency towards
an equalisation of the rates of discount on the various Bourses,
the rise of great commercial unions such as the Zollverein, and
the multiplication of direct steam navigation routes, has reached
what may prove a period of transition, and which has reared a
highly artificial structure of wealth, liable to be shaken by small
accidents, this mutiny is most serious and dangerous.   Of our
pre-eminence in wealth it is well to reflect that we have no entail.
Roughly speaking, we are rich because of our abundance of
skilled and trustworthy labour and of capital—two things not to
be chained to the soil.   Let workmen demand exorbitant terms
of capitalists, and it may be they will transfer their capital,
mobilised as it now is, to other countries ; let capitalists not
answer the fair demands of workmen, and the best of them
may migrate with ease to our half-peopled colonies, or to the
United States.   The histories of many other commercial States
—of Holland in particular—remain to warn us.   Placed like
us in a country naturally poor, a race of frugal seamen, fishers,
and merchants, reared like us an artificial structure of wealth
within their sea-menaced land.   In the middle of the sixteenth
century Guicciardini, though fresh from Florence and Venice, can
find in Holland matter for surprise ; in the middle of the seventeenth century, Amsterdam and Antwerp were among the wealthiest cities in the world; Dutch fleets floated on every known sea
as the carriers of the world; Dutch factories dotted the coasts and
islands of Asia from Balsora to Japan; and for a time there was
no country that could vie in riches with that heap of mud and
sand, that "indigested vomit of the sea."   Partly to the jealousy of the English Parliament and of Colbert, and to the growth
of the commerce of other countries, but still more by reason
of the discouragements given at home to the growth of capital,
and of the inducements to send it abroad, that artificial fabric
tottered ; and so it has come to pass that Holland, once the
mart of the world, the carrier of the nations, is now an agricultural country, with almost a peddling commerce—a warning

that pre-eminence in wealth, such as we possess, is not held on a tenure that is proof against the consequences of ignorance and disregard of the conditions of pre-eminence.*

Not that Political Economy alone can lead to a settlement of the questions that disturb industry. Here, as everywhere, more is requisite than a good chart, even if Political Economy were the complete chart. There comes a time when want of knowledge proves less destructive than want of desire to use it, and perhaps in regard to social questions that time has arrived.

* Since writing this I have observed that M. Thiers, in a recent speech, has employed the same comparison to enforce the same lesson; and I take the opportunity of at once escaping the charge of plagiarism, and shielding myself with his authority.

CHAPTER II

WEALTH.

BYRON speaks half of the dismal truth when he says, "Poverty is slavery the world over." The splendid exceptions which we meet show only that certain men of heroic stuff can rise above poverty, not that poverty raises ordinary men ; these it crushes and maims. One of the oldest and noisiest of cants of which this world is full is the cant about the benefits of poverty. Perhaps nobody believes it ; but how ready many of us are to enlarge on the inexpressible blessing of having nothing ! This cant is the cardinal doctrine of asceticism. It is the cry of all the Senecas that ever lived, whether they have come as Roman stoics, preaching in purple and fine linen, and with carefully pointed epigrams, the vanity of riches, or as Puritans, the modern stoics. The gospel of indigence is one of the commonest, most Protean, and abiding misrepresentations of Christianity. Yet an instinct, not to be preached out of existence, impels men to gather wealth, as an instinct impels bees to gather honey. Moralists and preachers notwithstanding, man goes to the mill, or the field, or the sea, as the bee to range over the wild thyme or clover. Surely for grown men it is time to cease talking as if there were affinity between brown bread and any of the cardinal virtues. For observe what wealth implies. How many things are impossibilities without wealth ? Civilisation, and all that it carries in its lap— leisure, knowledge, culture, the fine arts, and, vastly more momentous, the hope of a better lot, for the millions that must now labour on unenlivened by rays of worldly prosperity, happy if they can deaden their desire of that smoothness of life which all of us at some time or other dream of—are possible only with a large accumulation of wealth. Without much of it there is no immunity from famine. Without a certain amount of it men live short lives. Our ancestors, being poorer than we are, lived lives that were on an average shorter than the lives lived now; and if things march as we desire and hope that they will march, our children will live longer than we live. To the increase of wealth we owe in great part political emancipation; to the poverty of the world we owe the very existence of slavery; for, as Aristotle long ago remarked, if the chisel and axe could work of themselves there would be no slaves. And when a country becomes so wealthy as to be able to yoke wind, water, and steam, so that the chisel and axe work of themselves—when a country attains a state in which skilled and versatile labour is in demand, slavery is rendered unremunerative and antiquated—in his own interest the master frees the slave. Arts, in all but the most rudimentary forms, are impossibilities without considerable wealth. They are, as Alfred de Musset says, *fils d'oisiveté*. Though not by any means the sole condition on which depends the rise of literature, though great events and ideas must be fermenting in men's minds before a literature arise, a stock of wealth is essential to the genesis of all kinds of literature, save, perhaps, poetry; and we never find reflective poetry budding until society is settled, and, so to speak, is in easy circumstances. History, as distinguished from humble chronicling, and science, presuppose vast resources—leisure, libraries, costly instruments. As a matter of fact, certain of the experimental sciences can be pursued only by very wealthy persons, or by persons with endowments at their command. Even religions are not independent of wealth. In modern times, at least, they have been propagated with the aid of costly machinery. Missionaries come home every now and then to warn their countrymen of the missions that must be abandoned if money be not forthcoming, and of others that might be planted if liberality were shown. Therefore, though it may be of trivial moment whether this man is wealthier than that, it is of consequence that this age should be wealthier than any former.

Some may think that there is no longer a strong motive for accumulating more wealth; a fairer distribution of what already exists would suffice. To which suggestion the economist must answer, without by any means pledging himself to defend every iota of the present method of distribution, that the world is still poor, and that if all the wealth that exists therein were equally divided among mankind, poverty, instead of being utterly effaced, would be universal. All mankind would be put on short rations. No man would have plenty. It cannot be too strongly impressed on political thinkers that the general state of things, outside a small circle of States, is destitution. Europeans are so familiarised with the sight of abundant crops, rich cities, and other marks of wealth, that they do not bear in mind that poverty is, as it always has been, the normal condition. Even were the riches of a country peculiarly wealthy, such as England or France, equally distributed among its inhabitants, the share of each person would be surprisingly insignificant. Divided equally among the inhabitants of the United Kingdom, its wealth would for a time give every person at most £20 a-year. The annual profits on British capital have been computed at £110,000,000, and this sum divided among 11,000,000 labourers would give £10 to each.* As regards France, M. Chevalier showed by figures that the whole wealth, if equally divided, would give to each sharer an income of about £9 a-year ; and our surprise remains, even after we prune the fact of the exaggeration with which M. Chevalier invests it, through forgetting that the present incomes of adult males have to support them, their wives, and their children. True it is, that if this be so, those that now sit at the foot of the table must be fed with few and wretched scraps. But, passing from this point of view for a moment, we observe that the first effect of an equal distribution of wealth—the crude panacea for social evils of shallow visionaries—would be to make everybody poor, or nearly so. Each would have the miserable satisfaction of knowing that nobody was well off. The next effect, soon making itself felt in famine, or at all events in dearth, would be an almost complete stoppage to the creation of wealth. The disastrous history of societies that have tried an equal division of wealth—all communistic societies—prove, if the thing needed proof, and if a small knowledge of human nature did not suffice to establish, that it is this inequality of riches that is one of the strongest and steadiest motives to industry, the mother of wealth. Equal distribution would have to be maintained by violence ; and, if so, the rights of property would receive such a shock, security in the future would appear so uncertain, that men would hesitate to labour to produce that which they

* Professor Leslie's *Land Systems*, p. 374. The *Economist*, in 1863, estimated our annual savings at £130,000,000 sterling.

might never enjoy. Unless a revolution were effected in their
nature, men would labour little if they knew that their enjoyments would not be proportioned to their exertions ; and if they
saw a competence secured to every one that came into the
world, they would multiply recklessly. The total resources of
the community would in time be diminished, and the recipients
be increased. So that, after an equal division, there would be
the option of starving, or of allowing inequality, with all its
evils, to be re-created.

The great inequality between the rich and the poor of our
country—the terrible gulf between the rich man and the
Lazarus of our day, into which charity pours waggon-loads of
good deeds in vain efforts to fill it up—is viewed with hatred,
partly from a latent feeling that the rich man has appropriated
something which, but for him, the poor man would have enjoyed. And if this feeling were always based on a correct apprehension, hatred would be pardonable, or, at all events, more
pardonable than it is. Now, this feeling is often generated by
a mistake. Those fine houses, and carriages, and pictures by
the best artists, and umbrageous avenues, so cool in summer,
sheltered in winter, and beautiful at all seasons, so enviable in
the eyes of the poor man, far from having been pilfered from
the common heritage of the race, generally owe their existence,
as articles of value, to their owner, or those whose representative he is in law and morality. They are generally the results
of the savings of the owner himself, or those whom he represents, and consequently they are no more enjoyed at the
expense of another than the health of A is enjoyed at the
expense of the health of B. Though to consume articles of
luxury is not the most laudable manner in which to expend
wealth, and though it would have probably been better to
produce something which would permanently augment the
stock of wealth, these houses, carriages, and pictures, are clear
additions to the wealth of society, not subtractions from or
illicit divisions of it. True, inequality of wealth may be carried
so far as to become a serious social evil—it is so carried ; and,
looking at wealth as an instrument for the creation of human
felicity, its accumulation in few hands is to be deplored,
because a man does not grow happy just in proportion as he
grows rich ; and after a certain point, which varies according to
men and circumstances, increase of wealth means increase of

sorrows. There must be some income, which, on an average, yields the greatest enjoyment. Suppose that some Asmodeus of the worlds that are within our breasts found, by gazing therein, that increase of wealth meant increase of happiness until the figure of £400 a-year was reached, but that, after that figure was passed, cares came in numerous troops, and that increase of wealth thereafter only brought disquietude, then it ought to be the object and desire of us all to see as many people as possible with £400 a-year. But it would next be discovered that the best way to create a great many incomes of £400 a-year would be to give every facility for the creation and enjoyment of incomes of £4000, £40,000, or £400,000 a-year. Few might attain these higher figures, but the possibility of attaining them would be found necessary to the general attainment of the lower. They are prizes which spur on the idle and the ambitious. They constitute a natural system of patents, the rewards of unusual skill or industry. They elicit industry, just as the hope of promotion makes the soldier brave. The few who attain to the higher figures will not do so at the expense of the less fortunate; in most circumstances the attending evils will be all their own. Since men have ceased to acquire in any great degree wealth by open force or fraud, inequality of wealth becomes more and more the effect of inequality of merit. No two persons have merited the same prize; therefore, no two obtain it. Only let not the Legislature, by laws of entail or primogeniture, by depriving females of the right of inheritance, or power to earn wages, or retain them when earned, endeavour to increase the inequality. And, as the guardian of the weak, as the protector of the right, let it not permit parents or relatives to exaggerate natural inequality by putting their young sons, daughters, or dependants to work which will render them inefficient workers, and doom them to be miserable hewers of wood and drawers of water. It is impossible to refer here to all the advantages of inequality of distribution in creating differences of character, variety of pursuits, etc.; but it may be observed that inequality of wealth, the natural outcome of allowing men and women to use their talents and opportunities, and consequently not to be prevented unless by injustice and by treating them as slaves, ought to be viewed with less odium when it is seen that it serves as a sort of insurance to society against famine and destitution. Were

this country peopled by a race of small proprietors with modest
and uniform means, one bad effect, however many might be
the good effects—and small properties have very many good
effects—would be a liability to suffer when years of calamity
come round. We are wont to attribute the immunity against
famine enjoyed by modern societies, in cheering contrast to
ancient and mediæval societies, to free trade, which enables us
to go and purchase food in a foreign market when the harvest
fails us at home. But free trade notwithstanding, there is no
purchasing without means; and as small proprietors have,
and can have, only a small surplus available, as they do
not export, and do in reality live much from hand to mouth,
and from week to week, it is to be feared they will not be
able to benefit by the abundance that is to be found abroad.*
Among such a people actual subsistence generally approaches
bare necessaries. They will, when drought comes, or when the
autumn is too rainy, have to suffer starvation under various
names and in various shapes. But, in such a time of need,
a society with a large element of very wealthy people will
have savings to fall back upon; and these savings will procure food, part of which will go to the poor in the form of
wages, or of charity given voluntarily, or through the
machinery of a poor-rate. The immunity from famine long
enjoyed by England and Scotland is ascribable in part to this
cause. The distress in Ireland, chiefly peopled by cottars or
small farmers, and the well-known liability to distress of
Belgium—fostering the famous *mauvais gré* of Belgian history—
are partly ascribable to the absence of it. To reconcile ourselves to this inequality, it is to be observed that, as Bentham
remarks, the greater the fund for enjoyment the greater is the
fund for defence.

It may seem superfluous to explain the nature of wealth, a
word that is in everybody's mouth. Yet we are assured by the
majority of economists that the grossest delusions have been
entertained regarding it. The common teaching of economists
is that some of the wisest of our species—Bacon, Raleigh,
Locke, and Voltaire, for example—taught the wildest and most
pernicious delusions, and that nations, and our own amongst
others, launched into bloody wars, solely from not knowing what

* Some of the aspects of the above questions were cogently stated a few
years ago in the leading columns of the *Pall Mall Gazette*.

wealth was; and to-day there passes current among our merchants, it is said, and among those of us who should be most conversant with wealth, language that indicates ignorance of its nature. Some of these assertions are true. Wealth is not synonymous with money—with pounds, shillings, and pence. These and such-like coins are varieties of wealth. They are the measure, and they themselves are a part, of it. Wealth itself is the sum of all things useful and agreeable that are valued by men. The confusion of wealth with money, gross and incredible though it seems when nakedly stated and stripped of plausibility, possessed, it is said, the cultivated minds of Europe for centuries, led to bloody wars, created hosts of pernicious laws and treaties, and lingers still among us, propagating delusive notions regarding currency and commercial crises. Economists say that this confusion was the foundation of the so-called mercantile system, which once domineered over the trade of every civilised nation, and which to-day is not extinct. Enormous were the consequences which, we are told, came to pass. Viewing wealth as synonymous with gold and silver, legislators, it is said, desired to introduce as much of these metals and to let out as little as possible; and they, therefore, laboured to export a great deal of the goods of their own countries, in order that they might obtain balances in gold or silver, and to import very little of the products of other countries, in order that no balance in money might be due to them. To secure these two ends a vast legal apparatus and vast armies of functionaries were called into being. Laws were passed to prevent, or at all events to obstruct, the entrance of foreign goods into the home market. Others were passed to encourage exportation by bounties, or drawbacks of taxes on articles sent abroad. And to enforce, or rather to attempt to enforce, these laws for smuggling—a profession which successfully eluded or openly defied the law—soldiers, wars, and much fighting were required. To this confusion of money with wealth, of the reality with the shadow, economists trace many of the greatest mistakes in colonial government. We desired to "make most of the money centre in England." Wishing to export all that could be exported, in order to be paid in money, Great Britain, and other European countries possessing colonies, forced them to trade only with the mother countries; and, to take our North American colonies for example, we monopolised their trade,

c

until in our attempt to deprive the colonies of the slight compensation of immunity from imperial taxation, we drove them to revolt, and lost for ever at York Town about a quarter of our empire. Economists do not indeed hold that the mercantile and colonial systems of trade owed their birth, duration, and extension, to no other causes than this error, or that this error was logically carried out in our dealings with foreigners and colonists—to carry it out logically would, economists admit, have been to prove its falsity by the startling absurdity of the consequences to which it committed us, and there were certain excuses for those systems of protectionism and monopoly which no longer exist ; but we are told that one of the causes which originated and maintained these systems was a misconception of wealth. I shall have hereafter to express my disbelief in the existence of the mercantile system. But as it is certainly true that men did and do attach an exorbitant importance to money, I have thought it right to state at the outset the views of most economists on this head. It may be stated that the exaggerated sense of the importance of money appears to-day in the peculiar prominence given to the amount of our exports as compared with our imports, in the undue alarm exhibited in mercantile circles when money is largely exported, in the complaints that France has taken, under the treaty of commerce, less of our goods than we have taken of hers, and that we are consequently, to our great detriment, exporting a balance in gold or silver. "Three-fourths of city men believe that we should export much and import little," said an eminent city man to the author ; and if this belief imply also a belief in the mercantile system, it still flourishes. Lest it may be disbelieved that any man ever seriously maintained that his country was impoverished by sending abroad money and receiving a fair return in merchandise, I shall quote the words of an acute writer, fully acquainted with Political Economy, according to the light of his time. It is Voltaire, treating of the causes of the poverty of France, who speaks, and his words are these :—

"We have to pay to our neighbours £160,000 for one article, and £200,000, or £240,000, for another, in order that we may put into our nose a stinking powder ; coffee, tea, chocolate, cochineal, spices, cost us more than £2,400,000 a-year. All this was unknown in the time of Henri IV., with the exception of spices, the consumption of which was far less. We burn a hundred times more wax candles, and we take more than half of our wax from the foreigner, because we neglect hives. We see a hundred times more diamonds on the ears, necks, and hands of the women of Paris and our great towns than belonged to all the ladies of the Court of Henri IV., including the Queen. For almost all these superfluities we have had to pay money." This reasoning made a profound impression on Voltaire ; anybody who perceives that one kind of wealth, which it would be folly to hoard, was exchanged for another kind of wealth, should be impressed only with its absurdity. And, to prove that the present age is not free from these errors, it may be stated that the French Minister of Finance, in 1856, threatened, in a grave official document, to punish those who destroyed "the general equilibrium of our monetary system" by exporting coin.

From the confusion of money with wealth, or, as I prefer to say, from the exaggerated importance assigned to money, flowed the pernicious maxim that "the profit of one is the loss of another," —a maxim sanctioned by Montaigne, Bacon, and Voltaire, but false notwithstanding. When two or more men play a game of hazard, and one wins, somebody must be out of pocket at the end of the game ; when any farmers leave the market with more money than when they entered it, somebody must leave with less. These obvious facts induced first economists, accustomed to look most intently at one kind of wealth, to say that the same held good of all trade, and that if one nation or person profited by trade, another must be a loser. Hence a fancied antagonism of interest between men and nations. And yet we may easily see that Bacon was wrong. A, a joiner by trade, wants a saw, would give anything for it—certainly would give that spade which, useless to him, lies in the corner of his shop. B, who lives next door, and is a gardener, regrets much that a saw is not a spade, as he has the one article and sorely needs the other. The joiner and gardener talk with each other about their wants ; a bargain is struck ; the spade and saw change owners ; both men are thereby enabled to earn their bread ; and "the profit of one is the loss of neither." In this bargain we see at once the fallacy of the Baconian maxim, and all commerce in miniature.

A very different error to be guarded against is the error of considering the population of a country as necessarily forming part of its wealth. Able-bodied men and women are a country's best wealth, it is often said, and all other riches are not to be compared with an abundance of stout arms. " Every existence," says a living French writer, " is *per se* a blessing." " Every birth increases the living capital of society." This doctrine is frequently met with, and is often vended when emigration or population is under discussion, by people who deplore emigration as a loss to our country, no matter how the person who emigrates was occupied at home, or who extol every increase of population as an addition to the wealth of the country, without regard to the manner in which the new-comers are to live ; but the doctrine is an error when these arms are not engaged in producing wealth. When men are idle, or wasteful, or dishonest, so far are they from being wealth, and so far are they from increasing the wealth of a country by swelling their numbers, that there cannot be a surer method of increasing the national wealth than to get rid of them. " Like hills of ants, or fleas—the more the worse." I am aware that with even this restriction I may seem to commit an error in classification, by comprehending the industrious and skilful in the wealth of a country, and there may be cited the authority of Mr. John Stuart Mill, who lays it down that " the people of a country are not to be counted in its wealth—they are that for the sake of which wealth exists." But, as Mr. Mill himself proceeds to include personal skill among the various kinds of wealth, and as the including of skill and similar personal qualities is in practice tantamount to what I have said, there seems no reason to refuse to consider an industrious artisan a part, and a very important part, of the wealth of a country. It has been computed that the United States get an annual tribute of £30,000,000 from the Old World in the shape of emigrants ; the computation is perhaps, in regard to certain years, not unreasonable. If the industrious part of the population be omitted from the category of wealth, we arrive at a singular conclusion. Every inanimate instrument of production, and all the lower animals that help men to obtain wealth, indisputably rank as wealth. Yet labour, the instrument of instruments, the sole source of wealth in the opinion of English economists, is ignored more than a nail or hammer—that which forms all instruments of production is treated as if it produced nothing. If man is the end of production, he is also a means ; if he consumes, he also produces; and to omit him from the category of wealth, is to fall into an error almost equal to that which I have already indicated. At the same time, accepting Mr. Mill's own basis, that the people of a country are not wealth, because "they are that for the sake of which wealth exists," one cannot refuse, as he would refuse, to term slaves wealth. Was the Carolina slave, forbidden to traffic on his own account, and liable to be put to death at any moment on evidence that need not be given on oath, or was the Roman slave, owned by a master who was not shocked by the brutal maxims of Cato, "that for the sake of which wealth exists?" Clearly not; he was a mere chattel, and, like other chattels, part of the national wealth.

To continue the elucidation of the definition of wealth.—In the widest signification of the term, and in the view of the subject which it is profitable for a moment to contemplate, wealth comprehends all that can be of service or delight to man; and thus the very stars which people the firmament, making night beautiful, so be it there are men to gaze upon them, and to be enraptured by them, the air, rendering life possible and pleasant, the sounds of birds and waters, and the melodious voices of men, the colours of flowers and skies, and whatever else enlivens this earth, equally with the gold of California and the wheat of Illinois, form part of human wealth; and the world grows richer as it obtains greater store of such things. Men have boundless wants; wealth is all that can gratify them. In some countries Nature has of herself done much. In the tropical countries she has given spontaneously all that is necessary for life. In Brazil, mankind sits down to a feast gratis; and, like a too indulgent mother to her child, Nature there so loads man with benefits and favours that she ruins him with kindness. But as we pass to the north, or rather, as we pass from one isothermal line to another, we find countries less and less endowed with natural gifts, until we come to those where man is an exotic, and life a prolonged and dubious struggle with hostile elements. The like dissimilarity holds with regard to beauty, an item of wealth in this wide acceptation. Look at Holland, and then turn to Italy or Greece. Flat and monotonous, with little colour, and steeped in an atmosphere that seems made to deaden beauty, Holland is naturally a country where there is nothing to attract and delight the eye; and

almost the sole beauty to be found within that land are the
buxom damsels that smile on the canvas of Gerard Dow,
the cattle of Albert Cuyp and Paul Potter, and that air of
comfort and neatness, the product of industry, which ranks in
pleasing effect almost with fine scenery and works of art. For
Italy and Greece, on the other hand, though art, ancient and
modern, painting and architecture, have done much, their rich
vegetation, and gorgeous colours on sky, and earth, and sea, and
above all, that pellucid air in which all objects are set, to their
eternal adornment, have made these lands beautiful from of old,
independent of the mouldering Coliseum and Parthenon, the
aqueduct arches that strew the Campagna, or the Campanile
Tower of Giotto, that catches the entranced eye at Florence.
This, the widest sense of wealth, includes all things that can
gratify the wants of man.   Now, of these things there are two
kinds sharply distinguished—things that are found in limitless
abundance, and things that are more or less scarce, or obtained
with labour.   The air we breathe, got in limitless quantities
without trouble ; water, to be had in abundance—these are
examples of the first ; the food and money we obtain with
difficulty ; pure air in a large densely-peopled town ; water, say
in Lancashire or Mid-Lothian, capable of driving a mill—these
are instances of the last, which, being at once rare and useful,
people set a value upon : in other words, people will give something for them ; they are exchangeable.   I have mentioned the
important word "value."   It behoves us to know clearly of what
we speak.   It is laid down in books on Political Economy that
there are two kinds of value—value in use, and value in exchange, the one of which is possessed by useful articles that are
obtainable in limitless abundance, while the other is a quality
possessed by articles which are useful, and are obtainable with
more or less difficulty.   Unless an article possesses value in use
—unless it gratifies some want, natural or acquired—it cannot
be endowed with value in exchange.   Another division relates to
gratuitous utilities, that is, utilities which are without value in
the economical sense of the term, and utilities that are not
gratuitous, and do possess economist value.   Jean Baptiste
Say has expressed the same idea by the division into natural
and social riches.   It is with utilities, not gratuitous or social
riches, that we shall have to deal.
      Not a little has been written with regard to the propriety of

including what are called incorporeal riches within the domain of Political Economy. The controversy has been agitated chiefly in connection with a subject which we shall by and by have to consider—productive labour. Some economists have declared that there exist no riches but material riches ; others say that these form but a portion of the subject-matter of Political Economy. The former are wont to affirm that it is essential to the very idea of wealth that it should be material ; the latter affirm that such a distinction arbitrarily excludes things which agree with those included in all but non-essential points. It appears to me that things which cannot logically be opposed are here placed in false opposition ; and legal readers will at once perceive the truth of this observation when it is stated that this false opposition resembles that which the Roman lawyers, confounding, as Leibnitz has remarked, fact and law, erected between *res corporales* and *res incorporales*, and that the whole domain of wealth is very similar to, though not absolutely identical with, the *res* of Roman law. The first were the subjects of rights or obligations—they were for the most part objects of property. The last were rights. He who owned the one generally owned the *plenum dominium ;* he who owned the other owned one or more of the rights making up the *plenum dominium.* Now, the distinction between material and immaterial riches is parallel. For the most part articles of wealth consist of a cluster of useful qualities, and he who owns or sells them all owns or sells the *plenum dominium.* But any number of these elements less than the whole, or the possession of the whole for a limited time, may be designated, by a slight looseness of language, immaterial wealth; and he who sells one or more of them, sells, either permanently or for a time, so much of the *plenum dominium.* A slave and a piece of land are both material riches. The temporary services of the former, and a lease of or mortgage on the latter, are immaterial wealth. So with the incorporeal hereditaments or choses in action of English law. So far as they are objects of sale, all particular estates fall within the latter category ; so do all services ; they are saleable qualities, fewer than the whole. In this point of view the demand for a Political Economy of services and of immaterial wealth acquires a rational and justifiable character. The science has not expanded to its natural dimensions until it considers the sale of portions of the *plenum dominium*, and while the area of the science is enlarged by this addition, the inclusion of much of the present contents is justified ; for how can the sale of labour be classed as a phenomenon of exchange if we are not to look at labour itself as immaterial wealth ? The growth of this species of wealth is enormous, and for many reasons. It has come almost to be a law of history that over fewer and fewer things is the right of absolute ownership exercised. Instead of enjoying the full dominion of any article save tangible articles, or those capable of being used only once, people have, as a rule, only a right to levy a certain rate on it. I am not able to give exact figures with respect to national debts and public investments, partly constituting, of course, a portion of immaterial wealth ; but I find them estimated, in Fenn *On the Funds*, at five thousand five hundred millions sterling ; and these figures should serve to fill one with a sense of the vastness of those interests which may be designated immaterial wealth.

How deal with this branch, it may be asked, in a valuation of national wealth ? If it consists of charges upon another country, it is a clear addition to the national wealth. Of this description, for example, are foreign securities owned by Englishmen. We may say the same of immaterial wealth, consisting of the only saleable qualities composing the *plenum dominium* — such, for example, is the skill of workmen. On the other hand, so called immaterial wealth, consisting of only one of the saleable qualities constituting the *plenum dominium*, ought not to be included in the catalogue of items composing the national wealth, or care ought to be taken that we do not count the same things twice over. It is almost unnecessary to observe that mortgages and the dividends paid to home fundholders ought not to be reckoned as clear additions to the national wealth.

CHAPTER III.

LABOUR.

In the last chapter, several ambiguities in regard to wealth were cleared away, and its nature was described ; in this and a few subsequent chapters it will be shown how wealth is produced. The first and chief agent in its production is the labour of men. We may say, though with a liability to be misunderstood, which by and by will be removed, that in no other way can wealth be created. In the sweat of thy brow, with travail of mind and body, thou shalt earn thy bread—there is no other rule for nations and men to gather riches; and the greater part of bad Political Economy may be resolved into more or less ingenious and masked contraventions of that simple fact, sham devices for giving wealth to individuals or communities without calling upon them to be more industrious or skilful, quibbles that attempt to hide the effects of idleness, which are want and poverty. If a man will not work, he shall not be able to live—there is no escape from this simple command, except in one way, and that is to throw upon others the toil of producing, and to appropriate the fruits of it ; and hence we find that almost all the rest of unsound Political Economy may be resolved into promises of wealth gained at the expense, and taken out of the hands of others—ingenious excuses for filching the earnings of a neighbour, juggling tricks by which, with appropriate " Hey presto," the property of defrauded A becomes the property of fraudulent B.   Here, then, is almost the whole science in a nutshell, the rules for individuals and nations written on one's thumb-nail : to be rich there must be more industry, and if one relaxes industry one must grow poorer unless by robbing some one else, or unless some one else stop from robbing.   Here is the substance of the economical gospel for the poorest cottar or day-labourer, and for the greatest financier or merchant prince there is no other. Practical conclusions:—if any one promises to a class higher wages or higher profits, without asking it to work longer, or to strain its nerves and muscles more severely during a shorter period, he promises this increase at the expense of others; and unless he can prove that they are robbing it, he means, though he may not say so, that it should rob them. If any one promises greater material happiness, and yet takes means to discourage labour, he is probably feeding men with delusions. If Mr. Ruskin, or any one else, promises a minimum wage higher than the minimum wage now received—and what would be the use of promising only as much or less?—without indicating that one must labour harder or more skilfully in order to create a stock of wealth sufficient to ensure the promised fee, the proposal is to be received with doubting and mistrust: if we do not infer straightway that he proposes to rob others, we must at least insist upon his proving that he does not. Should it be promised that, working eight hours a-day, and not harder, you shall earn luxuries which could not now be earned in twice the time, we must make sure that he does not mean the spoliation of the wealthy. Should trade societies, or guilds, or corporations, make rules which will raise their remuneration without demanding more labour, they, of course, take the increase from others, and compel others to work harder, or to go with less. If, as all communistic and many socialist leaders do, men promise great abundance, and yet dry up the strongest and most permanently elastic spring of industry, the desire of bettering one's condition, the promise will prove to be a delusion when the excitement and hot fanaticism which usher these societies into life cool down to the commonplace indifference of after years. Upon this rock were wrecked Saint Simonism, Fourierism, and Owenism. Saint Simon would divide society into chiefs and workmen, subjecting the latter to a tyranny which would have crushed out the motives to labour, seeing the fruits of the common labour would have been distributed without any necessary regard to the amount of work performed. Charles Fourier, not making work a condition of remuneration, exaggerated the evils of the old Poor Law of England, which gave relief without endeavouring to check the growth of mendicancy; he also substituted for the present motives to activity, which everybody can appreciate, those abstract motives arising out of a collective interest, which only cultivated intelligences can adequately appreciate; and thus his system would discourage industry among all but a few heroic and self-denying men. Robert Owen committed a like mistake by restricting private property; private property was, according to him, the second person in "the Trinity of Evil;" and Louis Blanc, and also Mr. Ruskin—in this, as in most of his social dogmas, only a reproducer of the theories of French socialists—by proposing to give equality of wages without regard to equality of work being performed, commit, in a modified degree, the same mistake. Mr. Carlyle, and many English socialists and positivists, who would "regiment" industry, and remodel it on the analogy of an army, turning capitalists into officers or captains of industry, and labourers into privates, would weaken the motives to labour by cutting the close connection between it and the enjoyment of wealth, and by re-creating a group of industrial castes, which have often proved synonymous with inefficiency and idleness. They are, therefore, amenable to the charge of seeking to better the material condition of society by means that would injure it—of endeavouring to make men richer by means that would infallibly in the long run make them poorer. Most of these theories sin in somewhat over-estimating the influence of the unselfish passions. Those passions exist, certainly; but to suppose that the regular work of the world can be executed by them, is like proposing to use sandal-wood for fuel to feed engine-furnaces.

While labour is the first thing required to create wealth, labour must not be confounded with mere manual labour. Nor is it, as economists have often assumed, the mental and physical labour of men. In fact, the term itself is a legacy of a time when other motor forces than human labour were rarely employed. The labour that I speak of includes at once the drudgery of the ditcher or quarrier with spade or pick, the thought of the inventor busied in devising a spinning-jenny, or the means of economising the consumption of coal by a steam-engine, the merchant's hours spent pen in hand in his office, the clerk's ciphering of accounts, the judge's weighing and deciding upon evidence. Nay, manual labour, so far from being of chief importance in the production of wealth, we shall find to be of secondary importance as compared with other kinds of labour; and to forgetfulness of this truth we owe many delusions. Hence unqualified eulogiums of those who work with their hands, as if they alone had reared the fabric of national wealth. Hence complaints of the low remuneration of physical labour, and denunciations of those who earn much without soiling their fingers as mere drones and parasites. " The poor and working classes create all the wealth which the rich possess"—these words, uttered by Robert Owen, are the creed of a popular cult. Hence, or partly hence, too, a dim misgiving sometimes haunting the minds of those who live in ease and affluence, that the return which they receive for their present or past labour is exorbitant, and a fear sometimes starting up that labour may yet awake from its drugged sleep and rudely grasp its own. These delusions partially vanish, and the truth becomes manifest, if it be considered that the mere power to pull ropes, to raise weights, to strike with a hammer, or to work a lever, unaccompanied by directing intelligence, is almost worthless, so long as there are in this world water, steam, and wind, to drive machines that will pull loads, raise weights, strike blows, that put to shame the puny muscles of man. Mere amount of vital force, and *a fortiori* vital force as seen in man, are among the most insignificant forms of force ; it is their intellects, such as they are, that make men valuable labourers. Whatever their muscles do machinery could. Mere labour, so far from being valuable, is almost worthless without the power or will to direct it. What avails it that a man, Ulysses-like, ploughs the sand of the sea-shore ? Labour without directing intelligence may even be positively detrimental. Are not some of the striking inequalities in the remuneration of wages and labour seen to be just in the light of this truth, that we can increase riches only as we have intelligence ?

To judge of the share which mere manual labour has in the production of wealth, take the following facts in the history of industry :—The simplest form of grinding wheat is with a kern or two stones. Now, it has been calculated by M. Chevalier that our "productive power" in this branch of industry has increased since the days of Homer about 150 times, and that a task which would have occupied 144 persons in the household of Ulysses at Ithaca could now be performed by one person. Within 500 years it has increased nine times. And to what is this marvellous increase due ? To invention. The same cause has within 500 years multiplied the productive power of man in the working of iron thirty times. By Arkwright's invention, which dates from 1769, one man is now enabled to do what would have required formerly the united labour of many hundred men. Again, in the washing of gold, a single invention so increased the productive power of men that one man was enabled to do what would formerly have required the united arms and energies of 2500. Five hundred years ago, almost as many people were engaged in cultivating the land as now; but by increase of skill and knowledge the agriculturists of to-day produce eight times as much. Look at what steam, the lustiest child of invention, has done for us. The locomotive engines of Scotland alone are more powerful than the united strength of all its inhabitants. By the aid of steam a hammer can be used twenty thousand times heavier than that which a strong man could wield. It has been calculated that in Great Britain there is steam-power greater than the united bodily strength of a third of the human race.

Now, if mere manual labour, or its equivalent, be so common, so comparatively little influential in building up the wealth of a country, and if its economic value be chiefly due to the intelligence that accompanies and directs it, many of the striking differences between wages and salaries will appear to be natural. The value of any useful article rises in proportion to its rarity. The rarer, therefore, the talent, the higher the remuneration. A common workman may plead that he deserves to be paid at as high a rate, seeing that he works as hard and as long, as a physician. But hardness or length of hours is beside the question; it is rarity that is the determining point. Urging the plea of hard work, one might enter a jeweller's shop and demand as much for a quartz pebble as another man had got for a diamond, on the ground that the quartz took as long time to find as the diamond. The jeweller would laugh at the demand, and so may we, when a man who produces an article of less rarity and value claims to be paid the same terms as another who produces a more valuable article in the same time. Out of charity or caprice the jeweller may choose to give as much to the owner of the pebble as to the owner of the diamond; and an employer may choose to give as much to the blacksmith or navvy as to the engineer that directs him. But both will act from charity or caprice. One very common rule in many trades is assailable at this point—that is, an uniform rate of wages to all, without regard to the value of the work done. Of ten workmen, each turns out different values of work ; but the trade rules sometimes lay it down that they shall all be paid alike. Certainly in a few trades there is no distinguishing or separating the work of each man ; and it is then right and inevitable that they should be paid at the same rate, just as soldiers are. But these trades are few ; and in these no rules are required to enforce a practice that is inevitable. In other cases which it is fair to recognise, rank-and-file payment saves the men from the caprice or tyranny of foremen. But, in the majority of trades and cases, it is easy to distinguish and value the work of each labourer ; and when that can be done, the rank-and-file style of payment is an attempt in its way to compel the employers to pay the same sum for different values —the same for the pebble as the diamond. Professor Beesly has defended rank-and-file payment by the analogy of the army. This comparison is a favourite one with him and Mr. Ruskin ; while Mr. Carlyle, it is said, justifies the regulation. But the fact is, there is no distinguishing, except very roughly, the value of one soldier from another. If they turn to the left or the right about, they are probably both equally good. But certainly the War Office shows that it desires to substitute individual payment for rank-and-file payment in all possible cases, by giving extra pay to men who have served long and well, and who are, therefore, presumably better soldiers than their fellows ; and for those who have been undoubtedly engaged in work of peculiar difficulty, there is " batta," or extra pay.

This insignificance of the man who is merely a muscular machine, the vast importance of intellect in the production of wealth, is a fact fraught with far-reaching consequences. It tells the poorer classes, the proletariat, how they are to better themselves if they are to do so, and how they are to keep their: lot from becoming worse. Alongside the Gibeonite, Nature has placed terribly efficient competitors—steam and water, with preternatural power, ready to be yoked ; unwearied Titans that never sleep. All that muscles can do tolerably they can do well ; and, wanting only intelligence to be the superior of man, they seem to tell him that every day there is less room on this earth for ignorance and mere brute strength, and to prophesy an approaching time when people will be able to gain a livelihood only if well educated. To the intelligent workmen of this country the extension of machinery brings, as a rule, many advantages. It need not deprive them of work; or at worst it need deprive them only of coarse drudgery. But to the ignorant, those who sell mere muscles, who earn their bread by a trade that calls for no exercise of intelligence, this extension turns a stern face; I shall not be able to prove that the extension of machinery brings unalloyed blessings to them. And it is not enough that a trade should require some simple exercise of intelligence; for them machinery will sooner or later be forthcoming. For example, counting or checking figures can often be done by machinery. Registering machines are common in the arts. Thus there are machines which register the amount of liquor drawn off a cask, which measure calico and ribbons and carpets, and record the rate of speed of vessels and carriages, the number of strokes made by the piston of a steam-engine, or the coins struck by a die. This, then, is one of the chief lessons of Political Economy : to be paid well now, and still more hereafter, one must be intelligent, one must have brain as well as muscle to sell. Poverty and ignorance go together. The scientific vocabulary of Political Economy bears witness to the vast extension of machinery and the curtailment in the use of manual labour as a motor power. Labour and capital formerly not unfaithfully corresponded to the motor powers of producers, and to the materials on which they were exercised, or by which they were fed. But labour has now become an inconsiderable motor power ; steam, wind, and other varieties of mechanical power play every day a greater part; and the logical propriety of the distinction between labour and capital is being gradually effaced, if by labour we understand the forces employed in production. The only way, it would seem, in which the old distinction can be rehabilitated is by regarding labour as equivalent to intelligent direction, and by considering capital to be equivalent to the various forces useful for production and the articles helping us to utilise them.

All labour is engaged in producing motion. It can do nothing more. Creation and annihilation are meaningless or figurative words. The husbandman equally with the carrier, the merchant equally with the joiner, are engaged in moving certain pieces of matter. Nature does the rest. Nay, we have some reason to believe that Nature herself does nothing more, and that what we call mechanical, chemical, and electrical changes, are nothing more than various modes of motion. Here, then, is the correction of a very common error. It is frequently assumed that the labour of merchants, shopkeepers, and of all those who are called the intermediaries of society, is either totally unproductive, or is labour of a kind totally different from and inferior to that of a farmer or an artisan. And nothing is more common than to hear ignorant people speak of the former as parasites on society. But the truth is that the work of all of them is the same in kind : the latter performs certain motions with soil and seed, tools and materials; and the former does the same with goods. All of them agree in setting matter in motion, in bringing it whence it is not wanted whither it is wanted. The manufacturer or farmer moves the particles of certain bodies, the merchant moves the bodies themselves. The mere circumstance that the latter produce no physical change upon the appearance of the goods does not render their work useless ; for the man who brings tea from China—from a place where it is as if it were not—surely renders society a service without producing any physical change upon it ; and the man who brings goods to your door, even though not all the way from China, does a service of the same kind. If he renders no service, saves people no trouble, gratifies no public want, he will get no custom.

Deluded by a theory that all wealth comes from the earth or from agriculture, Quesnay and the French physiocrats refused to consider any persons productive but those engaged in agriculture, fisheries, and mines. Adam Smith, who was much influenced for good and evil by them, was influenced on this point also, and though his good sense made him recoil from extreme opinions, we find him designating the labour of a menial servant as unproductive. In order to get at the root of this controversy, let us analyse the phrase in question. " Productive" is an elliptical expression for "productive of wealth, or utilities not gratuitous." It is true that some writers have understood it to mean merely productive of utility; "to produce," says Destutt de Tracy, "is to give to things a utility which they did not possess." Destutt de Tracy's words would be liable to lead one to suppose that he considered labour which created gratuitous utilities as productive—a conclusion which conducts to manifest absurdities. Destutt de Tracy, and most of those who have defined "productive" as he defined it, really understood the creation of utilities that are not gratuitous ; and this, it need scarcely be said, is only another way of expressing "production of wealth." Mr. John Stuart Mill, substantially accepting Adam Smith's conception of productive and unproductive labour, does not bind himself to any one acceptation of the term ; but, on the whole, he prefers to consider "all labour as productive which is employed in creating permanent utilities, whether embodied in human beings or in any other animate or inanimate objects." This position, I submit, is, for several reasons, dubious. All of these reasons cannot be stated until capital is considered ; but, in the meantime, the following may be stated :—Generally, it is not a proper position to abide by one definition with the proviso that it may be occasionally rejected. Secondly, the chief advantage to be gained by limiting the term "productive" to those persons who produce a physical change in a substance, is increase of clearness and sharp demarcation ; but this clearness is blurred, the line of demarcation somewhat effaced, when Mr. Mill goes on to abandon his first position, and to extend the term "productive" to labour, indirectly or mediately, issuing in the production of material wealth. It then becomes impossible, or at least very difficult, to distinguish "productive" from "unproductive" labour. The distinction becomes a closet distinction. For who can tell whether labour, apparently the most frivolous or unpractical, may not help, "indirectly or mediately," in the production of material wealth when centuries have elapsed ? At first sight, a geometer's labours appear to have no bearing on the creation of wealth. Yet there is no certainty that events may not turn out differently, and that formulæ, apparently barren in practical results and removed from the affairs of the world, may not lead to some discovery in physical science which will be the cause of a vast increase of wealth. The Alexandrine geometers engaged in investigating the properties of the ellipse, might well seem labouring at a task which would never add one tittle to the sum of wealth. Yet to their labours we partly owe great circle sailing, and consequently, in no small degree, our extensive commerce. Boyle investigating the elasticity of air might seem an unproductive labourer. Yet to him we partly owe the steam-engine. There is always a difficulty, occasionally rising to an impossibility, to decide when a person is or is not a productive labourer in Mr. Mill's acceptation of the term. Accordingly, in the last census a different signification was given to "productive," all being such except those who were supported by the community, or not engaged in some remunerative occupation. Further, by confining the term "productive" to labour which effects some physical change, we are committed to incongruous results. For example, the skill of a violinist is unproductive, the skill of a violin-maker is strangely, indeed capriciously, productive, according to the above definition. Take the term in either sense —suppose "productive" an elliptical expression, with either wealth or value understood, the incongruity remains. The musician would be ranked with the mere *natus consumere fruges*. It will perhaps be found from these reasons that the distinction is placed on its true basis when he is reckoned productive who does that which is valuable, and he is unproductive whose labour nobody will give anything for. But these are not the only reasons.

We saw that there were two kinds of wealth, infelicitously termed material and immaterial—the former consisting of the *plenum dominium* of articles at once useful and more or less scarce ; the latter of one or more of the purchasable qualities included in such articles. Now, it appears that if we consider that productive, as Mr. Mill says, means productive of wealth, consistency will oblige one who accepts this view of immaterial wealth to designate much labour exercised upon no material object as productive. Let us take a capital instance. Only where slavery exists is the *plenum dominium* over men sold. Here, and wherever slavery is abolished, we deal only with immaterial wealth when human beings are in question—that is, only certain rights belonging to them are bought and sold, and are articles of value ; their services only for a certain time are disposed of. Now, it is clear that, from the above point of view, he is productive of immaterial wealth who sells some of the constituents of the cluster of rights of which every man is the owner; admitting the existence of immaterial wealth— and I submit that this unhappy term may receive a rational meaning—we are shut up to the conclusion that he is a productive labourer whose labour is saleable, or who brings into the market so much of this immaterial wealth.

Of course, if "productive" mean "productive of value or

utility," there can be little hesitation in divesting it of all necessary connection with labour exercised upon a material object; it cannot be disputed that labour for which we pay is economically valuable.

On the whole, we may therefore say that the confinement of "productive" to any narrower signification is arbitrary— so arbitrary, that the fact which should most strongly tempt one to believe that the mercantile theory ever existed is the fact that many have maintained that wealth—all that can gratify men's wants and that is not procurable in a limitless quantity— is synonymous with what is material.

It may indeed be said that "productive" ought to be applied to labour which, *par excellence*, increases the permanent sources of enjoyment. In the popular view of its meaning it is associated with increase of comfort and opulence ; and it is said that we ought to select for the term that meaning which best harmonises with an almost universal association. But deference to that objection, very proper in the mouths of those who think that it is a false Political Economy which regards only present increase of wealth, would suggest the application of " productive," not to all labour increasing the sum of commodities, but to labour engaged in industrial operations that are the bases of all others. It is manifest that if mankind, or a too large portion of it, engaged in certain pursuits designated productive by Mr. Mill, destitution, starvation, and misery, would be the swift fate of the race. Agriculture and the arts occupied in creating food and clothing and the means of shelter might, *par excellence*, be designated productive, seeing they are essential to man's existence and to the exercise of all other industries ; and, viewed in this light, the doctrine of the Physiocrats, that agricultural labour alone is productive, assumes a rational aspect. In this point of view all nutritive forces, or the equivalents of such forces, would be the sole objects of productive labour. Even if it be true that services do not add to the permanent sources of enjoyment, it is only a difference of degree that separates them in this respect from many kinds of material commodities, and the last again are separated by an equally wide interval from many other kinds. Further, many services do add as much to the permanent sources of enjoyment as many commodities ; if the utility of the one is evanescent, so is that of the other. If the first confer momentary gratification, so do some of the second ; and the antithesis between services as momentary enjoyments and commodities as permanent sources of enjoyment is scarcely correct.

Looking at the physical conditions of an efficient workman, we cannot fail to perceive that, whatever they be, certain races possess the qualities in an immeasurably greater degree than others do. Whether these differences are due to an inherent superiority in certain races, or are the accumulated effects of unanalysed circumstances, these differences are so great that the spinning-jenny is not more superior to the spinning-wheel than the European is to the Asiatic or African as a producer ; and if the production of wealth were to be the sole criterion of what is desirable, we should desire these races to be replaced by Europeans just as we desire the steam-engine to drive out inferior motive powers. The greatest economical improvement possible would be the peopling of the earth with Europeans. In strength, as in intelligence, no races can vie with the European ; and of these the best adapted for most kinds of labour belong to the Teutonic stock. As industry becomes more and more the occupation of the world, the supremacy of these races must become more manifest. But strength and endurance, their characteristics, are not the only qualities required of a producer. Nicety of hand, sense of beauty, tell also ; and some of these qualities seem to be naturally possessed in far higher degree by the Latin than by the Teutonic races, while others are possessed by certain Orientals in greater degree than by any Europeans. The muslins of India attest a degree of manipulative delicacy, perhaps explicable only on the theory of a transmitted aptitude.

The best economical state is, of course, one where there are no idle people, none who consume and do not produce, none who quit the world without at least replacing the value which they have destroyed. We are far removed from this state. And to mention only one of the drawbacks, it is a blot on even societies most thrifty, that nearly one-half of their members are compelled by the force of public opinion, petty hindrances, and positive laws, to live the somewhat ignoble and unsatisfactory life of consumers, or to curtail their powers of producing wealth. I speak not of any professed trades-union of recent birth and of a local character, but of that strong and universal trades-union which is almost as old as the

race, which has our earth for its domain, of which all men
are the members, and from which most women are the sufferers.
The one sex has appropriated the best remunerated and most
enviable of employments, those that bring wealth and honour,
and has permitted women to enter only a few professions
offering paltry rewards. This is not the place to characterise
the morality of this partially artificial separation ; but it is
befitting here to deplore the waste of labour, the frittering
away of excellent capabilities, the enforced idleness of so many
fingers and brains that might be busy creators of wealth. As
one contemplates these talents spilt on the ground, so to speak,
it is almost unavoidable to carry away the idea that free trade
between nations, improvements in taxation, and a settlement of
the other economical questions which now float on the surface,
may be of less moment in an economical point of view than ·
the complete breaking down of those legal and social barriers,
whether in the form of statutes or sneers, which prevent women
from entering what professions they choose. Clear these
barriers out of the way, and not only will there be a better
distribution of talents, those which are now wasted upon sew-
ing with a few pence a-day as remuneration, finding a congenial
and lucrative vocation in the lighter handicrafts ; but a large
portion of women who now produce nothing, economically *non-
valeurs*, and who may be excused for being such, seeing they
are emphatically told by their teachers that doing nothing is
their sphere, and seeing the professions to which they may
resort are monotonous, not lucrative, and far from inviting,
will be stimulated to do good work. Can the sisters of men
who earn £800 to £1000 a-year be expected to engage in
work which brings only £20 to £30 ? May we not expect new
exertions when they have the prospect little less tempting than
their brothers ? For men there always is, as Daniel Webster
said, " plenty of room higher up," while the inferior professions
are overstocked, and that circumstance constitutes an impulse
to the meanly-paid workman to toil on ; for women there is no
" higher up"—too often inactivity or a pittance is their miserable fate. It is not essential to the realisation of the above
hopes that women should prove to be possessed of the same
aptitude for labour as men ; enough if they do tolerably well
many things which men alone do perfectly, and if the field of
workers be enormously increased without any increase in the

expenditure.   Nor is it essential that there should be an utter
reversal of present social arrangements, and that all married
women, for example, should labour, to the detriment of their
children ; enough if most unmarried women, and married
women without children, should in some fashion help to add to
the stock of wealth.   This would be a change fraught with
far-stretching consequences.   The discovery of a mode of all
but doubling the producing powers of the males, without
necessitating any increase in the amount devoted to subsistence,
would seem to be the chief of economical improvements.   It
would render shorter hours of labour possible ; and celibacy
would no longer be encouraged, as it is, by an enormous bribe.
The Romans had, perhaps foolishly, their laws in favour of
marriage—we, by making it needlessly expensive, have ours
against it.*

There is another point which it is pertinent here to allude
to.   Economists have not sufficiently directed attention to the
bearings of diet upon the efficiency of labour.   They have not
availed themselves sufficiently of the teaching of physiology,
which has shown that a man's capacity for labour is a function
of his food.   Everybody knows that a navvy receiving twenty
ounces of bread, as many of meat, two ounces of rice, with
coffee and rum, is in a better working condition than a
French labourer, who consumes almost no meat.   Almost
every railway contractor has surprising stories to tell of
the wonders effected by a change in diet.   I do not know
whether he was perfectly right who said, "Tell me how any
people dined to-day, and I shall tell you what achievements
they will perform to-morrow ;" but it is certain that physiolo-
gists and practical experience have accumulated a number of
generalisations with respect to the connection between diet
and work, which economists ought to incorporate in their
teaching.

* The effect of the *Leges Julia et Papia* was to deprive the unmarried
of mere windfalls ; English society punishes pretty uniformly marriage in
the case of the middle classes.

CHAPTER IV.

CAPITAL.

In the last chapter, Labour, the first thing necessary to the production of wealth, was considered. The only other thing absolutely necessary is Capital ; and if its nature be thoroughly understood, Political Economy is known almost to the bottom ; almost all purely economical questions may be solved, and the greater part of future discussions consists of drawing deductions from the fundamental properties of capital. Its momentousness must, in the first place, be impressed upon the mind of every student of Political Economy. Man without capital is as purely a fiction of the imagination as a line without breadth or a point without magnitude. It is as essential to the continuance of life as air. It is the breath of industry. No people ever existed without it, and no people ever attained to civilisation without abundance of it. Declamations against capital are possible only by reason of its abundance ; and if it were now very rare, those who most loudly decry capital would probably be following, naked and savage, a scarcely more savage beast in some rude and trackless country.

We saw that labour was of two kinds—productive and unproductive : the former imparting a new value to some article or performing some service esteemed valuable ; the latter doing neither. The ploughman, the smith, the doctor, the merchant, it was agreed, were productive. Labour, again, which does not help to make men wealthier, which does not sell, was described as unproductive. Now, we shall find a similar and parallel distinction running through the other constituents of wealth besides labour. In fact, the distinction between productive and unproductive labour is only a particular and special application of the distinction we are about to draw ; and if Political Economy were not a practical science, or if it were investigated by persons who had no object in applying it, labour need not be severed from the bulk of commodities. Whatever wealth, labour excluded, is devoted to help to form new wealth is capital, or, as we might say, is productive wealth. The wages given to workmen, the tools and raw material employed, are capital ; all these help men to manufacture things which possess value in exchange, or to perform services which are held to be valuable. Capital, to put the definition in another form, consists of all that is necessarily consumed in order to produce wealth ; or, to vary the phraseology, it consists of all that is necessarily consumed by productive labourers—all that is necessary to the efficient performance of their tasks. "Necessarily" is introduced to remind one that expenditure capable of being foregone without appreciable injury to the work, does not rank as capital. How, then, should we answer one who asked whether a bottle of champagne formed part of capital ? The answer would depend on circumstances. If consumed by one who produces nothing, the bottle of champagne is assuredly not capital ; if consumed by one who produces something valuable, it is capital, or, to be accurate, so much of the value of it as would have bought equal nourishment forms capital, the rest being purely unproductive expenditure. The only person to whom the bottle of champagne is necessarily capital is the wine-merchant—only to the service to society which he performs is it necessary. Are we then to understand by capital only articles employed in producing material wealth, or are we to include those essential to the discharge of valuable services ? The above explanation shows to which opinion I lean, and my reasons are, for the most part, similar to those which induced me to regard as productive all valuable labour. Immaterial wealth, though an unhappy phrase, may be so understood as to cover a distinct set of facts deserving to be taken cognisance of by economists, and agreeing with immaterial wealth in satisfying desires. Wealth employed in producing immaterial wealth, consumed in the performance of services, may be fairly designated capital ; and science may here legitimise popular parlance, which undoubtedly considers the merchant's stock and the violinist's instrument as their owners' capital.

Mr. Mill defines, as we have seen, productive labour to be that which helps to produce material wealth. Now, this distinction, and the distinction between capital and non-capital, are parts of the same great distinction, and ought to march together; so that Mr. Mill ought to define capital as that which helps to produce material wealth. He does so, but at what cost? By a sacrifice of usage, to which, in defining wealth, he perhaps sacrifices scientific propriety. Usage certainly designates the instrument of the musician, the school-room of the teacher, as capital; usage will refuse to pronounce the instrument of the musician not capital, and the tools of the musical instrument-maker as capital. However writers may distinguish and refine, usage will consider the violin of the one and the chisel of the other as alike capital. And rightly so. Both are tools—both are employed in producing some new value; and that the one effects a change which the eye can discern, and the other one which the eye cannot discern, is a circumstance of not much importance to the economist. It is true that all this suggests that just as there is a certain kind of labour which may be styled *par excellence* productive, so there is a certain portion of wealth upon which production peculiarly depends, and which might be termed capital *par excellenc:*—such, for example, are articles of food, articles of clothing, etc.; in short, all those articles which are absolutely necessary to a continuance of production. Food, clothing, tools, and other articles formed by productive labour, in the sense Mr. Mill understands it, are necessary to every producer. It is impossible for countries to devote their energies to labour not embodied in these commodities—viz. all which store up or economise motor power—to continue wealthy. They will inevitably become poor. Considering this position from another aspect, I may say that it is the object of the economist to state the laws of the increase of valuable enjoyments; and he may therefore fairly regard as productively employed labour and commodities expended in conferring some valuable enjoyment, whether temporary or permanent. He will indeed attach most importance to an increase of the permanent sources of enjoyment; but he will not, for the reasons already stated in connection with labour, refuse to consider the food or clothing used by one who has left behind no material equivalent, as necessarily spent unproductively. Looked at in the point of view of the entire world, wealth and labour would alone be considered productive which resulted in some valuable service.

" But is not all this a discussion about mere terms, and,

therefore, of no practical consequence?" No; on the contrary, this discussion is daily assuming some tangible shape, and many important consequences hang upon it. For example, the Government of India erect barracks, forts, and bridges. Are these public works to be considered productive? Are they capital? One school, represented by Mr. Laing, maintain that they, or, at all events, the last, are capital. If these are productive works, they need not be paid out of the current revenue; if they are not so, it will follow that they should be paid out of the revenue of the year. This question is one of vast importance, upon which turns the raising of millions. Again, what railway meeting a few years ago passed over without a discussion of the charges with which revenue ought to be debited? The important point at issue was to be decided upon the principles we have indicated. The Court of Chancery, too, has sometimes to discuss the point. It will conduce to clearness to specify at this stage the chief and fundamental kinds of capital. One must premise, however, that what follows is no complete inventory. Capital is so much an ideal department of wealth, that frequently it is impossible to point out the articles forming the capital of a particular establishment. Thus, the capital of a company may consist of wealth not all "paid up." The chief varieties are three—food, clothing, shelter, and everything else necessary for the maintenance of the workman; the raw materials of industry and commodities necessary for the performance of valuable services; and tools and machines, from a rake to a locomotive engine. Under the second or third of these divisions will fall land, so far as it is used for purposes of production. This is, indeed, contrary to the usage of English economists, who put land, the representative of all other natural agents, in a category by itself. But two reasons, I think, warrant a deviation. In the first place, the classification of English economists with regard to this point involves an inconsistency; for, though laying it down— to take Mr. Fawcett as their spokesman—that "capital is all that wealth, in whatever shape or form it may exist, which is set aside to assist future production," and though, of course, viewing land as a portion of wealth, they exclude land from the kinds of wealth included under capital. In the second place, though rent, in the narrow and somewhat arbitrary signification given to it by Ricardo, has, like the price of all other natural agents, certain peculiarities, I do not think that this circumstance excludes productive land from the category of capital, especially seeing the differences in the laws that govern the profits of certain kinds of fixed and circulating capital do not forbid them from being all regarded as capital. Agricultural land, and all the other kinds of wealth enumerated above, agree in a fundamental and relevant point—they are employed productively. I might add, as a third reason, that the rent of land is, in old countries, in very great part, nothing else than the return on what is acknowledged by every one to be capital. According to some, not only are these material things capital, but knowledge and habits, so far as they co-operate in the production of articles or services esteemed valuable, form part, and a very important part, of capital. It is said that the teacher's knowledge and skill and experience are his capital. It is said that, having given to wealth the wide domain of all utilities not gratuitous, and having defined capital as all these utilities, labour excepted, employed in the production of other utilities not gratuitous, we ought to include within capital all the elements of thought, the observations, the fruits of reading, and the emotions, which the poet, for example, works up into epics, quite as much as the raw jute or cotton to be worked up into carpets or shirts. But why so narrow the idea of labour?

The conception of capital, which I have tried to elucidate, is different from what will be found in deservedly esteemed books. By capital, Jean Baptiste, say, for example, sometimes understands the entire amount of accumulated wealth, whether it is or is not devoted to production. Say seems to have needlessly spoiled a term which fitted a well-defined idea. At every turning in economical discussions we feel the want of a term which will save us from using the confusing as well as awkward circumlocution, that part of wealth which is devoted to production.—Capital supplies this want; why then spoil the needful term? And here it may be observed that, to complete economical terminology, a term which will stand for that part of wealth which is not capital, but which is consumed unproductively, is exceedingly wanted. Until the gap be permanently filled, unproductive wealth may be employed as a stop-gap.

Those who, like Mr. John Stuart Mill, have confined " pro-

ductive labour" to labour which effects some material change
on a substance, have, I submit, unjustifiably narrowed the term.
As has already been indicated, there is a very visible economical
impropriety in relegating to the same category the labour of
the maniac and that of a musician. This fact suggests the true
mode of regarding capital.

A moment's reflection on the nature of capital should dissolve
the greater part of the errors that encompass the so-called
Labour Question. Once the nature of capital is perceived,
some of the current prejudices respecting it are seen to be
ridiculous. These prejudices are old, for the Labour Question is
not new, as we are apt to imagine ; the battle between the
labourer and the capitalist but continues the strife between
debtors and usurers that we read of in so many histories.
How silly,* for example, to speak of capital as the enemy of
the labourer, when we see that capital is wealth to be given
to the labourer ! How silly to deplore the increase of capital,
when it means more food and clothing to the working people !
How silly to say that " capital is degrading the country," when
addition to the capital of the country means greater wealth to
the working people ! Working men hear their friends sometimes speak of the " tyranny of capital ;" they hear Mazzini
proclaiming that the great social evil of the time is the
" tyranny of capital." There may be some truth, or the dis-
tortion of it, lurking in the phrase ; but whatever tyranny
there may be comes of capital being scarce. A parallel
instance may save several words. A caravan passing over some
sultry desert discover that no water remains to support them in
their march save the scanty stores in the water-skins of one
man, and that, in the howling wilderness, where, as Collins,
describing such a scene, says—

 —— "rocks alone, and tasteless sands are found,
 And faint and sickly winds for ever howl around"—

there are no wells or hope of them. In the agony of the
future march the owner of the water-skins can exact for the
water whatever he pleases to ask—it is the only thing between
the people and death ; buy they must. But whatever were

* " Le capital c'est la honte accumulée. L'ouvrier qui épargne est
trâitre envers ses frères."—Declaration in a Paris Socialistic meeting,
quoted in Mr. West's Report for 1870. ﹀

the terms, there would not be one so foolish as to complain, when Schiraz' walls were regained, of "the tyranny of water"— to murmur because water had been found at all; for every one would know that the water had saved him, and that his suffering was due to the rarity of it. Just so with much-abused capital. Being here, and still more elsewhere, too rare, it gives the owners of it the power which is wielded by every one who possesses that which is at once a necessity and a rarity; and this power may rise to the height of "tyranny" when capital is very scarce and labourers too abundant. But increase the amount of capital—transform this rarity into abundance—and this power or "tyranny" vanishes. Labourers can do nothing without food and clothing to keep them alive; and when capital is rare, as it has generally been, if our measure be the necessities of men, labourers bid eagerly for the use of it, and wages fall. Certainly, until the limit of the productiveness of the soil is attained, any event which produces a great destruction of capital tends to be injurious to the labourer. The civil war of America, for example, destroyed much; it cannot be doubted that the fact that some years afterwards articles had risen in the depreciated currency fifteen per cent more than labour did, is ascribable largely to the destruction of capital.* But capital is equally powerless without labour; and when capital accumulates capitalists bid for services, and wages rise. When population is sparse we witness what we may with equal reason call "the tyranny of labour." Such a state of matters was witnessed in England after the plague of 1348-9, which thinned the number of labourers; and it has been frequently experienced in our colonies, particularly in Australia. The statement of the relationship between capital and labour shows that there are two great modes open to workmen of preventing the so-called "tyranny of capital," which is, in fact, the power inevitably possessed by the owners of a rare necessary. Diminish or restrain their numbers; capitalists will bid for labourers. By leading peaceful lives that will encourage others to save, and by saving themselves, and by becoming capitalists—the meaning of co-operation—let labourers augment capital; its owners will again bid for labourers. In any of these cases two masters will be seen chaffering for one man, instead of two men chaffering for one

* Commissioner Wells, quoted in *North American Review* for April 1869.

master. I only state the same truth in a somewhat different
form when I say that, speaking generally, the greater the
amount of the existing capital, the greater the share of the
produce that will fall to each labourer. This produce is divided
among the capitalist and the labourer, and as profits—that is,
the capitalist's share—fall as capital increases, it follows that
the labourer's share becomes greater. It is looking at the same
truth from another point of view when we say that it is not capitalists who are the antagonists of labourers in the struggle for
the proceeds of industry, but that capitalists are the antagonists
of each other, and labourers their own rivals. This, of course,
runs in the teeth of many prejudices, and takes the piquancy
out of much popular invective. Nevertheless it is the truth
wherever competition is fully at work. For the capitalist is
prevented from being able to charge a monopoly price for his
capital only by the fact that there are others competing against
him, and willing, should he attempt to exact too much, to sell
the use of capital at a lower price ; and in like manner the
labourer is prevented from charging what price he pleases only
by the fact that there are other labourers desiring employment.

Let us now consider a little more systematically a few of the
functions of capital. No production of wealth is possible without capital, or, to use Mr. Mill's words, " the sphere of production
is limited by capital." This is a cardinal and almost a self-
evident truth, which may be translated into the vernacular by
saying that men cannot work unless they have food, clothes,
and the raw materials of industry, and cannot work to much
profit unless they have tools and machines. There is here no
mystery. The husbandman cannot raise a crop unless he has
wherewithal to support him throughout the winter, spring, and
summer ; the cabinetmaker cannot devote a week to make a
chest of drawers unless he has previously obtained food. It is
not the less true that we find production carried on without a
distinct class of capitalists. In the trade corporations of the
Middle Ages, and in those strange remnants of antiquity, the
arteles of Russia—and, in fact, in all small manufactures—the
capitalist and the labourer are identical. Peasant proprietors
or yeomen combine the two functions. The village carpenter,
or the village merchant, is at once a labourer and a capitalist.
Our professional classes exhibit the spectacle of wealthy persons
uniting in themselves the functions of capitalist and labourer ;

the doctor is a labourer quite as much as the farmer; but the former owns much of his capital, and the latter buys his. Indeed, only in England and the United States of America do we find a general separation of capitalists and labourers. Nowhere else do there exist vast masses destitute of capital. Nor is it to be desired that the bulk or even a large part of society should want it, and should thus be free from the ennobling ties with which property binds a man. He that owns something, be it little or great, has given hostages for his good conduct. He becomes conscious of hitherto unknown dignity and responsibility. For him life now is serious; peace and social order he will defend, for he defends his own. He looks forward with interest to the future; he looks back with a certain satisfaction to the past, which, on the whole, has dealt kindly by him; on the little handbreadth of the present his thoughts do not squat. He ceases to be the waif of circumstances. On the other hand, to be totally destitute of property is to be combustible material, ready to explode at the spark of revolution. "Something must man possess," says the philosophic Schiller, in Wallenstein, "or he will murder and burn." To be destitute of property is to leave no room for the humane parts of our nature to spring up; unstable and brutish, that people cannot excel; and a state of society in which the mass of the people own nothing but their bodies cannot be the goal of progress. We look back into the depths of a past in which the most of mankind were the property of others; nearer to us we see the majority masters of themselves and nothing more; may we not look confidently forward to a future in which they will own enough to make them masters of their fates? Already we see hopeful symptoms in the millions of deposits in the savings banks, the success of benefit and building societies, the growth of co-operation, and the rise of joint-stock companies with shares of small amount. And one indisputable benefit due to trades-unions is, that they have accustomed workmen, who never before thought of saving, to accumulate a reserve that may be used as capital.

Had it been borne in mind that production is limited by capital, many dark chapters would have been blotted out of the history of emigration. We should have heard fewer tales of emigrants, deluded by offers of cheap land, plunging into the backwoods or bush, and there finding the plenteous and rich land, the goodly and abundant timber, the full-volumed rivers capable of bearing fleets on their breasts, of little avail, and hopes of founding comfortable homes for themselves in the wilderness rudely shaken by poverty and disease. Dickens would have found no Eden Creek to describe its horrors. In nine cases out of ten colonies have failed by reason of the want of capital. In almost all young countries, with the exception of land, capital is rare; witness the fact that the rate of interest on deposits in savings banks, which is £2 : 10s. per cent in this country, is often, in many of our colonies, as in Queensland or South Australia for example, 5 per cent. Had governments perceived that the production of wealth is limited by capital, protectionism would perhaps never have risen to its present and still less to its past importance; for governments would not have been deluded into believing that it increased the wealth of the country to encourage one branch of industry with capital taken from another. Perhaps—though the consideration is not decisive—we should not have seen Russia exclude British cotton and other manufactured goods by means of import duties, the heaviest imposed by any European government with the exception of that of Portugal, and induce her nobles, by the consequent high prices, to withdraw capital from agriculture to invest it in lines of business utterly unnatural. Perhaps we should not have seen some of the people of the United States proud of having created, by a protective tariff, an artificial iron trade, in contempt of the fact that the more iron the less corn was produced; and States, and the believers in State omnipotence, would be less confident that misery was wiped out by a loan, or the proceeds of a tax distributed among the poor, if it were clearly understood and fully kept in view that production is limited by capital.

"All capital is the result of saving"—this proposition is of great importance, if to the exceedingly infelicitous term "saving" we give so wide a meaning that it will include the conduct of a man who buys a hoe instead of a gallon of beer, or who devotes an acre of land to growing turnips instead of turning it into a lawn. Only we must not confound mere hoarding with saving—the man who ties his money in a stocking and stuffs it below the thatch, does not increase the capital of the country,—the miser is a useless being. Harpagon hoards; Grandet saves. To be just to it, popular opinion has always held the miser in sufficient odium. Comic writers of all ages and countries, the mirrors of popular opinion, have ever held up to ridicule and execration the miser. Molière shows us a Harpagon rolling in wealth, yet cheating his own horses of their oats; Goldoni has his Trappolo nightly visiting vast treasures, yet eagerly picking up waste pieces of paper, and quarrelling with his servant for not buying large eggs. But popular opinion, and comedy, the mirror of it, have confounded in common execration him who hoards and him who saves, and they have reserved their praise for the spendthrift. Aristophanes shows us the hard-working Strepsiades at great disadvantage beside Phidippides, his horse-racing extravagant son; and if Harpagon is execrated by Molière, the extravagant Cleante is praised. The Middle Age prejudice against the Jew, so far as it was not due to superstition, was really an ignorant prejudice against saving. The eulogies on Louis XIV. of France, which we find in the historians and memoir-writers of the period, were at bottom eulogies on extravagance. How could the poor live if the rich were not extravagant?—that was then a favourite defence of luxury. The prejudice is still alive, for how often do we not hear the man who gives grand entertainments, keeps a carriage, and innumerable servants, praised as the benefactor of the poor, while he who lives quietly, and turns his gains into capital, instead of plate or wine, is held to be the enemy of the poor! How many a man persuades himself that such and such a piece of extravagance is right, seeing it is "good for trade!" Quite a mistake. The self-styled friend of trade wastes in private luxuries what might have been spent as wages, and might have produced fresh wealth. He who saves devotes his fortune to hiring labour, and creating the means of hiring it anew. Luxury benefits, unless by accident, only those who enjoy it; from saving ramify endless blessings to others than the economiser and his dependants. Luxurious expenditure I do not presume to term sheer waste—without its stimulus there would be little work; but, as far as the labourer is directly concerned, it is equivalent to waste. Luxury being the economists' enemy, it is, of course, a matter of solicitude to them that it should not exist to a great extent, or that it should take the least wasteful form. And I might here venture to observe that it is a question worthy of their consideration whether the severe restrictions placed upon games of chance, and the disapprobation with which they are visited, are not hurtful, seeing they divert

E

men of luxurious tastes from indulgence in manners not of necessity wasteful, to practices that must be so. There may be grievous evils attending *Rouge et Noire;* it may be right to shut the German gambling establishment; but a point to be noted is, that though wealth lightly acquired is in danger of being prodigally and luxuriously expended, the so-called losses incurred in games of chance do not imply any destruction of wealth, but simply a change of ownership; and we may well consider whether, in the event of gambling being rendered difficult or impossible, the passions which now find an outlet in it may not seek gratification in pursuits, the very essence of which consists of the annihilation of wealth.

Capital being the result of saving or abstinence, of self-denial, of the resolution to defer enjoyment, the person who has made the sacrifice naturally expects that he should gain by it. This gain he calls profit. If another person borrows that which it costs him self-denial not to consume at once, and which may yield him profit, he expects compensation, called interest. If risk is run, the lender requires indemnity, or insurance.

There is another truth regarding capital over which it may be desirable to linger for a moment, the more so, that a distinguished expositor of it, Mr. John Stuart Mill, has not, perhaps, fenced it round with due limitation. No explanations are required to show that while producing any article a workman is not supported by the money, or rather the money's worth of food, etc., given by the purchaser for the completed article. Manifestly, a shoemaker, while making a pair of boots, does not subsist upon what has not yet been paid to him. His capital must have been supplied by another than the purchaser. He must have lived on food, etc., which the purchaser did not give him. This truth Mr. Mill expresses in the formula, "a demand for commodities is not a demand for labour." This proposition in the above naked form is ambiguous. Of course, it is true that a demand for a certain number of shoes is not a demand for a certain number of shoemakers. In the one case the results of labour are bought, in the other case labour itself is bought. A demand for labour must no more be confounded with a demand for commodities, than a demand for steam-engines with a demand for that which they make. But when Mr. Mill proceeds to add that a demand for commodities "determines the direction of the labour, but not the more or less of the labour itself, or of the maintenance or payment of the labour," he draws an unwarrantable inference. For imagine demand for all manufactures to cease. Would the direction of labour alone be affected ? Would there be no less demand for labour ? Why, all demand for it would cease, except in the case of mere attendants. Returning to the primary conception of capital, we shall perceive, without any laborious search, the limitations to this truth. Capital is not distinguished from other kinds of wealth by any material peculiarity, but by the intention of the owner. The opposite idea, sanctioned by M'Culloch, leads to a confusion. It is not certain things that always constitute capital, but things put to a certain use, and that the production of other wealth. Consequently, by a mere change of mind, one may increase or diminish one's capital, and the amount of wages to be distributed—may increase it within limits, and may diminish it indefinitely. Now, the motives which induce a capitalist to alter his mind with respect to investment may be summed up in the state of the demand for commodities. If demand is small, and there is no hope of profits, he will perhaps spend unproductively what otherwise might have been capital. If the demand is great, he may do the reverse. Thus we see that demand for commodities may increase the amount of capital, and consequently the amount to be expended in wages ; and, therefore, though a demand for commodities may not have given or created the actual physical articles constituting the capital which supported the fashioners of the commodities, that demand may have caused the creation by others of capital, and, indirectly, of a demand for labour. To take a single instance :—A firm of railway contractors have finished a contract. They are about to discharge their workmen. Until another offer is made they will spend a certain amount of money unproductively, or they will lodge it with a banker, who, by discounting some bills of exchange, may transfer it to one who will consume it, or rather its worth, unproductively. But a new contract is concluded ; having got their bill passed, a certain railway company create a demand for labour ; the workmen are retained ; and a demand for commodities has determined the maintenance of labour. Nor does it appear to be correct that a direct hirer of labour is necessarily more influential in creating a rise of wages than the buyers of commodities. Most production is now carried on with a view to a future demand; and the purchasing of the commodities is the only reason why fabricators of them continue to be hired. Mr. Mill shows that the hirer of bricklayers employs labour himself, while the buyer of velvet merely decides in what kind of work some other person shall employ them—very different from proving that the former necessarily augments wages more than the latter. " There was capital in existence," says Mr. Mill, " to do one of two things— to make the velvet, or to produce necessaries for the gaining bricklayers, but not to do both." True, but there may have been wealth in existence to do two things, and the new demand may have created so much new capital.

In truth, capital, instead of being as rigidly fixed as the quantity of matter in the world, is, I repeat, capable of being indefinitely diminished by a mere change of intention, and is capable, within certain limits, of expansion. All the wealth that exists in the world consists of two parts—what could be capital, and what could not be so. But all the possible capital is never made actual capital: all the loaves, for example, are not consumed by hard-working, industrious people ; and consequently it is possible to increase to a certain extent the amount of capital by a change of intention. Every bag of wheat is potential capital, though every bag of wheat is not turned into capital. If the people of this country became, by a miraculous change worked in their natures, all at once as frugal as the Dutch, and, like them, could be induced to save laboriously without rushing into ruinous speculations, even when they had no better prospect than that of getting 2 or $2\frac{1}{2}$ per cent for their money, the wealth of the country might not instantaneously be increased, but the amount of capital would, and the wages of the labourer would very soon rise. This truth, perhaps never denied, but too much forgotten, should have prevented many controversies which still engage the learned. It should have prevented many discussions on the nature of credit. It clears up, as we shall see, some dark points regarding strikes and wages. It reminds us how, starting with the same resources, men and nations may yet soon attain to very different degrees of wealth. Again, this truth helps to explain the marvellous extravagance that is often witnessed in times of great commercial distress. It has been remarked that, in the midst of the Revolution of 1848,

when industry was paralysed and little gain was coming in, the
demand for popular luxuries was unabated; the reason was,
that people, by a mere change of intention, and under the influence of that heedlessness of the future which marks all
revolutions, had diminished their capital, changing it into
unproductive wealth. This possibility of expanding or diminishing capital explains how countries in time of war are
able to put forth marvellous energy, and to draw forth, as it
were, hidden resources. How, asks Destutt de Tracy, was
France, after the Revolution, able to make head against the
world, to keep up fourteen armies in a time of famine, to support enormous taxes, and to spend immense sums on public
works, when, under her ancient government, she was of little
account and nowise feared abroad? The secret of this trans-
formation, he answers, is to be found in the suppression of the
sources of unproductive expenditure. There being no longer a
vast idle class fed by the feudal duties and tithes, the resources
of the country were left free for other purposes.

We may notice what may be called the mobility of capital,
or the amazing power which it now possesses of transferring
itself from one country to another. Formerly, before railways
were common, and steam navigation had narrowed the widest
seas into mere ferries, when a small part of Europe and
America were the only countries that possessed roads or wheeled
vehicles, and when ignorance and prejudice, and wars and
treaties, and hostile tariffs and laws, such as the *Droit d'Aubaine*,
and the obstacles in the way of naturalisation or expatriation,
made intercourse with foreigners difficult and constantly liable
to interruption, the capitalists of one country could scarcely
expect to gain footing in a foreign country; and, restricted to
the home market, they took care, by protective and prohibitive
duties, to retain this monopoly for themselves. If labour was
dear, or taxes oppressive, or the laws in any respect unfavourable, they had to submit; if they were in danger at home, it
was madness or suicide to send their capital abroad. Even
if the workmen took to burning their premises or breaking
their machinery, as they now do to striking, there was no
escape. But, thanks to recent changes, and, in no small degree
to the facilities recently accorded to commercial concerns being
quoted on foreign Stock Exchanges, he who is not satisfied
with the returns got at home can go abroad himself or send

abroad his circulating capital with comparative ease : the world is before him ; let him choose. Hence, from a country like ours, where the annual savings are large, and where the average rate of interest is, on the whole, low, a vast amount of capital is yearly sent abroad—some of it spontaneously, other portions of it through the allurement of State guarantees—to construct Indian, or Russian, or Canadian railways ; to buy the deben-tures of foreign railways ; to relieve the necessities of needy European or South American States ; and to be invested in mines in Mexico, building schemes at Marseilles or Brussels, in meat-preserving establishments at Monte Video, or in what-ever project and place profits above the home rate are to be had.

At this stage of our inquiries it is well to analyse the simplest phenomena, and it is desirable that there should be no mistake about the meaning of capital being sent abroad. When we say that capital migrates or is sent abroad, we mean that funds which would have been employed in hiring English labour, are employed in hiring foreign labour, or sold to capitalists who will so employ it. By reason of this exportation there are fewer hirers of home labour, more of foreign labour. Sometimes there is an actual efflux of capital. But fixed capital, machinery, etc., is, as a rule, immobile ; and in most cases migration of circulating capital means that corn, and other articles of food, which would under other circumstances have been imported, are retained in the country of their production, or sent elsewhere than to England, to maintain foreign labourers and artisans. It means also that foreign securities held by Englishmen are ex-ported, and that bills drawn on foreigners are ultimately paid to foreigners. It means that more than usual of the goods ex-ported into this country—the great entrepôt of Europe—are re-exported. It means a diminution of reinvestments in England.

In connection with capital, I must not omit to mention a point generally omitted. It is a sweeping statement to make, but, with deference, I venture to affirm that the greatest fault of current Political Economy—a fault so grievous as to vitiate much of its teaching—is, that its cultivators have fixed their attention almost exclusively on the means of increasing wealth in a brief period. Wealth which, when expended, does not yield a return within a century, it would scarcely acknowledge to be capital, however magnificent the tardy yield might be. Circulating capital is with most economists something which will recoup its owner within a year at most ; fixed capital what will yield a profit to this generation or the next. That course, on the other hand, is economically good which is good for a time, however wasteful in the end—though it "scourges" the land or saps the energies of a people. Yet why should a science have as its horizon the immediate future ? That, apparently, should be esteemed capital which brings a return, though long postponed ; and if Political Economy, capriciously narrowed by some of its votaries to the study of the causes of an immediate increase of wealth, refuses to consider all late-flowering plants as productive, there will, we may be sure, arise a more comprehensive Political Economy, looking far beyond the present hour and day, and often counselling, in the name of the science of wealth, courses which for years, it may be for centuries, will bring no return. It was a considerable advance when men began to follow those courses which were economically advantageous for a whole nation, in preference to the interests of classes. Free trade, which taught us to seek that which conduces to the benefit of all nations, was at least an equal step in the march to a comprehensive Political Economy. And we shall make as great an advance when we look not solely to the advantage of this generation, or even to that of the next, but when we shall consider how the greatest permanent gains are obtainable. Hitherto this subject has been almost ignored. Political Economy has rarely been studied with an eye to this point, unless by visionaries. In unmerited neglect lie those agencies and influences that do not bring forth their offspring of wealth for centuries. Transient and permanent material prosperity are confounded. Hence almost all economic discussions are tainted with a *petitio principii*—they describe accurately enough, and with acuteness analyse, the modes in which wealth is produced without great delay ; they assume but do not prove that these are the modes in which the greatest amount of permanent wealth is to be got. They assume, for example, that the springs of industry will not lose their elasticity by constant use ; and, with rare exceptions, these authors never reflect that perhaps the total immersion of one generation in the pursuit of gain may doom others to sterility. In the track of sordid money-making often treads riotous waste ; those grand discoveries which are the dowry of the race never come to dollar-hunters ; there is an anxiety after lucre that overshoots and misses its mark; and the ceaseless chase of wealth may enfeeble and enervate the physical as well as the mental powers. So, why any certainty that the laws of production, as deduced from the experience of a few years, may not require enormous modifications when all the consequences of obedience to them have been matured ? Perhaps, when Political Economy is studied from this side, the divergence between its teaching and that of Ethics will be small. Slavery, for example, might be counselled by the political economist who looked only to the passing profit ; in a higher point of view, and having regard to remote interests, the economist, as well as the moralist, would condemn it. Again, it is apt to be esteemed a matter of no consequence, so far as its production is concerned, how wealth is divided ; and yet it is impossible to conceive a society composed of a few rich and a multitude of poor to be economically healthy. Ethics, the aim of which is to devise rules by which the utmost happiness, and, as an important part of it, the utmost mental and bodily health, may be obtained, can scarcely recommend courses of action greatly at variance with those recommended by Political Economy, understood in this wide sense. In these pages it will be our endeavour to keep these considerations in view.

CHAPTER V.

INDUSTRIAL EDUCATION.

Two of the preceding chapters have treated of the things absolutely indispensable to the production of wealth. They are
Labour and Capital. Here it will be advantageous to speak of
the chief conditions on which depends the efficiency of labour.
And this leads to the subject of economical education. Education is not here synonymous with the three R's, nor even with
the most complete mental culture : that is not the primitive,
and it is not the true, conception of education ; and it is a mark
of the low state of popular ideas regarding education, that it is
still commonly confounded with the benefits derived from books
and teachers, and that it does not comprehend the cultivation
of the whole cycle of faculties. Moral, mental, and physical
education are all required for the economical production of
wealth. " Moral," because wherever there is great store of wealth
there must be a people living to a considerable degree under
moral restraint, and possessed of a more or less accurate code
of duty ; and a land dotted with bursting stackyards, mapped
out into well-tilled fields, and noisy with the hum of looms and
the clang of hammers, is evidence that there is at hand no small
portion of the stuff out of which martyrs and heroes are formed.
Though fine names may not be given to the qualifications of
a busy people, skilled in many crafts and trades, producing
articles cheaply and well, it is patience and sobriety, and
faithfulness and honesty, that have gained for them eminence.
These are not, indeed, the tombstone virtues ; they do not
shine in paragraphs, or obtain statues and ribbons for their
possessors ; nevertheless these russet-coloured virtues are the
very salt of the earth. To begin with moral education, and to
appreciate its influence upon wealth by the magnitude of the
consequences of its absence, mark what would ensue if men
were somewhat less trustworthy than they are—if workmen

were eye-servants, masters slippery in their promises, and customers ready to cheat or slow to pay their debts,—if what a moralist has called " faith in common life" were less rife. Or, to make the importance of moral education more patent to the eye, suppose this state of things were general; the consequence ? Why, trade would flee our shores more surely than if war had ravaged them ; if carried to the uttermost, as we suppose, this carnival of vice would dissolve society itself ; if carried to a somewhat less pitch of infamous consistency, it would scarcely leave the wherewithal to live—certainly no superfluities to export ; and even if we had the latter, our customers, grown incredulous of our goods as well as of our promises, would not buy of us.   This faith in common life, seen in every action, is the ligament of society ; every man who commits his chin and throat to a barber bears witness that he lives by "faith in common life."   It has been all but demonstrated that a nation of thorough-going liars could not hold together.   This is an extreme supposition.   We turn now to the effects of less flagrant dishonesty, as seen among ourselves.   At intervals of a few years—generally ten—this country is visited by a commercial crisis ; business is brought to a standstill ; fortunes and reputations vanish away ; months, it may be, pass before things return to their old channels and confidence is restored ; and a potent cause of the majority of those crises is, that certain persons have so violated their engagements and the common maxims of prudence, that lenders, taking alarm, decline to make any further advances, and hasten to recover those which they have made.   A country subject to these crises, periodically liable to inability to fulfil its engagements, of course, competes at a disadvantage with others free from crises.   A permanent cause of inefficiency or costliness of production is the risk which is inseparable from the credit system of payment, so long as there are found men immoral enough to take goods without the certainty of being able to pay for them.   He who runs this risk must insure himself against the losses which the dishonest may bring upon him, and often the honest man pays the premium.   Look at another aspect of the matter : if workmen are not trustworthy they must be closely watched ; and, as watching is costly, the overseer's wages must be added to the natural price of the article.   If manufacturers or retailers adulterate their goods, those who are honest enough to sell what is good and genuine will be able to charge higher prices as remuneration for exceptional honesty and trouble. Countries where there is little of this faith in common life are consequently doomed to slow development of wealth. That we have had to import truthfulness and common honesty into India is one leading reason why that vast continent, with upwards of 160,000,000 inhabitants, and a rather rich soil, has had so little to export. One often wonders why a community of slaveholders do not outstrip in the race for riches communities which pay dearly for the service of every labourer. The wonder largely disappears in face of the fact that, slaves having few inducements to be faithful and diligent, and many to be the contrary, the onehalf of the community may be said to be engaged in seeing that the other half is so. A trade may be altogether or partly ruined by the dishonesty of a few of its members. Send watches to the East Indies with seconds-hands but no corresponding works,—no more orders come for many a day. The impurities which Irish flax-growers often mixed with their bundles of flax to increase its weight depreciated its value below that of other flax inferior in quality; and it is well known that American cotton was preferred to Indian cotton, not more from the intrinsic superiority of the former than from the mingled carelessness and dishonesty of the Indian ryots who prepared the latter. Fast modern traders think to grow rich by a judicious mixture of devil's dust; but that can succeed only if they are surrounded by traders who set their faces against devil's dust; and roguery can be profitable only when honesty is general. We saw that capital, an indispensable condition of production, was due to abstinence, to a sacrifice of present to future enjoyment; and this sacrifice—self-denial we may call it—implies a degree of self-restraint which is the result of moral training, and can be general only when the morality of a country is pretty high. This capacity to save may be called Pecksniffian morality by those who only esteem theatrical and somewhat flashy virtues; but it will be called so without due consideration, for, to sacrifice the enjoyments of the present to those of the future is of the very essence of true morality. To brave actual pain in order to avoid ideal pain is an element in all moral acts. Savage nations are little competent to this sacrifice; to them the present moment is everything. The Jesuits, who once ruled Paraguay, could with great difficulty prevent the savage Paraguayans from devouring the seed-corn—so alien to their habits was the postponement of enjoyment. Everywhere in Political Economy we shall see other instances of morality working out economical benefits, and of economists deploring the evils against which moralists and theologians battle. And this is natural; for the aim of morals being to better the condition of men, it cannot but frequently, especially if time be given, coincide with the dicta of Political Economy, which shows how men may obtain all forms of comfort.

A curious question, which is cognate to this subject, over which darkness reigns, but which deserves elucidation, is the influence exerted by various religions in stimulating or retarding the formation of wealth. On the face of the facts this influence is considerable. Certain religions, if firmly believed in and carried out, would almost doom their adherents to a mediocre position in wealth. Those which are ascetic in character have this tendency. How can he who believes that it is right to mortify his flesh in all things be zealous in accumulating earthly riches? Religions which paint this life as a matter of indifference, a moment of existence scarcely worth counting, or which inculcate fatalism, so far as they are acted upon in the deons, choke the growth of wealth; and more directly and manifestly, this effect may be produced by a superabundance of religious *fêtes* and holidays, breeding waste, and dissipation, and idleness, or by the existence of vast and costly religious establishments. The economical mischief produced by religious bodies, when they are as numerous as in Spain of the seventeenth century or Rome of to-day, is incalculable.* On the other hand, religion may, in an economical point of view, be a blessing. It may furnish new motives to industry, consecrating honest sweat, or it may, in the selection of feasts and holidays, make a felicitous economical distribution between days of work and days of recreation.

It is only of recent years that the influence of mental education upon the production of wealth has been appreciated. Past schools of Political Economy have been too silent about man; in the Political Economy of the future he will be almost everything. The theory of so-called "practical" men hitherto has been, that knowledge is an actual impediment to good work in the field or in the workshop, or, if not an actual impediment,

* Buckle's *Civilisation*, vol. ii. p. 65.

a superfluity. In agriculture that theory still possesses life; and this is the more excusable, inasmuch as the efficiency of education is perhaps less evident in agriculture than in manufactures. Raise the question among farmers, and you will be pretty certain to hear some one say, " Two men that can't read are worth three that can." Farmers are not the only people entertaining this opinion. When men are accustomed to possess a precious thing they are prone to despise it; and one of the fruits of the spread of education is a wide depreciation of its value. Just as the luxurious society of France in the latter half of last century generated disgust at civilisation, and prepared the frequenters of the *salons* to listen greedily to Rousseau discoursing of the privileges of the savage, whose life was an endless *fête champêtre*, whose drink was water, and whose thoughts were purity itself; so, abundance of schools, and colleges, and books, and lectures, and educational apparatus, has generated a real or affected distrust in them all. People—and the best educated most keenly—see what education has failed to do; they are apt to ignore what it has done. But I take it that at least all manufacturers who feel the spur of home and foreign competition, and who reflect on the conditions of pre-eminence, will admit that the period has come which Humboldt spoke of when he said, that " the time was not far distant when science and manipulative skill must be welded together." On this subject a mass of striking facts has been collected, showing that, for general purposes, educated workers are far more efficient than uneducated. To take only a few instances of the importance conceded to education in regard to manual labour: Sir John Burgoyne states that a sapper, who is an educated artisan, is worth, for the common purposes of war, three common linesmen. It has been calculated that, if the recruits to the army were fairly educated, one million a-year would be saved to the nation. Whether these and many similar statements which might be quoted are or are not perfectly accurate, it is manifest that unless there be some occult virtue in ignorance, education—that is, an increase of intelligence and command over men's faculties—must heighten the value of the labourer. In short, it may be taken for granted that education does make men more efficient labourers. What, then, is the existing machinery for imparting education to all? In England, Scotland, and Ireland, primary schools are tolerably abundant. An education rate will soon work much good in England. In Scotland, schools are, and long have been, particularly good and abundant : hence, or partly hence, as Lord Macaulay has eloquently shown, her thriving condition, in spite of a poor soil and a rude climate. But there are many obstacles to these schools being attended. Not prizing education as it ought to be prized, parents have been inclined to withdraw their children from school ; the labour market, offering to children wages that appear considerable to needy parents, has tended to withdraw the very poor who stood most in need of this education to work in the fields, cotton mills, dye and print works ; and Parliament has several times passed laws to restrain this tendency, and to prevent parents from thus maiming or destroying the minds of those who cannot protect themselves. The temptation is sometimes very great : in some rare cases these children can work as well as, nay, occasionally, if we are to believe report, even better than a man ; the little fingers of a boy, it has been said, with what degree of truth I know not, can "sharpen twice as many needles as those of an adult." The climbing boys of the beginning of the century are represented by the modern "boy" jockeys.

In order to check these evils a network of Acts has been spread across almost the entire industrial field, with the view of drawing children to school. The bearing of these Acts on education may be thus stated in the words of Mr. Redgrave, one of Her Majesty's Inspectors of Factories :—" *Every* child who performs any manual work (except in agriculture) is bound now to attend school concurrently with its daily occupation." None of these Acts touched agriculture; and it was contended with reason that many of the most terrible evils which were once rampant within the walls of factories flourished unchecked on our farms, especially where the gang system was common ; that, cut off from selling the whole of their children's time to manufacturers, parents sold it to agriculture ; that it was unfair to deprive manufacturers of children's cheap labour, and to allow farmers to use it ; and that, in short, to be impartial, and even to make the Factory Acts fully efficacious, the extension of the principle to agriculture was required. To ascertain whether these contentions were just, a Royal Commission was appointed in 1867, and ample evidence has been collected throughout the counties of England, sufficing to show that there are almost as good grounds for extending the principle to agriculture as to factories, and that parents might allow their children to attend school without much greater hardships than the workers in mills do. Enough of evidence has been collected to show that the old boast that the inhabitants of Britain, and their descendants in the United States and our Colonies, are the only people who do not allow women to engage in the arduous forms of field-work is now baseless, if it ever was true. There is the more need for an extension to agriculture of the substance of the educational provisions of the Factory Acts, from the fact that, as a comparison of the census returns of 1851 and 1861 shows, there is a tendency to hand over the work of agriculture to the young. Every observer may mark this movement for himself. Striplings who, twenty years ago, would scarcely be trusted to give fodder to horses or spread the litter of cattle, are now entrusted with a team or a " pair." This resort to cheap labour—which we take to be due to the rise in rent and wages, and the consequent necessity for seizing every opening for economy—is distinctly recorded in the census tables.

Of the young labourers it seems probable that those under ten might be prohibited from working for wages, and that between ten and twelve or thirteen, partial school attendance might be exacted as a condition of service. Some such provision would probably give education to thousands who now go without it. And though there is no ignoring the fact that in several counties of England the labourer might be deprived of, say £2 : 10s. in the year, or even more, if his children up to ten were hindered from going out to weed, pick stones, scare birds, run errands, " herd," as they say in Scotland, or " tent," as they say in Yorkshire, we rejoin that *De minimis lex non curat ;* that similar exceptional cases have been disregarded by the Factory Act, and need not be heeded in " agriculture ;" and that these miserable families will disappear by a better distribution of labour. They are chiefly to be found in districts where labourers huddle together in misery and oblivion of the fact that, a few counties off, wages, perhaps twice as high, are to be got for the asking ; and the domestic migrations which the silent social forces of the day are setting in motion, and those more artificial migrations which have set in from Devonshire to Yorkshire and elsewhere, will thin these pauper beds and level the wages of agricultural labour. Here I do but glance at the question of the propriety of the State meddling with the education of the poor. Rightly or wrongly, it is decided in this country that the State should interfere. And with good reason. The old theory—too often but a theory —embodied in the maxim " Spend me and defend me," that the relation of master and servant carried with it certain duties enforced by the strongest social sanctions, that the master was bound to see after the moral and physical well-being of his servant or apprentice, and that the servant was to look up to his master as a guide in all his conduct, has disappeared, and we have entered on a time when master and servant bargain as equals. Nobody should regret the disappearance of the former period. Mr. Carlyle and Mr. Disraeli—marvellous unison of opinion—whose books are full of sighs at its decease, and of dreams of its resurrection, would conjure it to depart if that ancient state of society did arise from the grave at their prayers. But security, such as it was in the relations of clientage and patronage, for the well-being of the poor, having disappeared, it has been greatly felt that the State should see to the fate of this shepherdless portion of the people. And, indeed, to suffer a father to ruin the health or stunt the growth of his children, is to abdicate the fundamental and chief duty of a State—the duty to protect. To suffer a parent to force a youth to labour as an adult is to revive the evils of the old Roman *patria potestas* without its advantages. In their recoil from the Tudor legislation for the organisation of labour, and in admiration of freedom of trade in labour and in goods, people gravitated towards the other extreme. They are, however, righting themselves : it is now a truism to say that, if the Elizabethan legislation injuriously interfered with the poor, the Georgian legislation, or absence of it, was injuriously indifferent to them. And, influenced by this recovery, Political Economy begins to cast off its fortuitous connection with *laissez faire.*

The political economist is concerned with primary education, inasmuch as it tends to make the labourer more efficient, and because, saving him from toil in tender years, it enables him to continue longer efficient. The economist must, therefore, desire to see the adoption of a measure which would most effectually spread primary education. And the foundation of such a measure would be to have one law applicable to children engaged in all kinds of manual labour, agricultural or manufacturing, with, as far as possible, the same simple rules for all. A bill to this effect was actually brought into the House of Commons by Mr. Adderley in 1860; but it was rejected on the second reading, the agriculturists being powerful enough to throw out that which they had forced the manufacturers to accept. Perhaps, however, eleven years' experience of the laxity, unfairness, and necessary inefficiency of such fragmentary legislation as hitherto has been applied, has prepared the public mind for one simple law. At the same time, one cannot anticipate that any legislative measure will suffice to make primary education universal. Even if these Acts received the utmost extension, many children would remain uneducated: compulsory legislation will be somewhat ineffectual unless backed by an almost compulsory consensus of opinion. Manufacturers often do not like to employ half-timers; preferring to dispense with children's labour rather than conform their establishments to the altered rules, they often discharge half-timers; parents and children themselves too often eagerly evade legislative provisions for their well-being; and they will continue to do so until it be a maxim believed at every fireside, that education is almost as necessary to a child as food.

The school may develop the general intelligence; but it is in the workshop that technical education, properly speaking, begins. Now, to the ordinary workman, the workshop or the factory must be the chief school; and in the recent discussions upon technical education, too much stress has been laid upon the advantages of a theoretical knowledge of science. I do not seek to underrate the value of it; but it is stating only a patent fact when I say that lectures, and experiments, and books, are to the ordinary workman of less consequence than the nicety and certainty of hand and eye that are to be got only by the actual handling of tools—*Fit fabricando faber.* The workman's technical education must be mainly his apprenticeship.

CHAPTER VI.

INDUSTRIAL EDUCATION CONTINUED.

THE preceding chapter pointed out in general terms the influence of education on the production of wealth, and briefly described or indicated the existing machinery for imparting it. We pass now to the machinery for imparting industrial knowledge and skill. At present, the chief instrument of technical education is apprenticeship (*apprendre*), and formerly it was almost the only instrument. This subject has been neglected by economists, and their neglect is singular, as some of the most interesting and immediately momentous questions of Political Economy fall to be considered in connection with apprenticeship. It will be desirable to speak briefly of the history of apprenticeship, more especially as it will be possible to judge of some cognate questions only when we know how apprenticeship arose. Adam Smith has truly observed that we find no trace of it among the Greeks or Romans; and in neither Greek nor Latin is there any specific word to denote it. This is not surprising in view of the economy of the ancients. To be an apprentice supposes that one is preparing to be a master workman, and as there were few or no master workmen among the ancients, as their industry was largely in the hands of slaves, apprenticeship was naturally unknown. Moreover, as Michelet has well pointed out, so long as the skilled Syrian or Carthaginian slave, a ready-made artificer, was to be had, there was no need at Rome of providing this school of technical education; it was only under the Empire, when the rude Dacian; and the Scythian were the slaves of the Romans, that the want was felt. Apprenticeship arose in Europe in the Middle Ages, probably about the twelfth century; and the rise was almost simultaneous in several countries, owing to the then similarity of social circumstances of the European States. It was an offshoot of the corporations which then arose throughout Europe. These guilds, or trading corporations—traceable, some think, to the Roman *collegia*—were natural institutions at a time when it was the interest of the craftsmen to band together to resist the oppression of the noble ; and the corporations, formed with this object in view, received privileges from kings, who protected them, if for no other reason than that they found them useful milch cows, and serviceable in balancing the power of the nobles. All comers, of course, were not allowed to share corporate privileges. They were, in truth, jealously guarded. A noviciate was required before one became " free of the trade," and this noviciate was the apprenticeship, which generally lasted from five to seven years. Indeed, so far as England was concerned, the famous Statute of Apprenticeship, passed in 1560, in the reign of Elizabeth, declared it illegal to exercise " any craft, mystery (*mestier*, old French for *metier*), or occupation," then in use, without having served an apprenticeship of at least seven years to the " craft, mystery, or occupation." In the exercise of that power of changing a law manifestly unjust which English judges at all times have assumed, and which, since the days of Holt and Mansfield, they have openly exercised, and in the name of " common right," the Judges of England did much to mitigate the cruel absurdity of the law : they explained it away ; but nominally it remained in force until 1814. By this famous Act the whole of England was given over, bound hand and foot, to close corporations. The most proficient might not practise a trade to which he had not served an apprenticeship under a member of some privileged body. Frequently one could exercise one's trade only in certain towns. He that could make shoes for the inhabitants of York was deemed unfit to make them for the inhabitants of London. As Sydney Smith has remarked :—

" Woe to the cobbler who, having made Hessian boots for the aldermen of Newcastle, should venture to invest with these coriaceous integuments the leg of a liege subject in York. A yellow ant in a nest of red ants—a butcher's dog in a fox-kennel, a mouse in a bee-hive—all feel the effects of untimely intrusion ; but far preferable their fate to that of the misguided artisan who, misled by sixpenny histories of England, and conceiving his country to have been united at the Heptarchy, goes forth from his native town to stitch freely within the sea-girt

limits of Albion.   Him the mayor, him the aldermen, him
the recorder, him the quarter-session would worry.   Him the
justices, before trial, would long to get into the tread-mill;
and would much lament that by a recent Act they could not
do so even with the intruding tradesman's consent, but the
moment he was tried they would push him in with redoubled
energy, and leave him to tread himself into a conviction of the
barbarous institutions of his corporation-divided country."

In the direct and confident language of the time, possessing
unbounded belief in the efficacy of legislation to mould facts,
the statute was passed in order that "idleness might be banished, husbandry advanced, and a convenient proportion of wages
yielded to the hired servant both in time of scarcity and in time
of plenty."   In the language of to-day, this statute was an
attempt to organise labour, one of the vastest and most magnificent attempts ever conceived and sanctioned, an idea which
could have entered the minds only of the spacious-minded statesmen of the days of Elizabeth.   Not that it had no precedent, or
that it was the first attempt to organise labour; it was part of a
system which dominated for centuries.   A long list of laws had
been passed, beginning with the famous statute of labourers in
the reign of Edward III., but the scope of them all was limited
compared with this the last of them.   It is interesting to note
some of its provisions, if only to observe their similarity with
the proposals of modern organisers of labour.   The Justices of
Peace were to regulate the rate of wages within their divisions:
this is part of every organiser's scheme; Mr. Ruskin would
endorse the principle.   Many kinds of workmen—such as shoemakers and tailors, and cutlers and cloth-weavers—could not
be hired for any term less than one year.   This, if I am not mistaken, is the very thing which Mr. Harrison and Professor Beesly
want.   This statute was found to work intolerable tyranny,
and those who would organise industry by legislation ought to
remember the fact.   Such parts of the statute as related to the
number and quality of apprentices, and the rate of wages,
had, indeed, fallen into desuetude long before 1814, and the provision which required every one to have served seven years at
the trade at which he was employed had been so explained
away that apprenticeship at any trade was held to be sufficient.

These guilds, which seem an inevitable stage in the development of industry—a stage beyond which, unfortunately, certain

countries never advance—were to be found all over Europe. In Scotland they were not so powerful or tyrannical as elsewhere; three years was there a common period of apprenticeship. In Germany they were especially powerful, and in Munich they lately lingered with almost all their absurdities, looking in the midst of the surrounding freedom tenfold more absurd and vexatious than ever. It is, I believe, of Munich that the story goes that it requires a dozen men to make a wheel-barrow. Saint Louis, Henry III., Henry IV., Colbert, the organising minister of Louis XIV., gave the French guilds privilege after privilege, and made them obligatory. In the insolence of monopoly they played all conceivable freaks, and did all possible harm to industry. They were embodied laziness, caprice, arrogance, and stupidity. Turgot, the great minister of Louis XVI. —in this, as in so many other respects, ahead of his age—complained of the "*dispositions bizarres, tyranniques, contraires a l'humanité et aux bonnes mœurs*" of the regulations of the corporations, and tried to destroy them; but though condemned at a *lit de justice* in 1776 they saw Turgot's fall, and lived on until, with so many other relics of feudalism, they were swept into destruction by the Constituent Assembly. Henceforth no term of apprenticeship was exacted in France. With the repeal of the Act of Elizabeth in the reign of George III. freedom of trade at home may be said to have been established. The repeal of that law was a measure well-nigh parallel in importance to the repeal of the Corn Laws in 1848. It left no legal restrictions as to the time or necessity of apprenticeship, except in the case of certain corporations. But what law has ceased trying to do, the customs of many trades, and the rules of many societies, have attempted to reinforce. Seven years is the term of apprenticeship still required in the printing, and many other trades. Men refuse to work with those who have served less. They look upon the latter as intruders. Some trades leave the question open, but certainly very many insist on a minimum time of service necessary to make one free of the society, or "legal to the trade." Thus the Operative Masons' Society is open only to those who have served five years; no one is admitted into the Coachmakers' Society unless he has served seven years as an apprentice in a coachmaker's shop. And not only do these trade societies insist upon a long apprenticeship, but they also, and with more unanimity

and emphasis, insist upon the number of apprentices not exceeding a certain fixed proportion to the journeymen. Thus, in
the building trade, men have insisted that each firm or employer
should have only seven apprentices; and the glassmakers allow
only one apprentice to three " chairs," each " chair " being composed of four persons. And I would observe that the societies
of barristers and advocates are amenable to the same charge.
They obstruct those who have not undergone a regular noviciate,
or who do not comply with certain rules, by a kind of " rattening," which may be mild, but which in principle does not
differ from the " rattening " employed by trades unionists.

The first charge that may be brought against the present
system of apprenticeship by economists is, that in almost every
trade the period is too long; and it is easy to select cases in
which the charge can be substantiated, if it be improper to
keep as a scholar and novice one who has long been able to perform journeyman work. That printers should be apprenticed
seven years is grossly absurd; if the object of apprenticeship
were solely to teach the trade as quickly as possible, one
third of the time would probably be enough. It is said,
however, that in most trades the time cannot be shortened
if the master is to be compensated for teaching his apprentices. This, however, is very much a theoretical objection;
and, as a matter of fact, the only privilege the ordinary
apprentice derives from his indenture is to be allowed the run of
the shop, and to have an opportunity, not of being taught by
others, but of teaching himself. In France, he is called a
" knowledge-catcher;" the term is accurately descriptive, for if
the apprentice is to be taught at all he must " catch " knowledge. Direct instruction is almost unknown; and often the
apprentice owes nothing more to the master than the habit of
keeping regular hours, and of finishing one thing at a time.
Then, as a matter of fact, the master in a few months at most
is able to remunerate himself. So much for the masters' plea
for prolonged apprenticeships.

It is easy also to show that the workmen's pleas for long
apprenticeships are unsatisfactory. They are accustomed to
maintain that a prolonged apprenticeship is a security for good
workmanship; they forget that, as a matter of fact, the quality
of the article is not to be judged by the private history of the producer, that the times in which apprenticeships were most stringent

and prolonged were not distinguished by specially good work, and that the history of industry contains a long list of names—such as Arkwright and Smeaton—going to show that men not bred to a craft may yet do for it what those bred to it could never do. They further say that, as journeymen have really to teach the raw lad, it is just that the latter should refrain for a period from competing with his instructors. Now, though this is not a fallacy, it is a fiction: the instruction is mythical; if it be real, let the instructors set forth the items for it, and charge for it directly, instead of resorting to an indirect charge, the proceeds of which may come into other pockets than those of the instructors. As to limiting the number of apprentices, that is, of course, to prevent so many human beings obtaining knowledge, and to expose a country or district to the danger of losing a trade.*

It may, indeed, easily be shown that many of the arguments for long apprenticeships are resolvable into selfishness; but those who choose to brave this charge, and are indifferent to it, are impregnable. It may be shown to workmen that by insisting upon a long term of preliminary service an artificial monopoly is created, and that the prospects of their own class, it may be of their own children, are sometimes impaired; but we do not see that if to sell in the dearest market be avowed as the rule of life, irrespective of all considerations, which it is not, if there be no thought for the morrow or the interests of others, these restrictions can be proved to the satisfaction of those who benefit by them to be bad. Openly avowing that they care neither for the interests of their own class nor even for those of their children, acknowledging no considerations but those of selfishness, they can be reached by no arguments. It is vain to point out that a long term of apprenticeship is hurtful to their classmates; they know and acknowledge it. It is in vain to plead that every man has a right to sell to the best advantage his skill, however acquired; they deny it wherever his skill would affect their pecuniary interests.

The economist's test of the propriety of these restrictions is—Are they necessary to ensure a supply of good workmen? Is it

---

* "These barriers, for the keeping out of incomers, keep in those who would be out-goers." See Mr. Chadwick's Address as President of the Department of Economy and Trade, Social Science Congress, 1864.

impossible to train good workmen in less than seven, five, or
three years? and the answer undoubtedly must be that, if all
other than economical considerations are waved aside as extraneous, as monopoly in some form or other, this necessity does
exist. If the test be, What is the shortest time, compatible
with their circumstances, in which the children of the labouring class can acquire a trade? the periods of apprenticeships
are far too long; and this much the most intelligent friends
of these restrictions will grant. It certainly seems unnecessary that all persons should be compelled to enter trades by
the same long avenue; and even granting that a protracted
period of apprenticeship is necessary to remunerate a master
for teaching an apprentice, it seems perfectly practicable and expedient that there should be alongside of the present system, a
more general custom of paying premiums, in return for which
masters would undertake to teach their trades in the shortest
possible time. Why should there not be special schools for imparting education in special branches, in imitation of those
established at Mulhouse? Certainly one who looks with un-
biassed eyes must admit that apprenticeship, as a system of training, is wasteful and inefficient, and that it resembles very much
the education in our schools thirty years ago, before the labours
of Pestalozzi and Dr. Bell had come to maturity. Instead of
keeping steadily in view as the chief end how to teach as
quickly as possible a lad to handle the tools and perform all the
work of his trade, every other end is preferred. The masters
wish to prolong the apprenticeship, so that they may pay for
journeyman work only an apprentice's wages. The workmen
wish to prolong it in order to exclude as many as possible from
the labour market. The apprentice himself has no stimulus or
interest to learn quickly. Thus there is a general league in
favour of inefficiency and tardy acquisition.

But a fundamental charge is brought against apprenticeships. Their destruction, not their reformation, is desired by
some. It is alleged that apprenticeships are unsuited to the
shifting conditions of modern industry, which require men to
be able to adapt themselves readily to the changes caused by
machinery and the discovery of new processes in the arts; that
without apprenticeships men would be able to learn two or
even three trades in their youth; that they thus would be
rendered independent of fashions and vicissitudes; that these

long years of serfage are alien to times in which short engagements are the rule; that they encourage idleness; that men
thus lose one or two years of their lives; that many trades get
on very well without apprenticeships; that there is no necessity
for their continuance elsewhere; and that, in short, to use the
words of Mr. Nasmyth, a very intelligent witness before the
Trades Union Commission, the apprentice system is "the fag
end of the old feudal system, and ought to be abolished."
And these assertions do not lack converts. At present, whether
for a time or for ever, the tendency is to discredit apprenticeship, particularly under indenture. In America, where an
eager competition for labour brings to the apprentice all the
privileges of a journeyman, apprenticeship is almost unknown,
and in France also there is a decline. M. Baudin, one well
qualified to speak upon the subject, stated in evidence before
a Commission appointed by the French Government to examine
the state of technical education, that only 1 in 15 of the apprentices who came under his notice in Paris were bound to
their masters by more than a merely verbal contract. Another
proof of the change is the fact that people are loudly bewail-
ing it. As to this country, Mr. Godfrey Lushington, a stout
advocate of the retention of apprenticeship under indenture,
speaks no more than the truth when he says:—" In nearly
every trade of the United Kingdom the system of apprenticeship under indenture is giving way before a system called
apprenticeship which is really not under indenture, and often
not even in writing." The potter's trade is an instance of a
relaxation of the apprentice system. In that trade, in which
formerly seven years was the prescribed period, it is now not
unusual to hire a boy for a year, to give him at first weekly
wages, and then pay him by piecework at a lower rate than a
journeyman. Not to multiply instances, the same holds good of
the joiners of London. Is this tendency, all but universal, to be
regretted? We think not; and though it would be rash to ·
pronounce a sweeping opinion—though the practice suitable for
one trade and country may be utterly unsuitable for another—
there is reason to believe that a constant succession of highly
trained workmen would be obtained, though apprenticeships
were everywhere shortened, and in a great number of trades
were wholly abandoned. Apprenticeship is, in truth, the resort
of people who are too poor to procure instruction, except by

mortgaging themselves for several years. It recalls the position of the Roman debtor under the early law. The course of its prevalence and continuance lies in the total destitution of a considerable portion of the population; and as this destitution is diminished, or as the labourer can attain credit, apprenticeship will disappear. The custom of dispensing with formal apprenticeship, and of paying a lad for work done, and charging him for work spoiled and instruction actually received, will be sure to spread. It is the opinion of many authorities, Adam Smith among them, that this ought everywhere to be adopted; and there are many manufacturers who will affirm that, given a lad of fair intelligence and strength, there is no trade or craft they know of in which he will not make himself useful in a few weeks, and will not remunerate his employer for wages, nominal at first, and ascending as he grows in skill; that it would suffice to empower the employer to mortgage a lad's future earnings in order to make good breakage and waste; and that there are no reasons, monopoly apart, why masons and carpenters should undergo an apprenticeship any more than farm-servants. On the whole, I venture to endorse this opinion; and this much is certain, that, if regard to economy is observed, a long apprenticeship will sink, from being the only mode to being, at most, one of several modes of learning a trade, and that it will be less and less customary to buy instruction with raw labour.

The chief school of technical education must be the workshop: it is there a workman must learn "to cut a plank with a gimlet and bore a hole with a saw"—the well-chosen test of a good mechanic. Still, theory is not useless, even to the humblest workman, and in proportion to the difficulty of his work it becomes necessary. Theoretical knowledge is often a short cut to practical knowledge, and "the rule of thumb," the national idol, must not have all our worship. For example, the man who knew the smallest smattering of mineralogy would never insert a slab of freestone in a wall so that the pressure of the superincumbent masonry should be through the planes of cleavage; but an uneducated mason might labour for years without discovering the fact. Technical education has never been entirely neglected, for our Universities have always furnished technical instruction to the lawyer and the doctor. And this generation is not the first that waked up to the necessity of technical education in the arts : we read in Gibbon, for example, that the Emperor Constantine, finding the Greeks had so degenerated that architects were not to be found capable of carrying out his ambitious plans for the new capital, Constantinople, directed the governors of the provinces to train a number of young men to be architects.

The Paris Exhibition of 1867 brought prominently to view the importance of technical education. Jurors and visitors generally returned to this country with the news that, instead of standing at the head of almost every department of industry, we now stood indisputably at the head of only some dozen ; that we had certainly improved since the Exhibition of 1851, but that France, Belgium, and Prussia had improved much faster, so that we were relatively declining ; and it was the almost unanimous opinion of jurors, men of science, manufacturers, engineers, etc., that we are being overtaken partly by reason of the attention bestowed by foreign countries upon technical education. " See," said these judges, " what has been done by technical education ! Our engines are no longer indisputably the best ; the locomotives made by M. Schneider at Creusot, are as cheap and as good. Krupp's steelworks, at Essen, can produce work quite equal to English work. Zimmerman produces tools which rival those made by Whitworth. Twelve years ago, there was scarcely a steam-power hosiery machine in France, and now the French are making as good work as we are. Wurtemberg and Zurich firms send in tenders for locomotives lower than those sent in by English firms, and Belgian cotton yarn has been sold in Manchester. Our advantages in abundance of coal and iron at our doors have been so counterbalanced by intelligence and economy, that France, with little coal and less iron, can compete with us." What will happen, it may forebodingly be asked, when the United States, with vast coal and iron-fields, will become, as it must sooner or later become, a manufacturing country ? It must be granted that there prevailed wild delusions touching industrial education, delusions now fading away. It must be granted also, that much of this self-vituperation and depreciation was the fruit of vanity. We were foolishly surprised that the despised foreigner could do anything so well as Englishmen. The old prejudice that one Englishman was of superior prowess to two Frenchmen, lingered in the form of a belief that he was superior to two French workmen.

We forgot that our exceptional prosperity and superiority were largely due 'to Watt and Arkwright, and the exceptional measure of peace and good government which had long been ours, but which for some years we have not monopolised. Our self-depreciation was not discriminative. Far from going back, we had not remained stationary, as reference to almost any department proved ; we had slowly been progressing in paths in which we were the pioneers, while foreigners, aided by our example, were progressing swifter. It was forgotten that technical education was only one of a hundred causes of the progress abroad. It is also true that the degree of attention given by foreign Governments to technical education, and the effects of that attention, were exaggerated. M. Louis Reybaud, a distinguished French economist, has shown that the French system of technical education has actually little influenced French industry. In 1863, M. Rouher, then Minister of Commerce, stated, in a letter to the Emperor, that the International Exhibition of 1862 proved that there was danger of France being outstripped in the race of industry by her competitors, and the chief impediment, in the opinion of M. Rouher, was the absence of a complete system of technical education, notwithstanding the existence of the *École Centrale des Arts et Manufactures.* As the labours of the Commission appointed in consequence of that letter had not borne fruit by 1867, the favourable appearance of France in the last International Exhibition cannot be ascribed to attention to technical education. As to Germany, where technical education is carried to a high pitch of excellence, we know that certain parts of the machinery for developing technical education have failed. I only condense a mass of trustworthy testimony when I say that the *realschulen,* or technical and practical schools, have not been altogether satisfactory. Lads from the Gymnasia prove quite a match for the *realschulen* pupils, even in industry. " I have often found," says Liebig, " that students coming from good colleges will speedily leave the pupils of industrial and polytechnic schools far behind them, even *in the natural sciences,* though the latter, when compared with the former, were at first giants in knowledge."

At the same time there are unquestionably two sorts of advantages to be got by technical education, and they are so important that they constitute sufficient justification of it. It is well that a man should understand the nature of his tools and the material with which he works, and that his eye should be so educated that he will not require to waste time in ceaselessly testing his work with the square or straight line. That a joiner should know at what angle the knife of his plane should be set, and should be able to perceive something of the reason ; that a stoker should know the theory of combustion ; that an engine-driver should be acquainted with mechanics ; that a dyer should know something of chemistry ; that a miner should know with what rocks coal is usually found, is well, unless there be some potent virtue in ignorance. Now, how is this knowledge to be got ? By mechanics' institutes, was the favourite answer thirty years ago ; but it has been proved that the answer was incorrect, or too sanguine. Instead of being schools of practical science, they have become, in great part, places where pleasure-loving audiences are amused with panoramas of the Holy Land, the Christy Minstrels, mesmeric or electrobiological quacks, a miscellany of bad smells and cheap fireworks dubbed chemistry. Mechanics' institutes have somewhat failed to accomplish the original purposes and the wonderful results expected by their founders and promoters, from many reasons, of which these are the chief :—The want of sufficient primary education to enable their frequenters to benefit by lectures,— a want which has effectually prevented their spread in France ; the choice of the form of lectures, eminently unsuited for beginners, in preference to teaching by class-books and examinations ; the prominence given to abstract sciences ; and the imprudent disregard of the occupations of the people to be benefited. Let us avoid these errors. Primary education being pre-supposed, let classes be taught from text-books and regularly examined ; let those sciences and parts of sciences which are of use in the arts be taught ; and instead of teaching the carpenter astronomy, with which he has no concern, teach him mechanics and drawing. Let not the teaching be gratuitous unless in rare cases ; the payment of a small fee wonderfully stimulates the attention. The aid given by the Science and Art Department to teachers of science and to pupils, in the shape of grants, medals, and exhibitions, will help. The prizes offered by Mr. Whitworth place, as it were, in the hands of every working man the possibility of obtaining an excellent scientific education. They make a royal road to knowledge, and run omnibuses on it. We come to the second advantage of technical education :—It trains men, qualified to be the overseers of others, ready to avail themselves of scientific discoveries when they are of service in the arts, and to form what the French call the *état major*, or staff of industry. Employers complain that such men are not to be had at almost any price. Employers with three or four hundred hands assert that, if their foreman were to die they could not replace him out of that number. Men so skilled in chemistry as to be able to pick up hints from scientific journals are scarcely to be procured. The colonies call out for scientifically-trained engineers ; but they do not come. Nor will these and similar men be found in sufficient abundance until we possess technical universities or schools, or until our existing universities, ceasing to run in a mediæval curriculum, erect special machinery for teaching the theory of the arts. There are the *École Polytechnique*, the *École Centrale*, the technical universities at Zurich and in Wurtemberg, the *Gewerbe Schule* of Berlin, to imitate and improve upon. Of course, the State has been requested to interfere, and its niggardliness has been complained of, but without just cause. Abstract sciences, purely theoretical knowledge, branches of learning which are not concerned with money-making, may with some excuse ask State endowments ; but to nurse with endowments technical education, which, if it be worthy of the name, and if one-half of what is said of the demand for persons possessing it be true, will enable those that receive it to enter lucrative professions, seems out of the question.

CHAPTER VII.

MACHINERY.

CONTINUING the survey of the means by which the production of wealth is made more effective, I come to machinery. The name may be retained, although it is apt to convey an idea far narrower than what is intended, and to conceal the fact that it refers to all expedients for economising human labour,—successful modes of rotation of crops as well as steam-engines. It is useless to spend much time or space in proving the advantages of machinery. He who speaks of machinery as an evil, proposes, though he may not know it, that we should till the earth with our finger-nails; employ a sharp stake or stone, and he commits himself to the threshing-machine and the sewing-machine. No sane man, weighing his words, ever attacked machinery as a whole. The Swings who burned the threshing-machines thirty years ago in England, the Luddites who from 1710 to 1820 broke the stocking and lace frames in England, in defiance of the punishment of death, the shoemakers of Staffordshire and Northampton who opposed the use of the "closing"-machine, the workmen of Lyons who broke the Jacquard loom, were enthusiasts for machinery: they went through blood, fire, and crime, in their enthusiasm for the flail, and the awl, and the unimproved loom. They were fanatics for imperfect machinery, a machine being only an excellent tool. To destroy machinery would be to cut off the right arm of man, and it is only in comedy that this is proposed as an advantage. Nevertheless, no mechanical invention of much consequence has been introduced into use without encountering strenuous opposition; for a time this resistance has frequently succeeded, so that the biographies of inventors, from Lee to Hargreaves, seem to cry out in unison, "Cursed is he that inventeth." " He giveth men blessings, and they reward him with curses." " Take your

invention elsewhere," was Colbert's remark to a man who came
to him with an invention which was to perform the work of ten
men ; and Colbert is not singular in his observation, or the man
in his fate. " What would you have me do with the mules and
muleteers that ply between Penote and Vera Cruz ?" asked
Santa Anna, a former President of Mexico, of those who proposed to make a railway between these towns ; and in this
country a similar question was asked of Stephenson by Colonel
Sibthorp, who saw in imagination highways overgrown with
grass, inns shut and tenantless, all horses useless except to be
boiled down into glue, coachmen, and guards and ostlers and
postboys wandering about in hungry idleness, and the screaming
locomotives followed by the curses of the crowds whom they
had ruined. The change has been consummated ; we see and
enjoy the consequences ; and they are an increase of traffic, more
inns, more horses, and an army of servants, of which the coachmen, guards, and postboys would not form a company.

All opposition to machinery—meaning thereby all mechanical
devices or forces used in place of human labour—may be
resolved into attempts to make the production of wealth difficult, to set up artificial obstacles to the attainment of wealth,
to make men poorer than they need be. A way of obtaining a
certain article with half the former trouble and labour has been
discovered ; men are enriched as surely as if a handsome present
had dropped from heaven ; but the makers of the article in the
old way stand up in their places and say, " We cannot allow so
much labour to be saved ; we insist that the articles shall be
made in a more laborious manner than is necessary, and therefore that you shall pay more for it than there is any need."
So acting, they impoverish men as surely as if they had stolen
the present. We read in Michelet that the boatmen of the
Rhine destroyed the bridge built by Charlemagne at Mayence,
doubtless in order that they might continue to have the privilege and profit of ferrying travellers across. Suppose—to carry
the illustration nearer home—you live on one side of a stream,
and a town which you have often to visit is on the other, that
a bridge is built by which you cross in two minutes and for one
penny, instead of in ten minutes and for the payment of two-
pence, and that the boatmen insist that the bridge shall be shut
up ; this real event and this hypothetical event correspond with
the conduct of those who oppose machinery. And like those who

would compel men to go the long road instead of the short, to pay dearly for an article that is to be had cheaply, they are to be branded as extortioners. If not so, they are beggars, and, like Gil Blas's beggar, they beg carbine in hand. In a modified degree, the same is of course true of those who, like the spinners who limited the spindles in Hargreaves' spinning-jenny, would hinder the use of certain complicated machines, or who would oppose the fullest extension of machinery. All who oppose machinery in any degree endeavour to impoverish mankind; they set up obstacles in order that they may be removed, and dig valleys in order that they may fill them up ; they compel men to go the long road, and would shut up the short one ; they are in league with dearness and famine, and they work in concord with hail and frost.

The two advantages of machinery consist in rendering more easy what was without machinery possible, and possible what was before impossible. It increases the means and wealth of society, and renders mankind more able to meet any calls made upon it. Hence it follows that, even if it were true that machinery threw labour out of employment, the most economical course would probably be not to resist, limit, or postpone its introduction, but to introduce it as quickly and as completely as possible. Society may be a gainer even should it give in pure charity all that the discharged men have previously received in wages. Among 50,000 men £2,000,000 are distributed as wages for producing the value of £3,000,000 ; a machine or set of machines is invented by which the services of these men are dispensed with, and goods of the value of £6,000,000 are yearly produced. Let the cost of the machines, or the yearly charges to pay their cost, be £1,000,000, society is wealthier than it was the previous year by £4,000,000. It could, therefore, give to the men thrown out of employment in charity £2,000,000—the amount of their wages—and, nevertheless, would be £2,000,000 wealthier. Nay, this does not fully represent the increased ability of society, for, subject to the quantity of potential capital in existence, the discharged men, entering into other lines of business, would multiply and cheapen other articles, and thus further increase the ability of society. For the sake of precision, let us value this second increase as a gain of £1,000,000. Then, society gains to the amount of £3,000,000 after paying away £2,000,000 in

charity; the men thrown out of employment receive more than
their old wages (£2,000,000 + x, their new wages); and—
which is a third advantage—their wages will probably go a
greater length, for, if consumers of the cheapened articles, they
will participate in the cheapness. Such in theory—and these
figures are not " packed"—may be the marvels produced, such
the blessings spread, by machinery !

The experience of the past by no means proves that machinery dispenses with labour; with a few exceptions it is
one prolonged illustration of the contrary. The most thickly
peopled countries—Belgium, Great Britain, etc.—are countries in
which machinery is largely employed. It must seem almost an
insult to the understanding to tarry long in elucidating what
must be clear to such as know how this country and many others
now maintain ten times as many persons as they did in the reign
of Elizabeth; that steam and machinery have made us what we
are ; that we owe it to machinery that we are not living in the
squalid poverty of the Andaman Islanders; that, take away
machinery, and we take away life itself from nine-tenths of our
people, for we take away the means whereby they live; that we
find that in exact proportion as a country avails itself of
machinery, does it employ labour; that Lancashire alone
employs as many hands as all Scotland did in last century.
Suffice it to mention, for the benefit of those who have not considered the matter, the following circumstances, which render it
clear how machinery has increased the demand for labour :—In
the first place, every machine, in order to supersede manual
labour, must be able to produce more wealth, must be able to
cheapen corn, clothes, houses, etc., and this new increment of
wealth is so much more available for the payment of wages.
The more capital a man has got, the more labourers he can employ;
machinery increases the capital of society, and enables it to spend
more on wages. Secondly, workmen are required to make machines,
and it will sometimes happen that the number thus employed will
equal the number thrown out of employment. Thus, locomotives,
railway carriages and trucks, stations, and permanent ways,
require an army of functionaries for their maintenance and construction that out-number the coachmen, guards, etc., thrown
out of employment. Thirdly, by cheapening articles and services, machinery may, and often does, beget such a demand for
them that far more hands are employed about the machines

than were employed formerly when the work was executed by the hand. This is the common economical defence of machinery, and there is much force in it, though we must remember that cheapness does not always lead to an increased demand, and still oftener leads only to a slight increase. We must also remember that this argument comes ill from those who consider the amount of capital at any moment as absolutely fixed, and who are hence bound to say that the required capital for paying the additional labourers must be taken from some other field of employment. Those, however, who bear in mind that capital may be increased up to the amount of the existing wealth, can employ this argument with perfect consistency. Not, perhaps, fully bearing in mind that "the distinction between capital and wealth, which is not capital, lies not in the kind of commodities, but in the mind of the capitalist," Mr. Mills is led to underrate somewhat this argument. The extension of railways is an illustration to the point. On a high computation, 20,000 or 30,000 persons were employed about the stage coaches in their best days. These have been superseded by locomotives; and such has been the development of traffic that it is not too much to say that upwards of 1,000,000 persons are directly or indirectly supported by railways. The fourth advantage is, that machinery, besides enabling men to perform better and more quickly that which they could without it do expensively and slowly, and besides extending the demand for labour in fields previously narrow, enables men to do that which they could not do at all without machinery. Coalmining would be utterly impossible without machinery; water would flood the ways, foul air would suffocate the workers. Many substances in the arts that were formerly worthless are now utilised. Papin's digester has made nutriment of useless bones. The electric coil and the galvanic jars have given us telegraphy, which has given man a new sense. Here also may be mentioned the effect of machinery in throwing into the far future the exhaustion of mines and land. Thus the impending exhaustion of the Harz mines has been averted by the introduction of machinery. When hand and horse labour have done everything they can for the land of this country, machinery will step in to do more, and to utilise nooks now abandoned to Nature. The clay soils of England will be better and more generally cultivated; and if steam is not suitable for effecting improvement,

owing to the risk of breakage by stones, it is admitted to be
admirable for effecting sowing in good time, and for loosening
the subsoil without bringing it to the surface. As another instance, take the effect of machinery in gold-digging : plots that
were worthless in the days of the simple bowl and water are
now highly remunerative. It may be added, that machinery
becomes more and more necessary, and may be one day absolutely essential for the existence of the human race, compelled
as multiplying men are to resort to less and less productive
soils. Our auxiliaries, machines, may yet be the plank that
will save men from destruction. Fifthly, machinery cheapens
articles of general consumption, and thus is equivalent to an
increased demand for labour and an increase of wages. Cheap
clothes, cheap food, cheap travelling, cheap luxuries—all are due
to machinery. And this cheapness may be of the greatest consequence ; it may determine whether an article is to be consumed
or not by multitudes. By machinery a factory girl is enabled
to wear dresses which a duchess sixty years ago would have
envied. Sixthly, and lastly, by increasing the demand and
enlarging, and thus steadying, the market, machinery renders
men more independent of fluctuations in employment. These
considerations, and the first and fifth of them especially,
explain how the extension of machinery is compatible with,
and productive of, an extension of the demand for labour ; and
all of these considerations are to be found implied in the fact
that machinery makes mankind wealthy, and that just as
a rich man is enabled to hire more labourers than a poor
man, so society, enriched by machinery, is enabled to employ
more. Take now an instance that will be a pocket compendium
of the advantages of machinery. Into no branch of industry
has it been introduced more extensively than into the textile
manufactures, and into none of these more completely than into
the manufacture of cotton. Mr. Baines, from whose book on
the *History of the Cotton Manufacture* I take some of the following figures, estimates the number of persons engaged in
the cotton manufacture in 1760 as little more than 40,000
persons. In 1785, Pitt estimated the number of persons
employed in all branches at 80,000 ; in 1787, when machinery
had begun to be brought into use, the number was 162,000,
according to Mr. Baines ; in 1831, Mr. M'Culloch estimated
the number supported at 833,000 ; in 1835, Mr. Baines was

able to say that the manufacture supported 1,500,000 persons. According to a recently issued Parliamentary paper, the number of persons engaged in the cotton factories amounted to 401,064; and if we add to these auxiliaries and dependants, the number will perhaps be swelled to more than two millions. And, moreover, there has been an increase of wages. In 1760, the average weekly wage was 5s., according to Mr. Baines; in 1859, Mr. David Chadwick estimated it to be 10s. 3½d.; Mr. Edwin Chadwick estimates it in periods of full work at 10s. 6d. to 11s. Take one more fact. In last century, Indian cotton undersold English cotton in English markets. That was the pre-machinery era. To-day English cotton clothes the people of India.

Is it then maintained that the introduction of machinery has been attended by no hardships, that machines have been unalloyed blessings, and that the enemies of machines are never sufferers? No; far from it; and one of the reasons why Political Economy has hitherto been discredited by the working classes, and has been accused of being the systematised selfishness of the middle classes, is, that economists have too often been afraid to look steadily at these inconveniences and hardships, have hurried past them with a vague commonplace, or have hid the stern facts from their gaze behind a screen of paltry sophisms, through which unsophisticated common sense and sharply-taught experience looked scornfully. Sometimes improvised to quiet the disaffected, the arguments of economists have been occasionally wanting in accuracy. They should have been content to assert at most that a balance of advantages was generally at once obtainable, and in the long run was always obtainable, by the introduction of machinery. It is idle and cruel to attempt to ignore hardships caused by men being thrown out of employment by machinery; and while we deplore the general folly of resistance, while we perceive that those improvements will make their way into use sooner or later with the irresistibility of the forces of Nature, we should sometimes pity, rather than harshly censure, the resistance; and we should ask ourselves whether society has washed its hands of the future of these men when it interposes between them and starvation only the workhouse. Frankly speaking, the poor in their resistance to machinery have frequently recognised their foes; they have not also seen that the foes were irresistible. In the unwritten annals of the poor are many tales of tragical suffering produced by machinery; and it is open to serious consideration whether charity has fulfilled its duties until it has organised measures for providing to the discharged men sustenance while out of employment, and guiding them, sorely needing guidance, to a livelihood in other places or trades. M. Chevalier proposed that a reserve of public work should always be kept to employ such men, and Mr. Porter proposed that the Government should aid their emigration : these proposals are sullied by their placing upon public shoulders that which should be borne by private shoulders. Certainly the persistent opposition to machinery, of which our history and the Statute Book bear so many traces, argues the want of some salve for these temporary and individual, but nevertheless real, evils. Nothing but good would come of measures of relief, were it clearly kept before those relieved that they were recipients of favours, and if mistaken charity did not seek to arrest the introduction of the machines. Until some such remedy is forthcoming we shall not do amiss in regarding the prejudices of the working classes as not wholly an evil. I have said that economists have slurred over these hardships. Take the following as an instance:—"Machinery never diminishes the demand for labour, and it merely alters the direction of the demand,"—and from this economists deduce the inference that machinery causes no hardship, or only a trifling one. Puerility and sophistry ! As if it were no hardship for the man who has been bred to weaving to turn to stonebreaking ; as if it were a light matter for men in middle-age to break with their fully-formed habits, to cut their moorings, and drift away in quest of a new port ; as if the hardships, temporary and disguised blessings as far as the race is concerned, might not be permanent and real so far as the individuals are concerned ! Machines never displace labour ! As if it were a little thing that the labourer had to go from Paisley to New York. You tell the brickmaker that this machine, which dispenses with his services, will increase the demand for labour, and you think to stop his mouth by this solitary assertion, forgetting that he will ask, " Will it increase the demand for my labour ? Will the change benefit me ? What avails it to tell me that my class is benefited, or that the wages of workmen as a whole are increased ; the interesting point for me is, will the change increase *my* wages, and that speedily ? Your arguments are dust and chaff to me until you have satisfied me that I shall obtain exactly the same wages as before, or more, and that I shall not have to undergo a painful apprenticeship when I am too old to learn well or easily, or to endure the want of employment. I do not deny that these machines will certainly benefit the race, but will they certainly benefit me?" I do not pretend to be able to show that such will always be the effect of machinery; but, at the same time, I would point out to the man who makes this objection, that the lot of those who suffer from the introduction of machinery is not wholly peculiar but very common. All social improvements are attended by some friction. In this world nothing can grow old without becoming venerable, and there comes no considerable change that is not a blow to somebody. Good is found as rarely in a pure state as the useful metals. There is a debit side to every event, and the world improves at all because certain events leave a balance to the credit of humanity. Every mechanical improvement, like all other improvements, strikes at the root of some vested interest. It is of the very nature of an improvement to render antiquated some process and those who perform it; if a better method has been found, it follows that the old has been brushed aside as outworn. Specialists, in particular, run a risk of seeing their professions vanish; and a grand cause why the middle classes do not raise a complaint similar to that raised by the working classes is that they are able to pass more readily to other employments. The professions of the middle class presuppose capabilities for other inferior professions; and the suppleness and agility of mind which education imparts to the members of the middle class, not to speak of the provisions which the more prudent make for an evil day, smooth their entrance into new lines of life. I add another cause of the lightness of the shocks produced by improvements, and it is this: improvements in law, medicine, etc., and other professions practised by the middle class, not being so indisputably improvements as those in the industrial arts, are apt to be introduced slowly, and thus those who stand by the old routine are allowed either to continue therein, or time is given them to change. When Harvey discovered the circulation of the blood, the practice of medicine was not instantly revolutionised. Practitioners still adhered to the old ideas; scarcely a convert over the age of forty was won by convincing arguments; and among Molière's doctors we have specimens of the old school. M. Diafoirus "never wished to comprehend or listen to the reasons and experiences of the alleged discoveries of our age touching the circulation of the blood, and other opinions of the same grain." Inoculation travelled slowly. Contrast this with the speed with which Arkwright's invention was brought into use, as soon as the Court of Queen's Bench, by annulling his patent, threw it open to all : within fifteen years the manufacture of cotton was trebled.

The above remarks have considered the bearings of machinery to the remuneration of labour. This forms part of a larger subject, the bearings of fixed capital—*i.e.* capital not consumed in one act of production—to the remuneration of labour. Every year enormous sums are sunk as fixed capital in the form of railways, roads, canals, and agricultural improvements. M. Horn, the French statistician, computes that £20,000,000 a-year are required for English, and £10,000,000 for French railways. Is the tendency of these improvements to augment or diminish wages ? Suppose that the funds are diverted from purely un-productive purposes, the tendency of these works is to increase wages, for these improvements, while subtracting nothing from the wages fund, bring, sooner or later, some return, available for distribution as wages, whereas, if spent unpro-ductively, they would have produced none. It may be, however, and in the case of vast works it is probable—that a large part of the funds are subtracted from other productive purposes ; and in this event it may happen that the new machine or work, created at the expense of a certain amount of floating capital, may soon replace it, with a considerable profit. Still, so far, the effect of the change is detrimental to the de-mand for labour, seeing capital is diverted from the creation of floating or circulating capital, with which wages can be paid, to creating things which do not serve for wages, though they may help to create in time the means of doing so. Industry, to put the matter in another light, consists of a series of steps which, when fixed capital is not present, is as follows :—Floating capital creates floating capital and materials for wages. But the rhythm may be changed into this :—Floating capital re-placed by fixed capital and not by the materials of wages, or by a small quantity ; for example, corn land may be turned into pasture ; railways may be laid down in vast numbers.*

* In the sessions of 1845, 1846, and 1847, Parliament sanctioned the

The working classes may, therefore, suffer from the introduction of fixed capital, though I venture to submit that undue prominence is given to these cases by those who do not point out that the capital required for effecting fixed improvements may be subtracted from unproductive, and is not always subtracted from productive funds. Had all the companies projected in 1865 and 1866 been floated, wages might have been seriously affected. To sum up :—The sole interest of the capitalist is to obtain certain produce regardless of the gross amount. The interest of the labourer centres in the amount of the gross produce. It is the customary contention of economists that in the long run a large net produce will be accompanied by large gross produce. This assumption, generally true, appears to be dubious and unwarranted if affirmed as a universal proposition.

creation of 8592 miles of railway. All this, of course, was not then made. Mr. Dudley Baxter on "Railway Extension and its Results." *Journal of the Statistical Society* for 1866, p. 552.

CHAPTER VIII.

DIVISION OF LABOUR.

THE efficacy of division of labour in the work of production might well have struck the most cursory, and therefore the earliest, observers—so gigantic is its efficacy and universal its presence. It struck Aristotle ; and Plato, in his imaginary sketch of a perfect State, assumes that " men, as soon as men resolve to live gregariously, must appreciate the advantages of dividing their various tasks, instead of every one doing everything." Adam Smith, however, was the first philosopher to elucidate in a very considerable degree the economical advantages of division of labour. Not that he exhausted the subject, for his remarks are scarcely more surprising for what they say than for what they omit to say.

Glance over society ; look around the community, the town, the village, the country in which you happen to live, and you will discern this principle originating and maintaining all parts of it, determining the condition of all members of it. Trades, various branches of them, and all classes of society —all are creations of the principle of division of labour. The differences between two nations, and between one period of history and another, are due in great part to the extent to which functions and labour are divided ; and that vague entity, called civilisation, is the product and embodiment of division of labour. Lowest down in the race of humanity, and standing to European societies in the same relation that an animal all mouth and stomach stands to man highly organised, are the Bosjesmans or the Sioux, among whom each man is his own farmer, clothier, cook, and policeman ; yet even among them there is a rudimentary differentiation of functions—the squaw does not go out to war, nor do the young men judge. Perhaps it will not be wrong to consider the separation between the duties of the sexes, and of the free man and slave, as the primary instances of this differentiation. Pass to another state of society, a little more refined, and a few trades begin to appear. The Homeric poems show us the monotony diversified by kings, chiefs, priests, leeches, slaves. Higher up in the scale comes the separation of society into castes : this arrestment—petrefaction as it were—of a certain imperfect development of the principle of division of labour, was exemplified in Egypt and India, in the latter of which there were four castes, split up into some two hundred sub-castes, and in the trading guilds, the history of which we have briefly related. As Mr. Maine shows, caste is the fate of peoples that lose their spontaneity, as it were, who indulge in dangerous self-satisfaction; who codify law, etiquette, usage, and organise labour too soon ; and who are, in fact, precocious systematisers. By and by the inhabitants of particular districts choose certain vocations, which they follow ; a Lancashire devoted to cotton-spinning, or a Pottery district is marked off; or an entire nation may specialise its industry ; and to this point we have reached. Now we so subdivide functions, that we begin to feel the evils of excess minutely, and see that it is not well that a man should be changed into a lever, and that his work should be as uniform as that' of a gin-horse. Men concentrate their lives on the heads of pins; the wish of the grammarian that he had devoted his life to the dative case is more than realised. Yet to what results this specialising has led !—by turning a wheel or pulling a string, men obtain for themselves all the necessaries of life. Marvellous result ! by signing one's name one may share in the wealth of the Indies.

Adam Smith's chapter on the advantages of division of labour has become classical, and it pointed out principles, too little noted until his time, throwing a flood of light on the mechanism of society. Nevertheless, it is imperfect, as will appear after a recital of the advantages which he mentions; and one grand imperfection is the fact that his remarks have almost solely in view manual labour, and that he has not sufficiently brought into light the truth that division fructifies every kind of labour, and that in all departments of life, in action and thought, men grow powerful by narrowing themselves. For example, literature illustrates almost as much as industry the necessity of division of labour. At the birth of literature, the same man is poet, historian, savant, prophet, philosopher ; in process of time he separates these functions, and science and history at least are improved. Each of these divisions is subdivided ; poetry is split up into epic, lyric, and dramatic ; and again each of these subdivisions is broken up into schools, pursuing different modes of treatment. The various sciences are subdivided according to the principle of the division of labour. Bell and Lancaster applied it with economy and success to teaching. In war, the counterpart of industry, being the business of destruction, while the latter is that of construction, division of labour is carried to a great and an amazing extent, and the result is, that the science of destruction is probably more perfect than that of construction. Government, now that affairs have marvellously increased in diversity and complexity, can be carried on only through minute division of functions, by separation of the civil and military and religious powers, and by endless subdivisions of these. And these are but illustrations, not a catalogue of the effects, of the principle.

The first advantage mentioned by Adam Smith is, that division of labour increases the dexterity of the labourer, and thus enables him to perform more work, and that better—a truth too obvious to be insisted upon. Man, in this point of view, is a tool. Now, a tool can execute only a few things well, and one must not employ the same blade as a trencher-scraper, a bread-knife, and a razor. Secondly, if a workman has to execute only one kind of work, requiring few tools, he loses little time in passing from one tool to another, and this is of great importance in engineering works, in which the boring, turning, and other machines require nice adjustment.* Even in small workshops this effect is of some consequence ; standing watch in hand, beside a village artizan engaged in jobs of all sorts, one is amazed at the time he consumes in getting his tools, and in passing from one to another. Thirdly, in the opinion of Adam Smith, division of labour is advantageous, inasmuch as it leads to the invention of machines for facilitating and abridging labour ; and he instances the familiar story of the boy who, being engaged to open and shut the communication between the boiler and the cylinder in one of the first forms of the steam-engine, tied a string from the handle of the valve to another part of the machine, so that

* Mr. Babbage makes a remark to this effect.

the valve opened and shut of itself, and allowed him to play. Division of labour also enables an employer to put each servant to what he is best suited for; a fact which furnishes the explanations of the intense and general demand in modern times for the labour of children and women—a demand which, as we have seen, is growing ; and we can well understand, though we may not approve of, the opposition of the manufacturers of England to the Factory Acts, in view of the fact that abroad children might be employed without restraint. Adam Smith forgot that the result of this differentiation is not only that men are enabled to execute more of a given kind of work, but that they are enabled to execute things entirely different in kind ; not only that it enables them to perform old achievements better and more quickly, but achievements previously impossible. Increase of dexterity does not cover the facts. We have to contemplate the case of persons born with peculiar aptitudes which would never have come to light, but which would have been stifled and destroyed, had there not been a very high differentiation of functions.

Just as it is advisable for a man to follow one pursuit according to the bent of his talents, so should one country take to one set of occupations, and another country to another, according to the nature of the soil, minerals, situation, climate, and the aptitudes of the inhabitants—aptitudes which may have been the creation of circumstances, but which, nevertheless, transmitted from one generation to another, are too deeply seated to be disregarded. It would be ridiculous for countries north of the 53° parallel of latitude to grow the vine, or for those north of the parallel of 51° to grow maize. It would be suicide and folly for Great Britain, with vast coal and iron fields, to imitate Poland or Central Russia, and to spend her energies in producing wheat for her own use and for exportation : her mineral riches, unparalleled by any other known part of the world for combined extent and accessibility, destined Great Britain to be a manufacturing country. This obvious principle is disregarded by Protectionism, which fosters manufactures where coal and iron are not easily accessible, and where countless acres hunger for the plough ; favours agriculture where metals and fuel abound ; laboriously creates a mercantile navy in a nation of landsmen ; and endeavours to realise for a people the old Stoical idea of self-sufficiency, not to be realised without injury to itself and others. Protectionists commit the same error in a less heinous form when they endeavour to develop any branch of industry for which a country is suited, at the expense of another branch of industry for which it is still better suited; and it is this form of error which is most common. Witness the United States developing their ironworks, Russia and Spain their manufactures, at the expense of their agriculture. It must, indeed, be admitted that one of the ablest and most renowned advocates of Protectionism, List, who may fairly be called the founder of the Zollverein, based his theory on the postulate that each nation was predestined to pursue a certain limited and well-defined number of branches of industry. It must also be borne in mind—though in the heat of the struggle round the Corn Laws, and while the memory of them was still fresh, it was barely possible to do so—that it is one of the peculiar triumphs of man to overcome the superficial unsuitabilities of Nature, and to infuse into exotic industries life and vigour, and permanence and beneficence, and that, running over the great branches of industry in any country, and tracing back their histories, one will find many of them to be exotics. Henry IV. of France fostered and developed the silk manufacture; and to-day it is the chief constituent of the French exports. Moreover, as men grow in knowledge and become possessed of that power over Nature which comes of knowledge, and as the process of manufacturing becomes so complicated that the cost of the raw material is a small item in cost of production, natural advantages go for less and less. At first Nature is everything; men's lives and pursuits are determined for them by the character of their birthplace. Like plants, they live only if they conform to the soil and situation. Transplant them and they wither. They must be a nation of hunters where wild beasts are abundant, pastoral and nomadic where these are scarce. But the labours and lessons of successive generations, together with travel and intercourse with strangers, emancipate men from the thraldom of the local peculiarities that were for their ancestors a destiny. Later societies, like the later rocks, are formed of the crushed *débris* of many societies. The plants and animals and manufactures of one country are transplanted to another. As in a garden or hothouse are gathered the plants of many lands, of multitudes of "botanic centres," so in the same land are gathered in the course of time the industrial habits and pursuits

of many peoples ; and the foreigners may perhaps in time grow
to greater lustiness and vigour than the natives.

I refer here to another modifying consideration, of which
more will be said hereafter. The rule for guidance is not wholly
a regard for present pecuniary gain; and it may be well to sacrifice
a little emolument for the sake of the moral and social advantages to be obtained by diversifying the occupations of a people.

We arrive at another leading cause of efficient production
when we name production on a large scale. It will be obvious
that this facilitates abundance and cheap production, and I do
not doubt that such facts as these will at once present themselves in crowds to the mind of every one—that a cotton-mill
containing 10,000 spindles may require a capital of £20,000,
and that a mill with 5000 spindles may require a capital, not
of £10,000, but of £11,000. The chief of the causes of this
efficiency, therefore, I shall briefly state. One of them is the
impossibility in some instances, difficulty in all, of applying
division of labour in small establishments. The village smith
must do everything, from mending a kettle to opening a lock.
He can live only because he is able to do many things indifferently well. Expense in management and control is saved
in large establishments. A farmer will, with much the same
trouble, manage a farm of 300 or 600 acres. Expensive
machinery can be introduced into large establishments ; while
expensive movable machines can be introduced into small
establishments only when there is a strong spirit of co-operation,
expensive immovable machines, such as stationary engines,
cannot be introduced at all. The farmer with fifty or a hundred
acres cannot be expected to possess the complete set of agricultural implements possessed by a farmer tilling 300 to 800
acres. The small producer cannot try novel methods and experiments, especially if the experiment must be conducted on
a large scale, before it is crucial and satisfactory. It is not to be
expected that a small Belgian or Tuscan proprietor will run the
risk of ruining himself in order to determine whether a certain
root or grass, or a certain method of cropping, is advantageous.
It was Lord Townsend that brought the turnip into use, and
Arthur Young, the apostle of large farms, and the practiser
of his doctrines, that introduced the Norfolk method of
rotation.

Division of labour is composed of facts which, looked at in

another light, are termed co-operation. To say that labour is divided is to say that there exists co-operation of labour. The converse, however, does not hold ; it is not true that wherever there is co-operation there is division of labour, for, in what Mr. Wakefield has termed simple co-operation—*e.g.* the lifting of a plank by several persons—there is no division. But what he terms complex co-operation—co-operating in different occupations—is only another way of looking at the facts encircled by the phrase division of labour. It may not be superfluous to observe that we will obtain a very inadequate idea of the character of co-operation, or division of labour, if we consider that it is exemplified only by workmen engaged in the same establishments consciously labouring for a common end. To appreciate the principle in its full breadth, we must see professions co-operating with professions, districts with districts, countries with countries, and one age with another. Complex combination or division of labour, it may be added, is not profitable under all circumstances. Demand must spread before division of labour can be largely employed. Again, into some professions, incapable of being broken up into simultaneous processes, division of labour cannot be introduced with completeness.

Division or specialisation of labour is only a part of a still wider principle. Man, in the view of Political Economy, is a tool, and as a tool he should be devoted to some special work. But the advantage of this specialisation is not restricted to man : all other tools and instruments, animate or inanimate, in the work of production, should be specialised ; and, instead of helping to perform several functions indifferently, each should help to perform one thing well. Thus, to take land as an illustration of my meaning, in a partially cultivated country, and indeed in all countries out of Europe and America, the portion of the soil intended to serve as roads is rudely and imperfectly defined ; and, to the great detriment of agriculture and locomotion, each foot passenger, horseman, or driver of a vehicle, chooses, in India say, his own route. As the country becomes civilised, the differentiation between the cultivated portion and the road becomes sharper, until fenced highways are substituted for straggling, indefinite paths. The differentiation does not stop here. All property is but an instance of it. The chief economical advantage of property consists in the advantage of specialisation.

Without lingering over somewhat arid generalities, I pass to one branch of the subject round which controversy has raged for centuries, and that is the subject of large and small farms. It will be observed that the question is not between large and small properties, for large properties do not ensure large farms, but rather between large farms on the one hand, and small farms and peasant properties on the other; the real antagonism is between *extensive* and *intensive* culture; any other contrast is apt to be a false one. The Romans were acquainted with the subject, for the contrast between Latium, densely peopled under a *régime* of small farmers, and depopulated under that which succeeded it, could not fail to strike them; and Pliny has embalmed his opinion of the change in the memorable phrase, "Large farms ruined Italy." In this country, the subject has called forth swarms of books and pamphlets since the days of Arthur Young; and no Continental economist thinks that he has done his duty until he has returned a verdict for *la petite culture* or *la grande culture.* The controversy has been barren and profitless, the discrepancies of opinion needlessly great, because the two litigants have employed entirely different tests of what is right and proper. There are three questions to be considered—What is ideally the best economical state for the present? what is the best economical state practicable? and what is the best state morally? and these three have been confounded. If purely present economical considerations are in view, and if the question be asked which of the two systems now produces the greatest results with the least expenditure of labour, Political Economy has said the last word, and the advantage of large farming over small farming ought long ago to have been acknowledged. For, in the first place, division of labour is possible to any extent only in the former, and though division of labour is not so profitable or practicable on a farm as in a manufactory, the principle does not fail in the former; it only does not succeed so well as in the latter. In the next place, production on a large scale in farming is more economical, just as it is in manufacturing, though the advantages are not so great in the one as in the other: there is a saving in management, in fences, in buildings, etc. Certain products, moreover, are out of the reach of the small farmer, unless he manages to induce his neighbours to club their resources; Gruyère cheese, for example, cannot be produced by the farmer of a few acres. And as to the

H

argument, so much insisted on by Mr. Mill and the advocates of small farmers in general, that they will expend almost "superhuman industry" on the land—which is, of course, true only where they are the proprietors—it must be remembered that every increase of produce is obtained by a more than proportional increase of labour—that is to say, that after a certain point doubling the labour will not double the produce, but perhaps may increase it merely one-fourth or one-eighth. Consequently, *intensive* culture is a comparative waste of labour so long as *extensive* culture is possible. And therefore, if purely economical considerations, having regard only to the immediate present, are to guide us, we should defer cultivating all Europe as Belgium is cultivated until all Europe is peopled as Belgium. Until that period comes, labour so expended will be misspent, in an economical point of view, for it might have been expended elsewhere to more advantage. But it is not enough to know which system will yield the greatest net produce with the least expense; that is not decisive of the whole merits of the two systems ; a further and equally important question lies behind—Under which system will the best race of men be bred and live? Under which will the average standard of morality, comfort, and happiness be highest? And the advocates of *la petite culture* rest their case on a more solid basis when they assert that small farmers, whenever they have owned the land they farmed, have been marked by sobriety of life, prudence, and all the work-a-day virtues, and that they have been the stablest pillars of support in those nations whose good fortune it has been to possess them. Property, as has been already observed, has a humanising effect; until men have acquired some property they are not tamed or domesticated ; and real civilisation grows as the number of those destitute of it decrease. It is not, therefore, a meaningless coincidence that those countries in which peasant proprietors have been most numerous have been the chosen abodes of patriotism. Niebuhr (quoted by Mr. Mill) says—" Wherever you find hereditary farmers or small proprietors, there you find order and honesty ;" and, with similarity of language as well as of opinion, Sismondi has observed, " Wherever are found peasant proprietors are also found that ease, that security, that independence, that confidence in the future, which assure at the same time happiness and virtue." The manly worth of the "statesmen " of England is not wholly a figment of poetry or an invention of romance. Slow to change, those small proprietors have often been the saviours of order. When all else has rocked in France, they have sometimes been immobile; and now, as the enemies of revolution avow, the greatest security against its repetition is the existence of a vast legion of peasant proprietors interested in the preservation of order. Plant the argument for small properties on these moral grounds—say that a long review of history and a broad survey of many countries attest that peasant proprietors have displayed singular worth of character, and that, on the other hand, large farming brings as an accompaniment a population such as the hinds of England, rude, unthinking, and ignorant—and the argument is not easily to be shaken; but do not say that small farming is in a theoretical point of view the best system—do not say that general want of capital, general isolation, general inability to try new methods, no division of employment, and a system which produces large results only when a man considers his labour and time of little worth, are the conditions in which the utmost wealth is at present produced with the least possible expenditure of labour.

These favourable opinions of the salutary effect of small farms on the general morals of the people, do not hold good when the small farmers do not possess the land they till, or hold it by a fixed tenure or for a long term of years; for experience and presumption alike assert that the cottier system of cultivation is morally and economically the worst that circumstances or man could devise. There the fate of the former is to scrape painfully together the means of a miserable livelihood, to slide into debt, penury, disaffection, and in the end perhaps into crime; and Ireland is a grand illustration and warning of the consequences of such a system long and generally pursued. It is true that the dense population of Ireland has intensified the evils that are to be ascribed to the system, and that several provinces of Belgium—the famous Pays de Waes, for example —attest that, among a people well educated, and accustomed to a comfortable style of living, and a standard set by neighbouring small proprietors, the cottier system may be productive of, certainly accompanied by, comfort. But it can rarely happen, at all events, where the land is let by competition, that the cottier's lot can be other than hard, barren of enjoyment and of hope.

Though large farms are, abstractedly considered, the best

economical state, it does not follow that they should be universally adopted in preference to small farms, seeing the fate of the
bulk of the population may be worse under the former than the
latter ; and I shall now point out a few other considerations
which should cause hesitation in recommending a universal
spread of large farms. Much heed and respect should be paid
to the custom of any country, for, if the custom has grown up
spontaneously, and has not been imposed by force, it is almost
certain that it is well suited to the district and character of the
people : the lower animals, and even the unsentient plants, we
allow to err rarely in their habits as regards food and shelter ;
why should we suppose that man, the most intelligent of
animals, the readiest of plants to adapt itself to situation, should
alone err grossly ? These customs are the growths of the wants
of the people, the slow and silent creation of experience ; and
they are not to be eradicated swiftly and without injury. And
we shall generally find, on close examination of agricultural
systems widely different from ours, that there is some good
reason for the difference, and that a sweeping condemnation can
come only from those who are ignorant of the circumstances.
Take France, for example : an Englishman or Scotchman almost
irresistibly infers, when he knows that there are twenty million,
out of a population of thirty-eight, engaged in agriculture, that
the proportion is outrageously great, and that there is no reason
in the world save stupidity and prejudice why the proportion of the
agricultural population to the commercial and industrial should
not instantly be altered to one-fourth or one-fifth, as in England.
But examine the products of the country, and the hasty conclusion is recalled. As M. Léonce de Lavergne, an unimpeachable witness, points out, much of the land in France and the
products are such as to require a far greater amount of manual
labour than in England ; pasture is not so good there as here ;
the products are more varied, and some of them—such as the
vine and olive—require all the attention a gardener gives to a
delicate exotic. " I know parts of our country," says M. Léonce
de Lavergne, " where small farming is the bane of the district ;
I know others where it is of inestimable benefit, and for which
the large system could never compensate."
    Again, there are soils which, but for *la petite culture*, would
never have been brought under cultivation ; and to recommend
the adoption of large farms as a panacea, is to doom large areas

to sterility. The subdivision of the soil of France is older than articles 826 and 832 of the Code Civil. It may, in most cases, be shown that the systems of cultivation in vogue have originated from a due appreciation of the circumstances of the country, and it is generally ignorance or want of reflection which conceals the fact. Destutt de Tracy, who shows a sense of this truth, does not happily apply it, and he attempts to explain the rise of large and small farms and *métairies* in the following manner : —" When land is fertile one person can produce a considerable amount of products. Now, if, *cæteris paribus*, the gains of every capitalist are always proportioned to the extent of his manufacture, here the gains may suffice to draw well-to-do people. . . . For their convenience, therefore, large properties are broken up into large masses, of which the usual size is about three to five hundred acres, with a good house at hand." Again, when the soil is unproductive, and when, consequently, the production is insufficient to attract large capitalists, proprietors are compelled to divide their lands into small portions within the reach of poor people, and the result is *la petite culture*. If the soil be still poorer, or if, by various causes, rural proprietors are few, the great proprietors form *domaines* or *métairies*, which, together with sufficient stocking, are generally entrusted to peasants, who pay half of the produce as rent. This theory, however, is eminently unsatisfactory. That large farms are found upon rich soils, and small upon poor soils, is in flagrant contradiction with patent facts. Destutt de Tracy's experience lay chiefly in France, and in a part of it unfavourable to the *métayer* system ; otherwise he would have been aware that the *métayer* system, which gives the tenant a motive to improve, is compatible with exuberant fertility. It is, moreover, unwarrantably assumed that small farmers always possess less capital than large farmers per acre, and that the profits of a farmer depend upon and vary with the fertility of the soil. That is a plea on which hypothec is defended in Scotland ; the evidence collected by the Commission shakes it. As to small farms or cottier-holdings, and *métairies*, they originate in different circumstances. If those dependent upon agricultural labour are numerous, an Ireland is apt to be the result ; but if they are not too numerous, and if the landlords are not in a position to hire them,—if the tenants be poor and not over-abundant,—the result is the *métayer* system, which may, as was the case in England, be developed into yeomen holdings. Any circumstance which increases the difficulty of the landlord cultivating his property himself is apt to lead to a form of *métayer* culture. It has been the target of much abuse —often needless abuse. It is not the *métayer* system that introduces poverty; poverty introduces it. English economists, who have found no words too strong to express their detestation of it, and who, not always with due account of dates, have favoured the world with ugly pictures of the miserable people who live under what Arthur Young calls the "most detestable of all modes of letting land," have not observed that these *métayers* ought not to be compared with the English farmers. The position of the former differs from that of the latter in the social scale ; and we find the true representative of the *métayer*, destitute of capital, in the English farm-labourer, similarly destitute. Place the peasants that till the Val di Nievoli, generally comfortable, secure in their farms, and often possessed of rude plenty, able to give their daughters dowries, and to drink indifferent wine, alongside the Dorset drudges, who labour for thirty years only to end their days in a workhouse, and then say whether the condition of the latter is so much more enviable than that of the former—whether it is not many rounds farther down the social ladder.* Moreover, there is this circumstance in addition, to be pleaded in deprecation of the diatribes of Young and M'Culloch,—besides confounding the effect of poverty with the cause of it, and forgetting that the *métayer* system may be the best possible in the condition of landlords and peasants, they do not bear in mind that the *métayer* system may be, as it proved in England, a stepping-stone to the foundation of a race of yeomanry.

If men were to be guided solely by present economical considerations ; if their immediate pecuniary interest was to be the one motive that determined their conduct ; if they were bound to quit their country whenever another offered to them higher wages and profits ; and if Political Economy approved of this ; then we should, speaking generally, wish for no small properties until large farming had covered the whole

---

* In the Reports of Her Majesty's representatives on the tenure of land (Part III. 36), I find the following relating to the *métayer* system in the island of Minorca :—" It does not seem to be the opinion that the position of the farmers of Minorca could be improved under any other system, as they are, for the most part, persons without capital, who would be unable to resist fluctuations in the market, and the years of bad harvest."

earth, and a packed population clamoured for food. But this is a fanciful state of things, and ought to be so. Men are not wholly the slaves of wealth ; they will not, and should not, cross the Atlantic for the sake of a few more coppers ; emigration, *per se*, is an evil, as the transplanting of a plant is ; population will, and should not, always spread itself over—though immobility is no virtue—the earth in the precise manner in which each man will gain most wealth ; and hence we have to consider what is the method of culture which will employ to most advantage the population that happens to be in a country. It will be seen that, according to circumstances, small or large farming is preferable. If the country be thinly peopled, and land be abundant, pretty large farms would seem to be preferable ; for why adopt the *intensive* culture so long as the *extensive* is practicable ? why spend upon twenty acres labour which would yield a third as much again if distributed over thirty ? And hence we find that most countries so circumstanced have spontaneously adopted it : Spain, for example ; and the United States, the slovenly culture in which is really wise and economical. Washington told Arthur Young that it was more advantageous in America to work ill a large tract of land than to till well a small space. Again, if a country be humid and suited to pasturage, or if it have no markets readily accessible, if it do not possess good roads, canals, or cheap carriage of some sort, small farms seem marked out to be the fitting mode of cultivation ; for what will be the use of a large net produce, the peculiar advantage of large farming, if there be no one to purchase the surplus ? Small farms seem in this case a necessity ; and we find in many parts of France, Germany, Switzerland, and Italy, an illustration of the truth. If, on the other hand, population grows remarkably dense, if a large manufacturing population spring up clamant for food, the option is to import food or to employ the intensive method of culture. We have taken the former course : Belgium has taken the latter. And, in proportion as population increases, must the importation increase, or the method of culture more and more resemble gardening. This holds good of parts of the same country as well as of different countries. Where population is sparse and land abundant and cheap, extensive culture prevails ; but as population increases, as we near great seats of industry, the tillage becomes intensive.

CHAPTER IX.

CREDIT.

Bless'd paper credit ! last and best supply,
That lends corruption lighter wings to fly ;
Gold, imp'd by thee, can compass hardest things,
Cau pocket States, can fetch or carry Kings ;
A single leaf shall waft an army o'er,
Or ship off Senates to some distant shore ;
A leaf, like Sibyl's, scatter to and fro
Our fates and fortunes as the wind shall blow.

IN these lines Pope has included the popular ideas respecting
the power of credit to accomplish marvellous feats. This
chapter will be an endeavour to give precision and accuracy to
these cloudy and incorrect ideas. Much of the difficulty that
envelops the subject is artificial. It has been obscured by
metaphors intended to enlighten it. What confusion, for
example, has been introduced by figurative words such as " in-
flated," " swollen," " contracted," etc., and all the other figures
which too often conceal want of knowledge or thought ! It
has been darkened with illustration and smothered by similes ;
credit has been compared—to the general increase of bewilder-
ment instead of edification—to roads, canals, waggons, and
numerous other vehicles ; to a potent alchemy which fulfilled the
dreams of Paracelsus ; it has been spoken of as a power mighty
and marvellous as electricity. The vastness of the results
accomplished by credit makes men ready to believe there is in
it something magical. Speaking of the national debts which in
his time began to take vast proportions, and giving countenance
to this delusion about the mysterious power of credit, Voltaire
said—" It is one of the efforts of the human mind in this last
century to have discovered the secret of owing more than we
possess, and of living as if we owed nothing." And this is

well in poetry or in epigrammatic writing; but we return to the region of solid facts when we say that, in all the length and breadth of it, credit is simply the power to use or abuse other men's goods, and whatever be the influence of credit in increasing wealth, it is to be resolved into or flows from this. So far as they are institutions of credit, the Banks of England and France and the *Crédit Foncier* are useful because they enable one set of people to use the money, or rather the goods, of another set of people.

This being the general nature of credit, let us inquire more minutely into its efficacy in production. Credit, in the first place, is useful because it frequently transfers wealth from those who would have employed it as capital, who would have used it to produce more wealth, but languidly or unskilfully, to those with a talent and a disposition for business. Take the case of a widow left with a little money, and unversed in business. She transfers her money to a bank; in return for a certain interest (though, by the way, the Bank of England gives no interest, and some of the English banks give interest only on considerable sums) she gives over for a time the purchasing power of which she is the owner; and the banker, for a higher consideration, sells this purchasing power to a man who may possess everything to succeed in business except capital to launch him. Had there been no banker to act as middleman, the widow's trusting ignorance might have committed this purchasing power to some unremunerative business, or to the undertakers of a Mexican mine, which might have ruined her and them. By the present arrangement this purchasing power may be employed in tilling a farm, or sinking and working a mine which will enrich instead of ruining the shareholders. She may become, all unknown to herself, a partner in some concern. In the next place, credit is the instrument by which wealth which would have been spent altogether unproductively, which would have been consumed without an equivalent being left in its place, or which would not have been consumed at all, or only after some delay, and would thus have been wasted, is transferred to those who will consume it productively and who will employ it as capital. In other words, credit, utilising the existing wealth, creates capital. Here is a rural district inhabited by cottiers or small farmers, with no bank in the vicinity. What remains to each after satisfying his prime wants must be spent in luxury, or be hoarded up ; the surplus, a tool as it were capable of creating more wealth, must be either wasted or left unused. These were the alternatives before the people of this country, until banks had penetrated into the recesses of the country ; they are still the alternatives before the peasantry of France in Departments in which the Bank of France has not yet opened branches. A bank is established in the vicinity ; these surpluses, these savings, as they are termed, are entrusted to the banker ; * uselessly small savings are gathered into one large mass ; the banker sells it to others ; these do or may turn it to productive purposes ; and thus credit and banking bring it to pass that the tools which would have been spoiled or lain useless are employed in producing more wealth. The peasant or farmer, to put his condition before and after the introduction of banks in another light, possessed a surplus which he could not use productively in his own business ; he refrains from consuming it ; he hands over the use of the surplus to an intermediary, who may sell it to a productive consumer. These two functions of credit are included in one phrase when we say that credit utilises to the utmost wealth, or that it transfers unused purchasing power to those who will use it productively. In modern times all banks perform these two functions ; some of them, such as the London Joint-Stock and private banks, or the Bank of Hamburg, may not issue bank-notes, confining themselves to receiving money on deposit and discounting ; and some, such as the Bank of Amsterdam, as originally constituted, were merely public safes; but in modern times, to collect wealth and to distribute it, to act as middle-men between lenders and borrowers, to bring wealth whence it is not wanted whither it is wanted, to be the lake that first drains the uplands of the superfluous wealth, and then by the sluices of the discount-counter lets it out to irrigate the parched plains, is the work of all banks.

It would not be proper to slur over the assistance to production rendered by credit, by its enabling producers to dispose of their goods quickly. The seller finds the buyer without

* The term deposit is unhappy, seeing it is apt to convey an erroneous idea of the relation of the banker and his customer. The money deposited by customers with their bankers is not a deposit, but a loan ; it is money which the banker may deal with as his own, notwithstanding he is bound to pay it on demand.—Levi's *Manual of Mercantile Law*, p. 213 ; Grant on *Banking*, p. 2.

delay ; machinery and fixed capital are consequently utilised to the utmost, and floating capital is quickly replaced ; the work of production is rarely interrupted ; and the circulation, to employ an expression which pictures the steady flow of goods in their various stages of manufacture, through the hands of the various intermediaries, and also the passage of remuneration from one party to another, is kept going. Credit, generally taking the shape of discounting, thus acts as a fly-wheel. As soon as goods are manufactured they find a market not limited to the persons at once desirous to purchase, and possessed of sufficient wealth, but so widened as to include those who possess only credit and this desire. A pays B for raw cotton not in gold, which he may not then possess, but with a bill at three or six months' date. A presents the bill to a banker, who cashes it— that is, gives him some of the unused purchasing power lying in his hands or at his disposal. B, probably before the three or six months expire, has worked up the raw cotton into a manufac- tured form, which, being sold, enables him to redeem his engage- ment to the banker or assignee. But for credit, which utilises purchasing power lying dormant, so that buyers are forthcoming, the raw cotton might long have remained unsold in A's hands, and B's machinery stood still until he had obtained sufficient ready money to purchase. Such an instance illustrates Lord Overstone's dictum, that " the whole principle of banking is to transfer capital from the inactive accumulator to the active and energetic person who wants capital." Banks, to put the matter in a different form, may be regarded as the collectors and dis- tributors of purchasing power. They are the intermediaries between certain kinds of lenders and certain kinds of borrowers. It is often said bankers are dealers in money ; but though they certainly require money, dealing in it is not their business: they do not, as a rule, discount in gold, and only an infinitesimal portion of their deposits is in the form of money. They deal in the equiva- lents of money, or currency. Another definition of their province is "dealers in capital." And this definition is defective only inas- much as it is incomplete. They are the instruments by which wealth lying unproductive is set in motion and transmuted into capital, and by which capital is passed from one hand to another. But they deal directly with capital only to a small extent ; and the banker's chief office is to receive A's title to a certain value, and to sell this and other titles to B, C, and D. For debts payable *à terme*, the banker usually gives debts payable on demand. The difference between the price at which titles are bought and the price at which they are sold constitutes the banker's profit. Professor Price is right when he describes bankers as dealers in debts; but we may, without inconsistency, admit that they deal in capital also, if for no other reason than that, through their instrumentality, wealth which would have been consumed unproductively, or would have been suffered to be idle, is productively consumed.

Credit helps to economise capital; in particular it helps to economise gold and silver. By means of bank-notes, a leading form of credit, we are enabled to dispense with much of coin. The Chinese, who have invented everything and perfected nothing, invented bank-notes. In Europe, they were first issued by the Bank of Sweden. Now they perform much of the work of commerce. Every civilised country employs them more or less. In Scotland they have all but superseded gold; and in Ireland notes are sometimes preferred to sovereigns—the person who tenders five sovereigns not always faring so well as he who tenders a five-pound note. The principle upon which notes are issued is this:—A person, or number of persons, believed to be wealthy—having "credit," as the phrase is—issue promises to pay in coin £1, £5, etc., on demand. The public, relying upon the fulfilment of these promises of payment, receive these notes, which thus take the place and do the work of coin; while the banker, keeping a reserve in coin, enough to meet all emergencies, which is popularly estimated at one-third, but which really varies according to the nature of the times and of the banker's other engagements, is enabled to sell far more purchasing power than he receives or owns. For example, if his deposits amount to £240,000 received in coin, then, setting aside his own private fortune, or the called-up portion of the capital of the bank, if it be a joint-stock concern, he may be enabled, to take an imaginary case, to sell to his customers purchasing power equal to £160,000 in coin, and £240,000 in notes. His profit by this arrangement is obvious; while he buys the use of only £240,000, and that at a low rate, he sells the use of £400,000, and that at a high rate. The profit or advantage gained by the community is only a shade less obvious, for the banker's paper notes perform the work of the £240,000 deposited with him, and release society from the necessity of providing 240,000 sovereigns, with the exception of 80,000 kept by the banker as a reserve; and even as regards them there is economy, for these 80,000 sovereigns suffer no wear. Certain other functions of banks remain to be noticed. Banks are of service in keeping money safely. The famous Bank of Amsterdam, founded in 1609, and one of the first to be established in Europe, was intended to relieve the Dutch merchant from the care of hoarding his money at home. Another function of banks is that of facilitating or dispensing with the transmission of money. For example, the Bank of England enables the Government to avail themselves of the taxes as soon as they are collected, and before they are transmitted from the provinces to London. " One of the most important services," says Mr. Hankey, late Governor of the Bank of England, " performed through the branch banks, is the remittance of the revenue, which is paid over by the collectors at the various places of receipt to clerks attending from the branch banks for the purpose. Credit is then immediately given to the Exchequer account in London, so that the revenue is made available for the public service with the least possible loss of time." The business of the Indian banks consists chiefly of exchange transactions. Further, banks save trouble in the presentment of bills. Lastly, it is no inconsiderable benefit that they enable the Government to reduce the National Debt. They are the bankers of the poor; the deposits in the savings' banks enable them to come into possession of consols which, subject to the interest of $2\frac{1}{2}$ per cent paid to depositors, may be converted into terminable annuities, with the effect of redeeming part of the principal of the Debt.

Credit gives rise to what are called bills of exchange, which still further, and in a far greater degree than bank-notes, economise money and utilise wealth. In any state of society, however economically undeveloped, lie the germs of future economical improvements. To speak of the invention of bills of exchange is perhaps erroneous language: men had not to go to Egypt or Phœnicia in order to learn that fire burnt; neither was commerce indebted to Italy for the ideas of bills of exchange. It is natural that we should discern in antiquity the germs of future economical improvements. The references, however, to bills of exchange are few. Isocrates and Cicero are almost the only authorities. These bills, which were first brought into extensive use in the thirteenth or fourteenth century, were at first bankers' drafts, intended to save the cost and risk of transmitting coin; and they were at first intended, as the name records, to dispense with the transmission from one country to another. The agents of the bankers of Florence, Lucca, and other Italian cities, who collected the Pope's dues in all parts of the world, instead of forwarding the money to the Pope's Exchequer, sent drafts on their principals. In process of time, bills were employed to dispense with the sending of money from one town to another in the same country. Thus, if A, a merchant in Newcastle, owed £1000 to B, a merchant in Bristol, the former would not send 1000 sovereigns, by post or otherwise, to the latter; but in the event of there being a merchant C in Bristol, who owed £1000 to D, another in Newcastle, A would pay £1000 to D, and thus buy his debt, while C would hand over £1000 to B; and thus, without one single coin passing from Bristol and Newcastle, the debts between these towns would be paid. Of course the process of settlement in actual business is pretty sure to be more complicated, and the offset will not be always so complete; but the above instance explains the principle of settlement. In course of time, as these bills came to be recognised by the law as a satisfactory discharge of debts, and as Courts of Justice became emancipated from the Common Law doctrine that debts were inalienable, they were drawn not only between persons in different countries and towns, but between different persons in the same town. In most trades it is customary to give credit to purchasers for three months; in others, such as the wine trade, for six months; in some for even two years; and if producers "lay out of their money so long," they would either require much larger capital than they now require, or they would be obliged to contract their business. But traders trade upon debts. They draw a bill upon their debtor, and presenting the bill to a banker, they receive from him the amount of the debt, minus the interest of the sum for the time that is to elapse before it is paid. This process, called discounting, really signifies that the discounters lend so much to the holders of the bill. The bill, as we may remark, is in the form of a letter or mandate, by one person, called the drawer, ordering another person, the drawee, to pay a certain amount at a certain date to a third person called the payee; and if the drawee agrees to comply with the order by writing "accepted," he is the acceptor. Those persons into whose hands the bill may pass previous to its being paid, and who put their signatures on the back of it, are called indorsers. The acceptor is legally responsible in the first instance; the various indorsers are regarded as new drawers. Another form of the bill of exchange is what is called an accommodation or fictitious bill. While a real bill supposes an actual transfer of goods, an actual debt contracted, an accommodation bill supposes no such real debt: one person undertakes, as a favour, or from various other motives, to accept a bill which apparently shows that he is in debt to the drawer, on the express understanding that the acceptor will not have to pay the bill when it matures; and the advantage of this arrangement is, that on the faith of the double credit the drawer is enabled to get the bill discounted and to raise money. The connection may be still farther complicated, for the drawee of one bill may redraw a bill upon the drawer. These bills save the use of money; where money was used, bills are now used. Instead of paying a debt by money, people pay it by other debts; instead of sending money, they send bills, which, when drawn upon a foreign country, are usually drawn in parts or sets.

In regard to foreign bills of exchange, a few words of explanation, partly with a view to point out that under a show of difference they perform the same services between different countries as inland bills do between different towns of the same country. Suppose that a London house has ordered and received a cargo of sugar from Brazil, and has, therefore, occasion to transmit £5000 to a Rio Janeiro house. The former, instead of sending specie by the mail, and thus incurring expense and risk, goes into the bill market or Exchange, and buys of some bill-broker a bill upon a Rio Janeiro house, and transmits the bill to its correspondent, who presents it or gets it discounted. Thus two debts are discharged without the passage of a single coin; the Rio Janeiro creditor is paid by the Rio Janeiro debtor, and the London creditor is paid by the London debtor. Supposing the liabilities of two countries to be equal, and the bills expressive of the debts to mature at the same dates so as to cancel each other, a settlement could be effected without the intervention of money, and the foreign exchanges would then be at par. Such simplicity, however, is not realised in practice. Exports may not balance

imports; one country may be habitually the debtor of another,
and owing to the necessity, from the exportation of coupons,
of paying dividends to the latter, the exchange may regularly
be "against" the former; debts equal in amount may not
become due at the same date; and loans may take place
with the effect for a time of tending to make the rate of exchange unfavourable to the lending country—an effect by and
by neutralised by the influx of dividends, and still more quickly
so if, as is usual in the case of foreign loans, they are repaid by
sinking funds. Such circumstances complicate the problem;
and another element of difficulty is the circumstance that the
trade of various countries is curiously interwoven. A debt due by
the United States to England may be satisfied by a draft on a
German house indebted to a New York firm; it is possible that
the German house may ultimately pay the debt by a draft on a
St. Petersburg house or a Riga merchant. All this, termed the
arbitrage of the exchanges, not to speak of blank credits or the
international equivalents of accommodation bills, tend to render
the rate of exchange at any moment a false guide of the state of
indebtedness of any two countries. Hitherto we have spoken of
bills payable at sight; but a fresh element has to be taken into
account in the case of bills at three or six months' date. The
rate for bills payable at sight can never rise above the freight
and insurance chargeable for remitting bullion, together with the
expense of packing, and will not sink below that term. This
limit in time of peace is small. In time of war, however, when
the transmission of bullion is either impracticable or perilous,
the preference for bills over coin may be intense, and the premium
may be considerable. In these circumstances, to send gold out
of the country may be impossible. Take as an instance the
state of Paraguay during the last war; though Lopez had
treasure of his own, the difficulty of transporting it induced him
or his mistress to try to extort a bill of exchange from a Scotch
doctor. In regard to bills which are orders to pay a sum of money
after three or six months in another country, it is necessary to
take cognisance of the rate of interest abroad. He who buys the
bills gives a present sum for a future sum. He therefore gives
so much less than for a bill at sight. The bill is to be honoured
in another country; and if the rate of interest is there rising,
subjecting the buyer to the necessity of paying interest at this
augmenting rate to his foreign creditor, he will make a further

deduction. This element, particularly if there is reason to apprehend a serious disturbance of the price of money, if the bills run long, or if the credit of the drawers be not unexceptionable, affords great scope for variations in the rates of exchange. The differences in coinage must also be taken into account.

Lastly, to these elements must be added, in the case of transactions with a country whose currency is debased, or whose paper money is depreciated, the premium on bullion, which may vary indefinitely. This has been termed the nominal exchange, in contradistinction to the real exchange existing between countries with an undepreciated currency.*

The subject of the foreign exchanges has always been esteemed one of the most knotty economical problems. I shall not attempt to elucidate the whole subject : enough if a few difficulties are removed. And the chief vanish as soon as we perceive that the movements of bullion present no peculiarities except such as are derived from its portability, universal use, and durability. When bullion abounds here and is scarce and in demand elsewhere, it will be exported; when the circumstances are the opposite, it will be imported. If some prime article is required from abroad, as corn in 1847, and there are not commodities to procure it with, bullion will be exported. Again, when the rate of discount is high in a country, bullion will be attracted if the difference is considerable and there is good security. Another important fact to be noted with regard to the exchanges is, that a persistent fall of the rate of exchange below the limits of the real exchange indicates a depreciation of the currency. A depreciation is of course also attested by the difference between the market price of gold—that is, the amount bullion-dealers give for coin—and the mint price, £3 : 17 : 10½.

It remains to speak of the signification of the terms, "favourable" and "unfavourable" exchange. No doubt these terms were invented by people who believed that an influx of bullion was beneficial ; now, however, they may be regarded as expressive of simple monetary facts, and as neither dyslogistic nor eulogistic. The above enumeration of the influences acting upon the rate of exchange, however brief and imperfect, will enable one to judge of, in part, the worth of the theory

---

* "In the Southern States the exchange on London actually rose to 400 per cent."—Goschen on *Foreign Exchanges*, p. 100.

I

upon which was built the Bank Act of 1844. Its promoters wished to regulate the paper currency by the exchanges. It was argued that an issue led to an augmentation in prices, consequently in the first instance to an augmentation of the imports, and by and by to an export of gold together with an unfavourable state of the exchanges. To curtail this the framers of the Act provided that as soon as gold quitted the country, or rather the Bank, the issue should be contracted with a view to lower prices and bring back gold. It will occur to most people, even before they are fully acquainted with the Act, that this cause of indebtedness, one among many, is comparatively insignificant, if influential at all; and it will perhaps be thought a more effectual mode of attracting money is by raising the rate of interest sufficiently high.

Promissory-notes also serve as a substitute for coin. We are told that they originated about the end of the sixteenth century among the merchants of Amsterdam, Middlesburg, and Hamburg, and that they were first used in England by the goldsmiths in the seventeenth century. After strenuous resistance on the part of Courts of Justice, they became negotiable like bills of exchange. Bank-notes are in reality only a form of promissory-notes. As its title implies, a promissory-note is a promise by one person, called the " maker," to pay on demand a certain sum to another person, called the " payee." These notes dispense with money in the same manner in which bank-notes do, the only real difference being, that promissory-notes being usually the promises of private persons, whose means are known only within a limited district, and bank-notes the promises of a person or body of persons whose means are likely to be more widely known and trusted, the latter are likely to be received more generally, and their circulation is apt to be wider and more unquestioned. Cheques are another substitute for money; and in countries where banks are common, and where people have grown accustomed to place with bankers their reserves instead of keeping them at home, cheques dispense with the use of an enormous amount of money. Cheques are, as every one knows, orders by a banker's depositor to pay a certain amount to a third person, or, as is usual in practice, to transfer a certain amount to a third person's account. Comparing them with bills of exchange, they are bills drawn by a depositor upon his banker. How influential cheques may be in dispensing with the use of money is patent, if we consider that, if all persons kept their money with a banker, and the same one, there would be no necessity for any money except for carrying on small retail and international transactions, and for the banker's reserve. Every consideration points to cheques becoming probably the chief and almost sole instrument of credit.

Is credit capital? Credit, the ability to borrow, is assuredly no more capital than the wheel and axle which raises the bucket from the well is the water which the bucket contains. Under this much-controverted phrase, however, is concealed the question, really sensible and interesting, Whether credit does more than transfer wealth from one place and person to another place and person? M. Say, in consistency with his conception of capital, Mr. M'Culloch, Mr. Hankey, M. Wolowski, and Mr. Mill (though the last qualifies his statement), affirm that credit merely transfers capital. Now, certainly, a transference of wealth is all that credit accomplishes; but, at the same time, this transference is frequently, though not always or necessarily, from those who would spend wealth unproductively, or who would leave it unused, to those who employ it productively. Here is a horse kept for pleasure, and never employed at farm-work ; it is wealth, but not capital. Some one who possesses credit borrows it and yokes it to a plough ; the horse is now capital. While merely displacing wealth, credit may create capital.

Does credit affect prices? Do the bank-notes and the bills of exchange which execute the work of gold and silver ever raise prices? There cannot be any doubt that credit acts most potently on prices, as the following considerations prove :— Prices depend on the effective demand that exists for commodities, and the attainable supply of them. When credit is imperfectly developed, and before banks are known, the only purchasers, if we leave barter out of account, consist of the actual possessors of money. Extend credit, draw deposits to the banks, offer facilities for discounting, and many who do not possess money are placed in a position to purchase, and for every one buyer there may be created two. Not merely every one who has money, but every one who can get money, or its equivalent, is a possible raiser of prices. The producers sell not merely for actual coin, but for bills. Presented to a banker, a bill is discounted, and procures the seller a certain portion of unused purchasing power lodged with the banker. This multiplication of potential purchasers may, and probably will raise prices; and if confidence be abused, worthless and reckless men obtaining the command of funds, the prices of many commodities may rise to an extravagant height. Some of these rises have become historical: witness the rise of prices which preceded the break-up of Law's system. It may be further asked, Which of these forms of credit affect prices most? The sums being equal, bank-notes are the most effective forms of credit. The area of circulation of an inland bill of exchange, a promissory-note, or of a cheque, is, as a rule, comparatively limited compared with that of a bank-note; and the same usually holds of all countries where banking is fenced round by restrictions intended to secure the convertibility of the note. Under most of the existing banking systems notes are issued by large corporations, for the solvency of which the State takes laborious precautions, and the character of which is widely known. Hence, as a rule, a note circulates within a wide area, or among many persons, without question, whereas bills of exchange, being based upon the soundness of private firms, are apt to have a more confined circulation. Of course, however, some inland bills circulate as widely as bank-notes, and good foreign bills of exchange are accepted more universally than any notes. Again, the period during which a bank-note circulates and operates upon prices is usually longer than the period of circulation of any other form of credit; and it is an obstacle to the use of bills as instruments of exchange that they vary in value, that one must watch their *echéance*, and that they require indorsement. Made for convenient sums, notes are made to circulate; other forms of credit are not. At the same time, partly from legislative obstructions to the fabrication of notes, and partly from certain inherent defects, they, as a matter of fact, are feeble elevators and depressors of prices compared with cheques and bills. Their amount and value are comparatively small, the total *fixed* issue not being much over thirty millions; and, unless where an inconvertible currency exists, their action on prices is comparatively slight. Cheques, provided their drawers and holders keep their accounts at the same banks, may exercise a still more powerful influence on prices than bills. No doubt there are certain legal restrictions, such as the fact that the cheque must be presented within a reasonable time, standing in the way of their operating so influentially on prices, amount for amount, as bank-notes. Touching the general theory of prices and the value of money, it may be said here that they, in the case of a purely metallic currency, vary inversely with the amount of money in existence, in the first instance, and the *efficiency*, or "rapidity of circulation," to quote Mr. Mill's phrase, of the individual coins. When credit comes into vogue as a purchasing power, referring to the general principles of values, we may say that the value of money will depend on the quantity of goods offered for sale and the demand.

The effect of credit on prices leads to the subject of commercial crisises, and is the cause of many. Many crisises run through the following phases :—Trade has been going briskly ; people have been ready to lend, and particularly ready to borrow ; bills have not been scanned closely ; there is abroad a general expectation of high profits ; prices are rising ; every one has money or the reputation of having it ; companies are started to send fire-irons to the equator and fans to Greenland, to "develop" the resources of the Sahara, or utilise the sewage of San Francisco; everybody can borrow; people are reckless and hopeful. Suddenly into this world of bubbles falls a disconcerting *incident. Some scrupulous banker refuses to discount an adventurer's bills ; there is a general pricking up of ears and a rush upon debtors ; the adventurers, all who are trading on borrowed money, tumble first, knocking down each other as nine-pins do. Even solid houses topple, for, being prepared only for ordinary calls, expecting no general and simultaneous rush of creditors, they may be forced to shut their doors, when, give them a little time, and only let their debtors be as forbearing as usual, and these houses would pay every farthing and leave a substantial balance. People then dread credit in almost any form ; they wish to handle gold. They, therefore, may come to the banker and instantly demand cash for their notes, to the great inconvenience and danger of the banker, who is prepared to meet no extraordinary emergencies. So far, however, as banks are concerned, the rock which has most usually proved fatal, as attested by the experience of this country and America—though the fact is ignored by legislators, who have laboured to secure the convertibility of the notes, without regard to the disposal of the deposits—is not the return of their notes upon banks, but the withdrawal of their deposits, the sudden necessity to meet liabilities usually far greater than those which their note-circulation implies. It was the reckless way in which the bankers of the United States dealt with their deposits that caused so many failures thirty years ago; with deposits liable to be withdrawn at any moment they made loans to be repaid at distant dates; it is the traditional care of the Scotch banks to invest a considerable portion of their deposits in securities which can be swiftly turned into money that has been one of their most solid buttresses. Unfortunately, and often of necessity, bankers think themselves 'ompelled to take steps which, in these times of excitement, are apt to heighten the confusion, and for very safety they are compelled to do that which sometimes leads to their own ruin. To keep off the ceaseless requests for loans coming in the form of requests to discount bills, they are obliged to raise the rate of discount. Gold is wanted, and if the bank did not sell it on onerous terms, its coffers would be speedily emptied. A bank is not, as has been well said, "a monetary providence" bound to satisfy all demands; but this act of self-defence, making loans dear and scarce, must not be lightly adopted, for a brusque rise may intensify the confusion which may spread to depositors, who, by withdrawing their deposits, may drag down the banker.

This is, perhaps, the type of commercial crisises : they are usually preceded by a reckless extension of credit, and followed by the reckless contraction of it—before them people put too much faith in each other, after them too little. Such, perhaps, is the type of all crisises. It is, however, necessary to impart greater precision to our explanations. In the first place, distrust is seldom or never complete, so that all forms of credit are "blown upon;" certain corporations and firms of tested soundness and long standing ride through all storms. One is apt to say that in a crisis all credit vanishes; but, as a matter of fact, this is an ideal pitch of anarchy, to which the commercial world never attains. In the climax of the storm the notes of the Banks of England and France are freely accepted. The very sight of them has sometimes calmed panic-stricken minds. The *Economist* has happily observed that an English crisis may be regarded as a time at which people will accept nothing but Bank of England notes. In the next place, it is well to observe that under the term "crisis" are classed very different phenomena, originating at bottom in very different causes. Every commercial convulsion is loosely spoken of as a crisis; a temporary glut of any article of merchandise passes in common parlance for a crisis; the same is true of a general fall in the prices of public securities. But withheld from such convulsions, so far as they do not disturb confidence, the word ought to be confined to seasons in which credit is wounded or destroyed. By what then are commercial crisises produced? In political events they may originate. Revolutions have frequently induced them; those which occurred in France in 1830 and 1848 are cases in point. What more consequential? Who knows in those days what the morrow may bring forth? Who, therefore, is not desirous that as much as possible his property should be in the form of ready money instead of the titles to it? Depositors may withdraw their share of a bank's resources. Gold may be in request. The prospect of war usually engenders a shapeless fear, preying upon many more than those whose property is in danger; one has witnessed the outbreak of hostilities between France and Prussia cause a momentary depreciation of all foreign securities, and even tend to lower considerably Consols and the shares of home railways, owing to enforced realisations taking place. Securities, unless of an excellent character, may be in little repute, and from the consequent desire for gold may spring a crisis. Bad trading and a few startling failures may engender this distrust, and may lead to a dislike of all but gold and the best forms of credit. The business of the commercial world is conducted by substitutes for gold, on the assumption that there will prevail mutual confidence, and that there will be manifested no hasty and universal desire to realise. At certain times this assumption proves false. What confusion would ensue if suddenly, in a week or a day, our railway trains and omnibuses were brought to a stand? In the confusion and annoyance consequent on our being compelled to fall back on the few mail-coaches to be had, we may read the analogue of the confusion of society when it is compelled to abandon payment by bills and cheques, and to transact most of its business by sovereigns or notes. It may happen, and this is another variety of crisis, that they are directly traceable to the efflux of bullion. Indeed crisises are generally preceded by unfavourable exchanges. A famine or a bad harvest, failure to procure a staple article of consumption in the usual quarter, or large loans, may necessitate the exportation of specie; and debtors finding growing difficulty in obtaining coin, creditors being unusually eager to obtain that which is in demand, and fear arising at the low reserve left to make good the various obligations to pay in gold, a crisis may arrive. In 1863-64 the operation of these causes was strikingly and fatally illustrated in this country and in France. Accustomed to obtain cotton from the Southern States in return for our goods, but obliged by the Civil War to seek supplies in India, Egypt, and other countries, where a taste for our goods had been little cultivated, we had to pay for the cotton, and pay for it dearly, in gold or silver, the universal merchandise. In France, injury to the silk trade necessitated exportation of specie. The effect of this necessary exportation, together no doubt with other causes, was to rarefy money and bring on a monetary crisis. And here I may say that a monetary crisis which is not a side aspect of a great destruction or serious want of capital, or grave wound inflicted on credit by reckless trading, can scarcely fail to be very prolonged, especially now that the electric telegraph can apprise distant countries possessing supplies of gold, of our wants; and the fact that the crisises which we have witnessed of late have extended over a considerable time is proof that the antecedents were not mere want of gold. For if there be abundance of commodities, a country can scarcely remain long unprovided with money. No merchandise is so easy to obtain within a limited period and to transmit as gold. Unless confidence has been deeply wounded, from a merely monetary crisis there will be a quick recovery. Not want of coin, but scarcity of floating capital, may create a commercial tempest, and this scarcity may be either absolute or relatively to the mass of engagements. Suppose, first, that a vast quantity of capital has been sunk in works which will not increase the wealth of the country for some time —in railways, bridges, harbours, mines, drainage, irrigation. The temporary consequence is a destruction of so much capital without a return. The world is for the time impoverished; capital is dear, and money is not to be had; the funds available for lending are reduced; the stock of articles which would have procured money is less than usual; and in the difficulties experienced in obtaining loans, with the necessity for them increased, a crisis may set in. In 1847 it is estimated that nearly £150,000,000 was engaged to railway purposes, and the consequence was a serious panic. Again, a crisis may be brought about by over-speculation. Let us understand clearly what is meant by over-speculation : this is a word so often used that its meaning has become indistinct, like the superscription of a much-worn coin. In particular, one must divest himself of the idea that it is of necessity immoral and injurious, though, no doubt, now when the rate of pure profit is low, and when the standard of *haut ton* is set by the possessors of vast inherited wealth, it often is gambling. Within bounds, speculation is a perfectly legitimate procedure, for it is buying in the expectation of a rise, the procedure of every sagacious trader. It is beneficial in its action, for society is thus saved from fluctuations in prices from one extreme to another. It is only when traders neglect fair chances, and exaggerate the prospects of gain, and turn traffic into a game of chance, that speculation is detrimental, and is productive of crisises. Perhaps a new market is to be opened, giving a favourable outlet for some commodities, or a country that formerly supplied us with some staple article is likely to fail in furnishing us with a supply. Traders buy up these articles, in the expectation of a rise of price. Such is speculation. In times of speculation there is almost what one may call a spirit of irrational imitation; and, prompted by the sight of persons speculating on perfectly legitimate contingencies, others may speculate upon goods in the price of which there is no good reason to expect a rise. The conduct of a mob is often more unreasonable than the character of any single member of it; and in these times of over-trading there is abroad a spirit of extravagant hopefulness of which no one man is the originator, and every man is the victim. If, as the French say, *tout le monde* is wiser than anybody, he is sometimes also more foolish. Men literally go mad with avarice in these seasons. Few perceive that their behaviour is unreasonable, for the bulk of men confound reasonableness with frequency. Men may then give £300 for the root of a Semper Augustus tulip, or may buy South Sea stock at eight hundred and ninety per cent. Of course, the frenzy by and by cools. Men wake up to the dangers they are running. They desire to sell. The particular goods or stocks formerly in request are thrown on the market, and prices fall more quickly than they rose. A universal settling day arrives, with ruin to those who speculated boldly, and it may be to those who stood aloof. The varieties of crisises would not be exhausted if mention was not made of those which are produced by the efforts of designing men. The designs of a band of New York stockbrokers in 1869, frustrated only by the Treasury coming to the rescue, showed that it may be in the power of a clique to bring about a monetary crisis by buying up gold. Not that such a contingency is possible—certainly probable—in this country; it could happen only in a country where a paper currency exists. It is frequently observed that crisises become more frequent as credit extends, and there may be detected a fatalistic tendency to acquiesce in them, as the inevitable price at which its benefits are purchased. This pernicious doctrine is discountenanced by the case of Scotland. Nowhere, probably, is credit more spread : no country can boast of so many branch banks in comparison with the population ; nowhere is coin so completely replaced by paper. Yet, with the exception of such disturbances as were ascribable to those prevailing in England, and of that in which the Western Bank was destroyed, Scotland has not, for upwards of half-a-century, been the scene of a commercial crisis. This and many other misconceptions would vanish, if for credit were substituted what ought to be its synonym—trust. It would then be felt that credit is not of a homogeneous character ; that in a country where morality and caution were developed, credit might ramify widely without danger, and that if the commercial world contained fewer gamblers, and worse than gamblers—if there did not prevail a feverish passion for wealth and an intolerance of moderate profits—it would be spared not a few of the shocks to which it is now frequently exposed. It is not the number of men trusted, or the extent of credit, but the nature of the men trusted, the quality of the credit given, that determines the frequency of these crisises ; and unless it be inevitable that trading should be conducted with as little regard to moral considerations and reasonable chances as it now often is, we need not resign ourselves to an increase of crisises, or to their decennial recurrence. And until that improvement be effected, ingenious regulations with regard to banks will be of little avail to abate the evil. That belief in machinery, the idolon of economists, impels them to look for a remedy for crisises, as for all other economical evils, in some ingenious arrangements ; they do but make well-planned structures out of rotten materials so long as men have not a lofty scorn of failing to fulfil their engagements, so long as bankruptcy is not disreputable, and so long as 3 per cent is scorned. Here Bills will not keep off earthquakes, nor will any mechanical device avert a crisis. According to a common doctrine, crisises are repeated every ten years. This also is a pernicious and false doctrine. It has the effect of creating uneasiness every ten years, and of be-getting overweening confidence and want of caution during the interval. This generalisation arises from the desire of men for uniformity—from their tendency to make it, if they cannot find it. As a matter of fact, crisises have not occurred decenni-ally. Not to insist upon the truth that not a year passes without a crisis of greater or less magnitude occurring some-where, we do not find that, if any one country be taken, it has experienced them at such intervals. To take England for an example, it suffered from commercial crisises in 1793, 1797, 1857, 1861, 1863-4, 1866. Is not indeed the single fact that so unforeseen and irregular a thing as war frequently brings on a crisis, enough to discredit the theory, even if it were not discredited by the most elementary consideration of the nature of credit ?

The giving of credit implies that the borrower can give some security that the loan will be repaid. Sometimes it is land or other property, which an owner mortgages or pledges ; some-times bills of lading or dock warrants, or Government securities, are the gage ; sometimes mere business talent or a good reputa-tion is regarded a security : it is one of the latest developments of credit, ascribable to Herr Schultze-Delitzsch, to lend upon the security of labour, so as to enable those who possess nothing but their arms, to borrow and to rise to the position of capitalists. Hence credit is divided into two sorts—real credit and personal credit. The former is chiefly exemplified by credit based on land, and credit based on personal property; of per-sonal credit we have numerous instances. The former, as we find it in its rudest germs, is granted only in the event of an actual transfer, nay even of a sale taking place. The Roman law brings us back to a time when people did not understand lending on the security of an article which was left in the custody of the borrower. That law, particularly valuable as a history of the growth of economical ideas, seems to show that all transactions were evolved out of a sale, certainly that a loan was regarded as a sale. Both ownership and possession were, in the early state of the law, handed over by the pledger to the creditor ; and it is almost superfluous to observe that, according to the common law of England, a mortgage is regarded as a sale. In only one department of credit is there now-a-days to any extent a deposit of a gage or surety—pawnbrokers exact this security.

Often real credit appears not in those forms which in Roman law were called *pignus* and *fiducia*, but in the form known to it as *hypotheca*. The creditor, instead of actually receiving the article, and obtaining the possession if not the ownership of it, has a lien upon some article the property and possession of which are left with the debtor. Advances may be made on deeds ; and, indeed, the most common of all the forms of credit is the advancing on the *titres* to property—for such bills of exchange may be considered. From the nature of his business it will be readily inferred on what security the banker is accustomed to lend. With a mass of liabilities maturing at an unknown time, he is compelled to lend chiefly on securities readily convertible at no distant date. Government securities will be favourites, and he will prefer Consols, always marketable, without the risk of serious depreciation, to terminable annuities, for instance.

It may be well to refer more particularly to a recent development of personal credit, by which those destitute of property obtain the command of capital. To Herr Schultze-Delitzsch is due the honour of conquering the difficulty embodied in the brocard, "*Plus cautionis est in re quam in persona,*" and of imitating on a large scale banks for advancing money to workmen. It was in Eulenburg that the first of these banks arose ; they are now spread over Germany. It appeared to Herr Schultze that the sole obstacle to workmen receiving loans was the uncertainty, owing to death, ill-health, ill-luck in applying their borrowed funds, and dishonesty, of the loan being returned with due interest, and that this uncertainty could be banished from such transactions if the security becomes corporate instead of personal. If each borrower was under unlimited liability for the whole debts of the corporation, creditors could scarcely fear to lend, and the principle of the credit banks is to buttress each debt by the security of the whole society. The maximum of security and responsibility is obtained by letting nobody borrow but members, by sanctioning only such advances as are likely to be employed in production, and by making the whole association responsible. Each debtor is unlimitedly liable.

The result has hitherto been a great success. According to all accounts, the members of these associations, now to be found throughout Germany, have prospered exceedingly, and capitalists who have lent to the credit banks have rarely found their trust abused. Almost unqualified praise is the due of these banks and their founder. In particular, he deserves praise for endeavouring to wean the German workman from the seductive arguments of Lassalle, who advised him to look to the State for the requisite capital. Herr Schultze deserves to have, and perhaps will have, imitators here. At the same time it must be observed that the onerous terms upon which loans are received, and the heavy liabilities incurred by the fact of membership, will perhaps deter the best class of our artisans from availing themselves of these credit banks; they could more easily obtain advances by means of a cash-credit account, supposing their character and skill were unimpeachable.

Lending upon land, or *Crédit Foncier*, is the most important part of real credit. On the faith of landed property a certain loan is granted. There may be no special institution for lending upon landed security. That is, broadly speaking, the case in this country, where the mortgagee is chiefly dependent upon the same banks as the trader, almost the sole difference being that for certain purposes the landowner may obtain government loans—on terms, by the way, very easy. But in several foreign countries there are special institutions for granting credit to landed proprietors somewhat similar to the famous and unfortunate National Land Bank of 1696. Among the chief facts which led to the establishment of the *Crédit Foncier* and other land banks was the circumstance, apparently denoting something wrong and rectifiable, that the rate of interest on loans upon personal security was considerably lower than the rate required of borrowers upon landed security, and that that which might prove utterly worthless was esteemed a better security than that which could not lose its value. The payment of interest at the rate of 6 to 8 per cent when the land yielded only $2\frac{1}{2}$ to 3 per cent on the purchase-money, stimulated the development of landed credit. Could not this be amended? was the question put with ardour some eighteen years ago in France; and encouraged by examples of the Silesian land banks, and convinced of the truth of the old maxim, *Plus cautionis est in re quam in persona*, many concluded that it could. The result was the

Crédit Foncier. The difficulty of borrowing except at high interest, M. Wolowski and other founders of the *Crédit Foncier* believed to be largely ascribable to the landed proprietors of France being often unable to repay the principal in a short period; obliged to lie out of their money for a long time, with perhaps no certainty of ever receiving it, lenders protected themselves by charging a high rate of interest. To rectify this it was the object of the promoters of the *Crédit Foncier* to render repayment of the loan easy and gradual, and to give the lenders every facility for realising their mortgage. It was to "mobilise the soil," and "to modify the form of the debt upon land, converting a floating into a consolidated debt, and to procure to proprietors the funds they needed in improving their modes of culture and increasing their produce." A company (at first several *sociétés* confined to regions) was formed for the purpose of lending to proprietors sums reimbursable by annuities that included the interest, a slowly operating sinking fund, and the working expenses. The funds were raised by issuing obligations or debentures bearing interest at the rate of 3 per cent on the value of the mortgages. In the principle of such land banks there was nothing wrong. It is proper to facilitate the borrowing of money destined to improve the land by putting borrowers who can repay only at a distant date into communication with lenders who agree to that condition. It was quite gratuitous on the part of certain English economists to decry the *Crédit Foncier* at the outset as based on a bad principle. Probably, the utmost that was objectionable in it was its needless connection with the State. At the same time, extravagant expectations were certainly entertained with regard to this Company. It must never be forgotten that the chief obstacle to the obtaining of credit was the poverty of the owners of the soil, its indebted condition, and the fact that they had frequently more land than they could profitably use. Before the *Crédit Foncier* was established the rich landowner could borrow readily, and on easy terms; and no company can do much to eradicate poverty. Here, if it were permitted to enter into details, one might speak of the agricultural loan unions, institutions with a similar purpose, which have sprung into existence in the Rhine provinces; but, forbearing, I would say that in this country probably facilities for borrowing upon the security of landed property would be greatly increased if there was a universal registration of titles, together with the burthens upon the land. This, which is needed in order to facilitate the sale of land, is particularly required in order to facilitate mortgaging, because a mortgagee is more particular about the character of a title than a purchaser. The latter is generally content if the title is proved for twenty to thirty years back; the mortgagee demands a longer investigation, and that without scruple, seeing the expense of the investigation is borne by the mortgagor or borrower. In almost every continental country one has but to consult the register in order to ascertain the real owner of any estate, and the mortgages on it, with their amount and order. Thus borrowing is facilitated; but it must be added that a very real obstacle is the fact that owners have found it so easy to borrow, and have availed themselves of their power. Indeed, as if to tempt the landowner to mortgage his estate, the State has employed strong lures. It has offered him loans at a low rate of interest; it has allowed him, even if he had a life interest, to charge his estate beyond his life; and by singling out land as a security on which a trustee may lend without fear of being rendered liable to refunding, it has multiplied the number of lenders.

Credit has been introduced in this conviction because it aids production. Its panegyrists, however, do not always observe that it may also impede production; and probably there are times when the advantages of credit are in the whole country balanced by the disadvantages of it. I speak not of accidental or insignificant drawbacks. Whatever precautions respecting number of signatures or character of paper be taken, unsound bills will occasionally be discounted. But there are times when it is a general fact that the machinery of credit is worked in floating schemes that could never be remunerative. Showy prospectuses wheedle capital out of the pockets of the unwary to squander it. In particular, credit has been abused by those capable of offering the most generally acceptable security—landowners and states. The enormous mass of mortgages on land, impairing its efficiency as a rule—so enormous that an Encumbered Estates Act seems universally necessary—testifies how landowners have abused the fact that land may be readily hypothecated. And, worst of all, the existence of despotic or semi-despotic governments, fond of display or war, and able to mortgage the fortunes of their subjects to a limitless extent, is a perpetual source of abuse of credit. Capable of averting or adjourning the Nemesis that sooner or later overtakes the private spendthrift, and willing to offer interest, suspicious by its very amount and far in excess of that which honest commerce can give, they yearly enter the loan market, withdraw or raise the price of the sustenance of agriculture and manufactures, in order to waste it on armies, fleets, banquets, and all the equipage of pomp. In the money market, creedless, heartless, looking only to security and believing itself absolved from all thought of the object of a loan, States find ready lenders if they only squeeze with regularity the dividends out of their subjects; and it matters not whether the money will be expended in stifling the free life of Hungary or ministering to the vices or whims of an eastern despot. Such prodigal and potent States —and there are more than one that answer the description —must seem to the eye of the economist the incarnation of evil.*

* I cannot, however, but mention here with approval the protest signed by members of the London Stock Exchange against the Russian loan, issued with much effrontery after the disavowal of the treaty of 1856.

CHAPTER X.

REGULATION OF THE CURRENCY.

BEFORE passing to the chief subject of this chapter, a word or two about certain kindred matters. And first, a few words more about bank-notes and cash-credit accounts.

Bank (*banco*) was originally used as the equivalent for *monte*, a term for the funded debts of Italian cities. By and by it came to mean an establishment which received deposits and discounted bills. Though the name did not come into use until the twelfth century, the thing itself was known of old, for the Romans, with their fine instinct for all that was practical, had invented and practised banking in a rudimentary way. They were not, however, the first to employ bank-notes; this device, as has been already stated, was the work of the Chinese, who issued paper notes, called " flying money," about the year 807 A.D. We may suppose that the invention was generally unknown in Europe in the seventeenth century, and we may therefore credit the Bank of Stockholm, founded in 1668, with the honour of re-inventing notes, in order to dispense with the cumbrous copper currency of Sweden. Banking, as now understood, first becomes perceptible in England about the middle of the seventeenth century, amid the Civil War.

In 1729 the Royal Bank of Scotland brought into use cash credits,—a device so peculiar to Scotland, and so fruitful in good results, that we halt for a moment to describe these cash credits or cash accounts. The Royal Bank, and soon afterwards the other Scotch banks, began to give credit for sums not rigidly defined, but varying usually from £100 to £1000, £2000, £3000, etc.—though often without these limits,—to people of good character, able to produce at least two sureties whose credit was good and satisfactory in the eyes of the directors, so that the bank ran little risk of loss by the failure or

K

absconding of the person to whom an advance was made. It is not necessary to possess property, though that may suffice, to obtain a cash account; if the customer can satisfy the bank of his business ability, and, at the same time, can induce wealthy friends to become surety for him, he will be granted a cash credit. One advantage, therefore, is, that it enables men who want nothing but a little capital in order to rise to wealth, to start in the race with capitalists on nearly equal terms; and there is no place in Scotland, however remote, in which there is not some wealthy man who owes his rise to cash credits. Other advantages consist in the fact that the customer only pays interest from day to day on the amount which he has actually drawn out, and that a bank allows him to repay it in small sums, and in this way to reduce a considerable part of the interest of the advance from the time in which each of these small sums is paid in. Thus, if a shopkeeper has a cash account of £500, and draws upon it on January 5 to the amount of £100, he begins then to pay interest on £100; if he pays in, on January 6, say £10 or £20, he is at once credited with interest on that amount, and so on throughout the year. Such a system is admirably suited for men whose wants are moderate and fluctuating; it relieves merchants and persons engaged in business from keeping by them money to meet daily demands, to pay wages, or to pay small debts every now and then maturing. Cash credits are granted to persons in almost every rank of society. They have laid the foundations of many private fortunes. They have helped to make roads, build bridges, and dig canals. They have soberly done for Scotland what finance companies, such as the *Crédit Mobilier* and the *Société Immobilier*, have wildly attempted to do for other countries. By means of them land has been reclaimed, and the farming of the country greatly benefited. By means of cash-credit accounts each Scotch bank has fulfilled the purposes of a *Crédit Foncier*. These advances are not regarded as dead loans, for it is expected by the bank that its customers will be constantly paying in and drawing out,— "operating" upon their credits, as the phrase is. The greatest advantage of these cash accounts is, as we have said, that the customer pays interest only upon the amount which he has actually drawn, and the moment he pays back any part of what he has drawn, the bank allows him interest on the balance in his favour, so that he can use his credit just as he needs it. On

the other hand, by getting a bill of exchange discounted, one
uses the whole amount of one's credit, and pays the whole amount
of the discount at once, whether the money be required or not.
Considering these manifest advantages, it seems strange that the
use of cash credits has not spread. It must, however, be remembered that in Scotland the form of the bond, and the summary proceedings which could follow upon registration, gave
exceptional safety to this form of obligation. Cash credits are
in substance of the nature of accommodation bills. To the banks
the system is advantageous, seeing the advances are made in their
notes, which thus get into circulation—an advantage of considerable consequence at a time when few bills were discounted,
and before the Act of 1845 restricted the note-circulation.

We pass now to the principal subject of this chapter. In
1844-45, Sir Robert Peel undertook the revision of the whole
banking system of the United Kingdom, in a series of memorable
measures ; and these Acts, still the subject of much discussion,
—on the one hand extolled as masterpieces of wisdom, and on
the other hand loudly decried as manifest blunders,—form
the corner-stone of British banking. In order to ensure the
convertibility of the notes, to prevent over-issues—the bugbear
of the time—Sir Robert Peel divided the Bank of England
into two distinct departments,—the issue department, where
coin is given in exchange for notes, or notes for coin or
bullion; and the banking department, where bills are discounted, advances made, the dividends of fundholders paid,
and the Government salaries paid out. The issue department
was allowed to send out notes to the amount of £14,000,000,
£11,015,100 of which was represented by a permanent debt
due by the Government to the bank, and the remainder by other
securities, while for all notes issued beyond this sum the bank
had to keep an equivalent in gold. Thus the first effect of the
Act of 1844 was to declare that, as far as the Bank of England
was concerned, the currency should consist of an undefined
amount of gold or paper based on gold, plus £14,000,000 (now
£15,000,000, owing to the lapsed issues of other banks) in
paper based on the Government debt and securities.

Previous to the passing of the Act of 1826, the number of
partners in the Provincial banks of England and Wales was limited
to six, with the view of preventing competition with the Bank of
England, and over-issues by numerous banks. Now, partnerships

or companies composed of more than six partners, may carry on
business as bankers, and issue notes, provided they were established before 1844, and do not issue notes within sixty-five miles
of London. The Act of 1844, which now regulates the banking of
England, limited the circulation of notes to the average circulation
during the twelve months ending April 27, 1844 ; and, at the
same time, in order to bring about the extinction of the power of
the private and joint-stock banks to issue notes, and to do something with a view to accomplish the unity of the note, it was
provided that no new banks of issue could be established, and
that two-thirds of the circulation of banks which might relinquish
the right of issue, or fall out of the ranks, should pass to the
Bank of England, on obtaining the consent of the Government
under an Order in Council. The last provision has worked
slowly, for Mr. Gladstone stated a few years ago that at the
present rate four hundred years must pass before the Bank of
England was the only bank of issue in England. Supplementary
measures were passed for Scotland and Ireland. In Scotland,
where previously there had been complete liberty of issue, all banks
of issue then in existence were permitted to issue an amount of
notes not exceeding the average for the year preceding 1st May
1845, together with the amount of coin in their possession at
their head offices. Contrary to the English regulations, the
Scotch banks were permitted to amalgamate, and to issue notes
equal to the aggregate circulation of the united banks. The
Scotch and Irish banks, moreover, were permitted to continue
the issue of £1 notes, while in England no notes under £5 were
allowed to circulate. Looking at the net result of the Bank
Acts on the note-circulation of the United Kingdom, we find
that, as regards the Bank of England and the Scotch and Irish
banks, they set no limits to the amount of notes for which there
is a reserve in coin kept, but that the English provincial banks
cannot exceed their fixed issues on any pretext whatever. The
total fixed issue of the banks in the United Kingdom amounts
to rather more than £30,000,000.

 The policy of all these regulations has been much discussed,—
so much, in truth, that it is alleged that the question of the
Bank Acts, like that of free-will, has passed out of the region of
profitable debate. I venture to think differently. The truth
appears to be pretty plain, and to be substantially this :—These
Acts are productive of considerably more harm than benefit.

The reasons for this opinion are as follow :—In the first place, the Acts of 1844 and 1845 are founded upon no principle. They are purely empirical. Accepting the view of the bullionists, that no bank-note should be issued unless there be in the issuer's coffers gold sufficient to pay it whenever a demand is made, one must pronounce Sir Robert Peel's Acts to be wrong, for they permit notes to the value of some thirty millions to be issued without insisting that they shall be represented by a metallic reserve ; the Bank of England is at liberty to issue about £15,000,000 for which no gold need be kept; and if we be assured that this portion of the circulation is amply fortified by the equivalent of gold, the security of the Government, the same cannot be said of the £3,000,000 which the Scotch banks may issue without any equivalent in gold. Further, if these notes are adequately fortified, it cannot be shown why more might not be safely issued on the same security. Clearly these Acts are in defiance of the principles of the pure bullionists. Now, the only other rational principles which Governments can pursue with regard to the issue of bank notes is to leave them to the discretion of issuers, or to insist that the liabilities shall bear a certain proportion, discovered by reasoning or experiment, to the metallic reserve. Obviously the former course is not pursued ; as little is the latter, for Sir Robert Peel fixed upon a purely arbitrary amount of notes to be issued without gold in reserve—to quote an expressive phrase employed at the time, the banks were " pounced upon "—and the amount which they were permitted to issue was determined by chance. But, supposing that the fixed amount of paper currency was suited to the wants of the country in 1844—and it must be remembered that Sir Robert Peel originally proposed a different average for the county banks—is the amount suited to the wants of the country for ever afterwards ? Surely the fact, if it be a fact, that the issue fixed upon then answered twenty years ago, proves that it is not now suitable in our altered circumstances. A change in the clearing-house arrangements, the more extensive use of cheques, would greatly alter the amount of coin required. Moreover, as confidence in banks varies, as the rules of banking and the bankers' channels of investment alter, the quantity deemed safe to issue without a metallic reserve behind it, ought also to vary. In short, a sum arbitrarily chosen is arbitrarily continued.

A second objection to the Acts is that they fail to accomplish their objects. These objects have often been disputed; indeed, it is a curious and suspicious circumstance that the apologists of the Act are not of one mind as to the object which it is designed to effect. Such a circumstance proves that the array of authorities in favour of the Acts of 1844 and 1845 should go for little, seeing they pledge their authority in regard to different things. But an object, if not the object, was to render impossible the inconvertibility of the note. To quote the words of an apologist of the Act of 1844, its "aim is confined to preserving that portion of the capital which is used as a national currency, from being involved, directly or indirectly, in the failure of speculative enterprises;" that is to say, I presume, that the aim of the Act of 1844 is to make notes always convertible. It is accordingly frequently said that Sir Robert Peel introduced "a cast-iron system," rendering inconvertibility impossible. And certainly there is almost a moral impossibility of many of the notes now issued in the United Kingdom proving worthless; but this security is not due to Sir Robert Peel's legislation. Long before 1844 the Bank of England notes were perfectly safe, so long as the banking part of its business was safely administered. It is in fact to Peel's Act of 1819, not to that of 1844, that we must ascribe the perfect convertibility of the bank-note. The former Act re-established cash payments—in other words, it compelled the Bank to fulfil its promises. Since 1797 the Bank had been permitted to coin promises and to break them with impunity; and it needed but this assertion of the plain rules of morality to ensure convertibility in all ordinary circumstances. At the same time, the Acts of 1844 and 1845 do not, as their admirers frequently affirm, render the suspension of payments a physical impossibility; they give note-holders no new security. If there was a general presentation of notes they could not be paid; £15,000,000 stand uncovered. Still more manifestly would ruin ensue if the depositors took alarm and began to withdraw their money. It must be borne in mind that the metallic reserve is the reserve not for the notes alone, but for the entire liabilities, of which the notes form an insignificant fraction. Compared with the entire liabilities, the notes may be one in fifty or even a hundred. In the case of the Bank of England there is indeed good reason to believe that the bullion and securities in the issue department cannot be taken to be specially appropriated to the note-circulation. In the event of bankruptcy all creditors would fare alike. As regards the Scotch banks, it is also clear that the physical impossibility of inconvertibility has not been provided for by the Act of 1845. The holders of the notes possess no distinct lien on the gold which the banks are obliged to keep. These banks resemble a garrison occupied by three hundred officers and six thousand privates. Is it sufficient, in order to keep the garrison well provisioned and able to stand a siege, to furnish provisions for the former only? The gold kept by the Scotch banks is not earmarked, so to speak, but is exposed to the demands of all creditors of the bank; and of these the note-holders, when compared with the depositors, possess insignificant claims. What are a few millions in notes compared with deposits estimated at fifty to sixty millions? A mere trifle. If, therefore, the banks behave imprudently, and invest them in securities, the echéance of which is distant, or which are not safe; if the advances too largely take the form of dead loans; the result, in the event of an intense panic, would be ruinous to note-holders, notwithstanding Sir Robert Peel's care for their safety. As to the country banks, the failures and errors of which were insisted upon by Sir Robert Peel as justifying his legislation,—though some of these are attributable to legislation,—has the Act made disasters unknown? and was it not possible, if they were to be meddled with, to make them issue the notes of a central bank? Even at present, the security against country bankers erring grievously, and repeating the lamentable experience of 1814, 1815, 1816, and 1840 and 1841, consists of prudence, not due to any Act of Parliament. In fact, a legislation which professes to protect the note-holder, and which does not at the same time confer on him a lien on the reserve, or insist upon a certain proportion being preserved between the total assets and liabilities, is a delusion. It is like keeping the wind out of a house by hermetically sealing the keyhole while the door is left ajar. In 1863 Mr. Chase showed a sense of this fact in framing a banking system for the United States; and, as the granting to the note-holders of a special lien would have been detrimental to the depositors, he enjoined the bankers to keep in legal money 25 per cent of the notes in circulation and deposits in "the redemption cities." The French règle des trois signatures in discounting, also evinced perception of the necessity of looking to all the liabilities. These considerations and facts kept in view, it will perhaps be admitted that the precautions taken by the Bank Acts for the benefit of the note-holders do not make the convertibility of the note an absolute certainty.

It has been said that the object of the Acts was to prevent over-issues. Now, as the evidence of bankers, fortified by *à priori* considerations, shows, this evil is all but imaginary, unless the State forces its subjects to accept certain promises, or releases their authors from the obligation of fulfilling them. Of course, when cash payments are suspended, and when a government arbitrarily saves from bankruptcy those who do not discharge their promises, an over-issue may take place, and the value of paper may then fall indefinitely below gold. The American greenbacks, the inconvertible currencies of Italy and Austria, our own currency from 1797 to 1819, illustrate this contingency. The issue of notes is a sale, to which there must be at least two parties, the buyer as well as the seller, the customer as well as the banker ; and, consequently, unless these promises to pay are considered as valuable as, and more convenient than, specie, they will not be readily accepted. Or if they be accepted at all by persons desirous to obtain assistance on any terms, the notes will be returned to the banker, who in most cases is willing to pay interest upon them, and if he be not in a position to redeem them, he is ruined. If he emits notes which he cannot redeem, they are returned to him ; if, while keeping at par with gold, they are too numerous for the work they have to perform, they are, unless when hoarded, also returned. These are natural checks on over-issuing. They are the same checks which hinder a concert manager or a railway company selling too many tickets, that is, if we can conceive the *impresario* or company becoming bankrupt provided a single ticket-holder failed to find a place. They are sufficient in all ordinary times to prevent over-issues, and those who doubt this appear to believe, to quote Mr. Herbert Spencer, that bankers have "a longing to appear in the *Gazette* which law alone can prevent them from gratifying." Such over-issues, then, as have really been experienced, have happened when an inconvertible currency was in circulation ; and the vulgar terror of their recurrence arises from a confusion between the notes which are transmutable into gold, and those authorised falsehoods which are not transmutable. The vicious effects of the latter are tacitly assigned to the former, and inconvertibility is blamed under a misnomer. In any other sense than the above—the failure to fulfil promises—over-issuing is indeed meaningless, or a misnomer ; over-issue and convertibility are in truth contradictions. True, the partisans of the currency theory have endeavoured to attach a different signification to the term " over-issue." By it they do not understand a depreciation of notes as compared with gold, but general depreciation showing itself in a rise of prices ; and it was on this ground that Lord Overstone based his defence of the Bank Act of 1844. His theory has been pushed by M. Cernuschi to almost its logical result, as it was by William Cobbett before him. " The bank-note" says M. Cernuschi, " is a falsification of money," the modern invention for debasing the currency ; the greater portion of notes rest not on gold actually lying in the coffers of the issuers, but on *l'or supposé* ; the notes issued upon this fictitious foundation affect prices, tending to raise them, and the possessors of actual gold suffer by its depreciation ; so that, unless a sovereign be kept in the coffers for every note in the hands of the public, a fraud is perpetrated.* Less bold and open in his language, Lord Overstone entertained at bottom the same idea, for such was the meaning of his doctrine that perfect convertibility did not suffice to secure the country against an over-issue of paper, with the consequence of a rise in prices, an export of gold to purchase goods abroad, a rise in the rate of discount to arrest this efflux, and in its wake times of difficulty. From these premises ought to be deduced the conclusion that no notes uncovered by gold should be issued, and M. Cernuschi faces this logical result, while the framers of the Bank Acts of 1844 and 1845 shrank from it, and subscribed to a compromise destitute of any principle. But M. Cernuschi, bold though he is, is not so audacious as his principle ; he also shrinks from a part of the conclusion to which he is committed ; he fails to perceive the full breadth of it, which should conduct him to a condemnation of bills of exchange, cheques, and other instruments of credit, which are immeasurably more efficacious than bank-notes in acting on prices. The last can affect the market only by investing more people with the capacity of buying, and stimu-

* " Paper in England has *pulled down* the value of gold and silver to a level with itself ; and this *pulling down* of gold and silver money has created the appearance of paper money *keeping up*."—*Paine*, quoted in Cobbett's paper against Gold, 255.

lating demand, and bills of exchange do of course exercise
the same kind of influence with even more potency. It follows
therefore, from the above reasoning, that all forms of purchase by
credit should be repressed. Need I say that the boldest recoil
from this ?

Credit certainly may act upon prices ; it may introduce into
the market a great number of purchasers ; and the demand
rising, prices may rise also. Therefore, so far as notes facilitate the extension of credit, they may tend to raise prices.
But this influence will not be prevented unless all forms of purchase by credit are repressed, for notes influence prices only in so
far as they create new purchasers, and if the employment of one
form is impeded, another may be employed all the more liberally
—most probably will be employed, for the notes could go into
circulation only if there was a genuine demand for them. It
would be more correct to say that the value of certain commodities is raised by the extension of credit, than to affirm that
the value of the entire currency, paper and coin, is depreciated
by the liberty to emit notes unsecured by gold, for they alone
are the exponents of the true currency theory who believe
that prices are affected alike by notes, bills, book-debts, and
whatever other forms credit, or the demand it creates, may
assume. Moreover, the sole effect of these forms of credit may
be to economise gold. But for them there might be merely
more gold, and not necessarily lower prices. Further, are
high prices, the owners of gold getting little goods, necessarily
more regretable than low prices, the owners of goods getting
little gold ?

The relative insignificance of notes as an influence on prices,
and consequently on the exchanges, compared with other forms
of credit, and the previous analysis of the causes producing an
adverse state of the exchanges will tend to correct the idea that
they can be seriously modified by a contraction of the circulation
leading to a rise of prices, or that an adverse rate of exchange
is always indicative of a general depreciation of the currency.
A comparison of the variations in the state of the exchanges,
with the variations in the amount of bank-notes in circulation,
fails to establish any connection.

Extension of credit no doubt, unless when it simply enables
a country to dispense with gold which otherwise it would have
used, raises prices, tends to lead to an adverse rate of exchange,

encourages importation, and may cause an efflux of bullion. But when other countries have their paper currencies, equilibrium will be restored without the Bank Charter Act; and while a limitation of the paper currency may not prevent a rise in prices, the expedient of raising the rate of discount will. Since 1844 the issue and banking departments have been separated. In the former, as was stated, notes are given for coin, or coin for notes, and the bank discharging the office of intermediary between the public and the mint, coin is given for bullion. The banking department, on the other hand, receives deposits, public and private, and discounts bills. The two departments have almost no connection with each other, and they might, as it has been truly said, be conducted at different places. This separation has been extolled as an admirable device. The eulogists of this arrangement have not always been mindful of the fact that they condemn the Act of 1845 in praising this feature of the Act of 1844, for if this separation were essential, why was it not insisted upon with equal clearness in the case of all the banks that were permitted to emit notes? Why were not the Banks of Scotland and Ireland either prohibited from issuing notes, or compulsorily split up into issue and banking departments? Mr. Gladstone and M. Wolowski have defended, as Sir Robert Peel did before them, the separation, as impressing upon the public mind the wholesome fact that the issue of promissory-notes is a sort of public duty; but if this be true, why neglect to embody the same principle in the Act of 1845? It is hard to deprive partially the people of Scotland of the lesson that the issue of notes is a State function, and banking industry is a private vocation.

Perhaps the most serious fault of the Act of 1844 remains to be mentioned, and that fault is making every drain of gold from the bank, no matter what may have been the cause, the signal for a contraction of paper currency. This may produce incalculable harm. This part of the Act events have triumphantly refuted, and three suspensions give us a right to believe that in future this provision will be disregarded whenever the reserve runs comparatively low, and the demands for assistance are numerous and importunate. Already the ablest apologists of the Act ask the insertion of an expansive clause, which should empower the exceeding of the fifteen million limit in emergencies. They think the Act perfect provided it may be broken; such also

is the opinion of its enemies. It was the object of the framers
of the Act, as the former allege, to make a mixed currency
fluctuate as a gold currency. They desired that the mixed
currency should contract in those cases in which a metallic
currency would contract, and expand in those cases in which it
would expand.* They—the holders of this principle—failed
however to perceive the exact manner in which their model
does fluctuate. They thought that whenever a few millions
were exported, the number of coins in actual use was necessarily
diminished, and that prices necessarily rose. They did not
recollect that in barbarous, or semi-civilised, or retrograde
countries, employing a purely metallic currency, hoarding is in
vogue, and that exportation may draw from coffers, from
beneath the thatch or flooring, from stockings, from ingeniously
hidden bags, stores of gold which were formerly as if they were
not, but which, entering into circulation, fill the gap, and save
the country from extreme fluctuations in prices. They did not
observe that these private hoards had been superseded, that the
Bank of England had, with a currency largely composed of
paper, become the one hoard which supplied the wants of the
country, and that by providing that notes should fluctuate with
the amount of this hoard, care was taken that the currency
should not circulate as a purely metallic currency does. With
a number of hoards, a metallic currency is well calculated to
save society from the evils incidental to a disarrangement of
prices ; a metallic currency without hoards, liable to be seriously
diminished in a week or a day, is peculiarly unstable, and a
mixed currency which would imitate this instability cannot be
too much condemned. There are other reasons forbidding
every efflux of gold being the signal for a contraction of the
currency. When by any reason gold is scarce and a crisis
is at hand or in process, it surely is nobody's interest to make
many bankruptcies, and to break up as many producing and
distributing societies as possible. It is the interest of the bank,
and may be essential to its safety, to accommodate as many as possible in these times. Its own safety will be endangered should
a run upon its deposits " at call" begin, and this may be brought
about by chary accommodation in the way of advancing upon
bills, leading to the forced sale of Consols, and other desperate
expedients. When, therefore, a scarcity of coin is experienced,

* See Fullarton on the *Regulation of the Currency.*

when the commercial world grievously suffers from want of it, and when there is an agonising moment in which all persons desire to possess money, or the highest form of credit, it may be a bank's duty and interest not to diminish its advances, so far as this can be reconciled with safety. It should not treat all drains alike. The discounting department should be at liberty to exercise discretion, and to draw a distinction between drains that are temporary and sure to bring about a reflux, and those which are more permanent. The temporary want of money of a community really sound and wealthy should not fare as the wants of an impoverished community, or the drain which is irrevocable as that which will certainly be followed by a speedy reflux. To people that do possess abundance of capital, fixed or floating, it cannot generally be imprudent to lend, provided they are willing to accept notes. The mere fact that there is little gold in Edinburgh and Glasgow is not sufficient reason for the contraction of loans or paper to merchants of these cities; the fact that there happens to be less gold in England than usual is also not of itself a reason for contracting the paper currency of the country. Romancers have pictured men laden with gold, and yet unable to procure a morsel of food, or a cup of cold water, and these romances provoke a smile at the vanity of riches; but it is a still severer satire upon the vanity of riches, that people with abundance of mills, goods, houses, and lands, should in any conceivable situation be treated as really poor. Crisises are, as we have seen, marked by one or both of two wants—a want of gold in particular, or of circulating capital in general. Supposing there has been no famine or bad harvest, and that the resources of the suffering country have not been too much absorbed by works that will never return the outlay, or will return it only at distant epochs; supposing the country to be really rich—and an unfavourable balance is, as we have seen, no infallible sign of poverty—this withdrawal of coin should be the signal for the emission, rather than the diminution, of notes, the demand for fiduciary money being all the greater owing to the absence of real money. The temporary breach should be filled by paper, or, as in 1825, by exchequer bills, if and so far as that is possible. Interest in the long run depends on the amount of floating capital in existence, and even money cannot long be deficient if capital abounds. That notes will be accepted in times of panic we know from experience. A crisis extending to such dimensions as to bring about a distrust of the Bank of England's notes is now unknown. Events since 1844 have rudely extorted a confession that it was wrong to tie down the Bank to an issue of fifteen millions uncovered by gold, and to compel it by Act of Parliament to appear panic-stricken in times of panic, however foolish. Three years after the passing of the Act, it was found necessary to suspend it, and to permit the Bank to exceed this figure ; and the very knowledge that notes were obtainable sufficed to soothe the public mind. Signal refutation of a false theory ! In 1857, the next great crisis, the Act was again suspended, and an excess of £800,000 was issued. In 1866, the third great crisis since the passing of the Act, it was a third time suspended with the most wholesome result. Does not the experience thus obtained satisfactorily confirm the demonstration of reason, and make it abundantly clear that to tie down the Bank to a fixed and arbitrary sum is suicidally to sacrifice the means of salvation ? If it does not at once strike one as absurd that the Bank should take no account of millions of gold, the approaching arrival of which had been telegraphed, these facts ought to destroy any lingering belief in a principle which tolerates such a *reductio ad absurdum*. I am aware that the idea of curing or mitigating a crisis by an extension of bank-notes has been scouted by Mr. Bonamy Price as ridiculous ; but, ridiculous or not, here is the fact that three times the suspension of the Act has calmed or mitigated a panic. It may be, as he affirms, that it was "a mental and not a material relief" which was administered, that only "feelings" were touched, that the crisis was not cured according to rule, and that merchants behaved childishly in attaching any importance to the license accorded to the directors ; but neither in commerce nor in medicine must we say with Molière's doctors that "it is better to die according to the rules than to be saved in defiance of the rules ; " and the material fact remains, that this contemned measure effected good. Professor Price has also observed that if the Bank "had said to the desperate borrowers that they might have loans if only they would carry them away in bank-notes, the notes would have come in for payment in an hour or two, for the simple reason that the wants of the borrowers were not for notes, and that their need had not created use for a single additional note." But this statement, irreconcilable with many features of those times, is irreconcilable with some of Mr. Price's other statements. For example, speaking of bank-notes, he says with perfect accuracy, " Still greater yet is the eagerness to get possession of them, when, after money has become 'tight' panic has seized on commerce. At such times, men are disposed to distrust the strongest and best-moneyed banks ; they like to keep their money in their own custody at home. Merchants, whose bills must be met on pain of ruin, prefer to have the money under their own eyes, rather than intrust it even to the Bank of England, lest it might be lent to borrowers and not be forthcoming for their own wants. Most of all the countless banks in England arm themselves at such seasons with additional notes; they draw deeper on the Bank of England for them in various ways, and a larger issue must come forth. On the other hand, when confidence revives, or trade grows slacker, the now unneeded notes flow back to the bank." Speaking of 1825, he observes again with truth, that " the effort of the public was not to present Bank of England notes for payment, but to procure them—to take them away home to their strong boxes, to hoard them as the best and safest investment of floating funds." Is there not here contradiction ? And is it not plain that the desire for notes must expand in these times, if we reflect upon their character ? They are distinguished by a distrust of all but the very highest forms of credit. Men then trust only a few. They dislike almost all deferred payments. The work usually performed by a vast variety of instruments has all at once to be performed by gold and the very best forms of credit. The modes of economising coin which exist only in an atmosphere of trust are almost entirely and suddenly destroyed, with the exception of the Bank of England note ; and an instantaneous extension of gold coin being out of the question, a supply of notes that are esteemed as perfectly trustworthy will be accepted, and will probably pass into circulation to perform the increased work. Of course it might, at a certain point which prudence would indicate, be necessary to raise the rate of discount. Of course, also, if these notes were instantly returned with a demand for gold, this issue, if continued, would destroy the Bank ; but this contingency can scarcely happen, for at these times the demand for notes, the work to be done by them, has been notably augmented, and there is in these, as in all times, a preference given to notes if

the money be not wanted for foreign payments. And if there
be a flow of gold abroad, there are devices for arresting it; the
balance of payments may be reserved; gold may be obtained,
as it has been, of the Bank of France; a rise of the rate of
interest and the sale of securities may alter the current. If the
crisis is purely monetary, an issue of notes may all but cure it;
if, as is usually the case, the crisis is the culminating period of
rash speculation, or of a series of enterprises that are unproductive of and have destroyed much wealth, if there be a
scarcity of floating capital and the country be poor—even perhaps in these circumstances the permission to extend the issue
of notes may prove beneficial. Reasonable distrust expands in
these times into unreasonable panic. The sound creditor is apt
to be confounded with those who possess no substance. Deposits are withdrawn from well-managed banks. Bills, which
would be accepted in payment when men were cool, are not
looked at. Is it not right and advantageous that the Bank
should be in a position to come to the rescue of these sound
firms? Yes, we may answer, without entertaining an extravagant conception of the efficacy of notes, or without forgetting
that the crisis was produced by the want of capital. For debts
which the Bank knows to be good it gives notes which the public
esteems good. All this is demanding no entirely new duty; the
Governor, in 1866, admitted "the duty" of the Bank to support the mercantile community: it has become "the Bankers'
Bank." It is true that the duty acknowledged in 1866 has
since been strenuously disavowed, and it remains a moot-point
whether, in hours of difficulty, the Bank of England, possessed
of unusual privileges and resources, is to be managed as a private
bank, reaping high profits from a high rate of discount.

These do not complete the charges that can be brought with
justice against Sir Robert Peel's legislation. The Acts of 1844
and 1845 err on a fundamental point, and they do so in
common with the banking legislation of most countries. Convertibility into specie is admitted by most competent persons to
be a property of good notes—their forced circulation to be
a desperate measure. The debated question is, How obtain
convertibility? In most countries, even in those which plume
themselves on having adopted free-trade principles, Governments
have endeavoured to ensure convertibility by subjecting all
banks of issue to more or less supervision. In some countries,

such as France, only one bank is permitted to issue notes ; in others a limited number is permitted ; and in other countries again, all banks, conforming to certain regulations designed to secure the safety of the note, receive permission. The question of policy which here arises is ambiguously stated in the common question, Ought there to be free banking? Of the essential functions of a banker, the issuing of promises to pay is not one ; discounting and the receiving of deposits constitute the chief of these essential functions ; and the issuing of bank-notes did not originally constitute any part of the work of a banker, and may be, and often is, absent. Strict free banking, in the proper sense of banking, there is ; and it is difficult to perceive that there can be any question about it in this country, persons or companies being freely permitted to borrow and discount. I say in this country because in France the bank is bound down to make advances only after compliance with certain conditions. Ought private persons, without let or hindrance, or supervision of any sort, and subject only to the laws that are passed for the punishment of fraud, and the benefit of creditors in the event of bankruptcy, be at liberty to circulate notes? that is the really interesting question involved in the ambiguous expression free banking. And the answer must vary with circumstances to be mentioned. If the note is legal tender, if the State compels its subjects to accept the note in requital of a debt, or if the note resembles that of the⁓ Bank of England, and is a legal tender in part of the country, it is just that the State, taking precautions for the safety of those compelled by its authority to accept a promise of gold instead of gold, should see that the promise is sure to be kept, or that the acceptor will not suffer. The State has deprived its subjects of the right of judging of the quality of the promise ; it has solemnly said, "This piece of paper stands for five sovereigns ;" and this deprivation and this declaration are culpable imprudence, unless the State releases the acceptor from the shadow of risk. Notes thus forced upon men resemble money. Their issue may indeed be intrusted to private persons or corporations, just as coining may be committed to private hands ; but the emitting of legal tender notes, and the fabricating of coins, should be conducted according to hard and fast rules, dictated by the State, and designed to exclude inconvertibility from the list of possibilities. To praise free banking

L

in the sense of permission to issue legal tender notes without restraint is to abuse once more the much-abused name of freedom : it is to eulogise a system, or absence of it, under which a State forces upon its subjects promise to pay, with the precise worth of which it is unacquainted. But if we have in view notes that are not legal tender, such as the Scotch banks circulate, destitute of any credit except such as flows from the repute of their issuers, it is not clear why the State should restrain their issue, or dictate the terms on which these private notes may circulate. Such interference does not appear to be justifiable. Enough that private persons are not at liberty to send forth notes so closely resembling, in size, shape, colour, and engraving, legal tender notes, as to lead to mistakes, that when an issuer fails to fulfil his engagements bankruptcy or winding up should ensue, and that the precautions taken in regard to joint-stock companies should be taken in regard to issuers.

Why should the State forbid any one to promise to pay in gold, and permit him to promise to pay in commodities ? Why should the State forbid any one to promise to pay in gold on demand at any time, and permit one to promise to pay in gold three months afterwards, even though that promise be a mere accommodation-bill ? A bill of exchange, in all its essential qualities, resembles a bank-note; the latter, it has been truly said, may be considered " as a bill of exchange, or any commercial obligation whatever, which becomes due on the day or the hour on which it is delivered ;" and ought the State to limit the circulation of bank-notes, and to emancipate bills of exchange from control as to their drawers or acceptors ? Is it not, to put the question in a more general form, part of an outworn system, to dictate to grown men what promises they shall make ? Such notes as are not legal tender are not money any more than bills of exchange—certainly not more than a bill endorsed in blank ; destitute of intrinsic value, circulating at all merely on the strength of the good name of the issuers, they possess none of the attributes of money ; and they cannot be brought under State control under the plea of being part of the monetary system established or guaranteed by the State. It is said that as they increase the quantity of money really increases, whereas as bills of exchange increase the difficulty of obtaining money grows ; but if both are good, both are the equivalents of money. If notes are designated cash by bankers, so also are cheques and bills of exchange. One may as well, indeed, style a dock-warrant a hogshead of sugar as term a convertible note a piece of money. We need not oppose restrictive measures in the name of any general law of freedom. If it were clear that the unrestricted issue of notes produced much inconvenience and distress, these measures would be justified. But the burthen of proving that such would be the effect of freedom rests with those who, contrary to the general spirit of the time, to the political philosophy associated with economics, and to the ideas economists enforce in unqualified terms with respect to all other departments of life, assert that in regard to banking traders must be cared for by the Government or they will come to ruin.

Much more might be said to the disadvantage of the Acts of 1844 and 1845 ; in particular, one might speak of the mischief produced by withdrawing attention from more important matters of bank management to notes, of the panic apt to arise when the reserve falls, and of the waste in the resources by the division of the two departments of the bank ; but it is enough to mention the monopoly of Scotch banking given by the latter Act to a limited number of banks. In 1845 the Government declared that no other companies than those that happened to be then issuing should be permitted to circulate notes in Scotland ; and thus the profits, not inconsiderable, derived from supplying Scotland with its chief currency, were arbitrarily given to a certain number of private persons. On the face of the transaction, it appears that those thus favoured had no better right to the profits than multitudes of other persons who could produce equally good security. Between this and a measure enacting that nobody shall be permitted to sell tea or spirits except the tea or spirit dealers in business in 1871, it is difficult to perceive the difference in principle. Either the profits should belong to the State or to private persons indiscriminately. If the issuing of notes be a public function, why are the profits absorbed by virtually private persons ? Or if it be proper that the profits should flow into private purses, it has still to be shown that a certain number of persons selected according to no satisfactory or rational rule should monopolise the profits, which are not small, to the exclusion of others equally trustworthy. And the mere profits of issue do not express the whole of the fruits of this monopoly, or explain the steadily high dividends paid to the proprietors of the eleven

Scotch banks in Scotland, where, unlike England in this respect, a bank cannot hope to succeed unless it circulates notes. A purely banking company could not employ gold—generally unacceptable to Scotchmen; and if it purchased the notes of the favoured banks, it would compete with them at a serious and indeed fatal disadvantage. Thus the Act of 1845 has given to eleven companies, selected according to no rational rule, the monopoly of issuing notes, and, by implication, of acting as bankers for Scotland. In palliation it has been said that Sir Robert Peel's legislation was conceived in the hope that the Bank of England would become the solitary issuer in the United Kingdom, and that these anomalies were left in confident expectation that one by one the Scotch issuers would expire. But if ever such a hope was entertained, events have proved its delusiveness. Though only eleven now exist, of the eleven the Edinburgh and Glasgow banks were never in a healthier condition, and no excuse can be found for the monopoly in a hope that the unaided course of events will destroy it, and will transfer the right of issue to one public institution. The sole consideration that points in a direction contrary to the above reasoning is the undoubted fact that the Scotch banks have not generally abused their monopoly after the manner of monopolists, and that they have had the good sense to maintain, at the cost of their immediate profits, large capitals*—a fact to their credit, which may give the system a respite, but which will not, it is to be hoped, for ever preserve an arbitrary monopoly, the necessity of sending gold down to Scotland to be returned unpacked, and a species of " monetary feudalism."

* " After making allowance for the capital of the private bankers, the probability is that the English joint-stock banks are working with *at least* 12 millions less than Scotch experience proves to be necessary."—*Banking and Finance*, by a Bank Manager, p. 17.

" Neither the aggregate paid-up capitals nor the reserves, aided though these have been by premiums on new issues of shares, amount in the London banks to the totals for a similar number of the Scotch banks."—*Financier*.

CHAPTER XI.

MONEY.

MONEY is a machine, an instrument, a tool for accomplishing certain work; it saves labour, as a steam-engine saves labour; it enables men to accomplish that which would be difficult or impossible without it, as a hammer or a plane does. We shall thread our way out of the labyrinth of error that encompasses this subject if we grasp this elementary truth and follow it as a guiding line. Yet money is of such consequence in Political Economy, and, in some respects, is a machine of such singularity, that it deserves to be taken out of the category of machinery, and considered by itself.

Gold, silver, and copper, are at present the only commodities used as coin by the people of Europe and America. But they were not always the only commodities so used, and travellers and historians are full of references to substitutes employed in ancient times and among savage nations or rude societies. They tell us of oxen used in Homeric times and in the beginning of Rome, of horses and oxen used by the Germans of the Middle Ages, of salt used by the Abyssinians, pressed tea and silk by the Tartars and Chinese, of eggs in the Shetland and Orkney islands, tobacco used by the English settlers in the early days of the colonies of Maryland and Virginia, of martin and beaver skins by the Russian Government and in the Hudson's Bay Territory, of cowries or shells by the savages of Guinea and in India, of dried fish in Newfoundland, of iron in Sparta, and of dates in Persia. These expedients, all of them objectionable, though answering in a rough way the requirements of a small trade, become superseded by metals, as they become known; and local currencies are destined to give place to gold, silver, and copper, which are to become the currencies of the world. Wherever these metals have been found they have been prized. Children of all races like the same amusements : the Caucasian and the African child will clutch with equal delight a rattle ; and savages, who are children in their passions and pleasures, are pleased with the glitter and the sonorousness of these metals, which are to them beautiful toys. All of these metals, not being found and known throughout the world, were not from the first adopted everywhere ; and the geological character of the country, the nature of the mines in the neighbourhood, determined which of them was first employed. And so it has come to pass that the world is divided into two great sections, one of which employs silver and the other gold, the East loving the former, and the West, and the Anglo-Saxons pre-eminently, loving the latter. Gold, though first worked, is a mere upstart in comparison with silver ; gold is the standard only in a few countries ; to-day, silver is the standard money of about four-fifths of mankind. But gold is spreading, and seems to have an entail of the future ; the English sovereign has now a wider circulation than any other coin ; and, as much value in small bulk must grow to be a more and more essential quality, the circulation of gold must extend. These metals did not instantly pass from the category of ordinary commodities, bought and sold as they are after due examination, into that of coins, bought and sold without examination. " We have now taught them to accept also money," says Tacitus of the effects of Roman intercourse on the ancient Germans ; and here mankind required teaching—it groped its way to the use of gold and silver.

The disadvantages of pure barter, with no common article in which to express values, must be great, and if commerce were of the present extent and complexity, they would be intolerable. It is much for a merchant to know the prices of a long list of articles and varieties of articles ; but the human memory would refuse to contain all the proportions between the various articles of trade if there were no common denominator. Schulze, a German economist, has pointed out that he who would have to value one hundred articles, and who has now to bear in his memory only ninety-nine proportions, would, but for coin, have to retain 4950 proportions. Were there no commodity which everybody freely accepted on all occasions, men would spend much of their time in searching for a purchaser ; and when they had found one who wished their goods it would be surprising if the one wished to buy precisely as much as the other wished to sell. Men would be obliged to sell too much: he who had nothing less than a sheep would be unable to sell anything less, even though he wanted only a handful of salt; the owner of a cow might traverse a whole county before he could get a baker who would be willing to exchange bread for a cow; and though their real wants might be a few loaves and a few pounds of meat, the one would have to accept a cart-load of loaves and the other many stones of meat. These inconveniences, which would now be intolerable, it would be an anachronism to suppose were felt in the same degree wherever barter was in vogue; for if commerce be insignificant, population sparse, and its wants few, barter may be accomplished with comparative ease. So great is the convenience of a common denominator, that money of account— that is, an ideal coin, to which there is no corresponding piece of metal—has been invented by civilised nations. Montesquieu, in his "Spirit of the Laws," makes mention even of certain savages who invented money of account called macutes; but the truth is, be it reverently spoken, that the "Spirit of the Laws" abounds in hoaxes about the customs and laws in the kingdoms of Bantam, Macassar, etc., and one of these hoaxes is the macutes. To appreciate the inconveniences experienced by reason of the absence of a proper currency, look at what happened in England in 1696, and in France during the siege of Paris—merchants compelled to stop their trades, or to accept, and issue as money, paper and rags.

Gold, silver, and copper possess certain properties which mark them out to be the cosmopolitan currency; it is not caprice frozen into convention, or the stamp of the mint, that has gained for them their present place; and Turgot says well, "Gold and silver are constituted, by the nature of things, money and universal money, independently of all convention and law." They contain much value in small bulk, they are similar in quality wherever they are produced, they are indestructible, they are readily divisible, and yet do not suffer in beauty by division, and they are readily united; they are so scattered over the globe that the same expenditure of labour has, in the past at all events, generally produced about the same amount of metal; and being at once the most generally diffused and the rarest of metals, they are marked out by Nature for coinage, and they no more owe their employment solely to convention than the use of wood in shipbuilding is dictated by mere custom. I do not

add that another qualification of the precious metals is, that
they preserve a uniform value ; firstly, because if we take into
account not merely the discovery of mines but improvements
in mining and smelting, it is extremely doubtful whether the cost
of their production has been perfectly uniform ; and secondly,
because, even if this were true, the value of gold or silver
would be affected by every alteration in the value of the article
for which it is exchanged. To say that " money is not wealth,
but a right to wealth ; " to declare that " abolish all the money
in the world, and mankind at large would be as wealthy as before ; " to squeeze an admirable figure of speech employed by
Edmund Burke into the assertion of a fact, and to affirm in a
scientific treatise that money is " the highest and most general
form of credit "—expressions which we find employed by Mr.
Patterson and Mr. Macleod—is to carry the reaction against the
so-called mercantile theory to extravagant lengths. It is to forget
that though money is not coincident and co-extensive with wealth,
it is a part of wealth ; that, apart altogether from its uses in
currency, it is luscious and gratifying to the eye, as is attested
by the fact that gold and silver have been used as ornaments
wherever they have been found ; and that that cannot be credit
which it requires no exercise of faith to accept. Pearls are
wealth—so is gold ; and if the former were, like cowries, employed as currency, nothing would have occurred which would
induce us to say that pearls are " not wealth but a right to
wealth," or that pearls are " the highest and most general form
of credit." Even adopting Mr. Macleod's own arbitrary definition of credit, this holds good. " Credit," says he, defining
something very different, " is anything which is of no direct use,
but which is taken in exchange for something else, in the belief
or confidence that it can be exchanged away again." But this
definition does not include gold and silver, which all nations,
savage and cultivated, have declared do possess " direct use,"
inasmuch as they please the eye.

We have seen that one may economise coin just as one econo-
mises vehicles, by making frequent use of the same vehicle.
We may do so by means of bank-notes, bills of exchange, and
other expedients which we have enumerated. Another truly
marvellous instance of this economy is to be witnessed in the
London Clearing-House, in which the bankers balance their
liabilities, amounting to figures of astronomical magnitude, with-

out the aid of coins or notes. So far has this economy been carried in England, that, with transactions which must be immensely larger than those of France, the metallic currency of the former is not much more than half that of the latter, which, previous to the war, was about a hundred and thirty millions. The precious metals are procured with much toil, and it has struck inquirers in every age that it would be a great gain if they could be wholly replaced by something cheaper, yet equally or almost as efficacious. Hence swarms of visionary and ruinous schemes. This is a Serbonian bog, deeper and more fatal than that between Damiata and Mount Casius of old, in which have perished whole armies of dreamers and visionaries. Mr. Disraeli has said that this subject has driven more men mad than love; it is moreover a madness which cannot be cured by disenchantment. The odium, the bad associations which these failures have left behind, have rendered it hazardous to write on the subject, or to let fall any expressions favourable to the use of devices for saving gold. The man who speculates on the subject is suspected and his credit is injured; and to show a leaning towards paper money is commercial atheism.

As has already been indicated, there are those who say that banks should issue no more notes than for what they have a reserve in their coffers. This, they say, is the only way to insure the convertibility of the note : all others are more or less dangerous. So regulated, a paper currency is economical only because, and in so far as, the metal in the bankers' coffers suffers no tear and wear. I am not aware that this theory, the bullionist theory *par excellence*, has ever been put in practice, unless indeed by the Bank of Amsterdam, which kept a metallic reserve adequate to meet all its liabilities, in the shape of notes; certainly it is not embodied in the Bank Acts, which, as we have seen, permit the Bank of England to issue £15,000,000 without an equivalent in coin, and with no other security than the State, and the Scotch and Irish banks to issue a certain quantity of notes with no guarantee save their own prudence. This is a wide departure from the bullionist principle, and is adherence to another theory which may be formulated thus :— That banks, complying with certain regulations as to publicity, should be permitted to issue a prescribed amount of notes without any security beyond what prudence dictates. This principle, if principle it can be called, embodied by Sir Robert Peel in the

legislation of this country, has been adopted elsewhere, for the
banking systems of several countries have been modelled on
ours. In the United States the National banks, so called in
opposition to the State banks, are allowed to issue among them
$300,000,000, with no other reserve than that of an equivalent
in national debt bonds.

We arrive at another class of schemes when we mention those
which propose to dispense with any reserve in coin, and to base
a cheap paper currency on some articles other than gold or silver.
Such schemes are divisible into three classes—those which
would base a currency on a specific kind of property or article
of wealth other than the precious metals, those which would
base it on property in general, and those which would make a
currency inconvertible. According to the second, notes are to
be promises to pay in an unspecified something; according to
the first, they are to be tallies. The favourite form which the
first theory takes is a proposal to "coin" the land of the country into money. According to the most usual form of this proposal, land is to be valued at a certain number of years' purchase,
and notes equal to this valuation are to be issued. Such was
the idea at the bottom of the speculations of Briscoe and Cham-
berlayne, who, in the seventeenth century, proposed to enrich
England by a land bank. But the most famous embodiment of
the idea was in the system of John Law. A duellist, a debauchee,
a gamester, a fop, and a spendthrift, living hard and drinking
hard, with a pecuniary imagination which must have resembled
that of Balzac, Law of Lauriston, while squandering his own
fortune, meditated much upon renovating the public fortune by
supplying abundance of money, to the want of which he ascribed
the poverty of Scotland. In 1705 he submitted such a plan to
the Parliament of Scotland. The Parliament, however, rejected his proposal. In a rude fashion it was carried out in
France. The most memorable instance of the failure of this
device was given by the republican government of France,
which, needing money to pay the troops it hurled against
Europe, and with abundance of confiscated property in hand,
issued notes on the security of the church lands. The disastrous result of this scheme is well known. As issue after
issue took place, these assignats or bank-notes fell in value;
to no purpose was six years' imprisonment annexed to the
crime of estimating assignats at any other price than that

which was marked on them ; their fall continued ; and at last one might have many francs in paper in one's purse and yet have to haggle with a baker about a penny roll. It is true there were reasons of detail as well as of principle why the assignats should become depreciated ; a bad principle was badly carried out. Each assignat did not entitle its owner to the possession of some one piece of land ; it did not represent any specific thing, but was a vague charge on the national domains ; originally warrants which the communes were bound to accept from the bidders for the national property, and suited to circulate only in small quantities, and among the intending purchasers of land, the assignats were issued in large quantities ; they varied in value according to the quantity of property in the market and of paper afloat ; and their discredit was increased by forgeries. Had each been the title-deed to one piece of land moderately valued, the assignats might have served, with certain inconveniences, as a local currency, though, of course, the making of such a currency compulsory would be inexpedient. The errors in principle leading to this failure, and to that of the land banks established at an early period in the history of the American States, deserve to be examined, for there still appear pamphlets and projects conceived in total ignorance of these failures and their causes. Apart from the danger of issuing too many notes, seeing paper is cheap, the temptation strong, and accurate valuation of land difficult, there is in the first place the fact that land is a commodity liable to variations in value. Secondly, while the land of a country might perhaps be a satisfactory basis for the currency of a district, it could not be one for a large country, or for several countries ; for with what confidence would a merchant in Brazil be inspired by the knowledge that a bank-note of the Russian Government was based on land in Siberia or the Caucasus ? Thirdly—and this is the cardinal objection —while a bank-note convertible into gold is a security that the acceptor of it will receive whenever he pleases that which has the power of purchasing anything which he may wish, the acceptor of a note covered by land has the security that he will receive some one thing, which may or may not be what he wants, or even be convertible into it. You pay for a season theatre-ticket ; you present it at Drury Lane, which you desire to visit, and you learn that your ticket is for the Haymarket, to which you do not want to go—such, or very similar, may be the fate of one who accepts a note based on land. These are the reasons why coining the land of the country has been a series of blunders, and they destroy numerous other theories for resting the currency on some one particular thing. The last of these reasons, slightly modified, exposes the fallaciousness of those schemes which propose to issue paper notes to be "represented" by goods in general. The receiver of the note would have the security that he would be paid in *anything which the issuer might have or select ;* a very contemptible security in the eyes of one who wished *that which could procure anything he, the receiver, pleased to select.* A merchant goes to the bank to cash or " change " a £10 note ; the cashier is sorry to say that he cannot give gold, but he will be happy to give ten pounds' worth of rugs—that is to say, rugs which some one would consider equal to £10. Not being the " some one," the note-holder reckons that he has sustained a loss, measured by the time, trouble, and expense required to turn his rugs into gold. How far these difficulties may yet be overcome, is a question not to be lightly dismissed. Some of the impediments are vanishing quantities; but it is certain that hitherto wherever notes have been issued on land, or where certificates of debts secured on land have been turned into a currency, disasters have occurred. Mr. Macleod would bar the door against the very possibility of such an idea : one cannot, he says, buy commodities and have the price as well. But no such absurdity is involved in Law's project. The possessor of a title to a piece of property may sometimes sell it from hand to hand ; and those who would base a currency on land propose to do nothing more. There remains another scheme—a forced currency, such as existed in England previous to 1819, and such as exists in Austria at present. The value of such notes depends on their quantity. If the quantity of forced paper could be limited, it would be liable to but one objection, that the issuers of it would raise a forced loan—unless, indeed, as has been the policy of United States financiers, an issue should be made to accompany a formal loan or new taxes. It is pedantry to maintain that in no circumcumstances of national difficulty is such a currency justifiable and expedient. How far the evil connected with a forced currency, liable to be augmented, could be corrected by making the notes bear interest, is a question worthy of consideration. Could the quantity of an inconvertible currency, legal tender everywhere, be fixed absolutely, it would be superior to a metallic currency. But how are these conditions to be fulfilled? One view we may notice in this connection, seeing it is propounded by no less a person than Mr. Herbert Spencer, one of the profoundest thinkers of our time. In his *Social Statics*, and in his Essays, he has laid it down that existing dishonesty is the only obstacle to dispensing with metallic money; "amongst perfectly honest people paper alone will form the circulating medium." Granting that perfectly honest people would never commit mistakes with regard to their engagements, this is so far true, that these "perfectly honest people" would always be prepared with something which they considered an equivalent, and which really would be an equivalent in the eyes of somebody; but perfect honesty would be no guarantee that they would be prepared with what everybody would esteem an equivalent. To sum up the obstacles that prevent the success of projects for basing a proper currency on any other commodities than gold and silver, they possess inherent qualifications for the work which they perform, and no other commodity has yet been discovered capable of performing that work so well. One commodity which possesses certain of the required qualifications is not divisible without diminution of value; another is too bulky; the value of a third fluctuates; a fourth possesses only a local value; and so on with all commodities other than the precious metals, which can be selected.

Here may be considered some other questions relating to the regulation of the currency. And, in the first place, a word or two with respect to the unity of the note. Can more than one bank furnish the required security? Apart from the liability to pay a premium, such, for example, as the holder of Scotch notes in England is exposed to, that is the chief determining question if the issue of private notes ought to be regulated at all by the State, which I do not think is the case, unity of the note may be, if the State be the issuer, and if it have a vastly preponderant credit, a great advantage; and considering the circumstances of the country, those who confined the right of issue in India, for example, to the State doubtless did right. But unity of the note is a benefit almost solely so far as it insures convertibility; it is practically needless where the convertibility of the note is secured by other expedients. Unity of the note is, moreover, so far an evil, inasmuch as monopoly is everywhere the father of sloth and inactivity, as it is generally the child of injustice.

Had there been but one bank in Scotland, can it be doubted by those who have seen with what slowness the Bank of France, though pricked on by the Legislature, has spread its arms across France, that, instead of there being branches in every large village, they would be confined to the large towns in Scotland? With one bank of issue, it is highly probable that the facilities for discounting would be lessened. If there be competing banks, bankers' profits will be abridged; and if the issuers are obliged to cash their notes in a certain number of large towns—" redemption cities "—no serious inconvenience will be felt. We speak of competition as an evil; we say that it is the spirit of war carried into commerce; and so saying, we do it injustice. Our domesticated animals are our foes by nature utilised; among our most beneficial passions are some that are our moral foes utilised, and to one of these—jealousy or rivalry—bearing the *nom de paix* of competition, we owe much in banking as elsewhere.

With one bank of issue we should, then, possibly see the evils of monopoly appear. Add to which the probability of considerable fluctuations in the amount of currency, the intensifying of panics, and the tendency which the favoured bank has of becoming the one reserve.* But whether there be a limited number of banks of issue, whether one or more, the State should monopolise the whole or most of the profits, if profits are to be earned, and the system at present existing in the United Kingdom, according to which the fruits of what is alleged to be a public privilege are plucked by private individuals, often arbitrarily selected, and subjected to insignificant stamp-duties, cannot be justified. That the bulk of statesmen and economists should maintain bank-notes to be a form of money, and that our law courts should have decided that the *jus cudendæ monetæ* belonging to the sovereign extends to notes, while virtually private firms actually issue them, is a curious anomaly. If it be deemed necessary to exercise supervision over the issue of banks, and not leave them free to the dictates of their own interests, it might be well to allow any one to issue his own notes, provided he held a certain amount of Government securities—these securities being valued at a defined price—or to induce him to

* It need not be said that the English joint-stock banks trust to the Bank of England, and that its reserve is in fact becoming the reserve of the country.

make special arrangements with the State bank for the issue of its notes.

It may dissipate some prejudices against the former proposal, sanctioned by the example of America, to recall the fact that the using of Government securities as a reserve would be following out policy at present spontaneously pursued. For, as a matter of fact, the real reserves are not those prescribed by the Bank Acts—which, being liable to the demands of depositors, are sham reserves—but the securities which a banker can in general realise without delay or great loss.

Before terminating these observations on the currency of the country, let us refer to some modes of economising the cost of keeping up the coin of the country. One proposal, actually carried into effect in the Bank of Amsterdam two centuries ago, has, in one form or another, been suggested by thinkers of eminence. It is a piece of waste, not insignificant, that the reserve lying in the coffers of the Bank should consist to any amount of coined money. Would not bars answer the purpose as well? It has been suggested that, to ensure the metal not being taken out for circulation within the kingdom, the use of gold within it as an instrument of barter should expose one to penalties. But, without resort to this severe and grotesque measure, it might be a possible improvement in our banking system that the reserve should always consist more largely of bars. Secondly, it is not at all clear why the State should go to the expense of coining sovereigns to be melted down or to circulate abroad. Our own silver and bronze coins, and the currency of France, prove, if it needed proof, that coin may circulate at a value in excess of that of the component metal ; and if the amount of seignorage were happily chosen, it is not clear that the value of the sovereign would be depreciated in this country supposing the seignorage was obtained by reducing the quantity of gold in the sovereign. A seignorage would check melting down. A small turn in the rate of exchange would not make it profitable to export sovereigns. The change might be accomplished without causing, in England at all events, of necessity a depreciation in value, or without a breach of faith, provided the change was felicitously carried out. Almost the sole point doubtful with respect to Mr. Lowe's much-debated proposal on this subject was, whether he had chosen a proper seignorage. It may indeed be contended that there was inadvertence to the fact, that if seignor-

age be charged there is a new liability to depreciation or appreciation, provided the supply can be indefinitely increased or diminished. On silver coin a seignorage is charged, and to guard against
the above contingency, as well as to prevent our having a double
standard, the mint declines to coin for all comers. Why the
country has not availed itself of the economy which would be
effected by the use of one-pound notes, must be matter of surprise. There is no principle which makes them advantageous
in Scotland and Ireland, but hurtful in England ; and it is to
be hoped that we shall recur to notes abandoned under the influence of a panic. It may be here mentioned that the value of
a currency, the quantity of which expands at pleasure, will
depend on the cost of production or prospective supply, while
the value of a currency which does not so expand will depend on
the actual supply. Into the question of a double currency we
need not enter minutely. It may, however, be stated that with
two standards a country is so much nearer a state of barter.
Every time that a change occurs in the value or quality of the
metals, the depreciated metal is sent abroad,—the theory of the
distribution of precious metals, as of all other articles of commerce, being, that they tend to go whence they are least valued
whither they are most valued.

.   Ere we quit the subject of banking, it may be pertinent to
make a remark upon the conduct of it. The theory of banking
is a collection of rules founded on observing the habits of men
—carry in our hands this truth as a lantern to light the way,
and we shall be able to clear up the question of reserves. So
far as the issuing of notes is concerned, banking is founded on
the probability, falling little short of certainty, that every holder
of notes will not simultaneously present them to be cashed ; if
there was a probability of a simultaneous rush of note-holders,
no bank, not based on the currency principle—that is, no existing bank—could stand, any more than an insurance company
could, if all the policy-holders were simultaneously or in close
succession to die. The banker has to calculate what is the
highest strain he will be likely to bear, though, like a prudent
engineer who builds his bridge to support a weight greater
than what it will in all probability be called on to sustain, the
prudent banker will place his reserve above rather than below
this maximum. Now, just as it would not do for insurance
companies to charge exactly the same premiums on lives insured

in all climates and professions, to ask no more from the trader in Guinea than from a clergyman in the Isle of Wight, as their premiums must vary with the degree of risk, so banking companies should vary the amount of their reserves according to the degree of risk. What would be prudent in one country and period would not be so in another. Banking, in short, is not so uniform, the habits of men not so constant, that rules cut and dry for all circumstances regarding the proportion of coin to paper—rules expressed with the same precision as if they concerned metal and not flesh and blood—are to be framed. All of us, for example, have heard of the idea that a reserve of one third is a safe reserve. This idea, however, as I have already said, possesses no scientific value ; even if, on an average, it guarantees the promissory-notes of a bank, it need not suffice as a reserve for its other liabilities.

Gold and silver are less prized as they grow more plentiful, precisely as corn or cloth is—they undergo a depreciation in value ; and it is alleged that Europe has several times witnessed such a depreciation, and that at this moment we are passing through such an ordeal. Be the last assertion true or not, certainly gold and silver have several times been depreciated. To take an instance of fluctuation in their value from ancient history, we know that, when Julius Cæsar returned to Rome with the spoils of rifled Gaul, prices at Rome rose by reason of the sudden influx of money. Other instances there are in antiquity, but let them give place to the most memorable depreciation, that which took place after the conquest of Mexico by Cortes, and of Peru by Pizzaro. Though the Spanish conquerors gilded their motives with the lacquer of religion, and were seldom so profane as to murder and steal in any other name than that of the Most High ; though within not a few of them, high-souled men, worthy comrades of Columbus and Las Casas, worthy countrymen of Isabella, burned heaped fires of zeal, which their religion fed with fresh fagots, giving forth the smoke of resolutions to deal righteously by the Indians ; though many were moved by a desire, which only children can now comprehend, to peer into the corners of the yet unexplored earth, the motive that lay at the bottom of the hearts of the vulgar mass was gold ; and through hunger and thirst, and unfurrowed seas, in defiance of the tempests and sunken rocks of the Antilles, and the poisoned arrows of the Caribbeans, in heroic forgetfulness of the fate of

M

so many of their companions, that object was pursued. There
are times when heroism is cheap: it is to be had for gold. For
gold, indeed, these men laid down their lives in a truly heroic
way, and what more did the Polycarps or Cyprians? There
must have been abroad, shall we not say, a diseased conception
of the importance of gold, an *auromania*, a mental epidemic, to
which we find no analogue save in the *gemania*, that hunger after
land in all circumstances, which has been the curse of so many
countries in our day, the ruin of so many colonies, a malady
preying with more or less severity on them all? These conquests and this zeal told on the markets of Europe. But the
influence worked slowly and gradually. First, in Spain gold
fell in value by reason of the influx of the spoils of Cusco and
Mexico—so much so, that Queen Isabella was forced to alter
the legal relation between it and silver; subsequently silver fell.
From Spain the decline spread to other countries, and, in course
of time, to England. Contracts were thrown into confusion;
calculations were upset; the landed proprietors and the poorer
classes suffered, for they, as has often been noted, are the last to
discover a depreciation and to take due steps in virtue of it;
and we find that the English Parliament, in order to avoid a
recurrence of such confusion, passed in 1576 a law, declaring
that in any new leases " for life, lives, or years," the authorities
of the Universities of Oxford and Cambridge, and of the Colleges
of Winchester and Eton, should stipulate that at least one-third
of the rent should be paid in corn. There is some reason for
believing that these fluctuations effected even important social
and political changes.

It is alleged that we are now in the midst of a fresh depreciation of gold. Between 1819 and 1847, new gold-fields were
discovered and worked in the Altai and Ural Mountains; in
1848, the "placers" of California attracted avaricious crowds; and
in 1851, everybody or everybody's friend started for Australia.
The united effect of these discoveries, along with others less
considerable in British Columbia and New Zealand, was to flood
the markets of Europe with gold, which, perhaps, would have
speedily undergone an enormous depreciation but for the fact
that the East, India and China, then began to be opened to
European commerce, and to absorb no small amount of the
redundant coin. But when these markets have been supplied,
when India and China no longer absorb gold, the fall, it is

alleged, will be rapid and serious. What would ensue if this prophecy were fulfilled? A sovereign would be only in name what a sovereign now is. All contracts made previous to the decline and binding after it would be virtually broken. Fund-holders would suffer, unless the State, refusing to take advantage of this accident, altered the terms of the contract; so would debenture-holders; so would mortgagees; so, in fact, would all people with fixed incomes. All debtors and leaseholders would have cause to rejoice, all creditors to mourn; for the former there would be a jubilee. Wage-receivers would temporarily be injured. Such a confusion would ensue as has occurred but too often through the wilful debasing of coin. If the fall were sudden, buying and selling would be for a time well-nigh impossible; if protracted, they would be seriously hindered. Now, it is probable that for a short time at least after these discoveries there was a depreciation: the demonetisation of gold by Holland in 1850 was a consequence of it.

Whether there has been a permanent decline is the question agitated; and I would take the liberty of expressing an opinion that the problem has not been always rightly stated. Those who ask whether the value of gold has been depreciated, really mean to put a question different from that which they ask, strictly interpreted. Their question could be comparatively easily answered; that which they mean to ask is a problem exceedingly difficult. In order to prove that this is the case it will be necessary to anticipate a little of the theory of value. Value means a comparison of some one article with another article, or with several. In this particular discussion M. Chevalier, who has largely the merit of originating it, defines value to be a comparison of some one article with the generality of other articles of wealth; and the question whether gold has been depreciated is, therefore, tantamount to the question, whether a sovereign purchases more valuable articles to-day than in 1849.* If we find it purchases more, it has risen; if less, it has fallen. And this will hold good whether the influences at

* As an instance of the ambiguity which prevails with regard to the phrase "depreciation of value," I may refer to a letter from Professor Cliffe Leslie, in the *Economist*. He quotes from Professor Knies, of Heidelberg, a statement to the effect that railways in Germany had caused a real depreciation of money, by "its influx into places where prices were low from places where they were high." The former objects to a rise of price produced by an improvement in the commercial situation, the means

work operate upon gold or upon other commodities. One commodity cannot rise in value without the others for which it is exchanged falling, and *vice versa;* and it is all the same as regards value whether other things have grown scarcer, or gold has grown more plentiful. The effect upon value would be the same : the general purchasing power of gold would have diminished, and its value would therefore have fallen. If it be said that a fall in the general purchasing power of gold is no fall in its value, seeing its purchasing power has not decreased as regards all commodities, the question, put upon this basis, only becomes more easy ; the instantaneous reply will be, that according to this mode of looking at the question, gold has assuredly not been depreciated, seeing a sovereign does not purchase less of every article than it did previous to the discovery of the Californian and Australian mines. If, however, we regard value as synonymous with general purchasing power, the question presents no real difficulties ; a comparison between the purchasing power of a sovereign in 1849 and to-day will decisively settle it one way or other. And the result of such a comparison would show that gold had risen as compared with articles of manufacture, but had been depreciated as compared with raw produce. " Yes," or " no," would not be the answer ; it would be a specific account of the state of the case with respect to each article of commerce. Value is a mental judgment of which we must be fully conscious. We are the valuers of gold, as of all commodities ; we are the depreciators of gold, if it has been depreciated ; a fall in the value of gold would be a mental fact due to the producers and consumers of gold esteeming it less ; and prices attest our valuations. But in this controversy respecting the depreciation of gold are really involved much more difficult problems, which would seem to be these : Whether there is any influence at work acting directly upon gold, the tendency of which is to depreciate it ? and whether, if there is any such tendency, it is counteracted by opposite tendencies, also acting directly upon gold ? To answer these questions it will not suffice to know whether gold purchases to-day less of most, or even of all, articles, than before the discovery of the

of exportation, and the trade of a place, being designated "a real deprecia-
tion of money." That, he says, is not the usual meaning of the phrase.
If so, the usual meaning is badly expressed ; for there can be no doubt that
Professor Knies is strictly accurate.

Californian and Australian mines, for there will still remain the unsolved question, whether the causes of the depreciation, if depreciation there be, originated in gold or other commodities. Of course, one can off-hand decide that the cost of the production of gold has been diminished. But when one comes to inquire whether this influence is not neutralised by an influence of an opposite tendency also acting directly upon gold ? whether the increasing demands of trade do not, or will not, effectually counteract the greater ease in obtaining the precious metals ? whether the increased supply since 1850 counterbalances the scarcity experienced during the early part of the century ? we face problems most arduous.* Assuming a rise of the prices of many different articles of commerce since 1849,—and the results of independent researches appear to confirm this view,—there is a probability that the chief cause of this rise is the increase in the stores of gold, more especially as (to cite an argument used by Professors Cairns and Jevons) the prices for some years previous to 1849 showed a decline. But the probability is not of a very high degree, for we know that it is only since that time that many other agencies tending to raise prices have come fully into play. In order to eliminate all elements save the influence of the gold mines, Professor Jevons has selected fifty of the chief articles of commerce, and compared their prices in 1849 with their prices in subsequent years up to 1869. He finds a rise of 18 per cent. Hence he infers a depreciation in gold, due to the Australian and Californian mines. But the proof is not sufficient. M. Victor Bonnet observes that 1849 was the end of a commercial period of inactivity, and the beginning of a period of speculation, which carried prices to an exaggerated height, thus affecting the averages. Free trade began to operate ; railways were created. Moreover, what follows if we accept the average ? Nothing more than that some cause or causes have been steadily at work, and why should not this be the increase of population, or the increased facilities of locomotion, or some other widely-acting influence, and not the increased quantity of gold brought into use by the gold discoveries ? Indeed, it seems to me that the enormous expansion of payment by credit, superseding metal, and raising prices to even an exorbitant altitude, is a far more considerable factor than the

* See Rossi, vol. i. 196. Curiously enough, when he lectured, men were speculating on the possibility of money becoming scarce.

above. Without the intervention of a single sovereign or note, credit may augment prices. It is, moreover, a continuous and progressive influence; and if we were compelled to dispense with it, not all the gold which could be procured in the whole world would save us from an enormous fall in prices. Far from the gold discoveries being the only large cause acting steadily on prices since 1850, it is, in reality, perhaps comparatively inconsiderable.* As was pointed out in the *Economist* at the time, after the commercial disasters of 1866, prices fell on an average 20 per cent,—a fact significant of the effect of credit in raising prices, especially seeing the rise took place when a stream of bullion was setting, and for five years had been setting, towards the East. In further deprecation of alarm on this subject, it may be added that the supply of gold from Australia and California is by no means what it was in 1853 and 1856; that some day or other the redemption of the forced currencies of the world may absorb much gold; and that the large supply of late having been largely due to the fact that diggers were content to accept a smaller profit than they could command in other branches of trade, this self-sacrifice may one day cease.

* The following statistics, showing the growth of the business transacted at the Clearing House, are pertinent:—

	Total for the Year.	On 4ths of the Month.	On Stock-Exchange Account Days.	On Consols Settling Days.
	£	£	£	£
1867-1868	3,257,411,000	147,113,000	444,443,000	132,293,000
1868-1869	3,534,039,000	161,861,000	550,622,000	142,270,000
1869-1870	3,720,623,000	168,523,000	594,763,000	148,822,000
1870-1871	4,018,464,000	186,517,000	635,946,000	169,141,000

CHAPTER XII.

THE INFLUENCE OF LAWS UPON THE GROWTH OF WEALTH.

AT this stage I think it proper to speak briefly of the influence which laws may exercise upon the production of wealth. Obviously their fair and honest administration is of the utmost importance in the eyes of the economist. If there is no security of property, what hope that men will sow, or plant, or build, or perform any work the return of which is distant? If the labourer cannot be certain that he will receive his due, a goodly land may be converted into a desert. An influence upon which it may depend whether any wealth is produced ought not to be omitted from an account of the science of wealth. True, Political Economy may be conceived of apart from laws, and perhaps even apart from society ; the phenomena of production *per se*, it may be said, may be exhibited where there are no laws, and where man is scarcely gregarious. But in this world there do not exist things *per se ;* the facts of production, so far as they deserve study and examination, are always environed by law and society ; and it will serve no useful purpose to suppose production carried on independently of either.

Laws affect the production of wealth by their influence on the enjoyment of it, and on the distribution of it. As regards the enjoyment or possession of wealth, we shall consider that subject in treating of property, its various forms, and their economical advantages. It may, indeed, be objected to the importance here assigned to the agency of property, that it is forgotten that wealth has been produced in a state of society from which property was expelled, that Socialism and Communism have been realised, that they may be so again, and that we must not ignore the widely-diffused doctrine, ever finding confident supporters, that wealth will yet be produced, and mankind will yet live in societies in which no man will be able to say "This is mine."

This objection to the course of treatment which I have indicated is, however, untenable. Of all the forms of Socialism or Communism which have existed, or which have been conceived by any sane mind, the complete destruction of property has been a feature of none; the destruction or abridgment of private property has been a feature of them all. No communistic corporation has proposed that all comers shall freely sit down at its table and share its goods on equal terms. Frequently it has been proposed that society should be recast, and that the social units should be composed of thousands instead of families, as at present; never, unless in a vague and unpractical way, has it been seriously proposed to make the family or unit as wide as mankind. " This is mine " will become one day an immoral, and, by and by, an obsolete phrase—so-called reformers have often said it ; " this is ours " will be a phrase passing current in all communistic societies—Communists themselves have not denied it. On the other hand, though all, even the wildest speculators, admit that the Bosjesman or the Tartar may not with justice carry off the goods of the Englishmen, it is equally true that the right of the public to curtail private enjoyment is consecrated ; taxation is everywhere a fact. Thus absolute property and no property are both unknown.

" Property is theft," said M. Proudhon in a little book which he sold for some francs. In this, and a subsequent Chapter, I propose to mention a few of the economical advantages of this kind of stealing, to recite a few of the leading forms of property, and to consider some limitations upon its enjoyment. Jurisprudence, borrowing for the most part the divisions of the Roman law, has classified the varieties of property. Its divisions—*res publicæ, res universitatis, res singulorum, res nullius*—do not, however, exactly coincide with those which an economist would select, and they will in the following remarks be occasionally abandoned.

How property arose we know not ; but there is abundance of writers who state with much fluency and many details how it did. In the seventeenth and eighteenth centuries, when the theory of a Social Contract accounting for the origin of society and laws was in vogue, it was esteemed satisfactory to say that mankind sometime met somewhere one fine morning, and somehow decided that the land which had hitherto been held in common should be portioned out. And just as Dionysius pictures to us Romulus when founding his city haranguing his people on the relative merits of oligarchy and monarchy, so some of these authors transmit to us the skeletons of orations delivered by the patriarchs of mankind in the morning of the world, on the advantages of private property and things in common. Others relate how wandering shepherds, finding pasturage scarce, settled down to till the land, and how it was tacitly or avowedly admitted by his fellow-shepherds that any one who had " mixed " his labour with the land deserved to own it. Rousseau, writing in A.D. 1754, relates to the Academy of Dijon, with the minuteness and local colour of a special correspondent, how a certain man, one day many thousands of years ago, having enclosed a piece of ground, said " This is mine " (ceci est à moi), and found people simple enough to believe him. All which, the theory of labour and that of occupation, is very ingenious and amusing, being pretty enough hypothesis ; but the origin of property in land being an historical fact, the evidence being none, the possibilities being limitless, these speculations may be put away in the lumber-closet, where reposes the Social Contract side by side with so much dusty and discarded intellectual furniture, the spinets and high-backed chairs of the mind. To which place we may also consign the statements of those who relate which of the two kinds of property, movable or immovable, personal or real, was first created. Either account may be true for all we know. Lost history cannot be recovered by à priori reasoning ; and the origin of property in land, with all the details of it, supposing it to have originated in one way, is an incident of history which has sunk to a depth which the plummet-line of investigation will perhaps never reach. If a speculator can evolve from his consciousness the precise manner in which property originated, why not the precise date also ? Why not even the name of the person who originated property ?

Though the origin of property in land is sunk in obscurity, certain considerations may be safely submitted. So far as the question is psychological, one's footing is tolerably sure. The sense of property means the sense that one can control something. The sense of property arises first with respect to one's limbs and frame. These can be controlled by the will ; and " the baby new to earth and sky," learns to feel that they are his. By and by this sense of ownership extends to things less intimately connected with one. It passes to the child's toys which he alone handles, and to the mature man's acres which he alone may till. Whatever one may freely dispose of comes to be held to be one's own. Hence we see that those who allege that property is independent of society, speak rightly if they mean no more than that a solitary human being might feel himself a proprietor, since he was free to do with many things as he pleased. Hence we see also that the opposite school of publicists who allege that property is a creature of law speak rightly if they mean no more than that only in society where order is established, and where indiscriminate scrambling is prevented, could any one not endowed with remarkable strength or cunning be so completely left in undisturbed possession as to admit of the growth of this pro-prietorial feeling. And I would add that the above considera-tions furnish a reason for investing with proprietorial rights the maker of an article ; not only do you give it to the man who ought to be proprietor, but you give it to the man who has learned to feel during the making of it, while he had it completely in his power, that he is its proprietor. In these pages property in land is chiefly considered : owing to the duration of land, it illustrates most completely the subject.

The earliest documentary evidence reveals no trace of purely private property. All property is vested in villages, communes, clans, gentes, septs, families—such is the summary of researches extending from Hindostan to North America. " The oldest dis-coverable forms of property in land," says Mr. Maine, " were forms of collective property." In Hindostan, the villager possesses nothing more than a life-interest in the land which he tills, being sometimes unable to sell it without the consent of his fellow-villagers, and liable to see it thrown into the common stock. Such a description, slightly modified, comprehends the commune or *mir* of Russia : there, unaffected by feudalism, this species of joint property has subsisted to our day, to excite the wonder of those who fancy that society is a possibility only through some western form of private property, and the hopes of those who would substitute a form of communism. In ancient Rome, we can detect traces of this joint property, if not in the division of the public lands by the agrarian laws, at all events in the position of the paterfamilias as a trustee of the family, and in the right of succession possessed by the gens in certain cases. To pass onwards to more recent times and familiar countries, we know that the Highland clans, and the Welsh and Irish septs, maintained that the land was the property not of the chief, but of the entire body of clansmen and septmen. They could not be voluntarily inoculated with the feudal idea of property which associated some one person with every piece of land. Like oil and water, these ideas were mingled only after turmoil and agitation. It was in Ireland that they came into most violent collision ; and the conquest of that country by the English nobles of the reigns of Henry II. and Elizabeth was embittered, and the ashes of a strife of races long kept warm, partly by the fondness of the Irish for "tanistry," and the ignorant contempt of their conquerors for it and every other strange custom relating to land. "Tanistry," the custom by which the Irish chiefs had only a life-interest in the demesne lands, was not in the law-books ; the English lawyers despised it ; they styled it "a scambling possession ;" and the Court of Queen's Bench in 1608 did away with this mode of holding property. Regarded in an economical point of view, this was a salutary change ; and, indeed, one of the grounds on which "tanistry" was abolished was its prejudicial effect on public policy. With what heart indeed would one drain and till the land if one had no clear assurance that one's own blood would be the gainers ! The sloth of the hireling is a byword, and this implies a community of hirelings to one impalpable master, the clan. To call forth our exertions, above all, to keep them on the strain, we require that our own interest, or that of those who are very near to us—far nearer to us than the sept—should stand clearly before us as the winning-post stands before the eyes of the emulous runners ; the lists must be narrow and defined ; men go astray or loiter in the race when the starters give no clearer direction than the interest of the community. And with this mode of holding property, progress was barely possible. Such communities resembled the lowest of animals—the *madreporæ*, and such like—that possess no individual existence. In them, life was necessarily a dreary blank of uniformity ; one man and day the dull facsimiles of another.

Feudalism, the next great system of landholding, is still deeply interesting, because to it our landholders owe their titles. The great legal doctrine of feudalism was "no land without a lord or master"—persons, not communities, were the feudal lawyers' units. Feudalism has been traced back to the Roman colonists who received lands along the banks of the Danube on condition of turning out to repel the barbarians; such, we are told, is the first trace of the institutions that by the thirteenth century had covered the face of western Europe. But this view appears to be only a striking instance of the proneness of men nurtured on the lore of ancient Greece and Rome, to find there the parentage of all mediæval or modern institutions; and it is safer to assume that feudalism is the spontaneous growth of a given state of society rather than artificial and accidental development. Feudalism was essentially military, the creation of times when people lived for war, and when man's chief end was almost believed to be the cutting of throats, and peace to be an interval for sharpening knives. Conceive the Franks or the Burgundians headed by their kings and chiefs inundating Lombardy or Gaul. They appropriate the land of the conquered, each man receiving according to his quality. But they are to remain warriors; they are to live encamped in the country, ready at the beck of their chiefs to go to the wars; and, therefore, when the nobles receive their fiefs, as the gifts of land were called, they were bound by oath to serve the king; and when the nobles granted—which was frequently permitted—sub-fiefs to their vassals, they in turn were bound to serve the nobles. The result of this tenure was, that the whole proprietory of a country was one army, ready to be put in motion at the word of the king, he passing the word to his nobles, they to their vassals. This continued to be the theory and practice for several hundreds of years, until the rise of standing armies abolished the latter by dispensing with military service. In the reign of Charles II.—I speak now of England—a reign, as Mr. Buckle and Blackstone before him have remarked, so strangely fruitful in private profligacy and measures of public utility—feudalism, in theory as well as practice, may be said to have ended; all tenures held in chivalry were converted into free and common socage. Released from the obligation of performing military service and the payment to the sovereign of aids, reliefs, and numerous fines, the landlords were asked to pay an equivalent tax; and one proposal was, to impose a tax on all lands that had been held in chivalry, and the other, to commute feudal incidents into excise duties. The latter, a device for throwing particular burdens on the shoulders of the community, was successful, though only by a small majority so far as the House of Commons was concerned ; and for a time the landowners paid no distinct land-tax. After the Revolution of 1688, the tax was renewed. In 1692, the whole land was valued—the landowners, by the way, being permitted to assess themselves—and a land-tax imposed the following year ; in 1798 the tax was fixed at 4s. on the valuation of 1692, the owners being invited to redeem it. Thus we see that the law of England, drawing a distinction between landed property and personal property—for, though the land-tax of 1692 mulcted the latter also, it soon escaped—has always, save perhaps in the short interval between the passing of the Statute of Charles II. and 1693, distinctly recognised that the landowners, having special privileges, should bear special burdens ; and if we choose to view the land-tax as a fixed rent, similar to that imposed by Asiatic sovereigns, we may consider that the Crown or State in England, as so generally elsewhere, has never let go its hold on the land of the country. It has been pointed out that the landowners of France who held lands in chivalry also evaded the conditions of their tenure. They, too, with their vassals, were bound to serve the king in person in the field. They, too, were released from this service when the undisciplined bands of feudal retainers gave place to a regular army. Further, they enjoyed special relief from the ordinary taxes, and, to complete their iniquity, they monopolised the chief posts in the army.

The economical effects of feudalism were in some respects excellent. Every piece of land had its master. Every one of the owners could say, with some truth, of his land, " This is mine ; here I spend my labour without fear that another will reap the fertility which I have created." Society was organised in a certain fashion. There was a place for every man, an owner for every acre. The fiefs becoming in time hereditary, there was a strong motive to improve. And it is also to be mentioned, as a laudable feature of the feudal mode of landholding, that it grasped the idea which, in one shape or other, will appear in every dense society, and wherever power to do with land as one pleases might prove noxious—the idea which takes in the East the form of the doctrine that the government or sovereign is the ultimate owner—the idea which, in this country, is embodied in the common teaching that the State still retains some *scintilla juris* with respect to the land, and which may be, though not with complete accuracy, expressed in the language of jurisprudence by saying, that one may have *jus utendi* but not *jus abutendi*, with respect to land. Thanks to feudalism for abiding by the truth that the community at large may forbid land from being used contrary to its interest, and may exact from its possessors duties ; and later ages which suffered this truth to fall into abeyance may derive instruction from the contemplation of a system which converted each landowner into a trustee. A word or two about the holding of land by corporations. The prejudices against this form of landholding were perhaps reasonable in the feudal times, seeing land in mortmain might not yield its fair share towards the defence of the country. But it is probable that the impediments which still exist have subsisted long after the grounds on which they rested have been washed away ; and even were this an indifferent mode of tenure in an agricultural point of view, it would be difficult to justify the restrictions placed by the Mortmain Act on bequests for charitable purposes. Only a century ago it was held impossible for joint-stock companies to conduct any but the simplest business. Look into Adam Smith, and it will raise a smile to perceive that he is unable to recollect more than four trades—banking, insurance, the management of canals, and the supplying of cities with water by means of pipes or aqueducts, suited for joint-stock companies. He regarded them as a species of monopoly. He speaks of them as might Lord Eldon. We know that Smith was mistaken in regard to joint-stock companies, that many other trades besides these he mentions have been conducted successfully by them, and that, as the necessity for large capital accumulates, joint-stock enterprises will probably extend. We may perhaps recognise that their multiplicity is as necessary a stage in industrial history as are representative institutions. We know the cause of his mistake ; a theoriser living in the time of Henri IV. might have inferred that, whenever kings ceased to lead their armies, generalship would become extinct, and war cease to be a science, seeing it would be impossible to hire military genius. That mistake would be similar to Adam Smith's ; a too narrow estimate of the motives that move men rendered speculators incapable of conceiving how Napoleon could lay his hands on an apparently limitless stock of great captains, and rendered Adam Smith incapable of conceiving that there lay unused managerial and directorial genius ready to be hired. Modern commerce has brought to light a class of men fitted to be the architects of the fortunes of others ; men who have a keen delight and amazing skill in handling large affairs—true Carnots of industry, with wills powerful enough to send energy into the extremities of their departments ; and why should not these men, the true children of this century, take the lands of corporations in hand and make them no longer a byword? With the development of such men, some reasons for the maintenance of the statute of mortmain will disappear. And to this topic is pertinent a remark which admits of a wide application. I speak of that belief which too many economists have in the efficacy of certain kinds of political machinery, and of the little regard they pay to the character of those by whom it is worked. It has been the fault of economists criticising this mode of holding land in the light of the narrow experience of modern England or of modern Europe, to assume that this method is necessarily bad. The learned ventilate as gross superstitions in their books as beldames do beside the winter fire ; and a gross superstition, worthy of being ranked with witches and fairies, is the exorbitant faith of the learned in the efficacy of political machinery. It is a fact ceaselessly exemplified, that countries with institutions apparently the most opposed to economy, conquer their apparent disadvantages and grow wealthy. We freely own that men cannot import their institutions as they do cotton, and that a Constitution is not to be invoiced. It has come to be an accepted axiom in politics that the search for the best form of government is as fruitless as the search for the best shape of a house adapted to all climates. Enlightened Republicans grant that there are seasons, and periods and peoples, for which a monarchy is best. The judicious admirers of a monarchy grant the same of republicanism. It has even come to be disputed whether the long roll of political philosophers, from Aristotle to Montesquieu or Burke, have discovered one general proposition which holds good of all countries and times. This is freely granted in politics ; but when they pass to Political Economy, the persons who admit all the above lay down sweeping propositions respecting the inevitable effect of institutions and customs in all circumstances, and with these unbaked bricks of theory, that crumble when touched by the inquiring hand, they build up the flimsy fabric of a so-called science.

The Church—the greatest of all corporations within the bosom of the State—held vast tracts of land in mediæval times.

In England, Germany, Italy, and Spain, it was gorged, or would
have been so, if its stomach had not been bottomless, with the
gifts and bequests of nobles. Men make their heaven in the
likeness of their earth, and those who were accustomed to atone
to earthly tribunals for murder by the payment of a fine, believed they atoned to God for the cruel deeds done in a life of
blood and rapine by handing over to him acres for which they
had no longer use. The clergy were accused of pampering this
humour. The Middle Age caricaturists were fond of picturing
the monk whispering into the ear of the dying baron that St.
Peter would open with alacrity the door of Paradise to one who
had remembered him on earth. Purgatory alone yielded the
Church a rich revenue. Moreover, that ever-present fear of
the end of the world, the fear not of fashionable sentiment, but
a living dread that the world would suddenly dissolve, helped to
augment the estates of the Church. Nor was the Church always
a bad landowner. All the monastic institutions were not be-
numbed by a belief that virtue was a peculiar kind of lethargy.
The Benedictines and their imitators first sent abroad the idea
that the sun and rain, aided by a little scratching, did not constitute agriculture. They were the improving landlords of feudal
times. Among the great impersonal proprietors of mediæval
times must be ranked the State. Indeed we might consider
that it owned the entire land of the country, and that the
personal service exacted from the nobles, or land tax, attested
this fact. Here, however, I refer to those lands of which the
State possesses the *dominium utile*. In England, these lands
were formerly of vast extent. Reckless alienation, at last
stopped by law, has greatly reduced them. In some European
countries they are still of great importance. In Germany they
were so important that their administration formed the subject
of a special science—Cameral Science. In Russia they supported a few years ago more than 22,000,000 persons. It is
an economical question, difficult and important, whether the
State should retain direct possession of any lands. On the
whole, though the evils of loading the State with various functions are to be acknowledged, there is much to recommend the
retention of certain portions of the soil in the hands of the
State. Admitting that the State rarely improves, and is a bad
landowner, is it a trivial advantage to the inhabitants of some
of our great cities, and of London in particular, that they have

within reach of them Crown possessions over which the public has practically got a servitude? In later times, at least, our sovereigns have acknowledged more or less that they hold their castles, and domains, and parks, as the representatives of the public; and, if we consider the healthy enjoyment thereby received by millions, it will be felt that these Crown possessions are an economical blessing to the nation, and regret will be felt that so much of them, the true *Ager Publicus*, has been absorbed by private proprietors. One may find another reason recommending State ownership, in certain circumstances, in certain departments of France, or certain districts of Italy, subject to inundations, owing to the destruction of wood along the mountain sides, which causes the rainfall to pour suddenly into the valleys, and to flood the streams without warning, and it will be seen that there also State possession is desirable. To prevent inundations, the slopes that have been bared must be planted, and the woods that remain must be guarded. But to the private proprietor it may be a serious loss to forego so much pasturage, and to hazard such expenditure. He may not wish to wait for the slow returns of forestry. What cares he for these inundations? They sweep away herds and flocks, and houses, and crops, and human beings. True; but the scene of destruction may be a hundred miles away from his residence, and he cannot be expected to forego or postpone gains, to afforest or disafforest, for the sake of strangers. It is highly to be desired that the State, which may be trusted to resist the temptation to fell the woods, or suffer them to be injured by flocks at the risk of a devastation of the remote plains, should possess the slopes down which flow the waters that feed the dangerous rivers. Direct ownership by the State, unsuitable in most cases, may, in these circumstances, with a Rhone or a Tiber to guard against, become imperiously necessary.

We have not completed the list of impersonal proprietors, for we have not mentioned the "commons" and the property owned by the communes. Speaking under certain reservations to be stated, to leave land in common is to leave it waste— to allow roods which might have produced wheat or turnips to produce a few thistles for the village donkeys, a few blades of grass for the village cows, and to present an inviting encampment for every passing gang of gipsies or vagrants, to the detriment of the village linen; it is to have no drains and much

N

rheumatism ; it is to encourage loafing and laziness, vermin and
vagrancy ; it is to leave in pasture and fallow land what might
with greater advantage be in wheat.   That is the case in this
country ; and though some of these evils could have been
tolerated at a time when the land was of less value, population
less dense than to-day, in consideration of the advantage to
labourers having cows, or keeping pigs, or a few geese, now we
cannot indulge in this waste ; and in the interest of the very
labourer, it is expedient to enclose the commons.   We could no
more permit these vast commons of last century to exist than
we could the Corn-laws to continue ; and the chief stain on the
history of enclosures is not their extent or rapidity, but the utter
indifference to all interests except those of the lords of the manor.
Previous to 1695, much of the land of Scotland lay in common ;
but an Act passed by the Scotch Parliament in 1695, which
authorised the enclosure of waste lands, on the request of those
interested, has diminished the extent of the commons.   Indeed,
perhaps almost all that would be worth reclaiming has been
reclaimed ; here and there you come upon a hill or moor of a
hundred acres, adjacent to some village, serving only to feed
one or two "langelled" horses and a few scraggy sheep.   Contrasting it with the surrounding fertility, you regret the waste.
But regrets at this waste partially melt away when you find
that generally these acres would not repay the cost of reclaiming
them, or that they are the lungs of a district.   In England also
the process of enclosure proceeded rapidly.   In the fourteenth
century, to go no farther back, the waste lands were of enormous
extent, and over them the peasant could feed his sheep, pigs,
and cows.   Sometimes they had the right of " turbary," that is,
of cutting peats, and the right to " estovers," that is, to cutting
furze.   The commoners did not own these waste lands, but they
had well-understood servitudes over them.   As feudalism disappeared, as war ceased to be the absorbing occupation of the landowners, as the advantages of a large body of retainers vanished,
as commerce arose, as the rearing of sheep for the sake of their
wool grew to be profitable, as the Statute of Merton worked its
effects, these commons began to be enclosed, to the detriment,
temporary it may be, but still to the detriment, of the labourers.
In the interest of the poor, the Legislature occasionally resisted
this enclosure.   But since 1710, when the first Inclosure Act
was passed, the process has gone on with accelerating rapidity ;

and between 1710 and 1867, 7,660,413 acres were enclosed.
The cost of obtaining a private Act raised at first an impediment, removed by the General Act of 1845. It cannot be
doubted that all this enclosure, among the very greatest factors
in English history, was not effected without serious temporary
injury to the poor, and serious disregard of their rights.
Certainly such was the case previous to the General Inclosure
Act of 1845 ; rarely were the rights of the poor, unable to fee
a lawyer to state their case in committee, heard ; the common
was too often enclosed as if the only persons concerned were
the neighbouring proprietors ; the cottagers' geese, cows, and
pigs were ignored ; and perhaps the only hindrance was the
expense in obtaining an Act. In this country there is at
present no very clamant grievance regarding the ownership of the
soil ; but there are districts where the bare mention of the
enclosure of the commons suffices to call forth bursts of maledic-
tions. The Act of 1845 made a show of liberally providing for
these interests. Allotments for gardens were to be given ; the
cottager was to grow cabbages instead of rearing geese. So
much for promises ; what do the reports of the commissioners
tell us of their fulfilment ? Why, that of the 484,893 acres
enclosed between 1845 and 1867, only 2119 have been set aside
for the onions and cabbages of the cottage ; the rest have been
swallowed up in the domains of the lords of the manors. To
enclose these commons in country districts is generally proper.
But why should some neighbouring proprietor ever draw the
whole rent ? The memorial of the commons' rights, founded on
a tenure older than feudalism, should remain in the shape of a
perpetual charge, fairly valued, over the enclosed land, to be
devoted to parochial purposes. Instead of acquiescing, as a
matter of course, in the main proposals of an annual Inclosure
Bill, Parliament should jealously scrutinise its details, and insist
on ample reservations for purposes of recreation. For verily
men believe that in morals two and two make five when sums
are set in acres.

While in country districts it is advantageous to improve
the waste lands, provided they are not appropriated to the
benefit of private proprietors without due regard to the privileges which the commoners have lost ; provided they receive more
than a few acres for recreation or gardens ; so far from the work
of enclosing in the neighbourhood of our large towns being facili-

tated, it ought to be stopped, for higher than economical reasons.　There ought to be machinery in existence for stopping the
so-called " improvement " of waste lands in the vicinity of towns,
just as there is and should be machinery for facilitating its enclosure in the country.　Refusing facilities for enclosing of waste
land within fifteen miles of London, and devoting ten acres to
the recreation of the inhabitants of large towns, or the reservation of an allotment of one-tenth of the enclosed land for the use
of the public, does not suffice.　It is necessary to make the
maintenance of open spaces in the neighbourhood of our large
towns a part of public policy ; and, as an initial step, a survey
is perhaps desirable.　In the catalogue of indictable offences
there are included some more innocent actions than the destruction of those playgrounds of the people.

CHAPTER XIII.

THE INFLUENCE OF LAWS UPON THE GROWTH OF WEALTH.

(*Continued.*)

HITHERTO we have been considering the economical influence of laws, so far as they affected the enjoyment of property ; turn now to their economical influence by affecting the distribution of it. In order that they may not be detrimental it is necessary that there should be every facility for the passage of the soil from those who are unable or indisposed to extract the utmost from its pores to those who have the capacity and motives. There must be no legal impediments to the transference of the land from the heavily burdened to the rich and enterprising. As far as possible—and we shall see how far it is possible—landed property should be transferred with as much ease as personal property. There should be little friction. Otherwise, we as infallibly diminish the production of the country as if we managed to cover the roads a foot deep with mud, and to create an artificial barrenness in the fields which they traversed. Is this facility afforded to the transfer of landed property in this country ? Far from it. A system of conveyancing, the most cumbrous that ever existed anywhere save in this country at a former time, trammels the sale of all landed property, and in some cases practically locks it up. Here we permit land to be transferred ; we ought to facilitate its transfer, for if a man desires to part with his land the presumption is that he is not the person qualified to make the best use of it—probably he wants capital or is averse to using it. Some readers will ask, What pretext, not to say reason, is there for these obstructions ? Why should not land be transferred as coal or stocks are transferred ? Is not all the elaboration a device for snaring fees ? No doubt the artificially cumbrous character of conveyancing is one obstruction ; but, in the nature of things, there are some reasons why land cannot be transferred with the same complete facility as chattels are. The possessor of the former is only in most instances, that of the latter almost of necessity, the owner ; the possibility of a sale being null and void is greatly diminished by the fact that goods and chattels are of recent creation. They have passed through few hands, and the risk of a bad title is small. On the other hand, if they be money or promissory-notes, they change hands so frequently that it would be an odious obstruction to commerce to require the payee to prove his title. But land, an article of property subsisting for ages, may be held by one whose claims may be overridden by prior and better claims, and to his cost a purchaser may find that he has bought a worthless title. Indeed, to prevent vexatious litigation, a statute of limitation becomes here necessary. Hence possession is no certain or very strong presumption of real ownership. Again, movables are comparatively rarely mortgaged ; land is frequently so, and penalties of the law against concealment of encumbrances may not save a purchaser from discovering too late that he is a nominal owner, and that the rents are absorbed by an annuity or rent-charge. Or, to cite another conceivable case, an estate may be subject to Crown debts. These two circumstances—possession being no valid proof of ownership and liability to mortgages and other encumbrances— tend to render the transfer of land more difficult than that of most personal chattels or movables. I say " most," because ships are frequently mortgaged, and this fact has necessitated the observance of unusual precautions in the transfer of ships, and the consequent formation of a shipping registry. Perhaps to the two above causes we ought to add a third—the necessity of obtaining a minute and precise description of the piece of land for sale. Of a certain amount of East India stock one needs no further description ; the ship one proposes to purchase is demarcated from all others ; but with respect to an estate in land, an artificial division, one must have minute and accurate information ; and until a cadastre or official survey everywhere exists, this difficulty will be serious. To these hindrances have been added others factitious and artificial, and of these the chief is the want of a right system of registration. It can scarcely be doubted that the transfer of land in England would be greatly facilitated by the establishment of a system to which resort should be compulsory. Various attempts have been made to create registers which would furnish easily accessible and unquestionable evidence regarding all contracts affecting land. So far back as Cromwell's time the subject was mooted; but the attempt then failed, through the efforts, we are told, of "the sons of Zeruiah." Though the opinions of almost all competent and unprejudiced persons is that the value of land would be enhanced if the title was indubitable, so as to be readily alienable or mortgaged, and though this course has been followed in one form or another by the Hanseatic towns for several hundreds of years, by several European countries, such as Scotland, Prussia, France, and Bavaria, and by our colonists in Australia,—the landowners of England, perhaps partly influenced by their legal advisers, have so strenuously resisted the publication of the nature of their titles and obligations that these attempts have been frustrated. Afraid to submit their titles to official examination lest they should be "blown upon," they have stopped the progress of several measures, and never suffered any to pass which was not mutilated. Lord Westbury was indeed successful in establishing a Land Registration Office, to which landowners were invited to resort. But owing to various causes few availed themselves of the Act of 1862. Its operations were tedious and expensive; and had they not been so, the absence of compulsion must have wrecked it. Those who are sure they have a perfectly marketable article will not resort to the Act because their position will not be improved; those who are not sure will not take trouble and undergo expense in order perhaps to prove that their title is bad. The experience of this Act has shown compulsion is needed. It is probable also that the period of search must be reduced from sixty to thirty years at most. Yet another obstruction to the free circulation of land consists of the numerous complicated and remote interests in land, of which the law of England permits the creation. The cheapness of conveyance exhibited by Continental States is partly ascribable to their legal systems, which, built on the Roman law, are, as a rule, unfavourable to the creation of successive intervals of use; and until the power of the landlord to dispose of the land after his death, and to create concurrent particular estates in the soil, has been abridged, reform will be arduous.

The main lines of any satisfactory system of registration are clear, and they seem to run in these grooves : An official and compulsory investigation and declaration of title, once for all— compulsory because thus only will the dislike to register, arising partly from the natural aversion to publicity, and the fear of provoking neighbours who do not register, be overcome. And it is pretty evident, from the experience acquired in the working of Lord Westbury's Act, that an indefeasible title may be granted after a less protracted period of search than sixty years. Purchasers are satisfied with less when they purchase through the agency of a private conveyancer ; and in these days of publicity the chances of serious error through the search not having been carried back more than thirty or forty years are few. It should be incumbent on every landowner to register his title within a certain time—an approach to which ideal was made in a recent Ministerial bill ; it is no real hardship to compel one to prove his right to land, the rent of which he obtains. Whether the claims of any persons interested in the land other than the owner of the fee-simple shall be registered is a moot-point ; almost everybody owns that leases of considerable duration should ; but it is doubted whether other interests connected with the land should. Should mortgages and other beneficial interests be registered ? On the whole, it would seem, judging from à priori considerations and Continental practices, together with the analogy of the shipping registry, that no system is complete which omits them. In a modified degree the arguments which recommend registration of title recommend registration of lesser interests. It is open, however, to consideration whether, as Mr. Ludlow has proposed, the register of ownership should not be entirely distinct from that of charges. The power of the landlord to borrow, it is reasonable to expect, would be increased by a register of mortgages. If to these measures was added a Court which was empowered to display boldness in selling estates encrusted with encumbrances, and if the creation of remote and complicated interests was forbidden, it is probable that the transfer of land would become as easy as it is now difficult. Nay, it does not appear utopian to anticipate a day when land and all permissible interests in it will pass from hand to hand with an ease and expeditiousness almost approaching to what is exhibited in the transfer of a sum of money from one banking account to another. With these changes effected, the predictions made by a Lord Chancellor with respect to the

Transfer of Estates Act, that it "will make titles more simple and secure, and will diminish the expense attending purchases and sales," may be notably realised. The most eminent lawyers echo the discontent of the mercantile world at the cumbrous operations necessary to the sale of a few acres. Lafontaine should have given us a fable of a lion bound by cobwebs and mistaking them for cords; the fable would have had a pertinent application to the tyranny of conveyancers. A subsequent generation may not be able to repress a little contempt for those who suffered themselves to be hampered by the cumbrous and costly processes to be gone through before an acre can change hands. Of the evils thus inflicted there are none more considerable than the obstruction to the formation of small properties and the artificial protection of large properties. Irrespective of the stamp-duty, the conveyance of a small estate may cost as much as that of a large one—it may happen to cost more—and what may be of no account in a transaction in which thousands of pounds are in question, may be of vital importance when the price of the estate amounts to a few hundreds. £23 has been paid for conveying the value of £100; no more might have been required for conveying an estate ten times as valuable. Judge of the hindrance to the growth of small properties by the fact that a company which bought land in large masses and sold it in small lots was able to pay a dividend of 15 per cent. Professor Cairns states that, even in the Landed Estates Court, the cheapest conveyance that could be drawn for a few acres would cost, exclusive of stamp-duties, £10, and that a deed of conveyance, transferring a thousand acres, might not cost more. It is to be feared that this and many other evils will not be cured until a reform is effected in the mode of paying solicitors in the case of sales and of mortgages. At present they are paid by length—a shilling for every seventy-two words of a deed—without regard to the nature of the work; and the inevitable consequence of this false arrangement is, that in order to obtain adequate remuneration for their highly-skilled labour, they are obliged to resort to amplification and verbiage. Tautology and "feeble expletives their aid do lend" to increase solicitors' fees. Seeing the solicitor must enlarge the deeds necessary for the conveyance

* Quoted in Lord St. Leonards' *Handy Book of Property Law*, Eighth Edition, page 93.

of small properties, because the transferrer of large properties
will not pay proportionately to the importance of the transaction, it follows that the former pay too much, the latter too
little ; and thus, as a matter of fact, those who dispose of small
properties pay for the transference of large properties.   There
are other evil effects of an indirect character that flow from
payment by length.   For example, the bulky character of the
deeds is a hindrance to registration.   The effect of lopping off
all needless processes in conveyance can scarcely be exaggerated.   Take as a proof the statement made by Lord Cairns
in the House of Commons, to the effect that the Act
rendering the assignment of satisfied terms unnecessary, an
extremely small process, was tantamount to a saving of
£300,000 a-year.

Stamp-duties are a hindrance to the free circulation of landed
property.   In all forms such duties, though perhaps necessary,
are open to the objection of being taxes on capital, just as much
as a tax on steam-engines would be one on capital.   In their
present form they are objectionable, inasmuch as they fall with
disproportionate heaviness on small transactions.   Entails, by
their very nature, impede the free passage of land, and they are
in fact intended to do so.   As practised in England, entails or
strict settlements enable the owner of an estate to secure it to
as many persons alive as he chooses to name, and to the man-
hood of an unborn child ; by which device it might be possible
for a proprietor to determine the destination of his land for
nearly a century.   This fact, however startling, feebly represents
the power of the entailer ; for his successor, himself a victim to
the desire of founding a family, trained by precept and caste to
consider this a compensation for the deprivation of rights over
his property, and tempted by the offer of an allowance in his
father's lifetime, is disposed to renew the entail ; and thus there
is facility and temptation to create that which reason and law
forbid—a perpetuity.   The chance of barring the entail may
come round only once in fifty or even eighty years, and when it
comes the temptation to disregard it comes also.   The slightest
consideration should suggest that this locking-up of land is
economically bad.   Not to linger over the broad fact that the
amount of land saleable at any moment is diminished, and a part
of the resources of nature locked up, we may mention that the
owner, if he may be so styled, of an entailed property, not being

always able to sell one acre, the rise of a shipping or commercial town is all but impossible on an entailed estate, for many will not build on that which they cannot buy. Great mineral wealth, rich mines of coal or iron, in the neighbourhood, may conquer this advantage, and there people may be content with a short lease. But where these advantages are absent, and a good situation, an excellent harbour, artificial or natural, or a large dock—mere facilities of exchange and distribution, in short—constitute the inducements to form around them a large town, these advantages will not suffice unless freeholds can be created. Moreover, it was formerly impossible to grant leases, as these would injure the heir; this serious obstruction to good agriculture has, however, been removed. Then, mark the injury the land itself receives from entails. The occupier of an entailed estate or tenant in tail is not the owner; why should he, at all events towards the end of his life, spend his money upon it? You may answer, because his son, if not he himself, will profit by every rood that is drained or planted. But this answer is not conclusive, because the proprietor may have several sons, and as the land goes to the eldest son, the father's duty and inclination will move him to devote his money to portioning his younger children. Thus, a pernicious divorce is effected between the land and the capital that would fertilise it; the poor proprietor is tempted to burthen it; he cannot transfer it to wealthy capitalists who would make the most of it; the measure which creates an old family impoverishes the land; and the growth of an aristocracy is made equivalent to the growth of mildew.

A defence commonly set up for settlements, whether in the form of the English entails or the *fidei commissa* of countries which have adhered to the civil law, is, that the settlement is rarely irreversible. A settlement usually contains powers of sale, and if they are wanting, the Court of Chancery can grant them; the *fidei commissum* of German law does not perpetually bar the way. But "it is provided that the money to arise from any such sale, or which may be received for equality of exchange, shall be laid out in the purchase of other lands,"* so that at least as much land is taken out of the market as is put into it; and as to the powers of the Court of Chancery, they do not override the principle that the proceeds of the sale must be devoted to "the purchase of other hereditaments, to be settled in

* Joshua Williams' *Real Property*, page 284. Fourth edition.

the same manner as the hereditaments in respect of which the money was paid."* As to the *fidei commissa,* in some cases the intervention of the "family council," or even of the State, is necessary in order to break the entail. But, say the apologists of the law of entail, it is possible to tie up consols or railway shares, or all things *quæ usu consumuntur;* why attack the settlement of land when these settlements are permitted? with the aid of trustees all the incidents of entails may be reproduced in the case of personalty; why not attack all settlements? For one acre of settled land there is at least £10 of settled personalty; why call the former fact an abuse and the latter an innocent fact? But, in the first place, the land is limitless, and the fertile land very limited, while the population is limitless; and while it matters little who is the owner of consols, it matters much that the land should be owned by those who possess capital and adequate motives to spend it on the land. Secondly, to settle personalty the intervention of trustees is essential—estates in personal property not being recognised—so that it is scarcely correct to affirm that there exist the same facilities for the settling of personalty as of land. Lastly, in the case of much personalty,—such, for example, as railway shares or debenture stock,—the State regulates by special Acts the sources of income.

Dislodged from these various positions, and owning that it is economically bad, the defenders of the law of entail cast their case on the supposed right of every man to do with his own what he pleases, even should he indulge in folly and waste; a man can destine his land, as his cattle, to whatever purpose he chooses. That this argument, particularly captivating in this country, where property is esteemed the national ark, is untenable, may be shown if we suppose that every owner did as he pleased with his own, and set it aside to some unproductive object. Then the option before the community would be between starvation and an abridgment of the right to do with one's own as one pleases. But reflect a moment, and it will appear that the power to entail is not exactly the power to do with one's own as one pleases, even if that popular doctrine held good in law and morality. Property is the creation of law; but it ought to be in accordance with the rules of morality. Setting aside the purchaser or original improver of an entailed estate, and his im-

* 19 and 20 Vic., c. 120, s. 23.

mediate heir, each of those who succeed to it is equally entitled to it; and there is no reason, but many to the contrary, why one possessor should have more power over the land than another. This plain truth, however, is set at defiance by the Law of Entail. Though all the proprietors should possess equal rights, one of them finds himself merely a liferenter, and another a true proprietor—one can sell the estate, another cannot. Moreover, the degree of power over the estate does not vary according to the degree of relationship to the original owner—a rule for which something might be said. Can it be satisfactorily shown why the great-grandson of the man who improved a moor should be forbidden to sell that which the great-great-great-grandson may sell? But we need not base the argument on this narrow ground. Though the right of bequest is by no means so obvious as to have been universally granted; though, to take England as an example, it was not until the reign of Henry VIII. that one could generally name one's successor to personalty; and though not until after the Restoration did the power of devising real property become so common as it now is,—though the right is not natural in the sense of being ancient and universal,—there are ample reasons why the power of bequest, or controlling property after one's death, should, within limits, be permitted. If permission were withheld, the proprietor would in the end of his days too surely waste, at all events would not improve, property which was to pass to those in whom he had no interest, and towards whom, it may be, he felt positive repugnance. These reasons, which amply justify the right of bequest to persons in existence, do not apply to bequests to persons not in existence, whose character the bequeather cannot know, and in whom he can scarcely be very deeply interested. We need not continue the argument further than to say that entails diminish the number of real owners of the soil; and as it cannot be held that this decrease is other than economically hurtful, the law should forbid entails. Some will judge that the absurdity of the law must be evident, and that it requires no reasoning to expose it. They will conclude that these considerations are superfluous. They who do so will inadequately appreciate the indiscriminate reverence for property that prevails. We are so watchful of its rights that we defend more; we ring them round with walls which enclose more than their domains. They who treat the question as perfectly simple will inadequately appreciate the blind reverence for the wishes of the dead. We are an ancestor-ridden people. In regard to the disposition of the land, forefathers bully us, and dead men rule us from their graves. Each generation takes its seat at the banquet of life with equal rights to all with which nature has spread the board ; none may take his seat twice, and none may be excluded. So says reason, but the custom of this country speaks very differently : we may dispose of but half the courses (it is not exaggeration to say it) ; of the other half former generations have disposed, saying who shall eat this and who shall drink that. In this country every landowner may live two lives ; we submit that one is enough.

Of course there must be laws regulating succession to property. The history of jurisprudence shows that it has in time always been found expedient to grant considerable powers of disposition to the testators. The continuity of society, broken by death, is thus preserved as much as possible. A sense of connection between the present and the future is established ; and with the filaments of one generation entwining with another, the race becomes more nearly what poetry and philosophy have figured it—one man undying and ever growing. To cherish thoughts of the generations to come, in labouring at the accumulation of wealth, saves the world not a little from coarse wastefulness, and helps to lift men out of the mire of selfish indulgence. The acquisition of wealth is idealised, so to speak, when we can pursue gain, not solely for the gratification of ourselves or that of our contemporaries, but for generations unborn it may be. But he who would create a perpetuity is not content with the privileges of an ordinary bequeather. He asks to be permitted to create an entail—a very questionable thing in any form. But, more exorbitant in his demands, more confident in his own wisdom, more distrustful of his successors, more greedy of posthumous glory than the creator of a private entail, who would fetter only one or two generations, the creator of a perpetuity would fetter all generations to come. Such perpetuities are remarkable privileges. They ought, therefore, never to be granted except when the object is admirable, and such as all generations will approve. Can we permit any mortal to "lock up" a county eternally ? The world might become uninhabitable if full license of bequeathing were permitted. Suppose every man had a tomb erected to him—the supposition is Mirabeau's

—the consequence ? " If every man that ever lived had a tomb, it would be necessary, in order to find land to till, to overthrow these monuments, and to disturb the ashes of the dead in order to nourish the living."

Another restriction to the free circulation of landed property is the law of primogeniture. It artificially confines land in few hands, tending also to cause an unnecessary and noxious divorce between land and capital. According to this law, when a proprietor dies without having made a will, the real property, consisting of lands and houses, passes entirely to the eldest son, in opposition to the rule which regulates the descent of personal property. Of course the law of primogeniture intervenes only in case of intestacy ; be it beneficial or hurtful, a will can avert its action. Primogeniture is part of the same system as entails. Both are designed to keep together large properties in the same family. The entails constitute the private machinery for this purpose ; the law of primogeniture is the machinery worked by the State.* Primogeniture is of ancient date. It was not, indeed, known among the Celts. Among them, as Michelet says, the brothers' rights were equally great as their swords were equally long. But it early came into vogue among the Germans. It arose also in England, having been virtually established by the statute *De Donis*. The county of Kent was alone exempt from it ; there gavelkind, or the custom of equal division, prevails. In transmitting the estate to the eldest son, feudalism exemplified a widely working principle ; for it is ever found that when a particular public function is handed down in one family, the right of primogeniture sets in, and this tendency is witnessed alike in the village communities of India and in our own parochial offices.

No custom is so bad that people cannot hunt out reasons for it, and some have accordingly hunted out reasons to defend the right of primogeniture. Mr. M'Culloch argues as if the abolition of the right of primogeniture would necessarily diminish the size of farms, and therefore retard agriculture. A complete misapprehension; as if large farms were the inevitable accompaniment of large properties. He argues, again, as if the option lay between

* Jefferson, speaking of the abolition of the law of primogeniture in the State of Virginia, said—"Some years after the abolition of the law there were fewer carriages-and-six in Virginia, but a great many more carriages-and-pair."

the right of primogeniture and a law of compulsory division, such as has existed in France since the Revolution. A misapprehension again ! Few wish to enforce compulsory division ; what is wished is, that the law of equal division applied to personal property in case of intestacy should be applied to real property. But, says Mr. M'Culloch, the right of primogeniture puts the younger brothers to the healthy school of adversity ; and Lord Westbury repeats the same argument. Well, why exclude the unfortunate elder ? Primogeniture stimulates, says Mr. M'Culloch, proprietors to be economical and industrious, by holding out to them the hope of founding a family. Are the Dutch, the Belgians, or the Americans, who do not admit the right of the eldest, less industrious than we are ? Does the English landowner, who knows that the family acres will go to Harry, till them more laboriously than the French peasant who knows that his dozen acres will be split up among Pierre, Jean, and Jacques ? It should not be put out of sight that there are reasons to suppose that among those who marry young, as the aristocracy generally do, the eldest son is not likely to be the most capable of the family ; and, if a Grand Lama must be chosen in every family, pains should be taken to choose the best. But we should concentrate attention and indignation on the colossal act of injustice perpetrated by the law every time that a proprietor with several children, and, possessed of little or no personal property, dies intestate. The father dies ; and it depends upon the eldest son to say whether these, his equals in the eyes of morality, and of every law in Europe, save ours, shall be beggars, of the most wretched description ; those to whom cling the memory of better days and the remnants of costly habits. The law is condemned by the conduct of those who defend it, for few proprietors neglect to charge their estates with portions for the younger children. In the absence of a will, the law, curiously enough, does that which it would be considered immoral and shameful on the part of a father to do. The attempt to reconcile manifest injustice with the custom of primogeniture is, by the way, most injurious to the land, for in many cases the heir receives the estate so burdened that it is impossible for him to devote money to improvements. As to another objection, very common, that the abolition of the right of primogeniture would conduce to the creation of small properties, there is unfortunately not sufficient evidence to warrant it. At the same time, it is proper to observe that there is one form of primogeniture for which some-thing plausible may be said. In Scotland, when a farmer dies with an unexpired lease, the eldest son takes the farm—a lease being real or heritable property; in Ireland and England it vests in the executor or assignee—lease in these countries being personal property ; and it is alleged that the effects of the latter have been most pernicious. This interruption of interest, to-gether with the power and propensity to sublet farms, did much harm to the agriculture of Ireland. Against the present con-dition of the law respecting intestacy in the case of realty, it is, however, almost unnecessary to argue ; the number of those who defend the privilege of the eldest is diminishing, and the law will probably soon be assimilated to that regulating per-sonalty, which, though not perfect, on the whole deals fairly by the widow and children of the deceased.

With respect to personal property—to the alienability of pro-perty other than land—there are few, if any, systems of law which have retained, even if they ever possessed, the cumbrous and costly rules to be found in connection with the transfer of land. Personalty being of small consequence in an ancient state of society, and sales of it largely taking place between foreigners who traded according to the enlightened *jus gentium*, and not according to the law which bound fellow-tribesmen, the symbolical modes of sale and purchase, common in all ancient laws, did not fasten firmly upon movables, too unimportant to require publicity or formalities, or, if these forms were ever attached, plain necessities compelled men to destroy or evade cumbrous forms. In no sys-tem, however, has yet been completely realised the ideal contained in the famous sentence of the later Roman law—" Let all jural formulæ, verbal snares as they are, be abolished in the case of all jural acts." In the English law may be noted at least two leading exceptions to facility and rapidity in the transference of property. Jurists have generally exhibited an aversion to con-sidering a mere promise or pact as sufficient to bind two persons to the execution of reciprocal obligations ; and every one knows that by the Statute of Frauds writing has been held indis-pensable to various contracts, such, for example, as those re-lative to sums of the value of £10 and upwards. This excep-tion has not been allowed to remain unquestioned. Whether the simple repeal of the section of the Statute relating to this point would suffice, and whether the last state would not be

o

worse than the first—delivery in whole or in part, or tender of money, being then requisite—may be doubted. A second defect consists of the aversion to sanction the free transfer of obligations, debts, or rights of action. Rigid adherence to the rule that rights of action cannot be transferred would be intolerably embarrassing to modern commerce, and custom or positive enactment has greatly weakened or ignored the rule, as, for example, in the case of bills of exchange, promissory-notes, or "covenants running with the land." But this principle still stands a little in the way of certain commercial requirements. Here may be considered a controversy respecting the ownership of land, which begins to come out of books and to enter the highways of the world. Already strange opinions on this question exercise a powerful influence. "Equity," says · Mr. Herbert Spencer, occupying the Extreme Left, "does not permit property in land"—the land belongs to the community, says Mr. Spencer. Mr. John Stuart Mill, less extreme in his position, lays it down that property in land is justified only when the owner of it is an improver ; "when private property in land is not expedient, it is unjust ; the privilege, or monopoly, is only defensible as a necessary evil."

I anticipate the disgust with which many readers will peruse these statements. They will sound as sacrilegious words, not to be listened to — heresies too gross to be reasoned about. It is a characteristic, and, some may think, a virtue of the people of this country, to believe in the peculiar sacredness of the rights of property. Long immunity from revolutions, our respect for industry, have engrained in us a deep, a fanatical, veneration for the prerogatives of an owner. Factions are at an end, and the people are one, when a finger or a voice is raised against property. May this useful fanaticism long continue, if the alternative be a state of society in which he that labours shall in any degree, or under cover of any specious principle, be deprived of that which he produces. Yet this prejudice, being a prejudice, has an evil side, and produces an almost cowardly repugnance to listen to arguments that ruffle our notions of right and wrong. Strange, and significant of the manner in which opinions are formed, that people most dislike to have to defend opinions which they hold to be most defensible ! Let us, divesting ourselves of this prejudice, examine these theories. First, Mr. Herbert Spencer's theory : " Equity does not permit property in land." Why? Because, if one portion of the earth's surface may justly become the property of an individual, the whole of the earth may be so held, and mankind be elbowed out of the universe by one fellow-man—which is as little consequential as if one should argue that it was an unwise thing to walk two miles on the way to London, because it would be an unwise thing to walk all the way to London. Next, says Mr. Spencer, most titles to landed property are not legitimate, because they may be traced to violence and fraud. To which we reply that the same is true of much movable property, and that in all reasonable systems of morality prescription confers right. "Not only have land-tenures an indefensible origin, but it is impossible to discover any mode in which land can become property." Unfortunately for the strength of this argument, almost every reason that can be pleaded against property in land may be pleaded against every other kind of property; and unless we are prepared to deny that a man may own his legs, or any natural talents he may possess, we must grant that he may own acres. If property in land be, as Mr. Spencer says, morally impossible, how can it be held by one community against another?

As to the controversy with which Mr. Mill's name is identified—the right of the State to deal with the rent of land in an exceptional manner—it is perhaps wrong to attach much stress to the common argument, that "no man made the land." No man made the land in the literal sense of the phrase. No man "made" coal, or a table; no man "made" anything. As to the conventional signification of making, he who trenches, drains, and ploughs a moor, may as truly affirm that he has "made" something, as he who put together the wheels that form a watch, or sawed up a tree and constructed a table of the planks.* A better justification of the relegation of the landowner to a different category from that which the owner of movables occupies is, that the value of an estate is enhanced independently of the exertions of the owner, and that he, as Mr. Mill forcibly expresses it, grows rich in his sleep. In opposition, it might be urged, that if the landowner grows rich in his sleep he may also grow poor in his sleep, and that the same influences, independent of him, which in one set of circumstances tend to enrich him, may, in another set, tend to impoverish him. If commerce progress, and the demand for sites advance, and the consumption

* "Oui, l'homme fait la terre."—*Le Peuple,* par J. Michelet.

of food wax greater, rent rises; without moving a finger his rent-roll increases, and riches come and lay themselves at his feet. The growth of Liverpool and Birkenhead has, of course, enormously augmented the incomes of the Devonshire and Derby families; the Marquis of Westminster grows ever richer because London grows ever larger.* True, on the other hand, it is right to admit that, if commerce decline and population contract, the rent falls; and, if the declension continue, the landlord may cease to draw rent without being able to remove his capital to a better market. Further, it is true that landlords alone do not benefit in this way; for railway companies, which have acquired a monopoly of the best routes between certain termini, are equally, with landowners, the recipients of an "unearned increment,"—an increment not always fully intercepted by the legal limitation on fares. But, these admissions notwithstanding, the abnormal advantages reaped by the landowners of England— ever growing in population—through their monopolies are apparent; and I cannot better illustrate those advantages than by quoting from Mr. Patrick Edward Dove's *Moral Science*—a work which has effected great though silent influence on this question, and which will perhaps be one day rescued from obscurity—the following passage:—" If, in the heart of London, a space of twenty acres had been enclosed by a high wall at the time of the Norman Conquest, and if no man had ever touched that portion of the soil, or even seen it, from that time to this, it would, if let by auction, produce an enormously high rent." The vastness of the consequences of these considerations will be apparent at a glance. To Mr. Dove, and still more to Mr. Mill, we owe it that this question, fraught with vast issues, has been awakened, so that it shall never again go to sleep.

The reasons which recommend the establishment and justify the maintenance of private property in land probably will be found to be two. In the first place, it is desirable, as far as is compatible with higher interests, to gratify the expectations which spring up if a person has occupied a piece of land for some time, or has expended labour upon it. The sentiment of ownership germinates in the bosom of every one accustomed to rule the smallest morsel of land; and it would be wantonness to

* Take as an instance of this unearned increment the fact that an acre of land at South Kensington, which realised little more than £3200 in 1852, was sold in 1860 for £23,250.—*Times*, May 22, 1871.

do violence to this sentiment, and to expel the sojourner from his haunts, or from the fields he has fertilised, unless for some high object. In the second place, private property in land is recommended by the most potent economical considerations. Let all things be in common, and the earth will be a populous waste. Appropriation is imperative. No man will labour continuously for the enjoyment of everybody else. To draw forth all his energies, and to induce him to toil persistently, we must give him a corner of land, and allow him to hug it as his own. Then, be it shifting sand, or stony as the bed of a brook, there is no saying what he and his wife and children may make of it. But at every stage of society there exist interests conflicting with the above reasons for establishing and maintaining private property. True, in a young society, with population sparse, and an unlimited tract of fertile and conveniently situated land, these conflicting interests exist in an almost infinitesimal degree. There absolute ownership may be recognised without much harm. There exclusive possession by one man will injure nobody else. "Separate thyself:" "Is not the whole land before thee?" But when a people multiplies, there start up reasons forbidding absolute ownership, and these gradually obtain more or less recognition. Regulations with respect to servitudes arise; public opinion, perhaps the law, condemns the wasteful or noxious employment of the land; and both of the two reasons stated above for the recognition of the right of ownership are impaired. Granting that the improvers of land should possess it subject to no conditions, even supposing they have not exhausted it, their children have not the same right, and society or the State that permits and sees after the transmission of an estate to descendants, may justly step in and ask that for this service it shall receive a share of the heir's unearned reward. The improvers ought to receive a patent; but it need not be of perpetual duration. As to those who received their land by gifts from kings —and this is the origin of an enormous number of titles—it was not morally in the power of kings to gift away parishes and counties to private noblemen, unless perpetual services compensating for the loss to the nation were exacted of them, and unless a distinct understanding existed that the landowner was a public servant. Feudalism, to do it justice, recognised this obligation. William the Conqueror did not give his followers land for nothing. They were soldiers, public functionaries, and

the land with all the privileges attaching to it was their pay.
The land-tax and the obligation to serve as High Sheriff are
monuments of this fact. And is it not manifest that this, or
some such arrangement as this, was just? Why should these
barons monopolise the common earth, and exact tribute from all
who ventured to dig or sow therein, unless the monopolists performed to society a service equivalent in value to the rents
which they exacted, and fully compensated it for the taxes
thereby necessary? And now that the defence of the country is
committed to a standing army supported by taxes raised over
head, ought not the State to insist on a money payment that
will be the fair marketable value of the privilege of being landowners? The land-tax as at present valued is not an adequate
equivalent, and it never fully was. A public office has sunk
into a sinecure—the greatest, the most rampant, of sinecures. It
ought to remain a sinecure no longer, and a perpetual privilege
should henceforth imply perpetual service.

Whenever land becomes valuable owing to the augmented
demand for food or sites, the community at large ought not to
surrender its claims without demanding some equivalent. This
is but fair. It has next to be observed—and this is the second
reason which forbids absolute ownership in land in densely
peopled countries—that society cannot without peril, and indeed
certain harm, surrender all right of interference over the soil.
Conceive what might happen if one could do with a county what
one does with a house or flock of sheep! A landowner might
take it into his head to evict all the inhabitants of a county and
to turn it into a desert, or he might decline, as landlords have
declined, to suffer a railway to be made through his estates. If
capricious enough, he might lay a county under water. Or he
might hinder the inhabitants of one parish from conveniently
communicating with those of another. These and equally
detrimental events are quite conceivable if the landowner be
the absolute owner of the soil. And thirst for gain, the common
reliance against such caprice or tyranny, does not preclude these
contingencies, especially among men too rich to dread poverty,
or prizing political or other influence more than wealth. To
permit the exercise of this omnipotence would be to tolerate
evils counterbalancing the beneficial effects of property in land.
The State has, where public interests come into collision with
private, generally overridden the latter. Even in the present

English law of real property, it is established that the landowner
is not omnipotent ; " No man," says Mr. Joshua Williams, " is
in law the absolute owner of lands.   He can only hold an estate
in them."   More and more indeed do these conflicting interests
increase.   Ownership is transferred into merely the highest
among competing interests.   The *plenum dominium* is split up
into several parts, of which the so-called owner has probably
the chief; it is *valeurs*, not things, one owns.   What, however, is still far from being obtained is complete realisation
of the public interests affecting land, with the establishment of machinery for ensuring that these interests be not
injured by private proprietors.   An authoritative catalogue of
the chief public duties pertaining to landed property is needed.
The need of this catalogue grows.   Some checks there are,
but they appear to be inadequate.   A private proprietor may
leave waste land which could easily be made arable.   By refusing leases he may, for political ends, prevent the land from
being utilised to the utmost; to gratify pride, to shield himself
from the vulgar gaze, in order that he may be alone in the
land, and to be the solitary inhaler of the beauties of those
hills and glens given him in trust, he may seal them to the
public gaze, and may punish tourists curious about scenery, and
the botanist or geologist ; or he may refuse to sell sites for
churches, and may compel the adherents of a creed that he dis-
likes to worship on the highways—these are acts which, on
a just theory of property in land, violate the duties of the proprietor, and usurp most sacred rights.   They are violations, since
he has been placed in his present position chiefly for the sake of
the public, and from a conviction that it will be best served by
permitting him to hold the land ; and as soon as he behaves so as
to conflict with the public interest, as soon as he prevents the land
from being made the most of by others, as soon as he holds it to be
given for his own private pleasure, the public may come upon
him as a trustee who is abusing his trust.   To refer to the most
common and flagrant violations of this duty : That the landlords frequently fail to raise their estates to the highest pitch of
agricultural excellence is notorious.   A series of statutes actually
or lately in force is an indictment against not a few of our landlords.   Placed in their position in order to make the most of
the soil committed to them, they have at divers times induced

Parliament to compel tax-payers to lend at a low rate of interest money for carrying out their improvements. They have thus shifted a portion of their own duties to the shoulders of the community. Assuredly they ought to enjoy great discretion in the management of their estates, and it would be a relapse into barbarism were the State to prescribe, with respect to cultivation, rules as rigid and minute as those which each ancient Teutonic village community enjoined upon its members; but there are certain courses of conduct which are at present lawful, yet which, on any right theory of property, ought to be forbidden. To good agriculture leases are all but necessary. Unquestionably the most potent cause of the prosperity of Scotch agriculture has been the prevalence of leases. As a rule, their absence means the presence of slovenliness and want of enterprise. And no wonder. Think how commerce would flourish if a merchant might be turned out of his counting-house or warehouse at a few months' notice. It would perhaps be too much to compel every landowner to grant leases, for there may be rare cases in which that would be a mistake. But the presumption being against letting land on any other terms, it should lie with the landlord who refuses long leases to show cause for his refusal, and to prove that it would be to the injury of the land to grant them. If he cannot, he is guilty of a breach of trust. Again, if a tenant have a mind to reclaim or improve soil which he occupies, it would seem that it ought to be out of the power of his landlord to put a stop to these works unless it be shown that they are injurious, and are in reality no improvements; for in stopping them the landlord would be frustrating the very end of his existence. Further, it would appear to be right that the landlord should not only have no veto over real improvements, but that the tenant who effects them should be entitled, at the expiry of his lease, to claim the value of them, either in a lump sum or a rent-charge.* Even in Scotland, the land of good agriculture, there sometimes occur hardships to individuals, or injuries to the community at large, through the absence of tenant-right. During the last years of a farmer's lease he, if

---

* The Roman law regarded the right of the proprietor as so subsidiary to the cultivator's right of compensation, that it allowed any one to cultivate vacant land, and made the owner liable to pay compensation. See Finlayson's *Law of Tenures of Land*, 24.

uncertain of its renewal, and if prudent, will not go through the usual rotation necessary to keeping the land in good condition. And, if we take as our guide the principle that the rights of the landowner arise from the presumption that he is a land-improver, it would seem that there is no warrant for his turning to purposes of pleasure, for his enjoyment as a deer forest, or a grouse moor, or pheasant preserve, land that could produce more food if otherwise treated. Society may sanction wholesale evictions; but it should be necessary to prove that these evictions are for the general good. Nay, it would seem to follow that if the owner of wastes declines to reclaim them, and some capitalist offers to do so, he should be permitted to take possession, in virtue of the principle that he who improves best fulfils the ends which society has in view when it establishes and maintains property. Further, if the landowner mortgages his estate deeply, it is almost proof positive that he cannot fulfil rightly the duties of his position. In the belief that such a course would impair his usefulness, the law does not allow military officers to mortgage their future earnings ; and landowners are public functionaries. The Encumbered Estates Act was an acquiescence in this doctrine so far as Ireland was concerned, and Lords Cottenham's and Romilly's reasons for not extending the operations of the Act to England, where embarrassed landlords are not unknown, were not convincing. In regard to another species of monopoly, it may be here observed that need of similar intervention is beginning to be felt. In many instances the share capital of railways now represents only a small portion of the whole capital ; and the consequence is, that the shareholders' motives to make the most of property often now only nominally theirs, have been diminished.*

It will, however, be said, that every landowner ought to possess unlimited control over his land, inasmuch as he is the improver, or has acquired in a perfectly satisfactory manner, in a moral point of view, the rights of the original improver. This plea, however, does violence to a matter of fact ; for, not to say that many titles can be traced back to conquest, usurpation, and wanton disregard of the rights of the original improvers of the soil, one can point to vast tracts of land which prove highly remunerative to their owners, and upon which neither

* See Slaughter's *Railway Intelligence*, sixteenth edition.

they nor anybody ever expended one farthing—moors which, though remaining in their primitive condition, yield large rents; commons which have grown valuable by the advance of towns, etc. It may be true that these tracts have not become valuable independently of any labour; but the labour that has made them yield a rent has not been that of the present owners or their predecessors. And, even if it were true that all landowners had reclaimed from a state of nature the soil which they now hold, or that they acquired the rights of the early pioneers by a more satisfactory process than robbery or conquest, the plea would be defective, for it cannot be proved that he who turns moor into corn-land, or who drains a swamp, ought to dictate for ever the disposal of that reclaimed land. Granted that he has made good his possession against his contemporaries, why should he and his exclude posterity? He and his heirs deserve to enjoy it until they have obtained a liberal return for their outlay of labour; beyond that their deserts do not reach. They ought to receive such a tenure of the soil they have improved as will encourage others to do the like; that justly forms their letters-patent. In no society, probably, need the reward be perpetual possession; in most a concession of unqualified possession for a century, or even less, would suffice; and the only circumstances, perhaps, in which perpetual ownership is justified, are those in which the landowner is ceaselessly improving.

In touching landed property delicacy would have to be observed with regard to purchasers who concluded their bargains on the understanding that they were to be complete masters of the lands which they bought. Certainly the case of these, and all who were led to believe that they purchased absolutely rights which enlightened legislation may decline to recognise, ought to be considered carefully and generously. The State gave, so to speak, a warranty; it ought, therefore, to introduce no change without a long warning. But, while those who brought the land under cultivation should be confirmed in their enjoyment long enough to recompense them amply, and those who purchased should have all reasonable expectations satisfied, preparation ought to be made for the coming of that time when the landlord shall—at all events wherever land is valuable—be regarded as a public functionary or trustee, entrusted with the care of certain portions of the soil of the State, and bound to use it to the common advantage, and when the last and greatest of sinecures will be reformed. That consummation no longer seems at all so remote as it did a few years ago. It does not seem so serious a revolution now that liberal compensation is a maxim applied in all political changes. Legislation with respect to Ireland has educated most men into a belief that the landlord has public duties to perform as well as privileges to enjoy. The Duke of Newcastle's "May I not do with my own as I please?" —recalling the coarse excuse made by the landlords of the fifteenth century for turning their lands into pasture, to the ruin and beggary of many a farmer,—now sounds like a fragment from some Scald; the outpourings of a Norse savage rejoicing in brute strength. And yet how brief a period since that saying was echoed with approbation in the House of Commons !

It should not be forgotten that the Court of Chancery and the Legislature have made tentative gropings in the right direction. The power the former possesses of granting leases for twenty-one years, or of encumbering an estate with drainage and other charges by one who has only a life-interest, and the Court's authority to order sales in certain circumstances, are dim foreshadowings of a time when the landlord will occupy his position primarily for the benefit of the community. In fact, the Legislature has never been wholly wanting, we have seen, in its duties in this respect. The Statute of Uses, to recall another instance, which may have been passed for feudal purposes, produced beneficial economical effects. But more remains to be done. After the disintegration of the feudal land-code, the object of which was to enable the land to maintain an efficient soldiery, it seems to be the work of this generation to frame a land-code, built on the principle that the soil should be used to the greatest public advantage, and that the landowners should never sink into the position of the Bengal zemindars or Irish absentees, with no particular function except that of drawing rent and sponging on their tenants. Of course, to confound public interest with the maximum of production, and to make war on every breezy moor in the name of improvement, would be a mistake. Parks might be spared wherever their beauty was evident; many commons might be jealously hoarded. Nor in any satisfactory land system will the desirableness of identifying the cultivator with the soil be wholly neglected.   All recent history illustrates the tendency to strengthen this connection.   The commutation of English copyholds—once, it is alleged, mere tenancies at will—into freeholds, the fining of Irish landlords in case of evictions, and the legislation of Stein and Hardenberg, giving the Prussian peasants nearly absolute property, are victories which will doubtless be repeated.   As to England, the need of change in this direction is great, if only because it is dangerous that few should be directly interested in the rights of landowners.

CHAPTER XIV.

CO-OPERATION.

In a work which does not profess to be rigidly systematic in the treatment of Political Economy, it may be pardonable and even proper to turn to co-operation, which really forms part of a larger subject, already discussed—the efficacy of joint labour. Co-operation is one of those subjects on which it is impossible to speak or write without sorely displeasing some one. Side with the friends of it, and you are branded by its foes as an ignorant sentimentalist; speak disrespectfully or depreciatingly of it, and you are shallow, and the flatterer of shopkeepers and all its interested foes. To take up a middle position, and own that one sees good points in co-operation, promises which will yet ripen in rich fruit, but that one cannot put one's name to all the brilliant and romantic pictures of the golden future to be created by it; say that "thou shalt co-operate" is at most one of the least of the commandments; cast a little of the cold water of reason on these conflagrations of fancy, and the critic is liable to be informed that there is no medium, and that he that is not for co-operation in all things must be esteemed against it in everything.

In the first place, let us refer to co-operation in distribution. This form of co-operation, apparently at bottom a commercial movement, a design to add a few pounds to one's annual income, has been advocated, in this country at all events, with the fervour and fanaticism of a religious propaganda. It is not souls, but coppers, co-operation labours to save; "get on," be a wealthier man, take part of the profits which you help to create, get yourself a better coat and a better house—these are at first glance the carnal, though wholesome, maxims which co-operation enjoins. And yet, appealing to such low and incombustible parts of human nature, this movement has raised a breeze of unselfish enthusiasm which, turned to other purposes, might have filled the sails of a powerful religious sect. We have seen, and still occasionally see, men cast into the offertory of co-operation talents and opportunities which might have secured to them considerable private fortunes. In Rochdale, and many other places where it has taken root, there have lived men who have preached co-operation really with something of the untiring fervour and unconscious heroism of a Loyola, and who believed they carried within them a message pregnant with consequences affecting the eternal destinies of our race. Labouring in season and out of season, throwing their time, and their money, and their eloquence on the highways, with as much confidence of plentiful return hereafter as that with which the husbandman casts the seed into the furrows, true apostles in their way, they have been superior to the apparent burden of their gospel. The very machinery by which, as well as the spirit in which, co-operation has been propagated, resembles that of a religious movement. Co-operation has its catechism, modelled on that of the Church of England. " Rehearse the articles of thy belief," says the catechiser; the catechumen answers—" I believe that honesty is the best policy: that 'tis a very good world we live in, to lend, or to spend, or to give in; but to beg, or to borrow, or to get a man's own, 'tis the very worst world ever known. I believe in good weight and measure, in unadulterated articles, in cash payments, and in small profits and quick returns," etc. Co-operation has its hymns and its poetry, breathing encouragement to the co-operator, who is bidden

> " Faint not, though still our world be bent on gain,
> The present seeming as the selfish past ;
> High thoughts are not mere thistles on the blast,
> But somewhere surely sow the future grain."

The language employed by the friends of co-operation savours of a religious movement : " We believe in co-operation," " he was an apostle of co-operation," " the great cause," " desirous of hastening the time when all men shall work in noble brotherhood "—these are expressions picked at random out of co-operative literature ; and the language to be heard at a meeting of co-operators is wonderfully similar to that which one may hear at a Methodist camp meeting. I have before me the report of the opening of the new premises of a co-operative store.

After the announcement that the affairs of the Society are flourishing, a speaker pronounces an eloquent eulogium on co-operation, the great charm of which, to his mind, is, that it diffused " brotherly love." Co-operation has its tracts, in which it is shown how " Tom Joyful," using some such sensible arguments as that " the cause of the misery of the people lies deeper than any Government measure can reach, and the work of its removal rests solely with the people themselves," converts " Jack Sprag." It possesses a widely-circulated literature. It has its organs to fight for it, to spread news, to encourage laggards, and convert opponents. Co-operative prospectuses are full of a pious unction in their references to " the movement." And if there are no co-operative chapels or pulpits, no convocations or general assemblies, there are what correspond to them— meetings where co-operation is fervently preached, and congresses where representatives of this and other countries assemble to take counsel and give encouragement, to read bulletins of their victories, and to plan fresh campaigns, to shake hands, as it were, and bid each other stand fast, as if they held some Thermopylæ. Apparently aiming at a purely selfish end, the movement towards co-operation nevertheless agrees with religious movements in appealing to the generous and unselfish springs of human nature : teetotalism is inculcated by some ; co-operators insist on the duty of wealthy societies aiding the poor ; pit benevolence against selfishness, they say ; co-operate in the spirit of brotherly kindness—these are the commonest of sentiments in their mouths. At all which strange phenomena a superficial observer will be inclined to hold up his hand in amazement, exclaiming, " Such a fuss and enthusiasm about giving people a little more bread and butter ! Excellent, but unintelligible ! "

So says the superficial observer ; but those who are familiar with the history of co-operation know that this feature is very natural, and that it is fully accounted for by the character and designs of its originators. The origins of great moral movements are of necessity obscure ; in their case, dates are at best approximate ; and their sources resemble those rivers which are the exuberant oozings of some marsh, of which it is impossible to say when the reedy slime ends, and when begins the river, which is known by no name until it rolls along a stately stream. Such was the beginning of distributive co-operation in this

country—obscure, undefined, almost nameless ; yet, if we are
to name any originator, we must trace it to Robert Owen. The
early English co-operators were disciples of Owen ; to this day
the most strenuous co-operators are those who in youth were
leavened by his teaching ; those districts in which co-operation
has struck root most deeply have been those in which Owenites
were numerous ; and altogether English co-operation may be
said to have been constructed out of the *débris* of Owenism.
It is a waif from the wreck of a system of universal philanthropy.
There is luck in posthumous fame, and Robert Owen drew a
blank ; and so it happens that the name of one who made much
noise in his day, who was, unquestionably, one of the dozen
originating minds of this century ; who, to compare him with
another contemporaneous mind busied with similar problems,
displayed more worldly sagacity and practical wisdom in his
scheme of social organisation than Auguste Comte; who, unlike
most framers of ideal communities, could set in motion what his
brains conceived, has sunk with lead-like rapidity out of memory.
Enough at present to state regarding his creed, that its chief
article was, that " any general character, from the best to the
worst, from the most ignorant to the most enlightened, may be
given to any community, even to the world at large, by the application of proper means ; which means are to a great extent at
the command, and under the control, of those who have influence in the affairs of men."

Owen and his disciples were world-regenerators. They had
designs for elevating the poor, for eradicating the greater part
of crime and misery ; they were possessed by a thirst for reforming ; they felt, what every true reformer feels in the morning
of his career, that—using the words of Shelley, himself intoxi-
cated with the wine of universal benevolence—

> " The world's great age begins anew,
>   The golden years return,
>   The earth doth like a snake renew
>   Her winter weeds outworn."

And with such feelings, with such a task upon their shoulders,
nothing more natural than that the disciples of Owen should
follow a course similar to that of religious reformers. He and
his cause may have been unworthy of this zeal ; perhaps so ;
but how apt we all are to go out to see a reed shaken by the
wind, and to take the clamour of the village bellman for the

cry of a John the Baptist! Robert Owen had advocated the establishment of co-operative villages. His followers warmly took up this idea; the Cænobites and hermits of the fourth century retired into the wilderness of Thebais to lead a life of purity; and the Owenites, to estrange the young from the temptations of the wicked world, retired into the country, and tried their schemes at Orbiston. This was about the time of the birth of the movement; and already there was a co-operative magazine in existence. The break-up of the larger scheme was the making of co-operation. Men who had before been bent on reforming a world thought of getting cheap tea, and in the bitterness of disappointment they stooped from the heights of universal philanthropy to concern themselves with the quality of molasses. Into this channel flowed, and has continued to flow, the spirit that once fed political reform. In 1843, Harmony Hall was founded, at a cost of £30,000, near Romsey, in Hampshire. It also failed, and thus a new impulse was given to more modest enterprises. In 1844, the Society of Equitable Pioneers was formed at Rochdale. Since then, co-operation has been humbler and more successful. Its tardy development was due also partly to the state of the law. When "joint-stock companies were regarded as nuisances;" when one was held liable to the last farthing for the debts of a joint concern; and when limited liability was unknown, the facilities for working men forming joint concerns were small.

What is this co-operation? Is it a peculiar method of doing business, or is it a method of elevating the working classes? Is it purely trade, or a mixture of trade and philanthropy?—of benevolence and quick returns? At present it is such a mixture to a large extent. The Rochdale Pioneers have or had, in connection with their stores, an excellent reading-room and library, and Turkish bath; and they lend or lent out stereoscopes and opera-glasses. Attached to a Halifax store there is, I believe, a smoking-room. Then again, it is often a tenet of this semi-philanthropic system that co-operation is antagonistic to the sale of beer and spirits; thus the Artisans', Labourers', and General Dwellings Company (Limited), a sort of co-operative society, inasmuch as shareholders have preference of employment, and all workmen participate in the profits, announce that " no beer-shop, inn, or tavern, shall at any time be erected on any property of the company." In fact, the most zealous

P

friends of co-operation arc careful to insist that the movement does not depend solely on the love of cash, that it is philanthropic in its nature, that it is a challenge thrown down to competition, and that they hope to substitute a better *régime* than that which now rules trade. "What, then," asks Mr. Ludlow, formulating with much precision this question, "are the root ideas upon which ordinary trading companies are founded in our day? If (as we have always understood) those ideas arc unlimited competition and rivalry, then we are at rivalry—for ours are fellowship and association." "Does the ordinary industrial system of our time look to the production of material wealth as the ultimate end of trade? If it does, we can have no peace and make no terms with it, for we look first to the training them as sons, and brothers, and fathers." Too much evidence is preferable to too little; and, therefore, in further proof of this characteristic of co-operation, we may point to the proceedings at a recent Congress, at which co-operation was identified with numerous moral causes. One gentleman read a paper on the higher aim of co-operation, which he explained to mean the emancipation of mankind from competition. Mr. Holyoake contrasted co-operators with the vermin of competition. If this view be correct, if co-operation in distribution be the application of benevolence to trade, if it be the Christianisation of the market, a raid against Mammon, a synonym for a congeries of all sorts of virtues, it would be very easy to demonstrate that the appliances of co-operators fall ridiculously short of their aims. If the movement spread to the widest extent, all that would happen, one might fancy, would be that our workmen would possess a few shillings a week more wages, and would drink pure coffee and eat wholesome bread. These arc results not to be despised—indeed, we know of few better; but when a man gets a better breakfast this week than he did last week, he is not far advanced on the road to "fellowship and association," and to being trained "as sons, and brothers, and fathers." Men write essays on "the higher aims of co-operation;" its higher, and, as far as I can see, its highest aims arc high dividends. Charity, benevolence, the spirit of "fellowship and association," among the aristocracy of virtues, are not a whit more closely related to co-operation than to limited liability or farming. But it would be unfair to criticise co-operation as if it professed to be a complete scheme of social reorganisation ; to be just, a critic should attack or approach it on the strongest side, and co-operation is strong when it claims to be no more than an advantageous mode of doing business. And indeed, if it is to progress at all, the barnacles of " a bastard communism " must be scraped off the hull.

But, before looking at the strong side of co-operation, let us lodge a protest against the view of competition embodied in several of the sentiments which we have quoted, and in many more which we might have quoted ; and, in particular, let us endeavour to show the absurdity of opposing co-operation to competition. There is abroad an opinion that Competition— I give it a capital letter, for to diseased imaginations it seems a personal demon—is a monster crushing the poor. It is not alone the ignorant that are the victims of this delusion, for passage after passage from authors, from Sismondi down to Ruskin, might be quoted which paint competition as an evil power, terrible as famine. Talk of superstition having perished ! It still flourishes. The modern demonology is almost as large and false as the mediæval and ancient. Only, instead of goblins, witches, and brownies, men believe in powers of evil called Competition, the Tyranny of Capital, etc. One gentleman says that competition means " Devil take the hindmost," another that it is " a sort of vagabondage." To the excited imagination of some moralists it would appear that competition in modern times had been sent to vex mankind, as Æschylus tells us the monsters Kratos and Bia were sent to vex Prometheus. Competition, the basis of modern society, we are told, must be removed, if the most flagrant social evils are to be cured. Was there ever a more infantile delusion ? Competition means really cheapness ; the absence of it dearness, monopoly, and all the evils that flow from it. Without competition wages cannot rise, or the prices of goods fall. Certainly it is true that, while competition among capitalists benefits labourers, and *vice versa*, competition among labourers of the same trade injures them pecuniarily ; that is a true charge to bring against competition. But the only way to prevent these evils, so long as men remain what they now are, would be to prevent a certain number of capitalists or labourers from getting employment—in short, by perpetrating a gross act of injustice. Taking at their word those co-operators who rashly say that their principles are antagonistic to competition, we must conclude that they are in favour of mono-

poly, of the producers and retailers, be they private manufacturers or co-operative companies, storekeepers or shopkeepers,
charging what they choose to exact, and that their principles
are monopoly, with all its consequences. But that is really an
untruthful and cruel caricature of co-operation, which is not
necessarily at variance with competition—a caricature the more
cruel that it is drawn by some of its friends. In fairness also it
must be added that economists have been too prone to make points
in regard to this matter, instead of stating the whole truth. A
state of competition implies a state of economical imperfection.
It supposes that there is not an accurate adjustment between
supply and demand. It supposes that hands and machinery
are not fully employed. There is implied some superfluity or
want. Two gas or water companies supplying the same town,
with separate works, and with different pipes laid down in the
same streets, are an example of competition, and nobody would
consider that the most economical arrangement which could
be desired. It is waste, tolerated at all only because the
alternative might be a state of monopoly, with tyranny, sloth,
and inefficiency. Generally, it is not tolerated ; one company
only is permitted ; and in order to save the community from
the evils of monopoly, the Legislature encircles the occupant of
the field with restrictions, perhaps exacting a certain degree of
efficiency, and permitting a maximum dividend of 10 per cent.
But in large trades there is no neutralising the effects of
monopoly ; and the waste which accompanies competition is
mere dust in the balance when weighed against the evils which
are the certain fruits of monopoly. Mr. Chadwick has summed
up the conditions of the best economical state in a happy
phrase. There should be, he says, competition for the field, not
competition in the field. The possibility of this being realised
in a considerable degree, of the machinery devoted to producing
and distributing being always fully worked, is a basis for great
hopes as to the future of society.

CHAPTER XV.

CO-OPERATION—(*Continued*).

IN speaking of co-operation in production as being invented, one is liable to misapprehension. Co-operation, meaning thereby an alliance of capital and labour on the understanding that the furnisher of the latter shall share in the profits, or that the same persons shall furnish both, is as old as agriculture or manufacturing. Even to allude to partnership, Pothier, Puffendorf, Story, Kent, and other jurists, expressly include the alliance of labour and capital as among its forms ; and Mr. Lindley, in his philosophic treatise on the subject, virtually does so.* Troplong expressly mentions it among the forms of *Société en Commandité.*†

We know not in what time there have not been instances of servants directly interested in the profits of their masters. Jacob, in tending Laban's flocks, was a co-operator ; and, to refer to less familiar facts and more unquestionable instances, the Greek sailors in the Levant, the American sailors engaged in the whale-fishery and China trade, the Chinese traders in Manilla, the Cornwall miners, the lead-miners of Flintshire, the Cumberland copper-miners, have long been either equal or partial participators in profits. In Russia there has long existed *Artèle*, a highly developed form of co-operative production. There was, in fact, no room to invent what lay obviously before every eye. At the same time, it is only recently that co-operation has come to be regarded as a means of regenerating society. We saw how co-operation in distribution originated in England ; let us next see how co-operation in production originated. It was in France—the great social laboratory of Europe, the country where all such schemes are hatched—that co-operation was first announced as a principle capable of indefinite exten-

* Vol. i. p. 15.

† Quoted in Phillimore's *Jurisprudence*, p. 93.

sion, and of revolutionising society, one of the chief economic forces ; and it is in France that co-operation in production has been tried most successfully. All revolutions, as distinct from mere insurrections and tumults, have been preluded or accompanied by a ferment of ideas, as if all old things within as well as without were in turmoil, as if the ferment without were but the volcanic outcome of that which raged within. It was so with the great English Revolution. One who had voyaged over all human thought, has told us that it would be difficult to conceive of a notion or fancy in all the great departments of knowledge not anticipated by the men of that age. It was so with the French Revolution. Before the institutions of the Ancien Régime tottered under the blows of the revolutionists, there had been a marvellous outburst of intellectual life, and the speculations of Rousseau and the Encyclopædists, encountering traditional beliefs, had produced intellectual anarchy. The Revolution of 1848, though a small specimen, was perfect in all its parts. Like the strange and countless insects called into brief existence by the first heat of summer, theories portentous and sometimes ludicrous swarmed forth. Men wallowed in economical and political errors. It was the saturnalia of theorists. People printed what before they would not have spoken ; they spoke in the Constituent and Legislative Assemblies what before they would have been reserved about in private ; and of the few points in which those social reformers were agreed, one was that most things were very far wrong.

I would not be understood to say that co-operation had never been thought of in France before the Revolution of February, or even to deny that before that time it had strenuous apostles, and that it had in some slight degree been realised. For Saint Simonism and Fourierism had fixed men's attention on co-operation. One of the most flourishing societies in France, the large co-operative farm at Condé sur Vesgre, was founded in 1833, and was founded by Fourierists ; and, as M. Véron observes, in his treatise on "Working-men's Associations," M. Buchez in 1831 and 1832 developed the "idea in all its aspects." In 1834 a society of gilders was started under the auspices of the latter.* Of course, in France, as everywhere else, long before that Revolution, capitalists, desirous of securing the zeal of their men, had

* See M. Jules Duval on "Les Origines du Movement Co-opératif."— *Journal des Économistes*, Nov. 1867.

rewarded them by premiums varying with the rate of profits. But it certainly is true that until the Revolution co-operation in production had not laid hold of the popular mind.

Co-operation receives nothing more than justice when we admit that it was among the soundest of the new ideas. Men expected to discover new worlds and level mountains by the aid of co-operation. *Collectivité*, they said, was an unworked force. The Constituent Assembly, wishing to encourage it, voted £120,000 for that purpose; and a Commission was appointed to distribute the sum among workmen desirous of rising to the level of capitalists. Assisted by the Government, or trusting to themselves, about 100 such companies or societies were formed in Paris, and many others were formed in the provinces—in all, 300. By 1851 the greater portion of them had perished; and it is not uninstructive to record that those were most unfortunate that had borrowed their capital from Government. Twenty-eight received State assistance, and of these, it is said, only four succeeded. Perhaps they failed from want of an education in economy and self-control, such as might have been imparted in the process of scraping together their capital. Perhaps that education was the secret of the success of some of those that still exist. Perhaps the necessity of a struggle at the commencement is an admirable mode of winnowing worthless members. Of the 300, only 20, we believe, remain. Truly wonderful instances of manly perseverance and skill are to be found in the histories of these societies. For example, fifteen printers banded together to carry on business on their own account. They received a loan of £3200 from the Government, and set aside one-fourth of every man's wages to pay back the loan. In ten years the debt was cleared off, leaving a net capital of £6000. Eight working jewellers of Paris, aided by a Government loan, so prospered as in ten years to be doing business to the extent of £5600, and to be able to pay dividends to each man equal to twice his wages. Nine journeymen cabinet-makers, possessed of some tools and £5 : 10s., aided by a Government loan of £1000, formed an establishment which grew to be the first of its kind in Paris, turning over more than £16,000 a-year. We might cite not a few instances of laudable success on the part of other societies which did not receive loans on easy terms. The noble history of one company has been frequently told, but it cannot too often be repeated. Some fourteen pianoforte makers, who had failed to persuade the Government to lend them £12,000, clubbed together their sous, boldly started a pianoforte manufactory with a capital of £9, and carried it on with such success that in ten months their capital was raised to more than £1300. Forty operative whitesmiths and lampmakers of Paris started a business in 1848 with a capital of £10 ; in 1858 it had grown to £2000, producing £800 of profits. Beginning in 1848 with a capital of £14 : 10s., some Paris masons formed a cooperative association, which, by 1858, possessed a capital of £7200, paying handsome dividends. These masons have justly been said to occupy in France the honourable position held in this country by the co-operators of Rochdale. They have undertaken and executed with success and efficiency numerous vast works. Their society has passed beyond the reach of hostile criticism. Only we must observe that in the course of their career they have deviated in two important points from the principles of co-operation. Part of the capital is owned by others than the associated workmen, and these extraneous capitalists are faithfully paid their dividends. This is one deviation ; another is that the society employs occasional workmen called "auxiliaries," who do not participate in the profits. The former step the society was obliged to take, because the members could not among themselves muster the required capital ; and the latter was found necessary because the society was liable to receive extraordinary orders which could not be executed by the regular staff, and could not be declined except at the risk of a stoppage of all custom ; and these "auxiliaries" receive no share of the profits, because it is held unfair that those who have not borne the burthen of losses should reap any of the profits. Another society began with a capital of 1s. 7d. ; it did something still more wonderful—it prospered. Altogether, there are (or were before the late war with Germany) in Paris about thirty-nine of these societies.

Mr. Thornton, to whose book on Labour I am indebted for some of these details, states, on the authority of the late Max Kyllman, that of fourteen Parisian societies, the total number of members was 340, and the number of "auxiliaries" 618 ; that the average wages was from £48 to £60 per annum ; and that, besides their wages, members shared in the profits on the capital, which were nearly 23 per cent. In England, these establishments have not struck root. Co-operation in production, with the workmen identical with the proprietary, is in this country talked of, but as a considerable fact, remains to be realised. Scattered bands of tailors, hatters, shoemakers, plate-lock makers, struggle for existence; but their success, if they do succeed, is not so unquestionable, signal, and attractive, as to beget numerous imitators. The Rochdale Cotton-Mill, founded in 1856, is the boldest attempt of the kind ever made in England. At first, the arrangement was that the profits should be divided between the shareholders and the workers, a man who had lent £100 of capital getting as much as another who had done sufficient work to entitle him to £100 in wages. This arrangement lasted until 1861, when the shareholders grew weary of giving what they conceived to be superfluous re-muneration to the workmen, believing that it was unfair to give the wages of abstinence to those who had not abstained; and now, as no one save the shareholders participates in the dividends, the Rochdale Manufacturing Society may be considered to be an ordinary joint-stock company, with a pretty large proprietary. Co-operation has been applied in England to agriculture; it was Robert Owen's belief in his latter years that it was peculiarly applicable to agriculture. A Suffolk squire took it into his head that some of the hinds of Assington might farm a piece of land if they got a friendly push at starting. So he gave them the loan of £400, without interest, and handed over 60 acres to fifteen shareholders. They flourished; they paid off the debt; they added 70 acres to the farm; and they were able to pay a rent of £200. Under the auspices of the same gentleman, Mr. Gurdon, the Assington Co-operative Agricultural Association was started in 1854, to farm 70 acres. Mr. Gurdon again lent £400 on the same easy and liberal terms. This Association flourished also; the debt was paid off; and the farm was extended from 70 to 212 acres, at a rent of £325. About the success of these two experiments there can be no doubt, for the labourers and their landlord are fully satisfied : "No land," says Mr. Gurdon, "is better farmed, or rents paid more punctually, than by these labourers." Several years before, a like experi-ment was tried in Ireland, by a Mr. Vandeleur, but after considerable prosperity, it failed, owing to the insolvency of the landlord. In Germany the co-operative movement is growing to startling dimensions, and figures really astonishing are quoted in proof.

These above facts suggest the following important question:— Since all producing co-operative institutions, which would not be retrogressions, exposing workmen to an uncertainty from which they are now protected, presuppose the possession of capital, no less than an ordinary business conducted by a single trader, how are working-men to raise this capital? If every labourer and artisan in this country were possessed of a small stock of savings, co-operation might be generally feasible, but, at the same time, it would be largely needless, for one-half of the ills for which it is the prescribed medicine would have disappeared; thrift and prudence would have become universal; and with these virtues a universal utopia would have been reached. But, having to face the fact that the multitude live pretty much from hand to mouth, possessing no savings, how, it is asked, are we to get over this initial difficulty? Many have struck in with the ready answer, "The State will advance the requisite funds." This was the answer most acceptable to the Constituent Assembly of France, which, as we have seen, voted, under the influence of M. Louis Blanc, a sum of £120,000. In Germany, the famous Lassalle, leader of the German socialists, saw the perplexing question, and persistently returned the same answer to it. He told Herr Schultze-Delitzsch, then engaged in the formation of co-operative societies, that his labours were vain so long as his clients were destitute of capital, that to establish a co-operative society here and a co-operative society there was mere trifling with a task which could be executed thoroughly only by the State. The State must assist these nascent associations; they must absorb the whole working population; the State must be supreme in industry as in war. This scheme, in its ultimate development, was identical in its main lines with that advocated by Louis Blanc. Both of them aimed at destroying, or at all events injuring, what they would have called individualism. Let us linger for a moment over the proposition that the State should assist these societies. A ready reference to the State or the Government as the healer of wounds and solver of difficulties is the infallible sign of shallowness, and is the panacea of half-educated men; the first philosophers cut the knots of philosophical problems with a vague reference to Nature as the explanation of all, and those who have little more than passed the rudiments of politics, who are but children in political matters, put the State in the place of

Nature. They speak of the State as if it were a great final cause, a self-sustaining power, a source of wealth distinct from its subjects ; as if its resources were not theirs, as if its profusion were not their robbery. To crude speculators the State holds the same place as an idol does to the superstitious—both treat their own work as a god. This disposition to refer to the State in all difficulties is the sign of a feeble respect for, when it is not the sign of a feeble perception of, the rights of others, inasmuch as State interference means compulsion—force exercised towards others ; and, unless we can plead a powerful reason, this compulsion is tyranny and injustice. They would initiate this measure of reform by the perpetration of a signal wrong ; they would steal the stones with which to build their temple of justice ; and men would know the triumph of philanthropy by the presence of the signs which speak of war and invasions. This solution set aside as unjust, and the proposal to transmute the funds of trades-unions into the capitals of producing societies being inadequate, co-operation seems possible only to the very few who possess sufficient capital, or to the still fewer who possess sufficient heroism and self-denial to imitate the pianoforte-makers of Paris. Of course, all this may be modified by the creation of credit banks, such as those successfully established by Schultze-Delitzsch in Germany. These banks have demonstrated the fact that capitalists will lend with confidence on the security of labour. But these banks remain to be created in this country ; and in Germany they advance money at terms higher than those at which respectable private firms can borrow. Speaking, however, of this country in its present state, it may be said that few of the working-classes have capital enough to join a co-operative producing society, or facilities to borrow, and that of the few who have, a large percentage would prefer to employ their capital and skill in amassing a private fortune, to casting in their lot with a co-operative society, participating in its modest prosperity, enduring the risk inseparable to a mode of doing business still regarded as experimental and dubious, and suffering from the unreasonableness and stupidity of numerous colleagues, and this hindrance not invincible, will remain so long as co-operation is rare.

This want renders it difficult at present for co-operative societies to spring up in great numbers, and all but impossible for them to undertake, with any prospect of success, businesses

which require much capital. Suppose, however, workmen had
surmounted this initial difficulty; what then? Will not, it is
asked, divisions sooner or later break up every such society?
Will not the expense and inefficiency of management eat up the
profits, and the workman be left with the idle title of capitalist,
and the harsh fact of irregularity in the payment of wages? Is
not industry like warfare, in so far that its forces must be lodged
in the hands of a few who are all-powerful? Is not the whole
movement in defiance of the tendency of modern industry, to
specialise each man, and therefore doomed to failure as the latter
movement is to success? These questions embody a number of
current objections to co-operation. but they do not admit of a
sweeping negative or positive answer, since co-operation is compatible with the most diverse circumstances and forms of society;
and before pronouncing any too decided opinion on any scheme
of co-operation, it will always be advantageous to know who are
the co-operators. If the co-operators be few, and their capital
abundant, there is no reason why they should fail any more
than an ordinary partnership should — co-operation, then, is
mere partnership. If they be sensible men, ready to defer to
the wish of their manager, and if he know his business, there is
no reason why they should not succeed. Again, if these men
take to businesses in which the wages of labour form by far
the largest item of expense, and in which little "plant" is
required, they may succeed. The great present obstacle in the
way is the workmen's want of capital, and they may not always
be so destitute. Once get capital, and by and by workmen, who
are possessed of the same faculties as other people, will acquire
intelligence, forbearance under losses, habits of obedience to
their managers—if in the process of getting capital they have
not already acquired these virtues. Possessing capital, workmen
would probably come to possess the virtues of capitalists. Once
get capital, and there is no reason why co-operation should not
succeed in a vast number of trades. With a fair approach to
accuracy, the true verdict on co-operation may be summed up
in the dictum that workmen stand in need of capitalists, only,
or almost only, because they have not capital. That they will
remain always so destitute is doubtful.

More successful than the above societies are the industrial
partnerships, exemplified in the establishments of M. Leclaire, a
house painter of Paris; M. Dupont, a printer; M. Gisquet, an oil

manufacturer ; M. Beslay, a maker of steam-engines ; and Messrs. Briggs, colliery owners. All of these establishments give the workmen a certain share of the profits ; all of them vest the entire management in the hands of the original proprietors. In M. Leclaire's establishment he and his fellow-partners receive salaries, and in addition one-half of the profits ; their *employés*, besides wages, receive the other half of the profits, with the stipulation that two-fifths of it shall be paid into a Provident Society, and that he shall determine how much of the remaining three-fifths each person shall receive. The establishment has been worked on this principle for about twenty years ; M. Leclaire has thriven ; former causes of dissatisfaction with his workmen have disappeared, while they, besides receiving the full market rate of wages, have received no inconsiderable amount of profits. It is alleged, on credible testimony, that in all of the French establishments which we have mentioned the change has been satis- factory to the masters and men. In 1865, Messrs. Briggs, of the Whitwood and Methley Collieries, near Normanton, Yorkshire, were, in consequence of repeated strikes, induced to transform, under the Joint-stock Act of 1862, their concern into a limited liability joint-stock company, two-thirds of the shares of which they retained, selling the other third by preference to their *employés.* They also arranged that, when the net profits rose above 10 per cent, one-half of the excess should be distributed among all engaged on the colliery. In Germany the idea of co-operation in this form was applied with success to the cultivation of land, by the economist Von Thünen. Indeed, in co-operation strictly so-called, we are perhaps to look for a possible reconciliation of *la petite culture* with *la grande culture.* In the simple processes of agriculture, where directing or managerial skill tells least, lies probably the best opening for co-operation, not, as Proudhon contended, in the most complicated departments of industry.

The mere statement of such a plan should convince one that it may succeed in a large number of cases. The common objection, suggested by the term " bonus to labour," and running to the effect that this share is a purely gratuitous gift, which only a few charitably-disposed persons will make, is unsound, for the principle of the plan is, that by this extra pay the men will be induced to do more work, to be less wasteful with material, will be less inclined to strike, and generally will be more watchful of the interests of their employers than they now are. To put it on the lowest possible ground : Give a horse an extra feed of corn, and you need be no loser if you take more work out of the horse. Give the men a share of the profits, and you will not be a loser if your profits are increased, if your men be more vigilant and thrifty, less of the nature of eye-servants, less of the nature of the Scriptural hireling who flies when the wolf comes, less prone to strike or to be missing on Monday. There is no philanthropy in schemes such as Messrs. Briggs', or M. Euverte's Bessemer steelwork at Terre-Noire ; they are ordinary ways of doing business, it being for each person to determine whether the " labour bonus" will be repaid by the improved behaviour of his workmen. Indeed, if the English schemes fail, it will probably be because they have driven too hard bargains with the workmen, granting them bonuses too small to exercise any appreciable influence on their conduct.

Not a little has been done in the way of amending the law bearing upon co-operation. In the first place, it is now possible for a working-man to lend his savings on the understanding that his interest shall vary with the profits of the business without exposing himself, in virtue of the principle *qui sentit commodum sentire debet et onus*, to the onerous responsibilities which belong to a partner. Wishing to evade the application of the usury laws once in existence, the judges construed such a mode of borrowing as a form of partnership ; " if it was not a partnership," said Lord Mansfield in a famous case, Blexham *v.* Pell, in which a person had participated in " usurious " profits, "it was a crime." By the 28 and 29 Vict., c. 86, the workman who chooses to invest his savings in a particular business, on condition that the interest shall vary with the profits, and who takes care that the agreement shall be committed to writing, may be protected against the liabilities of a partner. In the next place, the benefits of limited liability, formerly granted capriciously, are now partially open to him. This advantage, it is perhaps well that workmen should know, they owe to Mr. Lowe more than to any one else. Much, however, has yet to be done. The history of the English law of partnership in recent times consists of a slow approximation of the legal idea of a body of individual men engaged in trade to the modern commercial idea. The former pedantically regards them as so many persons bound together as principals and agents, but bound by no other tie ; the latter regards them as forming an artificial person, a corporation, a *persona,* to whom each of the partners may be the debtor or creditor, and of whom we may say " the debts due to the corporation are not due to the members, nor are the debts due by it due by its members." The latter, it need not be said, is the more philosophical and convenient conception of a firm, and to it we are travelling. Chartered companies occasionally formed, were a movement in that direction ; then came the creation of chartered companies as a matter of course, though at great expense ; finally, in 1855, came joint-stock companies with limited liability. Of the defects still to be remedied the chief relating to co-operation is the prohibition to give limited liability to less than seven persons, and to allow shares to be divided. There seems no very substantial reason why these lines should be drawn, especially as shares are generally found to be vendible inversely as their amount. Again, it is perhaps needless to demand that the limited liability company shall always make known its character ; enough perhaps if it is registered as such. Mr. Cobden compared all other precautions to the old Saxon law of Kent, which enjoined that all bargains should take place in the presence of the priest, the bailiff, or the lord of the manor. Lastly, it is difficult to account for the refusal of the Legislature to recognise trading societies partly composed of persons with limited liability. The principle once admitted, this application ought to be so also.

It is said by some that this new bond between master and servant is needless, since their interests are already identical. Well, supposing this were the truth, so long as workmen do not believe it, this or any other new bond of concord is a godsend. But this alleged identity of interest is partly fictitious. It is true that it is for the interest of every labourer that there should be as much capital as possible, and for the interest of the capitalist that there should be as much labour as possible. But it is no more true that A, who buys B's services, has identical (pecuniary) interests with B, than that the man who buys a horse has identical interests with the owner of it. Of course, if the master overreach the servant, or the servant insist on exacting exorbitant wages, the offender may suffer in the long run, as the buyer of a horse may suffer if he drive too hard a bargain. People may be induced by this occurrence, or a succession of like occurrences, not to save so much as they otherwise would, and capital may be thus in the long run diminished, to the detriment of the labourer, just as the rearer of horses may be induced to leave off breeding horses, to the detriment of the buyer. But this "long run" may be a very "long run;" such a contingency is uncertain; and even if it should come to pass, there is no certainty that A or B, the offender, will be among the sufferers. *Mutatis mutandis*, the above holds of wages.

Co-operation in distribution was, as we have seen, designed to remedy the costliness of the existing machinery for distributing wealth, and to save the wholesale and retail profits. Its originators in this country were Robert Owen and his disciples, and the scene of their most successful labours is Rochdale—as Mr. Holyoake has said, it is the "Mecca of co-operation." We hear of co-operative societies as far back as 1795 and 1806. The early co-operative stores in England almost all terminated disastrously. The history of the Rochdale store has become classical. In 1844 a few flannel-weavers on strike clubbed together their twopences, and managed to raise £28. Starting with a capital of £28 and forty members, the Equitable Pioneers had, by 1867, acquired a membership of about seven thousand, and a capital of about £116,000 sterling, with sales to the amount of £280,000. On the history of English societies we need not dwell, since they have often been fully described, and it will be more interesting and instructive to mark the efforts made in other countries to replace private retail shops by co-operative stores. In France the Caisse du Pain was the first distributing society. It was founded at Guebuiller, in Alsace, by a number of workmen who banded together. The project succeeding, the store extended its operations to selling fuel, potatoes, shoes, etc., and to founding a bank for giving free loans. According to M. Eugene Véron, to whom we owe these details, the society was, a year or two ago, flourishing.

A more remarkable association is the Alimentary Society of Grenoble, which serves as a sort of omnibus kitchen for the poorer inhabitants. The payment of ninepence-halfpenny a year constitutes one a member; and the privilege of a member is to receive at the lowest price soup, bread, meat, vegetables—cooked, if cooking be necessary, in a common kitchen. Though somewhat depressed of late years, the society has none the less done considerable good. In 1857, the sales amounted to more than £5000 sterling. In Germany, as was already stated, co-operative stores are spreading. The idea, introduced from England, it is said, by M. Huber, has taken root. The chief of the co-operative stores is that of Hamburg, which, according to M. Véron, contains 2000 members. In Belgium the co-operative movement is also vigorous. The dividends of several of the Belgian industrial manufacturing partnerships are said to amount to 10 per cent. Co-operation has long ago penetrated to Switzerland, and the Consumers' Union of Zurich is firmly established. In regard to Italy, it may be mentioned that in Venice two stores, with a capital of more than £300, held by 450 associates, were founded some time ago ; and, according to recent statements made at the Paris Society of Political Economy, Italian co-operation is flourishing. The United States have, of course, participated in the movement.

These details suffice to show that co-operation in distribution is a large and growing fact. No limits can safely be set to its expansion. And it is no matter for marvelling that it should have succeeded. Were it only the circumstance that most co-operative stores, and probably all that are in a sound condition, both in this country and abroad, have insisted upon their customers paying ready money, it would not be wonderful that they should have undersold the former purveyors of the working-classes. And if they only abide by this principle, taking it as the first commandment of their commercial gospel, co-operative stores will effect no small reformation among the poor, not the least of whose curses is a fatal facility for obtaining credit at the little usurious shops that prey upon their necessities and thoughtlessness. If co-operative stores could emancipate the poor from this bondage, they would confer an incalculable blessing. If the co-operative movement be not, as its sanguine eulogists hold, destined to revolutionise the earth, it at least shows a desire on the part of the poor to better themselves, and a growing resolution on the part of the poor not to put up with the prices and qualities that happen to be got at the nearest shop.

It has been objected to co-operation, in all forms, that it is new-fangled, the sickly invention of *littérateurs*. Yet this charge against co-operation is hard to substantiate. In fact, one cannot help being struck with its antiquity and vigour, so-called co-operation being but a very pronounced form of a phenomenon which always has existed. Is it rare to find some portion of capital

Q

in the hands of the labourer? Setting aside England and the United States, it is the general rule. In slavery alone do the enemies of co-operation find their ideal. Each step from that state of society in which the tiller of the soil owns no capital, but is himself owned by his fellow-man, must be retrogression in their eyes. For the slave in time is transformed into a serf endowed with some *peculium* or potential capital; the serf becomes a yeoman. Or perhaps the slave is made a free labourer, who begins to own some capital, even if it be no more than his clothes and tools, and who in process of time will have furniture and savings, and no small stock of surplus wealth. And co-operation is but this ancient tendency becoming very pronounced. The parallel character of the great movements in the government of political and industrial societies is an instructive phenomenon which has not been sufficiently dwelt upon. Had it been so, the great things probably in store for co-operation would have more clearly emerged to view. The likeness between the earliest forms of both—some species of despotism and slavery—is obvious; and it would be easy to show that the narrowing of the gulf between the ruler and the subject, the destruction of divine right, the substitution of an intelligible and a definite bond for a limitless obedience on mysterious grounds, are accompanied by corresponding changes in the industrial world; the servant in time bargaining freely, and often on terms of equality, with his master, the definite and thin nexus of cash payments replacing the limitless obligations of feudalism. And the causes of the two changes are similar: "In a settled state of society," as Auguste Comte observed, "Government, strictly so called, is a mere extension of civil influence." We have seen the movement towards equalisation so completely developed in the political world that representative or partially Republican Government seems destined in one form or another to make the tour of the world; and there is reason to think that the parallel of this movement may be witnessed in industry. In the growth of the great railway and insurance companies; in the fact that "everything is now done by societies;" in the accumulation in the savings banks; and the growth of the habit of acting in concert, the chief desideratum for co-operation —we see the analogue of the rise of Parliamentary Government. Some of the same causes which have invested him with a share of political power are conspiring to invest the workman with a

share of industrial power. Indeed, such are the ultimate ·
prospects of co-operation, that it requires no artificial coaxing;
and when the Legislature goes out of its way in order to further
co-operation, as when, in the case of the Industrial and Provident
Societies Act, it exempts such societies from certain taxes, the
kindness is questionable.

CHAPTER XVI.

THE DISTRIBUTION OF WEALTH.

THE preceding chapters have in some fashion summarised and illustrated the laws of production. They have shown that the two necessaries to the creation of wealth are labour and capital. They have also indicated several of the ways in which labour and capital are rendered more effective for this end. We have seen how education has made man a more efficient producer; how machinery has gifted him, a two-handed being, with more than the fabled hands of Briareus; and how laws and customs relating to property have been instrumental in producing wealth. We have also examined the pretensions of co-operation to be an instrument of efficiency. This will perhaps suffice for the first division of Political Economy; let us now pass to the second division of Political Economy, the Distribution of Wealth.

The former part, treating of Production, was mainly at bottom an elucidation of physical laws; the only variable element was man, so far as he is an instrument of production. Here, on the other hand, we shall have to deal with uniformities that are not inevitable, with habits rather than laws, for it is men, capricious and mobile beings, who distribute wealth. This line of divergence suggests a difference of treatment. It seems to say that, while Production does admit of scientific treatment, Distribution must be a jungle not to be threaded. Since Ricardo wrote his *Principles*, English Economists, with the exception of the Rev. Richard Jones and Mr. Cliffe Leslie, have professed to pursue what is called the hypothetical method of investigation—that is to say, they have supposed man to be always actuated by a desire to gain the utmost; and, assuming this to be true, they have worked out the consequences. The conclusions will not be perfectly true, but, with slight and easily made conjectures, it is held they will be so. Mr. John Stuart Mill has most completely elaborated this theory, which is but a corollary of the still more general theory laid down in his *Logic*, that social investigations must be pursued in a deductive manner. In his *Essays on Disputed Questions of Political Economy*, Mr. Mill describes Political Economy as "essentially an abstract science, and its method as the method *à priori;*" and he adds, "Such is undoubtedly its character, as it has been understood and taught by all its most distinguished teachers." The second assertion might be challenged; the dissidence of economists on this point is enormous; some considering Political Economy an art, some a science, others an art and a science. Adam Smith would in any catalogue rank among the most distinguished teachers of Political Economy; yet sometimes he speaks of it as an art and sometimes as a science; and certainly his practice proves that he never considers it as a hypothetical science. But this question is subsidiary, and, passing it by, I may mention that Mr. Mill goes on to say that the science "reasons, and, as we contend, must necessarily reason, from assumptions, not from facts. It is built upon hypotheses, strictly analogous to those which, under the name of definitions, are the foundations of the other abstract sciences." Geometry presupposes an arbitrary definition of a line, "that which has length, but not breadth." In the same manner does Political Economy presuppose an arbitrary definition of man, as a being who invariably does that by which he may obtain the greatest amount of necessaries, conveniences, and luxuries, with the smallest quantity of labour and physical denial with which they can be obtained in the existing state of knowledge. It is supposed that "man is a being who is determined, by the necessity of his nature, to prefer a greater portion of wealth to a smaller in all cases," without any other exceptions than those which are due to his aversion for labour and his desire to enjoy costly indulgences at once. On reading these words, many will be tempted to exclaim, "Man, rootedly selfish, except that he is somewhat lazy and thoughtless! All of us worshippers of Belial and Mammon! An universe of greed, with a spice of folly! All of us carnivorous animals, with the distinction of liking our meat well done, while the lion likes his underdone! Vile calculators, slanderers of your species, men who teach selfishness· and call it science, there is no opinion in Mandeville or Rochefoucault more cynical, coarse, and false than the foundation of your teaching. Your supposition is an insult. Why should we not next have a science that supposes us all to be pickpockets, as well as one that supposes us selfish and greedy?" This indignation, though in spirit admirable and common, is a little misplaced and premature. Reserve this indignation until economists are caught affirming to be true that which they only suppose to be true. There is no such thing as an insulting supposition; suppositions which are with any show of truth described as insulting are disguised forms of insinuations or affirmations. Any supposition that is useful is permissible. If it in any way served the purposes of military science to suppose man a fighting animal, Jomini would have been entitled to do so, just as the geometer and the natural philosopher, for the purposes of their sciences, are entitled to assume that points have no magnitude, and that projectiles move in vacuum; and Jomini would be guiltless of inhumanity as long as he did not assert that men were sent into the world to send each other out of it, just as the geometer and natural philosopher would be guiltless of folly so long as they did not assert that points are what they are said in Euclid to be, or that the flight of projectiles is unimpeded by friction. Why, indeed, should the above assumption be regarded as offensive, when it is a fundamental principle of the law which rules us, that a "consideration" should be required or presumed in all dealings, and that a gift should be deemed an impossibility?

Let us here drop the thread of the argument, to draw attention to the light which is here thrown on many controversies that have raged on the subject of Political Economy, in particular to the light which is thrown on the battles between the plutocratic school, best represented by M'Culloch, and the philanthropic school, represented by Sismondi or Ruskin. The disciples of Ricardo were not always careful to recollect that they were dealing with abstract, not concrete, truths. I hate your "ifs," said Sterne; it was propositions with "ifs," expressed or understood, which Ricardo generally furnished; and from a similar hatred of "ifs," men in the course of repetition gradually rubbed down the hypothetical propositions of Political Economy into categorical propositions. They forgot they were dealing with the science that exhibits the laws according to which the utmost possible wealth is obtained at the least possible expenditure. Sismondi has coined a word which describes that province. The word is *chrematistique*, and it would be convenient to employ that or a similar word. But as wealth is not an end in itself, but a means to an end, he who took as the one aim of life the gaining of the utmost riches would justly be pronounced wicked and foolish. Even a gross intelligence would own that a man had behaved foolishly who had gained riches and missed happiness ; to the more spiritual intelligence he who had gained riches, but who had in nowise contributed to the happiness of others, would perhaps appear both wicked and foolish. The rules for the acquisition of wealth, at all events temporary acquisition, are not complete rules for guidance in life. Consequently, economists of the school of Ricardo, as such, do not enjoin ; the imperative mood is out of place in the mouths of those who adopt Ricardo's method and conclusions ; before the rules of Political Economy become rules of right action, certain ethical corrections must be made. Of all this most economists have been a little heedless, and any one bearing these distinctions in mind will find in their writings a rich harvest of fallacies ready to be reaped. Even Ricardo states as facts what would be so were certain non-existing conditions realised. Following the example, if not the justification, given by their great master, Adam Smith, other less cautious and lucid economists have inextricably interwoven precepts and exposition, exhortation and investigation. Probably no one could be named who has faithfully carried out Charles Dunoyer's maxim, " *Je n'impose rien, je ne propose meme rien ; j'expose.*" And what very many have done, there was some excuse for doing, for it is not to be denied that the sacrifice of technical propriety brings sometimes in its train large compensations. The reader's attention is riveted ; the writer catches animation from the living questions he introduces ; the incessant application of his principles to practice induces him to insert reservations, and often exposes to his view a lurking fallacy ; and all, it will be said, may be for the best if the economist does not sink into a mere pamphleteer. If the aim of economists be to show the laws according to which the utmost possible wealth may be obtained, we can understand that there will exist an apparent antagonism between these writers and others who seek to show the laws according to which wealth may most conduce to the wellbeing of a community, for they set before each other different goals, and consequently follow different routes. The speculations of the latter writers are a mixture of pure economics and ethics. Mr. Ruskin's speculations fall within this province.

Like Sismondi, he seeks to show how wealth should be created
and produced to make men happier and better. Both treat of
morals and legislation. Accordingly, the combat which has raged,
and still rages, between the two schools, arises from a mischievous
understanding. The parties do not really join issue; they
purpose totally different ends; and they fight, not as men with
foot to foot, but as midnight combatants who stab-where the
enemy is not, and deal frightful blows to empty space. Mr.
Ruskin seems incapable of conceiving that it is possible for pure
economists not to forbid what they do not enjoin, or not to enjoin all that they suppose. On the other hand, it has been too
much the fashion to scout as useless all such speculations as
those in which M. Sismondi and Mr. Ruskin have indulged.
That is to commit a mistake as gross as, and probably more mischievous than, the "sentimentalists" have committed. For they
perceive that the rules of Political Economy are not sufficient
guides to right action; that a science which, as hitherto taught,
in one of its departments supposes man rootedly selfish, is not
alone a rule of life for man that ought to be rootedly selfish in
nothing; and with pardonable indignation they rebuke those
who say or imply that the way in which wealth is distributed
by "covetous machines" is the way in which it should be distributed among people who should seek for riches only so far as
they render themselves and others richer in happiness. Similar
attacks have proceeded from the socialists. In their attacks
upon economists, the socialists have been, perhaps, far less dis-
creet; but, so far as their systems related to wealth, its creation
and its distribution, they had the same ends before them as the
"sentimentalists." Like them, the socialists planned methods of
production and distribution which, it was imagined, would most
conduce to the general well-being; and it is not surprising that
M. Louis Blanc, or M. Cabet, and Mr. Ruskin, should sometimes
arrive at similar conclusions. The prodigious nonsense—prodigious in quantity and quality—that has been talked or
written on this part of the subject must not pass as a proof
that reasonable doctrine is unattainable or is not needed. Because in their search after ideally better ways of distribution
many have plunged into errors, we should not dismiss equally
both search and searchers as useless.

Though the vulgar objections taken to Political Economy on
the ground of the direct immoral consequences of its teaching

are, for the above reasons, baseless, it must be acknowledged that, taught by narrow-minded men, apt to forget the hypothetical character of their science, accustomed to impute and enjoin mean motives, almost incapable of conceiving any other, and with somewhat sordid souls, and an exclusive veneration for wealth, Political Economy may be, and, I believe, sometimes has been, turned into a corrupting study, blowing into a fuller blaze of unrighteous zeal that exorbitant and unreasonable passion for wealth which is not the least of the sins of our time. Nay, there is a danger of such pernicious consequences coming to pass, even if economists faithfully bear in mind the nature of their reasoning, provided they do not again and again give warning that they deal with suppositions which ought not to be always facts. Evil may be done by not reproving as well as by approving. It has been laid to the charge of Tacitus and Machiavelli that " they corrupt the minds of their readers by not expressing the detestation and horror that naturally belong to horrible and detestable proceedings." A morsel of wholesome truth here. Such is the delicacy of conscience that, if we be familiarised with the mere idea of a course of action that is bad, without a protest being lodged every time that the idea is called up, conscience suffers, its keenness is blunted—without having approved the evil course, we are less able to resist it. To be continuously neutral is often at last to be false. It is scarcely easier to keep pure and let a continuous stream of noxious propositions pass through his mind, than for a man to remain sober and yet keep drinking spirituous liquors. Our moral susceptibilities flourish only by exercise ; and he who writes many pages and draws many conclusions on the supposition that men are thoroughly selfish in all their ways, may end by forgetting himself, and causing his readers to forget, that men are not so, and that there come occasions when the rule of buying in the cheapest and selling in the dearest market ought to be relaxed. How much greater, then, the mischief of ignoring altogether the hypothetical character of the science, and wilfully passing off hypotheses for proved truths ! It must be said in excuse of the popular prejudice against Political Economy, that it has, in this country at least, been associated with a system of psychology which, perhaps, takes a too contracted view of the motives which dictate actions, and which, above all, exaggerates the influence of purely selfish

motives. Human nature was assumed by some English economists to be simpler than it is. There was not sufficient cognisance of the fact that many men are, and whole ages have been,
feebly actuated by the desire to accumulate wealth. Man, we
were told, is so and so constructed, and will in certain circumstances do so and so. Man, the reader sometimes discovers,
meant the late Mr. M'Culloch.

It is one of Mr. Mill's many merits that he rarely so errs.
Possessed of wide culture, he does justice to the great diversity of
human motives. Viewing Political Economy as an abstract or
hypothetical science, he reminds us that its conclusions "are
only true, as the common phrase is, *in the abstract*—that is, they
are only true under certain suppositions in which none but
general causes—causes common to the *whole class* of cases under
consideration—are taken into account." But is Political
Economy an abstract science, and are its conclusions, as is
here affirmed, true only in the abstract, and not concretely?
With due deference to Mr. Mill, speaking on a subject upon
which he is a recognised authority, I submit that his answers
to these questions are a little too sweeping. His chief and
almost sole reason for his opinion is that induction is inapplicable
to Political Economy as to all other departments of social
science, because seldom or never can we make what Bacon calls
an *experimentum crucis*. A satisfactory induction being thus impossible, it is only left for us, reasons Mr. Mill, to select a cause
which largely regulates the production and distribution of wealth,
and to reason deductively therefrom as if it were the sole determining force. Thus will the problem be simplified. The conclusions will be true in the abstract, and, with due allowance
and correction, they will be true in the concrete. But is crucial
experimenting impossible? Is induction inapplicable to Political
Economy? Is it wholly an abstract science? In the province
of production induction is applicable and applied, and the
science, so far as production is concerned, is not abstract or
hypothetical, and its truths are true in the concrete. Take, for
example, the various propositions regarding the advantages of
the combination of labour. Every one of the familiar truths
mentioned by Adam Smith, Mr. Babbage, and others, was, to
all appearance, discovered by a course of observation or induction, and it is difficult to see how some of these truths could
have been discovered by *à priori* investigation. It is a familiar

law, esteemed by the majority of English economists to be of
the utmost consequence, that every increase of produce from
land is obtained by a more than proportional increase in the
application of labour—that is to say, doubling the labour does
not double the crop, but may increase it quite inappreciably.
This law, which is declared by Mr. Mill to be " the most important proposition in Political Economy," and which Mr. Senior
included among the four elementary propositions of the science,
was certainly never discovered deductively. It could have
been discovered deductively only from a knowledge of the
chemical properties of soil; but it has been familiar time out of
mind to people who knew nothing about chemical properties.
Inductively, any one with a spade and a plot of earth at
his command may find out the law for himself. Take again
that law to which Mr. James Mill first gave due prominence,
that in creating wealth man can do nothing more than move
matter. This law, concretely true, was of course inductively
discovered. Indeed, on examination it will appear that experiment is applicable to the whole province of production; for the
main part of the facts being the subject-matter of Chemistry and
Natural Philosophy, may be varied in that indefinite way which
makes experimenting so potent an instrument of discovery in
these two sciences. Man is indeed a factor in the problems;
but not man in all his complexity, but only on his physical side.
Mr. Mill tells us that the science supposes man to be wholly
immersed in seeking to be rich—that he is, as Mr. Ruskin says,
" a covetous machine," or, to cite a still better description, a
"predatory animal." A useless supposition, so far as production
is concerned. Every one of its laws, all the propositions relating
thereto, would remain true on the supposition that wealth was
only one and the smallest of a thousand pursuits. It would
still be true, for example, that capital comes of saving, that
it is consumed, and that it limits production. Now, why
fabricate and introduce a hypothesis absolutely useless, which
can be dispensed with, and no harm follow? There is no reason
for its introduction; and if so, its introduction is unreasonable.
Indeed, so far from being obliged to assume, when they treat of
production, that all men are wholly given over to the love of
lucre, economists are obliged to speak of a certain class called
" unproductive consumers "—that is, of a certain class which,
far from being determined by the necessity of its nature to

seek to accumulate wealth, is rather determined to get rid of it, and that as quickly as possible. Altogether, examination will show that induction is applicable and applied to one of the two great departments of Political Economy ; that it is not necessary to introduce any arbitrary definition of man into production ; that its truths are concrete, not abstract ; while the propositions of geometry—to which Mr. Mill compares Political Economy— are not strictly true of the lines, circles, and squares to be found in this material world, the propositions of production are perfectly realised wherever wealth is created. Perhaps it was unnecessary to argue the point at such length, for Mr. Mill concedes in his later *Principles* almost all I contend for, and virtually and tacitly limits the sweeping assertions made in his Essays. " The laws and the conditions," he observes in the former, " of the production of wealth partake of the nature of physical truths. There is nothing arbitrary or optional in them."

And here, by the way, one may notice that this conclusion shows the vulnerability of M. Comte's only plausible objection to Political Economy, grounded on the alleged impossibility of an analysis of the economical or industrial phases of society being effected, apart from an analysis of its moral and intellectual phases. In social phenomena there is, according to him, too much solidarity to admit of the study of any special set of facts, such as those connected with wealth ; we must look at the *ensemble.* Comte's criticisms, worthy of the consideration of economists who mix up theory and practice, laws and rules, without duly considering whether their rules are based on purely economical considerations, and valid if he had confined himself to saying that it was absurd to frame rules of conduct out of, and with regard to, economical considerations alone, confound the errors of economists with Political Economy, and his reasoning falls harmlessly on those who, keeping within proper bounds, seek to ascertain only laws and facts without dictating rules, or, at all events, without dictating rules inspired merely by regard to wealth. Granting it right to assert that the analysis of the phenomena of the distribution of wealth was profitless, since it issues, as we shall see, in some case only in conclusions relatively true—though, as Mr. Mill observes, relative truths may be very valuable, and, as Professor Cairnes proves, the grounds on which Mr. Comte objects to the isolation of economical phenomena are fatal to the modes of inquiry pursued in many physical sciences; the objection is neither just nor plausible in the case of the analysis of the phenomena of production, which issue in conclusions absolutely true. Social changes do not change them; social changes do but change the illustrations of them. Moral, intellectual, and political facts obey these laws; and, altogether, perhaps it is doubtful whether there is better reason for beginning with a study of the *ensemble* in the case of production, than in the case of one of its branches —say shoemaking. On the whole, economists may view with equanimity the attacks on their sciences made by Comte. Arguments which would be fatal to the pretensions of geology to rank as a science, are not dangerous; and those who repeat Comte's arguments on this head, ought to question themselves whether every one is bound by his somewhat arbitrary definition of a science.

CHAPTER XVII.

DISTRIBUTION OF WEALTH—(*Continued*).

WHILE men must conform in the creation of wealth to the laws of physical nature, they may distribute it in ways as diverse as their own caprices.   Indeed, it is spread abroad, not in one uniform way, but in several ways, and under the influence of several motives.   Selfishness is often the motive ; so sometimes is self-denial.   To consider only distribution by exchange, one man's rule may always be to sell his goods or his labour in the dearest market ; while another, through misfortune or caprice, contrives to sell them at the moment when they are least wanted.   To the great increase of complexity, the same person may, and generally does, follow one rule at one time, and another rule at another time.   Selfishness, laziness, stupidity, benevolence, are all at work.   With so many causes at work, with such consequent complexity of effects, it is held by most economists that it would be impossible to track out the laws of distribution inductively, and that, if tracked out, they would be too complex to be of use ; so that the only resource left to us, it is said, is to abandon the experimental method and employ the deductive method.*   Since wealth, it is said, is mainly

---

* Mr. Buckle has attempted to show that distribution is determined by physical laws as much as production is.   " In a very early stage of society, and before its later and more refined complications have begun, it may, I think, be proved that the distribution of wealth is, like its creation, governed entirely by physical laws."   Assuming that wealth will be divided between capitalists and labourers, he argues that the question of wages is a question of population, and ultimately one of food and climate.   It would be possible to detect several fallacies in this argument, and in the pragmatic historical conclusions based thereon ; but, on the face of it, the argument is marred by the supposition that " in a very early stage of society " wages and profits are the main modes in which wealth was distributed.   In ancient India, which Mr. Buckle had particularly in view, the distribution of wealth was determined by the degree of security which

distributed in the way of business by persons who desire to gain the utmost at the least cost, let us assume, for the sake of simplicity, they say that the distribution of wealth always takes place by exchange on the part of men always desirous to gain the utmost. The problems are simplified still more by taking into account only civilised nations, and by supposing that the social structure of them all resembles that of England—that everywhere society is made up of three distinct strata—capitalists, landowners, and productive labourers. A state of perfect competition—that is, a state of distribution by exchange on the part of the economist's ideal men—is supposed. " Only through the principle of competition," says Mr. Mill on this point, " has Political Economy any pretension to the character of a science." On the hypothesis that wealth is distributed by exchange among a people ever eager to gain the utmost, and with social arrangements resembling those of England, what will follow ? Such, according to most English economists, is the skeleton of all the problems in distribution. As regards one, and not the least important, part of the science, it was shown in the last chapter that it was unnecessary to suppose a state of perfect competition. We shall now see that it is unnecessary to introduce such a supposition into certain parts of distribution. But, understanding by competition distribution by exchange among people desirous to obtain the utmost on all occasions, let us reflect what Mr. Mill's remark implies. It tells us that Political Economy, the science of wealth, can render no scientific account of the ways of distribution other than by competition, in which wealth has been and is distributed ; that it deals only with the present and a little strip of the past ; that it has nothing precise or very intelligible to say of modes of distribution rife and prominent in great civilisations that preceded ours ; that it is built on a state of things perfectly exemplified only in a small part of Europe and America, in certain towns therein, in certain trades practised in these towns, and by certain members of these trades, and only on certain occasions ; that that which claims to rank in the hierarchy of science is but the theory of English commerce—at widest, the theory of commerce ; and that, if as many thinkers

existed, rather than by the facility with which food is obtainable and the heat of the climate. Probably the distribution of wealth is determined by physical laws, as much as, and not a whit more than, other highly intricate social phenomena.

—thinkers so diverse as Mr. Ruskin, M. Comte, and M. Proudhon—imagine, the "higgling of the market" is not always to
determine wages and prices, the formulæ of the science may re-
cede further from the truth than they now are. To the question, How wealth is distributed? the English economist replies,
"I can tell you how it is distributed by trade. In its length
and breadth I cannot answer your question. 'Tis true, at the
outset I gave you to understand that I would explain how
wealth is distributed in all circumstances—my subject was distribution. But I promised too much." The task was to render
an account of all the great and permanent modes of distribution
intervening between the creation and the destruction of value,
between production and consumption; only a part of this task
has been performed. It is true that Mr. Mill speaks of distribution determined by custom; but to crowd all forms of distribution other than by exchange into a *terra incognita* called
custom, is to carry analysis only a short way. Custom conveniently expresses exchanges by persons who do not, from laziness, ignorance, or good nature, take as much as they could get;
it happily expresses the regulator of the pecuniary dealings of
remote rural societies, in which the utmost gain is not invariably sought, and which are often, historically speaking, a species
of ruined communistic societies, still bearing evidence of their
primitive condition in the fact that no one buys in "the cheapest
market to sell in the dearest;" it would be spoiling a good term
to apply custom to the distribution of wealth by other modes
than exchange. Wherever it is prevalent, it may be well to
suppose that all bargains are transacted by "covetous animals;"
but it is inexpedient to suppose exchange to be where exchange
is not.

If it were not possible or necessary to inquire into modes of
distribution other than exchange, why keep up in books of
Political Economy a distinction between distribution and exchange? Why first treat, as Mr. Mill does, at great length of
the laws of distribution, and then in another book, and also at
great length, of the laws of exchange, when, if exchange be
co-extensive, as is implied, with distribution, the laws of the
one must be the same as the laws of the other, and the second
dissertation be a repetition of the first? No right reason can
be given by economists who consider only one form of distribution; but a right reason can be given by those who think there

are several forms. Economists' theory has been here much better than their practice. They have left a vast blank to be filled, and not without reason. But nobody has taken the trouble to fill it in. A far more accurate view of distribution is that taken by Plato in the *Sophistes*, where it is said that the acquisitive art (ἡ κτητική), the art by which men grow wealthy, the modes by which wealth is distributed, is divided into two parts—one carried on by voluntary interchanges, and the other by force in various shapes. This is an incomplete theory, but it is completer than that of English economists. How far were economists from perceiving the breadth of their science is attested by the fact that it is not long ago since Archbishop Whateley's description of Political Economy as the Science of Exchange passed unchallenged. Here lies a part of Political Economy, on which whoever embarks may almost say, in the words of Dante, "The sea which I sail is untraversed."

Wealth is now mainly distributed by exchange; but in past ages, in rude countries, and in unsettled times, wealth has often been mainly distributed by violence, or in virtue of superiority, resting upon conquest, or, it may be, upon birth. The farther we go back, we see the last two ways towering into importance; the farther we advance, exchange becomes the more potent agent. Behind lies a past dimly discerned through fragments of history or ancient law, or the still more ancient records of language, in which man appears to be little better than a carnivorous animal engaged in nameless and endless wars. Many circumstances conspire to make us incapable of conceiving how large a part on the stage of the world was once played by warfare. Extreme love of life, the growing appreciation of it, from religious, social, and economical causes, and our susceptibility to the pains of others—the first in its existing degree quite as modern as the third feeling—the prevalence of peace, the importance of industry, persuade us that strife and bloodshed, and general insecurity of life, and general exposure to the other horrors of war, could never be but unnatural and occasional; and when it does engage two nations for a few months, when civil war rages for a time, we seem to be witnesses of a moral cataclysm. Yet how different the truth! The ancient and the modern worlds, and, less sharply, the modern and middle ages, are demarcated by the broad fact that in antiquity and mediæval times men lived to fight, and that now they rarely fight

R

save to live. Hence the prominence given to military affairs
by ancient and mediæval historians. Hence the injustice of ex-
patiating on the folly of Thucydides, Livy, Tacitus, and Polybius,
for dwelling on battles, sieges, invasions, and conquests, to the
neglect of the substantial verities of history. These historians
filled their rolls with details of warfare, because it really was
the life of a nation, the great architect of national fortunes,
the supreme educator, at once consuming and unfolding the
energies of a country ; the great instrument of its rise or fall ;
bringing strange races into contact to struggle for mastery
and often existence ; transplanting the religion and habits
of one people to flourish among another ; blending mythologies and languages, blood and traditions ; and thus affecting
man deeply and permanently. When industry was in its
infancy, when it was often merely subsidiary to military
designs, how could historians of antiquity help becoming
merely the historians of the wars of antiquity ?   Apart
from them there was no progress—all stagnation ; and how
treat stagnation historically ? Really, so far as profane history
goes, we appear to be nothing better than tamed hyænas.
Great stress is laid on the rise of Christian and humane feelings,
which check our propensities for strife. They have their weight ;
but the world is habitually peaceful, mainly, perhaps, because
every race " has had it out," and knows its strength. Not the
least, rather the most, important part played by war was as an
agent in distributing wealth ; and, be it observed, this was no
fitful and insignificant action such as we all admit—no action
resembling that of the waves in casting up occasional waifs—
but a steady action, like that of the Nile or Ganges, bearing its
perpetual loads of alluvial matter to the sea. To give due
proofs and illustrations of this is difficult, because the material
is overwhelmingly abundant; and there is a danger of letting it
be understood that the few proofs and illustrations of which
space and patience allow the insertion are conterminous with all
that could be produced. Aware of this danger, and trusting
readers will fill in my suggestions out of their own knowledge,
let us glance at the records of the earliest European society we
are acquainted with. Look at the society depicted in the
Homeric poems, which may be pure fictions so far as Troy and
the wanderings of Ulysses are concerned, but which, nevertheless,
faithfully record manners that once existed, and probably those

of the time of the poet or poets—record them even more instruc-
tively than a history would have done, for ancient poetry, being
more philosophical than ancient history, dealing, like science, with
types, not instances, or rather with scientific or typical instances,
preserves what is general and valuable, and drops what is
particular, exceptional, and interesting only to a few. What
kind of society, then, do the *Iliad* and the *Odyssey* show ?
Piracy a recognised and honourable profession, about which it
is befitting to boast and ask questions ; men trading little and
robbing much ; piracy rife by sea and robbery by land ; plunder
a familiar and well-trodden road to wealth ; war and violence
pursued for the sole purpose of gain. Hybrias, the Cretan,
sings, " My wealth is my long spear and sword. With these I
sow, with these I reap." The spirit of many a turbulent
age is embalmed in these words. Even in the days of historic
Greece, when vulgar piracy was stamped with disapprobation,
it ceased to be a common profession, only to remain a common
crime. Greek history itself is but a tissue of wars, some of
which were potent agents in distributing wealth. To mention
two instances, and to refer only to money :—The Persian
wars led to the scattering of the vast hoards of Pericles ;
the conquests of Alexander scattered the still vaster hoards
of Darius. On a still larger scale was this agency illustrated by the Roman Empire, which is one long instance
of distribution by violence. Greece, Asia, Egypt, and Gaul,
were successively rifled. Cæsar wrung so much out of
the last as to lower the value of gold. At one time
Carthage had to pay a war fine of £600,000 ; at another
time, of £2,000,000. Antiochus was let off with a fine
of £3,000,000. The whole world, to speak in haughty
Roman phrase, gave its neck to the yoke, and tribute to the
conqueror. The wealth of the world flowed in an abundant
stream to Rome, not because it was the centre of trade, but
because it was the residence of force. In one point of view, the
Roman Republic and Empire appear as a gigantic apparatus for
the collection of wealth—the Romans as the tax-gatherers of
Europe, cosmopolitan banditti, men who took to the highways
of a world. When, guided by a few dim lights, we pass out of
the circle of Hellenic and Roman influence, and enter the
encompassing realm of barbarism, we find violence a still more
potent and familiar agent. Consider the enormous sums we

read of as garnered up by ancient Oriental princes, to remain in their treasuries until the hand of a stronger than the owner scattered the accumulations of a lifetime. Consider the oft-noted fact that rude nations, and especially the Orientals of antiquity, have been accustomed to carry as much as possible of their property on their persons, and that immovable property was rare with them. Consider that commerce was so insignificant that one province might be lavishly provided with the precious metals, while in a neighbouring one they might be scarce—that commerce could not have been important, since ancient law gives us glimpses of a time when contract and even individual property were all but unknown, and when *status* determined all a man's life, and joint and often indivisible ownership was rife. As to the Middle Ages, though the industrial *régime* arose in them, though in them we first see large bodies of freemen wholly engaged in peaceful pursuits, war was still rife, and in many places Europe was then almost as unsettled as the society in which Ulysses and Autolycus moved. Kings purloined the property of their subjects, subjects purloined crowns. Owing to plunder and ransoms war was a lucrative pursuit. The Norsemen, a race of thieves, shook thrones and founded others. Kings and nobles stole from each other, and they both combined to sweat the tiller of the soil. The feudal system was itself a military organisation ; and, speaking broadly, the feudal times were times of universal rapine. The two absorbing passions were war and religion, and it was a curious peculiarity of the religion of those times that it was frequently requiring somebody or other to be killed or plundered. Without passing to more modern examples, but considering these facts and not forgetting that the present differs from past times not only in the greater frequency of wars in the latter, but that they were then waged with plunder more directly the object in view, and were effected at less expense to the victor, we shall perhaps acknowledge that violence has been most powerful in distributing wealth, and we shall understand how Aristotle, with his eyes resting on turbulent communities, should have included in the earliest draft of Political Economy war among the ways in which wealth is acquired, and, consequently, among the ways in which it is distributed.*

* Ortolan, in his *History of Roman Law*, says in reference to the early private law, " That which we now call property bore a name very expres-

But we would carry away a dwarfed conception of the magnitude of this agency if we forgot that slaves have ever been acquired mainly by war. They have occasionally, indeed, been bred, but rarely—how rarely in antiquity Hume has shown ; and it is a proof of the dependence of slaveholding on violence that an instance can scarcely be cited in which slaves have kept up their numbers. Prisoners have ever fed the slave-marts ; such supplies as were got through the defaults of debtors or through gambling must have been small. If we include slaves in the estimate of national wealth, the influence of violence in the distribution of wealth is immensely magnified. The point which most conspicuously distinguished the industrial side of antiquity from that of modern society—the circumstance which begat the leading differences between them—was the prevalence of slaveholding in the former. For the ancient slaves did all that machines and much that beasts of burden do for us. Almost all the social arrangements of antiquity presupposed slaves. They performed all work, coarse or delicate, except fighting. Aristotle could no more conceive of a society without them, than we can conceive of a society without labourers. Greek, Roman, Egyptian—in short, all the civilisations of antiquity—were so far alike in exhibiting a fraction of freemen dependent for everything on a body of slaves originally procured and recruited by war. The slave-marts of Rome, Delos, and Chios, fed by a perpetual stream of captives, are the keys to the whole economy of antiquity. And as to more modern nations and times, need we say that, in the first quarter of this century, the colonies of every European power were dependent on slaveholding, that it lately lingered in the colonies of Spain and Portugal, and that, until recently, the staple occupation in one-half of the United States was carried on by slaves whose ancestors had been stolen ? Look where we may, we are reminded that slavery, especially in the view of the economist, is one of the biggest facts in the history of the world, and that the means by which it has, with few exceptions, been sustained, have in no small degree influenced the growth and distribution of wealth.

Let us speak now of another phase of the same agency : War, let us suppose, passes over some people. They are conquered.

sive of the then state of civilisation—*mancipium*, which was applied at the same time to the object of possession and to the power of possession itself (*manu captum*)."

They become the vassals or helots of some such empire as Rome or Persia, and henceforth they pay tribute in kind or in money to foreign rulers. Or a swarm of conquerors settles on the land, as the Mahometans did in India, and the Turks in Eastern Europe ; and for centuries the peasant gives the alien lord part of the produce, and the alien gives in return—nothing. No exchange here, but verily and unfortunately, much distribution. Birth, not conquest, may be the basis of superiority, and the peasant may give of his flock or crop to a chief whom he believes to be a distant relative of some god or demigod, or at least a man of peculiarly fine clay. Nor have we to go back to early times and rude men to discover examples of distribution in virtue of superiority ; all taxation, whether imperial or local, direct or indirect, illustrates this second mode. So also do all laws relating to inheritance. Judgments which determine the destination of wealth, bankruptcy laws, etc., illustrate the vast consequence of this agency. In Great Britain alone, it yearly causes a displacement of about £100,000,000 in the form of imperial and local taxes ; of the amount distributed in virtue of judicial decisions there are no means of judging accurately, but it must be enormous. For our means we are perhaps taxed as lightly as any civilised nation ; in Europe alone it is keeping within reasonable figures to assert that from £800,000,000 to £1,000,000,000 are annually raised by taxation alone ; and, instead of diminishing, this taxation, imperial and local, is growing, by reason of the tendency to widen the province of government—growing so quickly, and assuming such proportions, that complaints are heard to the effect that under a thin disguise the hardship and evils of communism have a prospect of being introduced, for there is hardening into the solidity of a fixed principle the hitherto loosely-held sentiment that the rich and the well-to-do are bound and should be compelled to see to the satisfaction of the chief bodily and mental wants of the poor. War, too, may help to determine the rate of interest, and may permanently raise or depress it in a particular locality. Thus the last war and the consequent indemnity, effecting a permanent displacement of wealth, may lower the rate of interest in Germany as compared with that in France, where previously money had been, on the whole, usually cheaper. And yet of this mode of distribution, now and always important, and destined to be more so, economists who professed to exhaust the subject of distribution have said nothing, or if they have, it has been in defiance of their plan. They had eyes only for distribution by exchange.

I am aware that certain economists have believed something was to be gained by resolving taxation into a species of exchange, and that Governments might be considered as bartering protection and other privileges for taxes. Such is M. Proudhon's view. It may be an instructive comparison—it is so—just as it is instructive to compare, as M. De Girardin does, the State to a gigantic mutual insurance company. But both are comparisons, and nothing more; and it would be as far from the truth to say that a man who was paying income-tax was engaged in bartering and performing his part of a bargain, as it would be to say that he was paying his insurance premium. Taxes have often been, and often are, raised on the plea of superior strength; they do not rise or fall according to the degree of protection and extent of favours accorded; as a matter of fact, taxes were originally in many Eastern countries, and in mediæval Europe, of the nature of gifts. Further, it is essential to the idea of exchange that there should be freedom on both sides; and taxes are of course raised *nolentibus volentibus.* Reciprocity between Governments and subjects is always a duty, no doubt, but not always a fact, and it is, moreover, not easy to ascertain when reciprocity is a fact. To resolve instances of distribution by taxation into exchange is similar to the behaviour of a jurist or moralist who should resolve all obligations into contracts. All tribute being a mere variety of taxation, of course illustrates this second method of distribution; and hence we see that it includes much of the so-called commerce of antiquity. The great corn trade of Rome, on which the Romans latterly depended for subsistence, was really no trade at all, for the corn fleets bore to Ostia, as a rule, only the tithes of Sicily and Sardinia, and the produce of Egypt, the imperial property. The second method of distribution includes also rent, as it was and is to be found in certain societies—not certainly rent as it is exemplified in a civilised nation, where it is a 'bargain, a process of exchange, the cultivator giving a certain sum for the use of the soil, but rent as it is exemplified in many Asiatic countries, where it is of the nature of a tax.

We now come to another great mode of distribution, also ignored by economists, or treated of as extraneous. Forgetting that their task was not accomplished until they had enumerated all the modes of distribution which intervene between the creation of value and the destruction of it, they have almost forgotten distribution in virtue of superiority, and they have usually ignored a third sort of distribution well demarcated. The two first methods are exhibited in virtue of our selfish instincts; but the theory of distribution would not be complete if we did not take cognisance of the vast influence which our unselfish passions exercise in distributing wealth. The "homo" of the economists is a being who never parts with anything without an equivalent; the "homo" of reality is a being not averse to charity, and with dependants, related to him or not, on whom he lavishes his wealth. How little, after all, any man can *himself* consume! The throat is after all but an inch or so wide— the world would have been revolutionised if its compass had been a quarter of an inch more! It is the dependants of the wealthy man that actually consume his substance. Reflecting that all charitable gifts, amounting yearly to many millions, all bequests, also amounting to many millions, and all distribution effected through ties of blood, come under this category, we shall discern that this third mode is as important as it is well defined.

The modes of Distribution are, then, these :—

(1.) Distribution by Exchange.

(2.) Distribution in virtue of Superiority, or Involuntary Distribution without an equivalent, or Ablative Distribution (including distribution by open violence, and by force embodied in law).

(3.) Distribution by Gift, or Voluntary Distribution, without an equivalent, or Donative Distribution.

These are the chief modes; but jurisprudence has always recognised two other modes—the acquisition of property in virtue of prescription, and the fact that the accessory follows the principle. In a complete treatise of Political Economy, the former might deserve consideration, and it would be interesting to point out the economical bearings of the various usages and laws determining the change of common property into private, or the reverse, and to criticise the terms of prescription fixed upon at a time when communication was imperfect and advertising was unknown. It would also be interesting to trace the economical history of the second principle, and to show how frequently, in virtue of it, or the kindred legal doctrine of fixtures, people have been, and still are, deprived of their labour and work. But both subjects must be eliminated from these outlines.

I anticipate the remark pretty sure to be made, that the so-called ablative and donative distribution answer to the Consumption of certain economists. This department, added to the science by Say, covers, it will be said, the same field of facts as the above departments, and it is needless to apply new names to things already designated. Now, the consumption of Mr. M'Culloch, the *consommation* of Say, comprehends and includes more than the above, and looks at the same facts from a different point of view ; while it describes the various modes in which value is destroyed, and treats of productive and unproductive expenditure, these departments, dealing with purely economical facts, and relegating to production the consideration of productive and unproductive expenditure, treat of the modes of distribution which precede the 'destruction of value. If I may be permitted to express any opinion upon a point respecting which great authorities are at variance, I think that Turgot, Rossi, and Mr. John Stuart Mill, are right in their belief that Political Economy consists of two great divisions, Production and Distribution. A tolerably well-defined science becomes an amorphous mass of nondescript discussions when its boundaries are enlarged so as to include the consumption of wealth. But those who introduced and have maintained the division of Consumption, had in view a real deficiency in the theory of distribution—they did not rightly fill the gap.

As to the theory of distribution developed so lucidly by Mr. Mill, and generally adopted in England, it may be observed that, with the single exception of Ricardo's writings, there would, were this theory strictly true, be scarcely one work of Political Economy, strictly so-called, extant. The *Wealth of Nations*, subjected to the above test, would fail to be enrolled as a work of Political Economy. Moreover, as regards one portion of the science, the province of taxation, unquestionably all writers have set themselves to investigate and expound the modes in which revenue ought to be raised. They have, as a rule, enunciated certain general propositions embodying their ideas of what is just, and they have systematised the diverse phenomena of taxation by grouping the facts round these rules. In fact, no writer ever consistently regarded Political Economy as a short mode of arriving at social statistics. Further, with respect to the phenomena of exchange, it cannot but be felt that the results to be obtained from a purely deductive treatment of wages or rent, for example, are often meagre, and utterly wide of the truth. Nor can there be much assurance that the results obtainable from the deductive mode of investigation will in course of time approximate nearer and nearer to reality. The accumulation of disturbing causes, such as Government loans of vast amount, the constant increase of inherited wealth, and the continued existence, perhaps augmentation, of a class proof against the motives of pecuniary gain, and open to other passions, materially and perhaps permanently mar the operation of mere selfishness to a degree which, unfortunately for the deductive mode of treatment, cannot be accurately calculated. It would be rash, for instance, to pronounce any opinion upon the question whether the chief of the four elementary propositions upon which Mr. Senior bases the science—that every man desires to obtain additional wealth with as little sacrifice as possible—approaches closer and closer to reality. It is also a circumstance which hinders considerably profitable investigation of economical phenomena, on the hypothetical method, that different systems of law have taken up various proportions of ethics, or have been built upon different ethical creeds, and that they may permanently retain their differences. No two systems of law agree as to what is fraud, and as to the circumstances which nullify contracts. The prætorian equity of Rome did not answer to the Chancellor's equity in England. Who knows by what equitable rules our law and freedom of contract may not yet be tempered, and whether *caveat venditor* may not replace *caveat emptor*? The limitations to the rule of buying in the cheapest and selling in the dearest market may multiply.

CHAPTER XVIII.

VALUE.

" ALL discussions are dull—a discussion on value dullest of all "
—under cover of this axiom of Frederic Bastiat, I would
endeavour to state what are the laws of value. These laws, if
such they can be called, are the explanation of the distribution
of wealth by exchange. These stated, the laws of wages, profits,
and rent, should be implicitly stated also. The complete theory
of value is the complete theory of distribution by exchange;
perhaps it is scarcely accurate to say, as Mr. Mill does, that the
consideration of value has to do with the distribution of wealth
" only so far as competition, and not usage or custom, is the distributing agency," for every instance of exchange, be it in virtue
of competition or usage, presupposes a valuation of the articles
exchanged, though it may be possible to ̦treat distribution by
exchange scientifically only when competition regulates it. In
endeavouring to arrive at true ideas respecting value, it is well
to profit by the labours of so many predecessors, even when they
do not happen to be strictly correct in their conclusions. It is
good to make of errors a bridge to the truth ; one learns the safe
course by marking the scenes of shipwrecks ; and, next to seeing
one's own errors pointed out, the best way to grave a truth in
one's mind is to see the encompassing mistakes of others marked
out. And one of the first errors which meets the inquirer into
the nature of value consists of the idea to which Mr. Patrick
Edward Dove gives expression, that value cannot be defined, and
that attempts to define it must issue in spurious definitions.
Now, why this alleged impossibility ? Have we not major con-
cepts that include the concept of value ? Far from being most
rudimentary, is it not rather complex and composite ? Is not
value a particular kind of mental judgment ? May we not define
it to be the comparative estimate of articles of wealth ? If this

be correct, the next step is to ascertain whether value rises and falls according to ascertainable laws, or whether its movements are capricious and wholly incalculable. The common answer is, that there is here no caprice ; and that value depends on the supply of articles and the demand for them. But it has often been objected that the latter part of this statement wants precision ; and, consequently, this formula has been changed for one which runs thus : The value of an article depends on the quantity supplied and the quantity demanded. "Depends" is vague. How depends ? A common answer given to this further question is, that value rises or falls precisely in the ratio of the supply of articles to the demand. This answer, however, is more precise than accurate. Obvious facts start up to contradict it. For example, supposing a harvest were deficient by one-fourth, prices would not, if there was no residue of the crops of former years and no importation, rise merely one-fourth; they might rise five, six, or ten fold.

Mr. John Stuart Mill, rejecting on these obvious and unassailable grounds this formula, has laid it down that the value of an article must be such that the supply of the article shall be equal to the articles demanded ; the demand must carry off the supply ; the true mathematical idea is an equation, not a ratio. "Demand and supply, the quantity demanded and the quantity supplied, will be made equal." "This, then," he adds, "is the law of value with respect to all commodities not susceptible of being multiplied at pleasure. Such commodities, no doubt, are exceptions. There is another law for the much larger class of things which admit of indefinite multiplication." What is the other law here referred to ? "In all things which admit of indefinite multiplication, demand and supply only determine the perturbations of value, during a period which cannot exceed the length of time necessary for altering the supply. While thus ruling the oscillations of value,. they themselves obey a superior force, which makes value gravitate towards cost of production, and which would settle it and keep it there, if fresh disturbing influences were not continually arising to make it again deviate." It is with diffidence that I offer any criticisms on Mr. Mill's theory ; but I venture to point out one or two apparent, or it may be real, flaws. It is an obvious, though perhaps not a superfluous observation, that we are left without a general theory of value which should state the condition determining the value of all articles, be they limited or capable of indefinite increase. Cannot these two principles be resolved into one ? Until they are so, a presiding law of value is wanting. We hear of two laws controlling the different species of wealth, and the one law is contrasted with the other. Supply and demand, it is said, do not determine the value of things which can be increased at pleasure, or if they do so only temporarily; on the contrary, supply and demand are governed by the cost of production. But cost of production is subsequently resolved into wages and profits; and as profits depend upon wages, and wages ultimately upon the supply of and the demand for labour, it follows that the value of articles capable of being indefinitely increased depends on supply and demand, and that the two classes differ only to the extent of the value of the one being determined by the supply of and the demand for themselves, and the other by the supply of and demand for the labour necessary to produce them. Further, when it is affirmed that the value of the latter depends upon cost of production, what is meant is, that sellers will not permanently produce such articles unless they are repaid with due profit, and that purchasers will not continue to buy them at a higher price than such as is necessary to repay the producers with ordinary profits; and this is equivalent to saying that the supply and the demand will tend to abate if these conditions are not realised. The seller does not exact much more than the cost of production, because the demand might fall off; the purchaser does not refuse to pay so much, because the supply might abate. It is the estimate or prospect of supply and demand which rules the value of such articles; and it is the same which rules the price of articles incapable of being indefinitely increased. In short, the theory of demand and supply is the general theory of which the other theory is a particular instance. It is true that in the case of the latter the actual amount in the market and the amount which could be brought into the market are sometimes identical. But this is not always the case; and the price of a water-colour by Turner is controlled by the fact that were it raised beyond a certain figure there would be no demand for it, and that similar pictures not for sale would be brought into the market. It may also be shown, from the very nature of value, that supply and demand must be the ultimate regulators of all articles of wealth. To value in exchange two conditions are necessary. An article must be in demand, and it must be more or less difficult of attainment; and according to the degree of utility and the difficulty in its attainment will be its value in exchange. Now, demand is nothing else than the current estimation of utility, and supply is a more or less perfect measure of the difficulty of attainment. The existing supply is, indeed, an imperfect measure of difficulty of attainment. But the prospective supply satisfactorily fulfils every condition of a perfect measure of difficulty of attainment, and I apprehend that economists meant by supply, not the actual quantity of articles in the market or in warehouses, but the quantity that could be exposed for sale within a limited time. Certainly that is Mr. Mill's meaning, for he speaks of supply as "the existing or expected supply." Give, then, to demand and supply this meaning—make them the measures of utility and difficulty of attainment—and the value of all commodities, be they capable of indefinite increase or not, is determined by supply and demand.

Instead of the value of freely produced commodities depending upon supply and demand, supply and demand, says Mr. Mill, depend upon cost of production; but supposing it to be true that cost of production determines the supply and demand, that would not exclude the useful doctrine that they are the proximate regulators of the value of all things. It appears to me that Mr. Mill's contrast is somewhat false. In supply, I apprehend, are included all those considerations bearing upon the actual or possible scarcity of an article which influence the mind in valuing it; and by demand, we mean either the quantity demanded or some inherent or acquired liking influencing our valuations. Now, far from contrasting supply and demand with cost of production, we should merely say that in certain cases cost of production forms one of the considerations summed up in the term supply. Cost of production, in short, instead of being contrasted with the first law, ought to be regarded as an instance of it.

In reference to his equalisation theory, the most novel portion of his exposition of the laws of value, Mr. Mill has admitted, with honourable and characteristic candour, that it sometimes fails. Besides those cases in which it is physically impossible for the quantity supplied and the quantity demanded at a given price to be equalised, labour affords us striking and frequent illustrations of the failure of this equalisation theory. Indeed, we may affirm that it is a permanent characteristic of many kinds of labour that this theory fails with respect to them in two respects. The demand at a certain price never takes off the quantity offered at that price, and the theory may be realised with different prices. The experience of most advertisers for unskilled workmen is, that scores offer themselves for each situation, and that the demand frequently fails to carry off a twentieth part of the supply. So far as certain trades are concerned, the rarity is to see the equalisation theory realised, even with the fullest competition. Aware that when his wages fall below a certain figure the workman's labour may become positively unremunerative, compelled by the nature of his business to employ a certain number or a certain proportion of workmen, or knowing that the demand for his commodities is defined, the most avaricious employer may not on account of the redundancy of hands reduce wages to such a figure that the supply shall carry off the new demand, or seize the opportunity of a dearth of employment to obtain two men at the former price of one. With the poor-house at his back, or, as is the case in America, with the certainty of obtaining a large tract of land whenever he chooses, or with a plot of ground to retreat to, as is often the case with the French agricultural labourer, the unemployed workman may not indefinitely undersell his fellow workman; for ten situations at 13s. a week, twenty may offer themselves, while not one may consent to accept the employment at a farthing less. Mr. Mill contrasts this equalisation theory with the popular statement that the value depends on the ratio between the supply and demand; and certainly there exists between these two doctrines the contrast always existing between what is frequently true and what is unmeaning. But here the contrast stops; the former is proffered as an answer to a question utterly different from that which the latter tries to solve. The popular theory attempts to explain why a certain value or price is attached to a certain article; the other theory states what is the *status quo* when a particular value or price is determined upon. The one offers a history of the circumstances that precede a sale; the other states the circumstances simultaneous with a sale, it being clear that this equalisation was preceded and caused by changes in the demand, and the estimate formed of the supply. The former attempts, however unsatisfactorily, to explain how the valuations of the two parties essential to, and involved in, a sale are made ; the latter states, with not complete accuracy, that a sale takes place when the two parties respectively supply and demand the same quantity. There is nothing in the equalisation theory to permit us to speak of it—though some writers have done—as determining price or value ; it imperfectly describes the essentials of a sale ; it does not tell why a particular price was hit upon by both parties.

In common with many economists, Ricardo maintains that labour is the foundation of all value, and that the relative quantities of labour expended on them determine the relative values of commodities. Stating his position in other words, I may say that, with the exception of commodities, the value of which is determined by their scarcity, the quantity of labour realised in commodities regulates their exchangeable value ; every increase of the quantity of labour augmenting the value of the commodity on which it is exercised, every diminution lowering it. To this position several objections may be taken. In the first place, it is not perfectly accurate to affirm that the "foundation" or "ground" of value is labour ; one might as well affirm that the source or foundation of all value is utility ; if value cannot exist without the former, neither can it exist without the latter. Then the theory does not include articles incapable of being increased at pleasure, and, right or wrong, the theory is therefore incomplete. Further, it is to be observed that labour itself is a commodity possessing exchangeable value. It is, moreover, a commodity capable of being indefinitely increased in a short period ; at all events, it is not one of those commodities "the value of which is determined by their scarcity alone;" and when Ricardo speaks of labour as "being the foundation of all value, and the relative quantity of labour as determining the relative value of commodities," we are left in doubt whether labour, "the foundation of all value," is the foundation of its own value—in ignorance of the determinant of the value of labour itself, certainly not one of those commodities the production of which is of necessity circumscribed. It is true that he

tells us that the price of labour is determined by the food, clothing, and other articles given for it; but this method of measure-
ment differs from that adopted in measuring the values of other
commodities. Logically, he was bound to deny—as Proudhon,
a holder of the same premises, does—that labour has any
value. Further, this term labour, used as if it denoted some
well-defined and homogeneous thing, is in reality a meaningless abstraction, until the quality of it is known. Labour,
the foundation of all value ! Whose labour ? On this head
Ricardo observes, in a not very satisfactory manner, " The
estimation in which different qualities of labour are held comes
soon to be adjusted in the market with sufficient precision for
all practical purposes, and depends much on the comparative
skill of the labourer, and intensity of labour performed. The
scale, when once formed, is liable to little variation." Here,
it appears, on Mr. Ricardo's own showing, and without insisting
upon the fact that the relative difficulty of certain kinds of
labour will ever be a moot-point, that the foundation of all
value is not labour, but the principle, whatever it may be,
which presides over the formation of this scale. Again, he
acknowledges that his principle, true of only a certain class of
commodities, is true of that class only in certain circumstances ;
for he admits that it is modified by the employment of capital
of unequal degrees of durability. Hence another deficiency in
the Ricardian theory of value.*

Let us, profiting by the discoveries and errors of others, endeavour to arrive at a satisfactory theory of the nature of value,
and of the laws that control its movements. And at the outset
I would say that the result will be modest ; little more will be
proved than that the precision and symmetry often obtained are
delusive. It is necessary to distinguish value, in the sense of

---

* Some of Mr. Ricardo's commentators and disciples have altered his
doctrine for the worse. Thus Mr. De Quincey teaches that Ricardo's theory
of value is compatible with that logical impossibility, a universal rise in
value. In "The Templars' Dialogues," one of the two novices asks, "On
Mr. Ricardo's principle, will not all things double their value simultaneously,
if the quantity of labour spent in producing all should double simultaneously ?" The dialogue continues thus : " *X.*—It will, Phædrus. *Phæd.*—
And yet nothing will exchange for more or less than before. *X.*—True ;
but the rise is not ideal for all that, but will affect everybody." This
singular proposition originates in a confusion between so-called real value
and exchangeable value.

S

general purchasing power, from value in the sense of power to purchase a definite commodity; and it will be well to consider the latter in the first place. In a certain sense the value of a commodity, or its power to purchase another commodity, depends solely on the demand of the owner or owners of the latter, or, in other words, on value in use in the widest acceptation of the term : that corn fetches twice as much gold or silver as it formerly fetched is due to the doubling of the demand of the owners of the latter. Of course, when we speak of purchasing power, that implies the demand of possible purchasers—effective demand is in view. This liking or demand, however, is a complex mental state produced by more than one cause. Were all kinds of wealth equally common, they would be valued according to the gratification they gave. Utility would be the measure of value ; value in use would be synonymous with value in exchange ; our appetites and wants would form a scale of value. But as commodities vary in difficulty of attainment, and as we prize that which is common less than that which is rare, these circumstances affect our judgments of the values of commodities, and we come to esteem them according as they are useful and difficult to obtain. The value of one commodity as compared with another, or its power to purchase that other commodity, will depend upon the opinion formed by the owner of the latter as to the utility and scarcity of the former. Analysing these determinants, we shall of course find generally that the purchaser's estimation of difficulty of attainment is measured by the quantity of labour that was actually spent upon the commodity—in other words, that Ricardo is generally right. Sometimes, however, the measure may be not that, but the labour that would be required to produce its like. The actual supply, or the number of articles in existence, is also generally a measure of difficulty of attainment. But not always : all of them may not be exposed for sale ; they may be incapable of being obtained at the hour fixed for consumption ; or their existence may be unknown to the valuator. Though perhaps all the influences acting on his mind in forming an opinion may be comprehended under the terms supply and demand, which are ways of looking at the rarity and utility of an article, every person will not be guided by precisely the same considerations. Peculiarities of temperament, individual likings, the urgencies of one's circumstances, will come into play ; and in the estimates of the supply one person will include that which another will exclude. There has been a very natural desire on the part of economists to put into mathematical shape the operation of the causes which lead one to form comparative estimates of value. The temptation has been peculiarly strong, because one of these causes, difficulty of attainment, can sometimes be mathematically expressed. Not indeed always. But even if it could always be so expressed, a further difficulty bars the way ; when one had learned the actual supply, one could not calculate with certainty what impression it would produce on the mind. Then, too, our appetites obey no laws capable of being numerically expressed ; consequently, demand and its workings are in the same position. From this it is an easy inference to the allegation that attempts to express by mathematical formulæ the movements of value must fail. A complete theory of value should enumerate the circumstances operating on the mind, and state with numerical precision the law of their influence. No theory of value does so. All the theories of value fail, for example, to enable one to predict the variations in the Stock Exchange of the prices of securities, of all things most ruled by considerations of pure gain. We ask for the means of discovering the value or price of anything : we are directed to means which can be got at only when the value or price is known. I know of a key, say economists, that will unlock the door ; but, by the way, the key hangs on a peg in the locked room. For example, it is stated that wages depend on the amount of capital and the number of the population ; but soon it is discovered that the former varies with the price of labour. These certainly are moderate results—that the value of commodities depends on the comparative strength of our likings, and these on our native passions and difficulty of attainment, and that the same quantities of labour will, as a rule, be exchanged. But is much more truth to be found in the so-called laws which writers have often set forth with much typographical pomp ? It is not altogether wonderful that men like Proudhon, and the founders of the " equitable villages," in the United States, find- ing no useful results obtainable from all this, have proceeded to reason on the assumption that wealth is distributed as it ought to be—that the same quantity of labour always purchases its like.

It is possible, indeed, in a number of instances, to impart

greater precision to the subject. The great majority of articles
are exchanged with a view to profit, and the condition of almost
every bargain is that the producer or owner receives at least as
much as he laid out—in other words, that the price cannot fall
below the cost of production—and that the buyer will not give
more than the labour which the possession of the article would
save him. In the long run, and to induce him to supply the
market, the producer must receive in addition the ordinary rate
of profit. Between these two extremes value fluctuates in the
generality of cases. But there are instances in which there is
an overflow of one of these banks ; and it behoves us to know
the circumstances and cases. Prices may fall below the cost of
production when the same or similar articles are produced by a less
amount of labour than formerly; such is the fate of men who possess a stock of hand-made goods, and who suddenly find themselves competing against an influx of machine-made goods. There
is another no less interesting and far less noticed group of cases in
which the value sinks below the cost of production. Literature,
so much of the work of which is executed by amateurs, or by
those who are moved to write by a thirst for fame, furnishes
numerous and daily instances of men selling the garnered results
of years of conscious toil and unconscious experiences for a mere
handful of coppers. What labour every good work of literature
implies ! It is coming to be recognised as a fundamental principle of literary criticism that literary artists can sell only their
own experience, that each line in their works is the memorial
of some sight or sound in their lives, that so-called creation is
really combination, and that the mind is incapable of doing more
than moving its stock of impressions, even as the hand is
incapable of doing more than moving matter. And if this is
so, if the artist sells nothing which he has not extracted
from books or life, what cost, in no metaphorical sense of the
word, does each work of literature represent ! If a good poem or a
novel requires as solid a basis of preparation as a history requires,
if each felicitous expression or thought is the result of some
mental exertion in the past, what gold shall recompense a
Milton or a Thackeray ? Milton got £10 for the *Paradise Lost ;*
and yet that work could have been accomplished only by one
who had perused costly books, made costly journeys and sojourns,
informed himself on the spot with respect to typographical details,
observed and lived the life of the gentleman of his time, and who

had been a cosmopolitan in manners and literature. To employ a somewhat vulgar word, and to associate somewhat vulgar ideas with a work of art, the outlay must have been immense. Still more obviously in the case of historians does value often fall permanently below the cost of production; the outlay involved in searching through libraries and purchasing manuscripts is still more palpable. His liability to loss is heightened by the fact that the historian cannot act like the manufacturer, who, finding a particular pattern distasteful, ceases to produce it—in the very title of his first volume, the former deposits with the public a sort of promise to accomplish, if life and health are given him, a certain amount of work, be his reward great or small, or none. Pecuniary loss is often the fate of books that are written by those who are in advance of their time. Contemporaries with us in body, they live, perhaps, in spirit among another generation, and, one might say, citizens of the future exiled to the present, they refuse to accept the ennobling crown from the hands of the strangers among whom they dwell; they comfort themselves with the hope that their harvest will ripen when the harvests of those who sowed by the highways have withered; they write for posterity; and unfortunately posterity cannot pay its friends with gold. Hear what M. Villiaumé, a distinguished French writer, says on this subject :—" I knew an artist who, having created immortal works of art up to the age fifty-five, was not certain of having bread the following year; he died at the age of seventy, with the artistic world filled with his name, and his family almost destitute. Nevertheless, his tastes and his style of living had always been extremely simple. Another of my friends, one of the most vigorous and brilliant writers of this century, author of a great number of books devoured by the public, had, having always lived with rustic simplicity, earned only £2000 in twenty years of a laborious existence. And the fact is that, before a good book can be submitted to the public, sometimes ten years of preparation are required, and during that time a man is little inclined to follow lucrative pursuits. In 1847, Lamennais told me that by working every day assiduously he could barely make £60 a year. I have seen recognised men of letters, useful writers, spend their life in meditation, to find themselves, in their old age, in spite of their always living soberly, in a condition bordering on misery. Some of them, it is said, have died of misery, or gone mad through despair, not choosing to prostitute their pen." Though these words are charged with exaggeration, and though they rhetorically conceal the many who find in their lifetime an audience that gives them bread in abundance without asking for flattery in return, they contain enough of truth to prove that the man of letters often sells his goods below the cost of their production, and to set one reflecting whether literature can be pursued as a profession, without injury to literature, the man of letters, and the public. The present arrangement may be the best possible; certainly if the only alternative were that system of patronage to which Dryden prostituted himself, and against which Johnson revolted, we should cherish the present arrangement, and be thankful that we live in times in which a man may be an author without first lying voluminously in prose or verse.

A third group of cases in which value often falls below the cost of production, is to be found in certain other kinds of wages. Each man is a machine, which requires a considerable expenditure to produce; but, as a man must live, he is often obliged to sell his labour considerably below what would be compensation for the outlay upon him. Taking the legal profession as a whole, and striking an average of the incomes, we should probably find that among advocates and barristers the remuneration is permanently below the cost of production.

Recapitulating the theory of value, we may state that it is determined by the estimated supply of articles and the demand for them among people who possess other articles of value; and that the value oscillates between the buyer's basis (labour saved to him) and the seller's basis (cost of production). The buyer starting from one basis and the seller starting from another basis, either giving, in the parlance of the Stock Exchange, an order "with a limit," move up and down until they meet. Altogether the adjustment of the price is of the nature of an experiment; between the two terms there is a debatable land; the precise point at which the pleasure of the one will square with that of the other can be discovered only by trial. ·

It is instructive to observe—if only to be warned of the peril of talking about "inexorable" or "unalterable" laws in this connection—how much it depends on almost fortuitous circumstances at what point a sale will take place. If the owner of a commodity is a monopolist, the value in that commodity of another will be the lowest capable of inducing the owners of the latter to sell; create competitors, and it may be the highest consistent with a profit to the owners of the former. *Cæteris paribus*, the party that can hold out longest will fare best; hence the advantage of the capitalist over the labourer. Choose a Dutch auction, and you may obtain one price; choose the English method, and you may get another.

There has been much controversy respecting the possibility of obtaining a measure of value, and various commodities have been named as conforming to the requirements of such a measure. In one point of view, as Mr. Bailey observes, every commodity may be a measure of value. If we know the relation of value existing between A and B, and the relation of value existing between B and C, B acts as a measure, enabling us to determine the relation existing between A and C. Again, when we wish to ascertain whether the relation of value between two commodities has changed, we are enabled to do so, by the medium of any article. Let A purchase B last year, and 2 B this year; the value of A in B has doubled, whatever the commodities be. But, not satisfied with this knowledge, economists have endeavoured to discover some commodity which, never varying in value itself, should always enable them to determine the causes of the fluctuations in the value of other articles. Such a commodity they have erroneously called a measure of value. Of course, it is not to be had. Corn or labour has indeed been suggested; but it is clear that other commodities could not rise or fall in value without corn and labour falling or rising, even supposing they were always produced under the same circumstances. What is rational in this inquiry is the search for some commodity which, produced by a constant quantity of labour, would consequently, supposing labour to be the sole cause of value, enable one to say in what commodities fluctuations of value originated. Though there is nothing self-destructive in the idea of such a commodity, as a matter of fact, owing to the constant variations in industrial skill, and the varying quantity of raw materials, no such commodity exists. Moreover, such a commodity would not decisively show that alterations in value originated in other commodities and not in it, because, even if produced by a constant quantity of labour, it might fluctuate in demand, owing to fluctuations in men's desires; and, consequently, to be sure that the causes disturbing value did not originate in it, we must assume that this commodity was produced by a constant quantity of labour in order to satisfy a constant demand. And, as Mr. Bailey has pointed out, every purpose which would be served by the possession of such a commodity would be equally well served had we a commodity produced by quantities of labour varying according to a fixed law ; and it may be added that the difficulty of ascertaining the constancy of the cost of production would probably be as great as that experienced at present in inquiring, without the aid of this so-called " measure," into the causes that affect values. The attempt to discover a measure of value in the sense combated above, is then vain. And yet, admitting the futility of this attempt, economists have tried to discover articles which approximately satisfied the conditions necessary to such a measure of value, and not a few have submitted that money is the closest approximation ; the truth being that all articles are equally near to, or, as one may say, equally far from being, a measure of value. The sole difference is that some tell with more accuracy than others— and money with most accuracy—where fluctuations in value originate. If the price of any article rise, one is tolerably sure that the cause is not in gold, but in the article for which it is exchanged.

CHAPTER XIX.

WAGES.

In treating of the distribution of wealth by exchange, we have to consider what is given for certain kinds of services—what is given for actual services (wages); what for the use of money or currency, or capital generally (interest); what for the use of land for a certain period (rent or hire).

This Chapter treats of the sale of services or wages. At present, they are one of the leading modes in which wealth is distributed in virtue of exchange. They have long been so. I do not hastily add that they must ever continue so, because there is a widely-diffused and firmly-held conviction that wages, a wage-receiving and a wage-dependent class, are transient phenomena, that they are evils to be temporarily tolerated because temporarily necessary, and because an advance on the condition which preceded them, and a stepping-stone to higher things. Perhaps I do not distort this conviction, though it is hard to state accurately in full that which is usually a latent postulate, when I say that many believe that they can discern in history a movement against which resisting nations and races must be wrecked, bearing away this social phase; that as slavery, in fulness of time, and when mankind had been broken to labour, was supplanted by serfage, and as serfage, when it had run its course, was abolished to leave men free to work as they pleased, so those who are now free in name, but in very truth the slaves of poverty, the mere tools of capitalists, will become free in fact; and that a condition in which a large portion of mankind are commodities bought and sold as bricks or logs, chained by their necessities, as once by law, to the soil, cannot be a permanent fact. This, it is said, is the divine drama, in which all the ages have played their parts; the drama, these social prophets add, is not completed, but we know what will be the happy outcome. "Having overthrown slavery," says Mr. Horace Greeley, "we must gradually outgrow the ineradicable vices of the wages system." And these vices are, in his opinion, the helplessness of the wage-receiver, a constant temptation to scamp his work, the hostility bred between him and the capitalist, and the rude approximation to justice which is possible under this system. The relation of the employer and servant is, it is said, a leonine relation. The truth contained in this denunciation and prophecy, founded on inference, perhaps not the least trustworthy kind of prophecy, will be discovered if we recollect that these evils and this transitoriness predicated of wages do not hold good of those who receive high wages for work that cannot be renumerated in any other way. The physician, the barrister, the judge, draw wages. That may be transitory which involves misery; but there is in these cases no sign of misery or abject dependence. Here there is no "humiliating oppression." Mr. Horace Greeley looks to the substitution of "association" or co-operation. But how apply co-operation to the bench? These prophecies and denunciations of wages must be pruned and trimmed; they are feasible only when those that utter them are satisfied with maintaining that it cannot be the fate of a large part of the human race to have nothing in this world but their muscles to sell. Here we reach more solid ground, as considerations previously submitted showed. That which most already possess, it is not utopian to expect that all will yet possess. Why should many millions for ever remain living from hand to mouth, not able to see six loaves ahead? Why should they for ever remain destitute of property on which to fall back when work is scarce? No physical obstacle bars the way. Turgot affirms that the workman must fail to get more than necessaries; whence this necessity? So much has been conquered; every man has got clothes of some sort; by and by it may become not rarer to meet a man without a coat than one without savings, and the total absence of capital of some sort may yet be held as complete a proof of incapacity for governing oneself as the total absence of the former. This language sounds utopian only if we look for the advent of these things in the near future, and if we suffer despair to set in when a few paltry centuries pass, and all is not fulfilled. In 1790 Barère presented to the French Convention a report on mendicancy and pauperism, in which he said that "the Convention ought to efface the word 'poor' from the annals of the Republic," and "make indigence disappear." Some economists expect like miracles of expedition. As if national vices could be blotted out like window spots with a few rubs! We allow a week for the cleansing of a village gutter, and we grudge a few centuries for the regeneration of a race. Here lapse of time must not pass for demonstrated impossibility, nor must failures discourage us. If we think of the ages that have gone without poverty being effaced, think also of the ages we may expect to come. And "years," as the Persian proverb has it, "are the father of miracles." Import into human affairs those sobering ideas of time which geology has taught us. The record of what humanity once was is the prophecy of what it shall yet be, the earnest of the blessings that are entailed upon it. When half mankind is concerned about luxuries, the time when the other half shall cease to be concerned about bare necessaries cannot be infinitely distant. Some, if they do not doubt, despise, that time; they sneer at the millennium, "when the earth shall be full of bacon." But those who, from an exceedingly high standpoint, bid us not make a fuss about hunger, are perhaps unworthy of being answered.

We pass to the theory of wages. According to one statement of it, wages depend on the amount of capital and the number of the population of a country. This opinion is mentioned only to be rejected, in the first place, because many things forming capital—such, for example, as the amount of land under cultivation, workshops, machines, beasts of burthen, etc.—do not necessarily tend to increase wages, but in some cases, temporarily at least, tend to decrease them; secondly, because population may increase without any decrease in wages, supposing the increase is among women, and others who do not usually work for hire. The next shape which the theory takes is that wages depend on the relation between the circulating capital and the labouring classes. This, though nearer the truth, is also inaccurate; for, to mention only one point, it leaves out of account the fact that the Lord Chancellor, not less than any bricklayer, receives wages, that the wages of the former must be considered as well as the latter, and that, as a matter of fact, fixed capital as well as circulating capital may enter into wages. A workman or servant receives his wages or salary in the form of money; but this money is transmuted into various articles, only a part of which may be

circulating capital. His 15s. or £15 a week may be spent in buying food, but it may be partly expended in buying a spade, or a
plot of ground, or a carriage, or a new office. Perceiving these, or
some of these, objections, some economists have altered the
mode of stating the doctrine, and have said that wages depend
on the ratio of the population to the wages fund. By the
wages fund they understand all that is given in exchange for
productive labour. Certainly wages are so dependent, but to
suppose that there is any fixedness in this amount, as the term
wages fund would imply, is to harbour a delusion. If fixedness is implied in the term wages fund, there is no more a
wages fund than there is a clothing fund, or a food fund, or a
beer or a tea fund ; it is no more the case that society pays, as
it is nowise more necessary that it should pay, a defined amount
for labour than that it pays a defined amount for sweetmeats.
Every employer of labour has the option of employing little or
much ; few always employ the same amount ; and what is true
of each is true of the aggregate. Mr. Baxter computes that the
10,961,000 manual labourers in the United Kingdom receive
among them an income of £334,645,000; but that income may
be increased or it may be diminished. Yet Mr. M'Culloch and
many other writers spoke of a certain amount of wealth being
"annually appropriated" to the maintenance of labour, as if
employers, imitating the Chancellor of the Exchequer, voted so
much at the beginning of each year ! The term "fund" breeds
mischievous delusions, and has been the parent of much fatalistic
doctrine as to the helplessness of wage-receivers to better themselves. Now, the only physical limit to the amount paid in
wages and salaries is the wealth in existence; the only moral
limit is that set by the necessity of the owners of capital receiving encouragement enough to make them save. There is,
moreover, one conclusive observation to be made with respect to
this and other doctrines we have mentioned. They are useless ;
if they have been applied to any use, it is illegitimately. Plainly,
it is impossible to know until after the fact, until the wages
have been expended, the amount of this wages fund—how, then,
determine anything regarding wages that is much worth knowing ? No doubt, theorists have freely employed this doctrine.
They have said, for example, that such and such procedure
could not raise or depress wages, since it affected neither the
wages fund nor population. But it is always open to ask, how

could they know the state of the wages fund? In what office could the information be had? Further, the other factor is not, strictly speaking, the population, but that part of it desirous of employment, and this, of course, varies with wages. All of these formulæ are vitiated by the attempt to reduce to a mathematical formula the laws of value. Besides, wages differ so much; the interval between the hind receiving 10s. a week and the Lord Chancellor receiving £10,000 a year is so vast that the average struck between the extremes is practically useless. Services differ so much in value that this kneading together of all sorts is like, in its wisdom and utility, framing a general theory of the value of all kinds of stones, huddling the pebbles of the brook and the diamonds of Golconda into one promiscuous heap.

The wise course is to recognise these enormous differences, and to consider each particular kind of work by itself, just as we recognise the difference in the value of each commodity. The first glance will reveal the fact that certain labourers are practically monopolists. Either from natural or artificial causes they are too few to compete with each other; or there exist certain well understood and observed rules forbidding or discouraging competition. In such instances wages will move up to the highest pitch consistent with the continuance of the demand. Other labourers at the opposite extremity are permanently redundant; as a rule, competition is always on their side, and their remuneration must be scanty. Yet it does not follow that their wages will fall indefinitely low—a conclusion implied in the common doctrine that wages depend on the ratio of the capital to population; a poor-law may buoy them up; in any case they cannot fall below the minimum which will keep them and their families alive. Nor does it follow that in this state of plethora every labourer will obtain some wages, however low; unless he is confident that he can increase the demand for his goods, the employer will not increase the demand for labour so as to absorb all that is available. Between the extremes of scarcity and redundancy, there are, of course, endless intermediate kinds of labour, some approaching to monopolies and occasionally becoming so, others always tending to redundancy. It also requires no profound investigation to perceive that the wages of certain kinds of labourers are liable to be influenced by influxes from contiguous kinds of labour; whereas there are other kinds severed by impassable barriers. An increase in the population, provided it be in the upper or middle classes, does not tend to increase the wages of day-labourers; it may on the contrary decrease them. On the other hand, an increase in the number of carpenters may lower the wages of cabinetmakers, and *vice versa*. Further, it is to be observed that certain kinds of labour have competitors not human; and though these form items of capital, an increase in them may have the effect of temporarily diminishing wages. If men stick by a trade, or a particular part of a trade, to which machinery has been successfully applied, and if they thus compete with machinery, plainly the latter influences their wages. Similarly with horse-power; if horses do what men did, the former, like all equivalents of human labour, influence wages. Again, it cannot help striking one that the various kinds of labour differ greatly in the rapidity with which they can be increased. Some, provided the remuneration is indefinitely raised, can be indefinitely recruited; other kinds, be the rewards what they may, cannot be increased, except after a considerable period. What pertinent inference is to be drawn from these facts? Little more than that they fortify this conclusion: It is useless to lay down a law respecting wages generally; each kind of labour must be considered by itself, and its value, so far as laws and other counteracting agencies do not prevent, like the value of commodities, will, when there is perfect freedom of contract, depend upon the demand for the particular service and the supply of labourers capable of performing it. A meagre result! Yet the only result perhaps attainable. As to the real remuneration of the labourer, that will depend on the proportion of the net produce which he obtains, and partly on the supply of the articles on which he expends his remuneration.

Those who are already acquainted with Political Economy will understand us when we say that the theory of wages may be stated in almost the same terms as Ricardo's theory of rent. The latter is, in fact, applicable to all commodities varying in quality and limited in quantity at any given time. Those who may not be acquainted with that theory we would ask to observe that every servant, from a Secretary of State earning £5000 a year to a boy that gets 4d. a week for scaring crows, is the possessor of a capacity for a certain work valued at so much; all labourers resemble the owners of land in Cheapside or Broadway and of a bog in Connemara. Now, just as there are some lands—

nay, whole countries—either by situation or soil, unfit to be cultivated or rented, so are there some men—nay, perhaps whole races—unfit to be hired. As there are some lands for which only a nominal rent is paid, so there are servants to whom only nominal wages are paid—children and old men, for example. As the rent of any piece of land may be said to be measured by the difference in value between the results obtained from it and those from the lowest kind of land repaying cultivation, so in a state of perfect competition, the wages of any man may be measured by the difference in value between what he produces and that produced by those who receive only a nominal wage. Indeed certain economists have agreed to designate the wages received by the possessors of exceptional talents by the name of rent. At the same time, little stress need be laid on this view of the matter. Ricardo's theory, thus substantially applied to wages, is itself of little use. Unimpeachable in theoretical accuracy, it seems made for another world than ours, and conducts to no very desirable terminus. The same remark may be extended to many other economical laws. Faultless to the eye, possessed of a severe beauty, they are too often fruitless, as the trees with which the frost illuminates our windows.

Adam Smith has enumerated five principal circumstances which determine the rates of wages. First, "The agreeableness or disagreeableness of the employments themselves." Calcraft may finish his day's work in ten minutes, yet he will be paid as much as a mechanic will earn in ten days. The profession that admits of a man smoking at any and every moment cannot be very remunerative. One is often astonished at the difference between the wages of an Englishman and an Oriental ; mark the manner of working, and one is less surprised. An Eastern traveller, mentioned by Greeley, states that he saw only one man in all Palestine doing anything, and he was falling off the roof of a house. Secondly, "The easiness and cheapness, or the difficulty and expense, of learning them (labourers) employments." Those who have undergone an apprenticeship of seven years will, as a rule, earn more than those who have served no apprenticeship. If they do not, apprentices will cease to present themselves. This, we believe, is exemplified at present in the shoemaking trade in those districts in which machinery is being extensively used. Without any long training, men earn, as riveters, finishers, etc., almost as good wages as those who have served the cus-

tomary period of seven years. The consequence is, they say, that
in the great shoemaking districts of Northamptonshire there is
a great falling-off in the number of apprentices. Thirdly, "The
constancy or inconstancy of employment." A mason whom frost
prevents from working all the year must receive higher wages
than a joiner, who can work from January to December.
Fourthly, "The small or great trust which must be reposed in
those who exercise them." Nobody will pay his cashier as he
pays his errand-boy. Fifthly, "The probability or improba-
bility of success in them." At least two out of three probably
fail at the bar. It is befitting and necessary that the prizes
should be high when the blanks are numerous. In a fair
lottery, the prizes equalise the losses, and, according to Adam
Smith, "the lottery of the law is," by this test, "very far from
being a fair lottery." This list is not perfectly complete or
satisfactory. Adam Smith takes no account, for instance, of the
fact that much work is poorly remunerated because partially performed by amateurs, who bring down the remuneration. Much
disagreeable work, too, is poorly remunerated, because paupers
are engaged in it. Neither does this list presuppose a right
mode of considering wages; it seems needless to give a theory
of wages in general, and then to state the circumstances upon
which the value of each kind of labour is dependent. The
general theory of wages, if it be worth stating it, is involved
in the general theory of value; and perhaps subsidiary theories
of utility could be better obtained by classing certain kinds of
commodities with certain kinds of labour than by classing various
kinds of labour together.

It is often said· that' wages depend on the price of food.
Professor Roscher lays it down that "a fall in the price of
articles of food and clothing is always followed by a fall in
the rates of wages, if the circle of the demands of the working
class does not enlarge in the same proportion; so also the
increase in the price of food must raise wages when their rates
scarcely suffice for the necessaries of life." This perhaps
is too dogmatic an expression of what is frequently realised.
The former result comes to pass in virtue of the readiness of the
labourers to marry in good times, and thus to increase their
numbers. Only let there be a good harvest, and the Registrar-
General's report will bear testimony to the number of marriages,
and by and by to the number of births. It is actually the case that

some thousands virtually say, "The quartern loaf has fallen in price; let us marry." At the same time no necessity forces wages to pass through this cycle. They might remain stationary in the face of a great fall in the price of bread-stuffs, if men did not commute their advantages, and hasten to bring into the world new competitors for wages. This evil is to be prevented by inculcating thoughtfulness, by persuading the working-classes not to rear families until they have the means of supporting them, by spreading a taste for simple luxuries among them, by elevating their ideal of comfort, and by reminding them that "a bit, a sup, a but an' a ben," must be provided for before a family is introduced into the world. One must try to teach them not to live brutishly in the present. The working-classes, in regard to marriage, are too much of the mind of the character in a comedy of De Musset, who says, "Next to the superfluous comes the necessary." This must be reversed.

It is not often that one event or century can work a change in the standard of comfort. Perhaps no signal instance of such swift success can be quoted except the French Revolution. This event, cursed by Burke and the reactionists as an insurrection of hell and the return of chaos, by abolishing corvée and other feudal privileges, by taking land from an effete aristocracy and a pampered Church, to put it into such industrious hands as Balzac has sculptured for us in Eugenie Grandet, by removing fear of the gendarme and the tax-gatherer, transformed "a people starved and stabbed in an untilled field," living on fern bread, pointed at by Malthus and his disciples as destined to multiply, so as to drink the very dregs of misery, and talked of by La Bruyère with ghastly irony as animals not human, into an industrious people with a high average of comfort, and increasing more slowly than any other nation in Europe. Excepting ourselves, no people has made so rapid progress within so short a time as the French. Not that the standard of comfort is very high among them, or that they live in a manner that is much superior to the style of living of the English peasant. The coarse scanty food of the French small proprietor strikes painfully an English eye : two-thirds of the French population live mainly on chestnuts, maize, and potatoes ; according to respectable computations, the consumption of bread and meat annually amounts to much less than is required for bare health. This

T

is sad ; but when we go back to 1790, we find a committee an-
nouncing to the Constituent Assembly that the presumptive
number of official poor was one million ; and M. Villiaumé, who
rates the number as nearer two millions, states that besides
these officially indigent classes, "one-half of the people often
wanted bread."

Labour is often spoken of as a commodity. The justice of
this language has been questioned by Mr. Frederic Harrison and
Mr. Ludlow. The former seems to think that this notion is at
the bottom of most of the false Political Economy of the time.
The labourer, he says emphatically, has nothing to sell. Of
course, in the sense given to immaterial wealth in a former part
of this volume, this assertion is not perfectly accurate. The
labourer sells immaterial wealth ; though he does not part with
the *plenum dominium*, he sells his services.

An interesting question here comes up for solution, and it is
whether the wages of various trades, in different parts of the
same country, are tending towards a level. We quote Mr.
M'Culloch's summary and endorsement of the views of Adam
Smith on this question. His words are these :—"When all
things are taken into account, the wages earned by the
labourers engaged in different employments approach nearly
to an equality," and he adds that the wages of labour are
now much nearer a common level than at the time of the
publication of the *Wealth of Nations*. In an essay which I
have consulted with much advantage, Mr. Cliffe Leslie has
demonstrated that the facts are different. Instead of approaching to uniformity, wages are in England actually more varied
than they were when Adam Smith wrote his *Wealth of Nations*,
though the settlement laws were then in full force. If we mistake not, M. Leonce de Lavergne has made a similar observation with regard to France. The reasons ? Mr. Leslie has
pointed out that the assumption made by Mr. M'Culloch, that
labourers freely pass from one employment to another, is grossly
wrong, that a bricklayer can easily become a blacksmith is a
pure delusion, and that there is, in fact, a much freer emigration
between some bordering grades of capital and labour than between different departments of labour. And Mr. M'Culloch is
not the only economist who has exaggerated the mobility of the
human mind and body, and the ease with which workmen can
pass from one employment to another; almost every economist

has been guilty of the same fault, in blindness to the same obvious facts. There are other causes of this inequality, and two of the most powerful of these are the extension of the division of labour, and the consequent separation in the value of kinds of labour in Adam Smith's time loosely thrown together, and the growth of railways and commercial cities introducing violent contrasts between urban and rural wages. Those who assert that wages must become uniform as competition increases seem to make the very questionable assumption that were labour valued by competition the diversities of it would be fewer than if valued by custom. The presumption is, I think, the other way. It is only in an era of competition that the nicer distinctions in the value of labour are apprehended; only then are the peculiarities of districts, making money value an unfair measure of wages, fully recognised; and it is in an advanced state of society that the economical circumstances of districts, once homogeneous, are most liable to be differentiated. At the same time, there is no reason to deny that the wages of labour of the same kind, in the same circumstances, are being equalised.

CHAPTER XX.

WAGES—(Continued).

A FAVOURITE cure for low wages and their consequences, frequently employed in the past, and still clung to by shallow minds, is to fix by law the rate of wages at what is called " a fair and just figure," so as always to give " a fair day's wage for a fair day's work." By this device it is hoped that wages will never fall so low that the labourer's lot will be miserable, nor will they rise so high as to breed extravagant habits; fluctuations in wages, with their demoralising consequences, will be avoided; society will be rendered stable; the cruel uncertainty of the life of the poorer classes, almost necessitating thoughtlessness, seeing calculation as to their future is frequently profitless, will give place to a happy certainty. And no doubt fixity of wages would be an immense social blessing. But what does fixity of wages mean? Suppose the law were again to do what it did in the year 1350, after the Great or Black Death of 1349 had ravaged England; suppose it did—what it did not do then— fix the wages to the advantage of the labourer, what, reducing this measure to its simple elements, would it denote? Why, if we consider that labour is a commodity, the value of which is the estimation of purchasers, we shall see that this decree would enunciate the tyrannical doctrine that the Legislature is to be controller of men's thoughts, and that a man shall be compelled to consider 15s. to be the equivalent of a service which in his heart he esteems worth only 10s.; and, to use a mild term, the measure would be a tax on the employer for the benefit of the labourer—an act of indiscriminate and forcible charity. But would this fixity of wages be always possible? " Always," because it is not worth considering whether fixity of wages could in certain circumstances exist; to every Englishman the necessaries of life have been guaranteed by law.

Clearly not always. The lot of the labourer would be improved only if the sum spent in wages was increased; but if men carried the increase to a certain point, and discouraged the creation of capital by depriving its owners of sufficient inducement to save, there would soon not be in existence wealth enough to provide this or any less fixed sum, and a measure conceived for the benefit of the poor would turn to their misery. Driven out of this position, owning that the law could not, except within very narrow limits, increase the total sum to be divided among the labourers, some have said that wages should be so fixed that, while those who now obtain high wages should in future obtain less, those who obtain low wages should obtain more; and thus the total sum spent in wages would remain what it now is, and yet none be miserably poor. The former plan would rob the capitalists; the latter would rob one fraction of the labourers for the benefit of another. The latter plan announces that unusual skill, great native talents for work, sobriety, and steadiness, uprightness, and all other qualities, acquired or natural, which make one labourer more valuable than another, shall be lost to their owner. With what consequence? These talents are stifled, these exceptional gifts are lost to the community, the sum of wealth is diminished, and the burden of supporting the poor of the working-classes thrown on the intelligent and industrious.

It must be stated, however, that history chronicles far more numerous attempts to fix wages to the advantage of the employers than to that of the workmen. There is indeed a period following the abolition of serfage when Legislatures seem inevitably to make efforts to fix wages. The reign of Edward III. saw in England the first of these attempts, that of George IV. the last. The Parliament of the former reign, filled with landowners suffering from the high rate of wages which were the consequence of the terrible pestilence that had passed over Europe with destruction in its hand, as when the Angel of Death passed over the houses of the Egyptians, fixed the rates of wages with the intention of cheapening labour, and annexed penalties to departure from these rates. The full history of that terrible time we shall never know; many of the ugly facts are buried, but enough remains to inform us that the pillars of society were shaken, and in some countries the very existence of humanity threatened. Froissart (quoted by Michelet) tells

us that "fully a third part of the world perished," and those
whom the disease spared it often transformed into beings of well-
nigh bestial carnality and recklessness. It began in Provence. It
visited Italy, raging with baleful fury in Florence : the readers
of Boccaccio's *Decamerone* will remember that it is in consequence of the plague that Boccaccio's ladies and gentlemen
retire to the country, there to weave voluptuous tales until the
pestilence or life depart : in that city alone perished 100,000
persons according to Boccaccio, and 96,000 according to
Machiavelli. The pestilence visited Germany ; it scaled the
Pyrenees ; and, crossing the Channel, it swept away, according to
one account, one-half of the people. Everywhere death, a scanty
remnant, uncultivated fields, and abandoned pursuits. Europe
thus turned into one charnel-house, and the hands that were left
becoming precious, prostrate labour asserted itself, demanded
privileges, resisted oppression ; and two of the fruits of its new-
born vigour were the English Peasants' war of 1385 and the
Jacquerie in France. Everywhere there were complaints of
the high wages and of the license of the labourers. The kings
and nobles of the land tried everywhere to get cheap labour by
prohibiting the labourers from asking, and the employers from
giving, more than the official rate : the statutes of Edward III.,
the ordinances of King John, the decrees of Peter the Cruel of
Castile, record these attempts. Attempts by legislators to fix
wages have usually taken the form of the imposition of a
maximum and a minimum wage. The famous statute of Elizabeth named a maximum wage, or, what was the equivalent of it,
put it in the power of the Justices of the Peace to send any one
to prison who did not accept employment at the official rate.

Recently the cry has been for a minimum wage. Most socialists,
who attempt a work very similar to that which statesmen
of mediæval times essayed, do in some shape or other demand
a minimum wage ; and it is a favourite and common proposal
for the relief of misery. Strange to say, one of the few
countries in which a minimum wage has been carried into effect
is England, the country where property is idolised, its rights
regarded as limitless, and in which socialism—an imported
heresy—has never taken deep root. The truth, however, is so,
for the old Poor-law of Elizabeth and that which succeeded it
in 1834 really established a minimum wage, seeing adults,
having always the alternative before them of the workhouse

or an allowance, need never accept wages which did not amount to that which charity gave them. And though the present English Poor-law attaches disagreeable accompaniments to the receiving of relief, the principle remains unimpaired— it is true that at this moment there is in force a certain minimum rate of wages. In France, about the year 1848, the demand for minimum wages took the form of "the right to labour." The workmen of Lyons, offering the choice of "bread or lead," and determined to die fighting or live working, asked the State to provide them with labour ; and the Provisional Government proclaimed, as the phrase is, "the right to labour." In September, however, of the same year, the principle was rejected by the Constituent Assembly. Much horror has been expressed at the doctrine, and the strictures passed upon it have been too indiscriminate, and would be fatal to much that passes almost unquestioned in this country. Certainly, if " the right to labour " is a short and pithy summary of a Poor-law— if it means no more than the statement of the fact that everybody not guilty of crime who is in danger of starving may, subject to certain conditions, ask of Society, or Government, its embodied will, bread or the wherewithal to obtain it, " the right to labour" is comparatively harmless. The principle which lies at the bottom of this right is that which lies at the bottom of all Poor-laws, more especially at the bottom of the Poor-law of England ; and certainly if we do not object to—nay, for three hundred years have gloried in—providing bare sustenance to the poor without always exacting of them labour of any kind in return, we should not, at least on the ground of leniency to the poor, object to their right after labouring to obtain sustenance. It may be said that the guaranteeing of labour is not the best form of bestowing public relief, and that the few instances of its application have been discouraging—both these assertions would be true ; but the arguments of Léon Faucher and Bastiat, conclusive against "the right to labour" in any other view than as a measure of pauper policy, are not conclusive against it in this sense. On the other hand " Droit au travail " is certainly not the best form of a Poor-law ; it imposes no check on the multiplication of paupers ; it does not sufficiently remind the pauper of his dependence. Permanently adhered to, it would be a pauperising machine driven by the State ; for if work could always be got by calling at some bureau, a stimulus to exertion and prudence would be taken away, and this coddling would deal a blow to self-respect, that cheap defence against poverty. There are, moreover, countries and seasons in which the congregation of vast bodies of idle reckless men is a menace to the existence of Government ; you put spades into their hands to-day, and to-morrow they change them for muskets ; there the right to labour may be the right to revolution. Madrid felt, shortly after the expulsion of the Bourbons, what it is to regiment and pamper its populace. Paris more recently felt still more bitterly the consequences of a like policy. If the right to labour be put forward as more than a right to a measure of temporary relief, if it be a claim for the average wages to members of all trades, if it be a request for superfluities and not bare necessaries given as alms, and if, in short, the right be not recognised as a favour granted in order to ferry one across some stream of misery that intersects one's path, it is to be condemned as injustice or folly. For if the State provide work for the upholsterer, why not for the physician ? and if we are all sure about obtaining good wages, why should we be particular about looking out for employment or keeping it when got, or why should we not all hurry out of disagreeable employments into agreeable employments ?

Among the devices resorted to during last century, and still more during the present, in order to raise wages and to resist falls, have been strikes. The very word is a warning that we tread mined ground, and that here it is impossible to satisfy all minds, or even to avoid irritating some. Invocations to the spirit of impartiality are useless. Mathematicians or entomologists may be perfectly indifferent as to the result of their investigations ; here are neither quantities nor insects to be considered, but a subject quivering with human interest. True, for a time there is a lull, and strikes are rarer than they have been ; the voice of reason does begin to be heard. Yet feebly. The surface seems cold and cindery : put your foot on it, and the cake breaks to immerse you in flames. At the very outset one may give offence by entertaining the very idea that strikes can, under any circumstance, do good.

Employers, as a rule, cannot speak of strikes with patience and calmness. To them strikes are unalloyed evils ; and, acting in accordance with the opinions of the employing classes, down to very recent times the Legislatures of almost every country have prohibited strikes, or rather the machinery which renders strikes practicable. One of the best recognised principles of the common law of England is, that all measures which "restrain trade," as the loose phrase ran, are unlawful; and as "restraining" trades, combinations for raising wages were also unlawful. Such was the loose and elastic doctrine of the common law—applicable, let me in justice add, to the combinations of masters as well as to those of men. It received a certain degree of precision from several statutes. In the reign of Edward VI. a statute was passed levelling a battery of fines and penalties against labourers who should conspire, covenant, or promise not to do work but at a certain rate, or to labour only at certain hours. Omitting specific mention of the thirty statutes passed between his reign and that of George III., it may be stated that by an Act passed in the reign of George III. all agreements between workmen in order to obtain a rise of wages were held to be illegal. But in the reign of George IV. these rules were annulled by the instrumentality of Mr. Joseph Hume, and the only crimes punishable were violence, threats, and intimidation. This Act was allowed to remain in force only one year, and the Act 6 Geo. IV., cap. 129, virtually re-established the pains and penalties of the common law, excluding from its action only those combinations which related to hours and rates of wages to be adopted, and, at the same time, punishing those who "molest" or "in any way obstruct." Striking successfully became in such circumstances almost impossible. It is not exactly correct to say that strikes *per se* or unions were ever illegal. They were only illegal in any sense when they were held to be "in restraint of trade." They were not illegal in the sense that they exposed parties to them to indictment. At present unions cannot be regarded as completely legalised, in the ordinary signification of the term, for with respect to contracts relative to union dues, the law refuses to enforce specific performance, or to award damages.

There are those who say that strikes must fail. It is needless to spend much time in refuting those who uphold this position by the assertion that there is a certain sum "destined," as the phrase is, "to be divided among the labourers," and that consequently the attempt to raise wages by any other way than by decreasing the labourers, or augmenting this fund, is futile ; for there is no sum destined to be paid to labourers. Nobody, or at all events few, destine a certain portion of wealth to the payment of labour, and all fluctuations have the effect of altering the total sum or wages fund. The strongest form which the argument against strikes assumes is, that the employers of labour are always stimulated to pay the utmost that they can afford to pay consistently with procuring fair remuneration ; for if they are receiving unusual profits, capital will flow in, or their rivals will outbid them and draw away their workmen. Still this argument does not satisfy one who coolly examines it. Even if we are to grant the existence of a state of keen competition, how is it to be instantly known that a manufacturer, a brewer, or a shipbuilder, is earning unusually high profits? Such knowledge cannot come in a day ; to suppose so is to suppose men gifted with powers of vision such as Asmodeus gave to the scholar of Alcala. Are we to believe that through the commercial world the news of high profits flies with as much mysterious swiftness as the fabled Phemé of the Greeks ? Secondly, this alleged omnipresence of competition, though an assumption, is not a fact, even in the long run. Even where there are no artificial monopolies, there may be natural monopolies. For the successful carrying on of a certain business, so much capital may be required that practically a few firms enjoy a monopoly ; a lucrative business may not be easy to learn, and the prospect of high profits may not suffice to induce people to overcome their repugnance to the necessary initial schooling. It is, moreover, not enough that mere capital should enter in order to stir up competition to the benefit of the labourer ; more capitalists and rivalry are required, and these cannot always be introduced instantaneously.

Profits, it is said, " seek their level." Yes ; but they are often long in finding it ; and though, if time be given, and if we put out of account insurance, and wages of superintendence, which must be permanently different, it will probably be the fact that any trade which returns higher profits than those returned in other trades will be invaded by capitalists who will ultimately lower the rate, this may not happen for many a day, and if the difference be very small, and insufficient to compensate the displacement of capital and skill from one business to another, the operation of levelling may occupy a very considerable time. And in the interval may not the workmen, indispensable to the employers, in receipt of unusually high profits, by standing out obtain a share of them, and so augment wages? Perhaps these considerations prove that it may be possible for profits to be different for a time in different trades, and that workmen may by standing out really obtain an increase of wages, at the expense of the extraordinary and transient profits. But will not the labourers who reap this unusual advantage instantly find competitors, others crowding into this happy nook? This objection to strikes, frequently put by their indiscriminate foes, exaggerates the mobility of labour, as other arguments exaggerate that of capital. If men could as easily pass from one trade to another as they change their garments, if it were not the fact that men rarely quit the professions they have once chosen, and that a new generation must grow up before an overstocked profession casts off its superfluity, this result might come to pass; with men as they are it cannot, and years may elapse before the exceptional gains of a particular trade be snatched from it. Another argument, frequently employed to demonstrate the inevitable futility of strikes, runs as follows:—If strikes ever benefit any workmen, it is at the expense of other workmen; for the portion to be divided among the body of them being fixed, if some of the working classes get more by striking, others get correspondingly less: the total amount spent in wages is never altered; and strikes may be described as devices by which 10 per cent of the working classes rob the other 90. If tailors, it is said, obtain a rise of wages, shoemakers or others get less. Here crops up again the idea of a fixed amount, "destined," as the phrase is, for wages. This idea is the keystone of the argument; and that keystone, as we have seen, crumbles at a touch. But, granting for the sake of argument that the amount available for wages is fixed, is there no escaping the inference that one class of labourers can get a larger share of this only by another class of labourers getting less? We are not reduced to that conclusion; there is another outlet, for, besides artizans and labourers, most capitalists do obtain wages. Of the 15 or 20 per cent which a merchant in fair or good business may be earning, and which, in ordinary language, will be spoken of as profits, only 5 or at most 10 per cent may be profits as economists understand profits; the surplus may be the wages due to exceptional skill and industry, or to the great risk or disagreeableness of the man's trade. So that, before this epigram about 10 per cent of the working classes robbing the other 90 passes into circulation as part of the good coin of science, we must "ring" it well on the counter of reason—we must examine whether it is not possible that the increment in labourers' wages may not have been subtracted from the wages, so to speak, of employers, and not from those of labourers. It is quite possible, in this point of view, for a portion of the working classes to obtain an increase of wages without diminishing the profits, properly so called, of their employers, or the wages of any other working men.

"Still," breaks in some questioning voice, "on the whole, it is true that the less profits are, the less goes in the shape of wages ; capitalists will save in proportion to their profits ; and if workmen benefit themselves for a time by squeezing high wages out of their masters, the sunshine will be but for an hour —eventually fewer labourers will be employed, and when its consequences are matured, a strike will be a demonstrated mistake." Which, of course, is true within limits ; true if wages so encroach on profits as not to leave a margin sufficient to induce capitalists to save. But as a universal rule, not so ; it is not true of luxuries that one contracts one's consumption of them in exact proportion as their prices rise ; still less is it true of the consumption of necessaries such as labour ; and when a man's profits fall owing to a rise of wages, it may—it does actually sometimes—happen that he will, if he can, enlarge his business, in order to maintain his old income and his old position in society. In the case of some kinds of labour certainly, and in the event of wages rising considerably, there will be a tendency to diminish the amount given in wages ; but it is no more universally true that a rise in wages, with a consequent fall in profits, will diminish the amount spent in wages, than that a rise in the prices of tools or materials will necessarily diminish a manufacturer's consumption of them. Is it rare to see a man accustomed to a certain style of living, when he perceives the rate of his profits diminished, and his business no longer returning sufficient to maintain him in this position, devote more capital than formerly with the view of keeping his income at the old figure ?

It is further said that strikes must fail because wages depend on the relations of supply and demand, relations which strikes do not affect ; "conditions," says Professor Wolowski, from whom we quote this argument, " which are as rigorous as the laws of fluids." On the same principle it might be objected that superiority could never be gained by fighting, seeing victory was predetermined in favour of the strongest. As if it could be always known what were the relations of supply and demand, and who was the strongest, without putting the questions to experiment! But is there not a change, or the equivalent of a change, in the supply whenever a strike occurs? Yesterday 1000 hands could be employed at 18s. a week; to-day there is a strike, and none can be employed at this figure. Surely a change in the supply!

Let us consider what a strike is, and it will be perceived that we argue for a truism rather than for any doctrine of dangerous novelty. A strike is a refusal to sell labour; it is standing out for a certain price; it is similar to the conduct of corn merchants or tallow merchants who decline to sell at a particular price, and wait until the market turns in their favour —conduct once punishable under the name of " forestalling," or " regratting;" and it would be strange that, if holding out on the part of the corn merchant is not always wrong, it should of necessity be always wrong on the part of the seller of labour. The only important circumstance separating the one case from the other is, that the labourer usually cannot hold out so long as the corn merchant; usually he is imperiously driven to sell at an early date; but that is a circumstance which, while warning the workman not to indulge often or long in strikes, does not peremptorily forbid him ever striking. It is true also that the corn merchants rarely or ever combine. But this forms no essential difference; combination happens to be essential to the efficiency of the refusal of the labourer. Those who hold that striking, or the power of striking, cannot in any circumstances cause a rise of wages, must in consistency hold that they rise and fall with no dependency on the will of the recipients. Increase of wages must come to the servant as rain comes to the farmer. Now, it is not true that competition of the capitalists is, as a matter of fact, universal and unconditional. It is not true that its action is instantaneous. It is not true that the knowledge of the capitalists extends to every occasion in which other capitalists happen to hire labour at advantageous terms. Nor is it true that every capitalist augments his business precisely as his profits increase. And, such being the case, it is not true that if men suffer things to take their course, and do not take steps to obtain an increase of wages, the action of employers will spontaneously give all that could be got.

The argument against strikes derived from the assumption that as there can be but one rate of profit, and as capitalists will not accept less than the normal rate, they will quit any trade in which labourers by striking have reduced the rate of profit below the average, possesses considerable strength so long as we suppose the combination of unionists to be small; it possesses less strength as we conceive the sphere of unionists extended; it possesses none if we suppose the sphere of unions embracing all countries and trades. Suppose that the combination is not local but universal—suppose, in the first place, that all the members of the same trade unite to attain their ends. The possibility of such a combination may be denied, and at present it certainly is impossible, there being little concert between the workmen of different countries. But, leaving out of consideration very distant countries as of little account, may we not hope or fear that some such concert will be established between the workmen of adjacent lands? The rise of working men's international congresses suggests to one that there is no certainty that alliances between the same trades of various countries may not be formed. If the Amalgamated Engineers extend to our remotest colonies, may they not cross the Channel? They may; and as those here controverted do not mainly rest their case on the difficulty of accomplishing such alliances, but upon a supposed principle in virtue of which strikes must fail, we may assume for the moment that there are faithfully-obeyed treaties between members of the same trades of all adjacent countries. What will happen in that event? A strike ensues in a certain trade yielding the average rate of profits. In the circumstances which we have supposed capitalists cannot profitably remove their capital to another country and there follow their business, because they will get no workmen to labour for them at lower terms. Nor, in these circumstances, will workmen from other countries, or other parts of the same country, reduce the rate of wages of the strikers to the old level by underselling them. Granting the existence of such a labour-league between the members of the same trade, it would seem that it was competent for them to attain their ends. "But the capitalists, being deprived of the ordinary rate of profits, will abandon the trade in which the strike has taken place, and will enter other trades, with the effect of reducing wages in that which they quitted to their old level"—such is the reasoning of not a few. But, if we are at liberty to enlarge the previous supposition, and to assume, in the second place, that the labour-league comprehends all labourers, it may be demonstrated that the reasoning is inaccurate. As there would be no transferring capital to a more remunerative business, as the same demands would be simultaneously made in every business, there would be but two alternatives open to capitalists—to comply with the terms demanded, or to suffer their capital to be idle; and as some profit, however small, is better than no profit at all, it would be strange if the former alternative were not accepted. Of course, it is extremely improbable that the second supposition will ever be realised. It is only the dream of a few of the more enthusiastic unionists. If it ever come to pass, it will be at some remote time. I only mention such a cosmopolitan combination as a possibility improbable, but fatal to the arguments of those who would prove that there is something in the essence of strikes which forbids their success. For the sake of completeness it must also be added that, according to all theoretical reasoning, a general and uniform rise in wages could not be shifted from profits to consumers. Nor, lastly, as the various rates of profits show, need the desire to accumulate be repressed or improved.

Strikes, *par excellence*, are accompanied by combinations. This is inevitable. Without combinations, most strikes would be utterly hopeless. Taken singly, each of two hundred men would be as insignificant a combatant against the possessor of £20,000 as the worm that lies in one's path. Scatter a regiment sufficiently, and two or three men may destroy it; Captain Bobadil promised to destroy a whole army in this manner; but knit these 200 men together, let the soldiers fall into rank, and £20,000 may fail to break up the one, and 2000 to put to flight the other. The truth, however, is, that it is deferring too much to a custom fruitful in error to discuss the efficacy of strikes in general. What nonsense or insipid and worthless formulæ would we not have if people discussed the possibility of raising the price of merchandise in general by the owners of it standing out! Labour, it cannot too often be repeated, is not one kind of merchandise, but thousands of

kinds of merchandise. The owner of one kind of labour is the
owner of what is a drug in the market, and it is useless for
him to strike; another sells labour which will be got from abroad
if he chooses to enhance its price, and it is dangerous for him to
strike; while a third, who sells labour of a kind which is rare and
in demand, may sometimes strike with impunity. In a trade
such as the builder's, by its nature almost independent of foreign
competition, the workmen have considerable advantages; in
such a trade as the lace trade, in which foreigners can readily
take part, success is difficult. If a trade necessitates the use of
machinery liable to be deteriorated by disuse, or if the stoppage
of the machinery causes, as in the case of a mine, serious
damage, the workmen, supposing they are compact, and supposing no substitutes are obtainable, fight at an advantage. A
colliery owner who may lose £150 to £200 by his works being
stopped for a day is in no hurry to provoke a strike. Workmen are, of course, also frequently able to dictate terms to a
firm with pressing orders on hand or dependent upon borrowed
capital. Many circumstances, in short, determine the impolicy
of a strike, and it is sometimes impossible to know these circumstances without unfortunately putting the question to trial.

But if it be possible for strikes to succeed, how happens it
that so few have been successful? How happens it that
scarcely one case can be mentioned of indisputable victory
to the workmen? At best, the records of strikes are but the
records of failures; the struggle of capital and labour resembles
that between regular troops and undisciplined mobs—the valour
of the combatants may be equal, but fortune resides with the
former. How is this fact to be reconciled with the possibility
of strikes to raise wages? These allegations are too unqualified,
and instances of success might be quoted. I have before me
an account of a successful strike by the breaksmen of the Erie
Railway. But, as a general proposition, the above is true,
though at the same time perfectly reconcilable with the possibility of strikes to succeed. Strikes fail not from an inherent,
essential, and necessary property of a strike, as is commonly
supposed, but, as a rule, from causes which might be removed:
first, the vexatious laws which made striking perilous; secondly,
the fact that it is usually far harder for a workman with a family
dependent on the labour of his hands to go without wages for a
month or six weeks, than it is for one who possesses capital, or

at least credit to borrow it, to go without profits for the same period. Most kinds of labour at present stand more clamantly in need of capital than capital of labour : for the one, striking is a question of existence ; for the other, of luxuries or profits. The labourer must sell, and the employer need not buy. Another cause is, that the combination of labourers is in all cases only partial. Rarely do all the workmen in the same trade combine ; never have all the members of the same trade in different countries done so ; and the very idea of all trades combining—which would, if the demands were not extravagant, secure a victory— has been little more than broached.

At the same time, these remarks would be *totally* misunderstood if they were read as an incitement to striking.' That workmen should have to fight for their wages is not a fit condition of affairs. Strikes are, as Comte says, measures of war, and as such rarely to be employed. These remarks are made with the intention of discouraging them in the belief that one most surely plucks an error when the ingredients of truth which it contains are frankly owned, and in recognition of that "element of decay," as it has been finely phrased, which lies "in any overstatement." On the heads of those who have often opposed strikes with sophistry, and who have never looked fairly in the face the grounds to which the working classes clung, lies much of the blame of those sad scenes which this country has of late witnessed—of barren months interpolated in the calendar, of opportunities and of resources suffered to lie fallow. For those special pleaders injured a good cause by their indiscriminate advocacy, and brought into disrepute sound reasons by introducing them in the company of impostors. There is no need of sophistry to discredit striking. Sufficient to remind the workmen that they must generally contend at a disadvantage with the possessors of wealth ; that in the generality of cases masters are urged by motives of competition to give the utmost, consistently with a continuance of saving ; that there is a danger, should demands be pressed, of trades and capital migrating ; and that a strike, being a stoppage of production, cannot but be generally injurious.

A remedy proposed for striking is arbitration. This is a laudable but somewhat inadequate proposal. When translated into asking some other body's opinion, arbitration does not seem a very potent instrument, though certainly it would often suc-

ceed if the arbitrator was a man of known gravity and uprightness. Men of repute, such as Mr. Mill, or Mr. Fawcett, or Mr.
Rupert Kettle, or Mr. Hughes, may ward off many a strike.
Probably before arbitration is of much service the arbitrator must
have authority to bind the disputants. So far back as the reign
of George IV. its advantage in trades questions was admitted
by the Legislature. In regard to most questions likely to arise
between masters and workmen, it gave the arbitrators the power
to enforce their awards on either of two disputants, and the
right to compel the other to refer the point at issue to arbitration.
Perhaps it was this provision, a little too arbitrary, which led
to the Act being not generally employed. In 1867 the Legislature, yielding to a very general desire, facilitated the creation
of Courts of Conciliation, a reference to which could be made
by mutual consent. The decree of the Court could be enforced.
What somewhat hinders the working of the scheme is the formalities required for the creation of the court, and the opportunities afforded for questioning the validity of its awards.

It is to be feared that these are remedies that will cure
only skin-deep wounds. Other medicinal appliances, more complicated and more delicate, more impalpable and less quickly
efficacious, and not so easily to be catalogued, are required to
purge the body politic of the humours of which strikes are the
outcome. No cunning mechanical arrangement, no conference,
no quoting of wages, no publishing of profits, will perhaps persuade workmen to abandon strikes wholly. You erect your
court of conciliation ; you bid disputants flock to it ; you promise
yourself the pleasure and honour of inaugurating a reign of industrial peace ; but too often, as soon as passions are fairly roused
and interests pull asunder, or when the arbitrator ceases to trim
and to split the difference, the old evils are in upon you—the
parties refuse to avail themselves of or trust the court. No
doubt this evil is provided for in a way by Mr. Kettle. The
history and plan of a court of arbitration are thus succinctly
stated by the Comte de Paris :—

"In 1864 the contractors in the building trade and the
carpenters not being able to agree, called in Mr. Kettle to settle
their differences. Six masters and six workmen met as delegates,
with Mr. Kettle in the chair. After a warm debate, in the
course of which each side was heard, they ended by agreeing so
well upon all the disputed points, that the chairman was not

once called upon to give his casting vote. Encouraged by so successful an experiment, Mr. Kettle resolved to develop this meeting of referees into a permanent institution; the masters on the one side, on the other the carpenters, plasterers, and after a time the bricklayers, came into his views, and their plenipotentiaries, under his direction, composed a set of rules regulating wages, which, it was settled, should remain in force for a year. All the masters who were represented at this conference were bound to have these rules posted up in their workshops, and to give a copy of them to every workman they engaged, explaining to him that they formed the terms of the contract between them. It was provided by one of the rules that all matters in dispute should be referred to a meeting of six masters and six workmen, sitting as a court of arbitration. This court derived all its power and influence from the fact that it was composed, not of mere delegates, but of real representatives; the members of it, therefore, were competent to decide all questions brought before them, without having to refer them to their constituents, who, on their part, were bound to submit to its decrees. In short, both masters and workmen having pledged themselves to abide by the decisions arrived at under the rules, the English law invested these decisions with legal authority; and, in case of resistance, they could be made a rule of court and enforced by the county magistrates. When once the rate of wages was by mutual consent unchangeably settled for a whole year, individual masters and workmen were bound only to adhere to the amount agreed upon, and all contracts, by which one party engaged to work and the other to find employment, might always be set aside in twenty-four hours, if either were dissatisfied."

Such a court is not to be despised. Then the employment of means to discover the actual supply of labour would dispense with strikes undertaken to find it out. That there should be better means of obtaining accurate information respecting the "produce" markets than the labour market argues some defect. To discover, however, a more thorough remedy for striking, we must know the nature and the cause of the malady, so far as it is a malady; and the cause is complex. It is well to say "so far as it is a malady," because strikes evince the presence of elements which are hurtful only in excess. Run down the history of any of the Western nations, and after one has traversed a few centuries of

turmoil and progress, in what other shape can one compress
more of the matter to be gleaned along the route than in this ?—
A privileged class struggling to retain their privileges against
an unprivileged class knocking at the door for admittance, and
at length forcing it open. Recall any considerable historical
fact, and it will be strange if it is not, directly or indirectly,
an episode in this struggle. "Those serious, though natural
enmities," says Machiavelli, "which occur between the popular
classes and the nobility, arising from the desire of the latter
to command, and the disinclination of the former to obey, are
the causes of most of the troubles which take place in cities."
Those "natural enmities" form half the history of States.
Well, so far as Europe is concerned, the door is opened.
Most of those privileges have been silently swept away in
England ; the French Revolution swept them away in France
with much bustle and bloodshed ; their reign was almost
finished in Germany when Stein virtually abolished serfage, and
permitted peasants to acquire the lands of nobles. De Tocque-
ville spoke of this tendency when he told his generation that it
was hurrying onwards, with footsteps not to be retraced, to
Democracy. Those rights are abolished, and the duties of
sustenance and help towards dependants, which were the correlatives of these duties, are also abolished. An aristocracy of
birth is elbowed out of authority by an aristocracy of wealth ;
and the misfortune which, in the meantime at least, we have
to deplore, is, that this plutocracy, having entered into the
privileges of an aristocracy, is still groping somewhat blindly,
tentatively, and with only partial success, to the code of duties
which are the moral correlatives of its privileges. The evils of
that old aristocracy—unbounded power and meagre responsibility—we are again in danger of admitting, and without check.
Our captains of industry, our cotton kings, are the modern
representatives of the Warwicks and Douglasses, with their
thousands of retainers ; but while the latter had a rude code
of etiquette of their duties to dependants, which in some rude
fashion they acted up to, there is no universally recognised code
of duties of employers to *employés*, or, if there be, it is conterminous with the legal enactments or decisions regulating the
relations of master and servant. Everywhere reigns the cruel
and crude fallacy that duties are extinguished by the fulfilment
of contracts. Now, those who admit the existence of an outer

circle of obligations, containing within it the narrow circle of
grosser obligations enforced by the law—whose morality is not
limited to a skilful and careful avoidance of the policeman—
will not be satisfied with an evasion of the gallows, the prison,
and fines. Take any system of morality one pleases, and
these external obligations face one. If morality is based on
religion, one must acknowledge that charity and benevolence
are as distinctly commanded as justice; the sole difference
being, that failure to render the latter is followed by temporal
punishment, while failure to fulfil the former is not. If one's
morality is simply enlightened self-interest, a well-informed
love of self, there are still motives why one should not stop
short at cash payments. And if you own, with more truth,
that in each or some of us there is a spring of disinterested-
ness, natural or acquired, you will need no behests to be laid
upon you, and kindliness will go out of you. Well, to do
what law and custom rudely did to better the relations of lord
and vassal, we require the growth of a code of etiquette which
will regulate the relations of the modern lord and vassal. It
should not be left wholly to each man to strike out a line of
conduct for himself; it is too much to exact of each one of men
steeped in business, that he should lay every course, from the
foundation upwards, of a theory of his duties to his dependants. Comte saw this want, and his sociology provides for it.
But his cure is worse than the disease. *La Société*, as arranged
by him, is minutely despotic. Still, the exaggeration of a principle is not the principle itself. It is not bad because Comte
misapplied it. The ordinary man must have some cut-and-dry
moral system ready to his hand. Reflect what, in a lower
sphere, etiquette does for the happiness of us all. Etiquette is
petrified politeness, fossilised considerateness ; and the salt that
was to-day passed at table in deference to usage was first passed,
we may well believe, by some Bayard or Sidney. Etiquette is
the chivalry of an early age, and the respectable mediocrity of a
subsequent one; and acts which were originally the efflorescence
of genius and high-souled generosity, coxcombs and boors at
heart by and by practise. Etiquette is a short cut to experience.
It is an artificial conscience : " each man makes his conscience,"
said Mirabeau : etiquette takes the work out of his hands. It
extorts from people that are clowns and selfish, acts that are
exteriorly polished and generous. Above all, etiquette, by

exacting from each one of us only imitation, and releasing us from incessant appeals to first principles, insures the world a high average standard of considerateness. Could we come to a rough understanding as to the duties of an employer, and have, in fact, a pretty uniform code of morality with respect to the relations of master and servant, we should reap benefits of a much higher kind than those which society reaps from its code of etiquette.

If only the rude and shapeless idea that more is due on both sides than the naked fulfilment of contracts, and that the only nexus is one of cash, received precision, we might hope for the disappearance of much of the animosity that now reigns between masters and servants. Setting aside a few loose and unfertile principles, securing nominal assent from all, consider how diverse are opinions with respect to 'the duties that spring out of this relationship. Practical ethics, a despised and neglected art, are nowhere more barren than with regard to the obligations over and above those written in the bond incumbent upon master and servant, *in foro conscientiæ*. Now, the consequence of this diversity of opinion is not merely to produce conduct which must be morally wrong. It unnerves even those who know their duty, and disqualifies them from performing it so faithfully as they would do, provided they were countenanced, stimulated, or punished, by a potent mass of homogeneous opinion. When such diversity of opinion exists, moral duties are performed with the inefficiency which we should witness in the discharge of legal duties in the event of there being different co-ordinate tribunals administering contradictory sets of laws. Those who are well disposed fall far short of their ideal, and those who are not so have no ideal. Public opinion, the sanction of moral rules, loses its influences when it speaks with an uncertain sound. It is sufficient here to insist that such duties do exist, that they are inadequately apprehended and stated differently, and that the principle which should preside over them is, that power should be accompanied by responsibility. If the doubt respecting these questions originated in the impossibility of settling them, there would be no ground of complaint. But the diversity, there is reason to think, is ascribable rather to carelessness or misdirected effort. We are ever rummaging in the affairs of remote planets, when duties at arm's length from us are unperformed.

This is not a direct or very certain road to the extirpation of strikes, and probably there is no such road compatible with the freedom to sell one's labour. Strikes are the sign of freedom ; they betoken the awakening of a healthy discontent, often the most efficacious elevator of man ; and they seem to be the price paid for this freedom. If they are now common and were formerly rare, it is chiefly because men are now in a position to sell their labour to the most advantage, and have acquired the disposition to use their newly got power.

CHAPTER XXI.

TRADES-UNIONS.

By an easy transition we pass from strikes to trades-unions. They are not, indeed, inseparable companions, for the most dangerous strikes of modern times—those of the Belgian miners —have been conducted without the organisation of a union, and there have been strikes in Wales to remind us that the connection is not indissoluble. Still, in this country, unions are the backbones of all successful strikes. It is uncertain what is the number of unionists in the United Kingdom. One estimate is 500,000, another 860,000. In a few trades—such as the tanners—unions are almost unknown, while in others, of which the engineers may be cited as an instance, they include the bulk of the workmen.

The two leading purposes of unions are to support men out of work, and to perform some of the offices of friendly or benefit societies. Let a member of the Amalgamated Society of Carpenters and Joiners—a favourable specimen, no doubt—be out of work, and he receives a certain allowance. While out of work, or "on donation," as the phrase is, he can draw on his society to the amount of £9 : 12s. a year. Should he strike, with the consent of the council, or, to quote the euphemistic phraseology adopted to escape the clutches of the law, should he "leave his employment under circumstances satisfactory to the branch or executive council," he is entitled to so much a week. One of the secondary objects of these societies is to obtain information regarding the state of trade and the demand for labour. Every month the branches send in to headquarters returns describing the state of trade, the strength of the society, and the burden on its resources ; and these returns furnish data to determine the feasibility of striking, and the best places to which to draft men out of employment. The proportions of the funds absorbed by strikes vary much. Thus, to take one extreme, the Amalgamated Engineers have, since the lock-out of 1851, expended almost nothing upon strikes, and the iron-founders only $2\frac{1}{2}$ per cent during ten years; while, to take another extreme, certain unions, such as the Sheffield Saw-Grinders, devote their whole resources to the support of strikes. Again, it was stated by the representatives of thirty English trades-unions that seven-eighths of their funds were allotted to benevolent or relief purposes, and only the remaining eighth to the support of strikes. Certain societies have shown in ways wholly indefensible their detestation of those who disregard their rules. A sadly long list of cases of vitriol-throwing, maiming, and blinding, attests the furious and brutal passions that have been enlisted in favour of unionism. At the same time, it must not be forgotten that the rules of no known union prescribe this form of persecution.

It is not easy to determine to what extent these malpractices are caused by unionism, and to what extent they are the effects of cowardice, meanness, tyranny, and cruelty, which would be displayed were there no unions. Similar deeds were committed with even greater frequency when there were no unions in existence, and villains do not require to enrol themselves in any club in order to be stimulated to crime. We do not burden the inherent character of the military profession with all the crimes committed by soldiers; we do not lay upon any cause the blame of all the crimes that may chance to be committed in its behalf. Still, having made every due allowance for inherent depravity, it is to be owned that corporations, whose morality at best is proverbially lax, such as unions, do too often stimulate vicious and unscrupulous men to violence. Members portion out guilt among them, and to have perpetrated the hundredth part of a murder or two-fifteenths of an assault, is a crime that lies lightly on the conscience. They do for "the society" things which they would shudder to do in order to compass private ends. More-over, they fancy themselves engaged in a war, and take to heart the deeds of violence which they commit as little as the soldier thinks of the enemies whom he has slain or wounded. Another difficulty experienced in apportioning the blame between the evil spirit which exists independent of the unions and that which is generated by them, arises from some unions coun-tenancing disreputable practices, without going so far as to enact positive rules enjoining these practices. Continuing the list of these disreputable practices, we may state that there are unions, such as brickmakers, that have steadily opposed the introduction of machinery, and have opposed it with violence. Manchester and its neighbour, Salford, have witnessed murders committed by men who not only objected to bricks being made by machines, but to any pattern of bricks being made by hand other than those 9 inches long, $4\frac{1}{2}$ wide, and 3 inches high. Even the Amalgamated Engineers desired in 1851 to restrict the use of machinery, inasmuch as they wished the new planing and turning machines to be worked only by men who had served or were serving an apprenticeship. Convinced, however, of the utility of machinery, or, as is more probable, taught that resistance is impossible, unionists have somewhat relinquished their futile endeavours to keep out machines; and a comparison of the Parliamentary reports of 1824 and 1825 with that of 1868-69 discloses a considerable improvement in this respect. More common is the attempt to limit the number of apprentices. Then, we find other unions objecting to piece-work. As the men do not, as a matter of fact, execute the same amounts of work, and as their work is not of uniform quality, it follows that masters who agree to this arrangement may, to protect themselves, take so much from the wages of the skilled and give it to the unskilled; and thus the artisan who does not know his business may fatten on those who do. A further effect of this measure is, as was pointed out by a witness before the Commission, that men who are too old to work as much as would entitle them to this average wage are thrown entirely out of work. Yet, if we except those brutalities, the criminality of which it would be an insult to expatiate upon, and which, like other vulgar crimes, are to be dealt with by the arm of the law, and if we exclude those which at once hurt the framers of the rules, we see not how the rest of the practices of unionists can be with consistency condemned by those who hold that pure unmitigated selfishness, with no regard for one's superiors or fellows, should rule the relations of master and servant, and of one servant to other servants; and the man who, in the name of " business is business," remorselessly turns off a servant without a thought of his future, practises the very principle he probably execrates when he finds it associated with unionism. Certainly employers who make use of " black lists " cannot with good grace cast a stone at unions.

Most unions have attached to them benefit societies, the objects of which are most laudable ; and one may hope that, when the lessons of defeat have been well conned, striking will sink into an incidental and subordinate object, and that numerous unions will be transformed into societies devoting their whole resources to relieve those thrown out of work, or disabled by accidents, to support the aged, to replace lost tools, and to satisfy that craving for decent burial which is the only immaterial passion of not a few of our poor. It is the hope that in trades-unions we have at length found that long-desired power which is to make the working classes provident as regards their future, which persuades many to look with forgiving eyes on the countless follies and crimes of unionists. And there is encouragement for those who entertain this hope, in the fact that, as the unions grow in age and wealth, they are found also to grow indisposed to strike, and that more and more they concentrate their funds on "benefit" purposes. Who knows but that unions, containing as they do about 700,000 skilled workmen, may not yet solve the problem of furnishing working men with the capital necessary for the establishment of co-operative societies ? The attention— no doubt slight—which they are giving to emigration is also an encouraging sign. True, it is to be feared that those unions which at present combine "trade purposes" with "benefit purposes" are in danger of insolvency. In fact, every such society must be potentially insolvent, for it has unknown and unlimited liabilities to meet ; and it is no answer to say that its resources are unlimited, inasmuch as it can at need make an extraordinary levy. If such a levy were made frequently, or to any great amount, the younger members would quit the society, and insolvency would ensue. At present, however, only a few societies promise superannuation ; and the safety even of these may be guaranteed if they raise by a few pence the weekly subscriptions, and fix a certain maximum to the amount to be devoted to strikes. It is also to be observed that unions, by means of "call-houses" and reports, facilitate the proper distribution of labour. Before 1855, no union, and for that matter no friendly society, could prosecute a member supposing he chose to embezzle the funds, it being a doctrine of the Common Law of England that a joint-owner cannot prosecute a joint-owner. In 1855 this state of matters was altered for the better, for it was enacted by the Friendly Societies Act that members of any society established "for any purpose which is not illegal" could prosecute a member.

But in 1867, the Court of Queen's Bench decided, in the famous case of Hornby *v.* Close, to the great alarm of the unions, that societies which were opposed to piece-work were established for a purpose that was not legal. The decision has been variously understood ; but it appears that the decision simply deprived certain Trade Societies of the benefit of the Friendly Societies Act. In 1868, Mr. Russell Gurney got passed into law a bill which increased the facilities for prosecuting embezzlement, and, according to some opinions, protected the funds of unions. That protection is on the eve of being accorded.

Here we are confronted with another agitation which unions fan. Besides agitating for an increase of wages, unionists frequently agitate for shorter hours. The nine-hours' movement at home, and still more so in the United States, has assumed gigantic proportions. *Distinguo* is an apt introduction to answering the question how far this agitation is feasible. The trade—its state, its prospects, the present hours of labour, the amount of the reduction in the hours—must be known before judgment can be delivered ; the judgment must alter as these data alter. If the present hours are so long as actually to injure the health, it may be that a reduction will increase the effectiveness of a man's work to such a degree that it may be to the profit of employers to diminish the period. Slaveowners, who have looked at this point with careful eye, know that there are a certain number of hours beyond which it is not remunerative to work gangs. In his lectures on Political Economy, M. Chevalier gives, on the authority of an employer of 4000 hands, a statement to the effect that the reduction of a half-hour in his spinners' time had been attended, contrary to all expectation, by an increase of 1-24th in the production. The Saturday half-holiday, equivalent to a general reduction in the hours of work, has, without contradiction, been followed by no diminution in production, for not only has it improved the health of our workers, but it has also secured more regular attendance during the week. The nine-hours' movement presents a difficult problem for solution, partly because it is impossible to ascertain to what extent, if any, the increased effectiveness of the labourer, due to the recruiting influence of greater rest and leisure, compensates for diminished attendance. Each person is the judge of the degree in which this compensation would operate ; the safest opinion seems to be that which expects least compensation. Assume the compensation to be null or slight ; the economics of the question are then simple. The request is a request for a rise of wages, for one may raise the price of a commodity, and of labour among other commodities, either by selling the same quantity at an enhanced figure, or by selling a less quantity at the old figure. The success of the movement, therefore, depends on the same circumstances as those which determine the success of ordinary movements for an increase of pay. Let the diminution in hours—that is to say, the increase in wages—be such that profits are seriously invaded, and that the capitalist prefers to eat his funds, as the French say, or to overcome his repugnance to change, and to embark his fortune in another business ; the movement is suicidal. Let the trade be an unskilled one, into which workmen may be readily introduced ; let it be a skilled trade in which there is for the time a glut of hands ; let it be one into which Belgium, France, or Germany, desires to embark, and possesses peculiar facilities and advantages for doing so ; let it be a trade into which machinery is tentatively creeping, ousting hand work ;— in the presence of any or all of these circumstances the movement is hopeless. On the other hand, let none of these circumstances be present; let the trade be compact, and all its members in brisk request ; let foreign competition be an impossibility, or in the far distance ; let the demand of their *employés* be not such as to disgust the capitalists ; and there is in the demand for a diminution of the hours of labour nothing extravagant or impossible. In the United States an eight-hours' movement has won a nominal triumph—eight hours is the time to be understood in all contracts not specifying otherwise, and the workmen in the Federal dockyards work only eight hours. The gain, however, is said to be illusory, for employers have proportionately reduced wages. There is a considerable impediment to the success of these movements in a very popular philosophy, which lavishes indiscriminate praise upon work. In these last days work has been canonised ; it has a liturgy ; priests sing its praises ; *laborare est orare* is the creed of multitudes who own no other; the ancients despised work, and we all but deify it. But when certain men have cleared their throats of a species of cant that at present sticks there to the impediment of truthful utterance, it will be acknowledged that if work saves some from being devils, it clips the wings of the rest; that, carried beyond a certain point, it is brutalising; and that it is a mockery and delusion to speak of moral improvement to those whose toil, creating a callousness only to be penetrated by coarse excitement, makes a man seek pleasure in flashes of dissipation.

Perhaps a fairer and more lenient estimate than that which is usual, would be formed of trades-unions if they were compared with other societies in high repute, which do not describe themselves as trades-unions, but which are so in substance. A few distinctions may, indeed, be detected between the unions of workmen and the societies of Lincoln's Inn and the Temple, the Scotch Bar and the Stock Exchange. It may be pointed out that the rattening which the benchers of the Inns of Court or the circuit mess may employ in the case of infringements of professional rules, does not amount to bodily injury or open insult. It may be pleaded with some truth that they do not compel recusants to enter their folds. Some of these societies may allege, with more or less truth, that they do not bar the entrance, so as to minimise the number of competitors, and there is no restriction upon the amount which a member may earn. Yet, discounting all this, we cannot fail to observe that they one and all agree with unions in imposing restrictions, direct or indirect, upon the modes in which their members may conduct their businesses; that they impose a minimum, and that as much as, or almost as much as, unions; and that they stand in the way of men who may be able to perform the work, but who have not acquired their knowledge or skill in the customary fashion. Set aside the heavy entrance-fees which lock out some who would otherwise enter, can there be found, for example, any union rule more exclusive, more manifestly designed to limit the competitors, than that provision in the entrance rules of the society of Scotch Advocates, which declares that no one can be called to the bar who has been during the previous year in remunerative employment? Could any arrangement be better designed to shut the profession to all but the rich and well to do? And if it be said that the object of this rule is to insure that every entrant shall have abundant opportunity for acquiring professional knowledge, the fitting rejoinder is, that unionists who object to the entrance of men who have not served the customary apprenticeship employ a similar argument : they too would persuade us that their conduct is prompted solely by a desire that every entrant should have had opportunities for acquiring professional knowledge ; and yet how incredulous are the critics of unions of these declarations, and with what zest they unmask them, and prove that these professions muffle selfish intentions ! The doctrine that each man should be permitted to do precisely as he pleases, and that skill is the main thing, that it does not matter how the skill is acquired, and that it is shameful to put obstructions, direct or indirect, in the way of entrants—doctrine which is remorselessly applied to unions—is forgotten when the societies of the middle classes are in question. In truth, there appears to be no substantial difference between trades-unions and these societies,—unless, indeed, the circumstance that the latter possess many privileges ; and the French National Assembly acted logically in at once breaking up trade-corporations, and introducing the freest competition at the bar. Trades-unions, let me add, are the modern manifestations of an old feeling. They are the counterparts of the castes of India, which, as Mr. Maine alleges, were nothing more than industrial occupations, with a religious sanction attached to them. These castes, as modern historical philosophy begins to admit, were not wholly pernicious institutions. They drew ringfences round those who had emerged from destitution, and did not permit them to be submerged or flooded by the surrounding masses. Little islands of comfort arose thereby out of its waters of misery. And the modern counterparts of castes have given the poor class the consciousness of their power ; inspired them with an *esprit de corps*, sometimes the generator of chivalrous and unselfish actions ; scooped a channel for their complaint to flow in ; and, in particular, have partially granted to the *ouvriers* that which the peasantry of Ireland desire under the name of fixity of tenure, and the peasants of India under the name of " occupancy." Such blessings unions seek to bestow, and the judgment pronounced upon them ought to be tempered by this knowledge.*

* One has but to read trade circulars—say in the wine trade—in order to find parallels to the selfishness of unions. Complaints respecting "the system adopted by foreign shippers of introducing themselves direct to the consumer," match the outcry of unionists against men who are not "legal."

Lock-outs are measures taken by masters to break the power of strikes. If assisted by those who are in receipt of good wages and in steady employment, the members of a large trade may long hold out, for the whole resources of a union are at their backs ; when one master, or a few, are pitted against the united strength of the men, it is not improbable that the latter may win ; and, attacking each of the masters singly, they may conquer all. To foil these tactics—to avoid being beaten in "a sectional struggle"—masters have on some occasions answered a strike by a general lock-out, and in the iron and shipbuilding trades masters' unions have been formed to retaliate upon the men. All the hands in a trade, or at all events all the hands in a particular district, have been turned adrift, and work refused until the men on strike capitulated. Obliged to devote its funds to the relief of its own members, all thrown by this lock-out on the union exchequer, one lodge, or set of lodges, can no longer assist another. The numerous pipes that fed the revolt are cut. A cordon is drawn round the strikers ; isolated, dependent on their own funds, they must soon capitulate if their masters do not soon relent. Attempts have been made to show that lock-outs stand in quite a different moral category from strikes, and that they are altogether more heinous. Mr. Frederic Harrison has denounced a lock-out as an industrial *coup d'état*," as " simply penal," possessing " a character of terrorism and aggression," " an abuse of power." He has said that masters " cannot fairly combine to punish their men for combining." This is to draw in morals an arbitrary line to the advantage of one's client. It is to insist that the cards be packed in one's favour. It may be true that " industrial wars, like national wars, have their own recognised code," and just as the code of international wars countenances all severity that tends to shorten hostilities, so would the code of industrial warfare, if it be modelled on, and be a correct analogy to, the code of international warfare, justify every measure that was thoroughly effective. And that lock-outs are effective needs no proof ; if facts did not demonstrate it, the complaints of those who have suffered from these measures of retaliation do. Mr. Harrison has said that the true parallel to a lock-out would be the case of masters consenting to the workmen's demands with the exception of one master, who, " with promises of assistance from the other capitalists," refuses, and of the union consequently ordering every workman in the kingdom to quit his work ; and this procedure would, he affirms, be universally stigmatised as a " wanton " exercise of power. " Wanton " it would in no respect be, if there were any reality in these promises ; and so far from being regarded as systematic " oppression and terrorism," we venture to predict that it would be considered as perfectly fair. If men throw themselves into any warfare, industrial or other, they must be prepared for the worst, and must not put their fingers in their eyes and blubber out " unfair " when their blows are returned with interest.

CHAPTER XXII.

POPULATION.

WAGES in any trade are determined by the supply of labour and the demand for it ; and the total potential supply of labour is the existing population.   It is, therefore, essential to state the laws of population so far as they are known.   Both Plato and Aristotle vaguely perceived the dependence of population on the available food ; and in order to keep the former within the bounds prescribed by the latter, they recommended, or at all events permitted, infanticide.   Indeed, so obtrusive and fundamental a fact as this dependence could not escape notice, and there were found in every age thinkers to announce the dangers of indiscriminate peopling.   De Maistre and certain Catholic economists, pointing to ecclesiastical encouragements to celibacy, have claimed for their church the merit of first fully appreciating the fact.

But the first person to consider population on its economical side with thoroughness, to describe almost exhaustively the causes which keep population within limits, and to demonstrate the hurtfulness of offering premiums with a view to increase of population, was the Rev. Thomas Malthus.   An English clergyman, a Tory, and a friend of the Government of the day, Malthus wrote his *Essay on Population* in the beginning of this century, in the wake of the false hopes excited by the publication of Godwin's *Political Justice*, to refute Godwin's thesis that the misery of his countrymen was ascribable to the negligence and tyranny of their rulers, to demonstrate how powerless the wealthiest and strongest and best Governments are to eradicate misery or to check its growth, to impress upon men that they may not with impunity introduce their fellows into this world without first taking care that seats and entertainment are provided for them therein, and to convince men out of the pages of history that temperance and forethought conduct to happiness, and intemperance and improvidence to want, disease, famine, and finally death. It lies with the people themselves to better their condition—this was the lesson Malthus taught, in refutation of those who said that poverty was a Government concoction : " A great command over the necessaries and conveniences of life," says Malthus, summing up the grand consequences of his doctrine, " may be effected in two ways, either by a rapid increase in the quantity and value of the funds destined for the maintenance of labour, or by the prudential habits of the labouring classes ; and as the former mode of improving their condition is neither in the power of the poor to carry into effect themselves, nor can in the nature of things be permanent, the great resource of the labouring class for their happiness must be in those prudential habits, which, if properly exercised, are capable of securing to them a fair proportion of the necessaries and conveniences of life, from the earliest stages of society to the latest." The doctrine from which those consequences are believed to flow runs as follows :—Man, like other animals, possesses the power to multiply far faster than the means of his subsistence ; within twenty or twenty-five years a people may double itself ; while population tends to increase at a geometrical rate, the means of subsistence tends to increase at an arithmetical rate. Two options lie before man, thus constrained by nature : People recklessly, and outstrip the means of subsistence, until " the struggle for existence " sets in, and famine, and disease or war (the positive checks), restore the disturbed equilibrium. In Asia, particularly in China and India, and in mediæval Europe, these were the instruments of decrease. Those great famines of which we read such incredible horrors in Boccaccio, and in the accounts of Indian travellers, were the executioners of Nature's mandates—the officers of a law as irreversible as that of gravitation ; while those torrents of Gauls that poured from the north to fatten the plains of Vercellæ ; those Asiatic hordes that traversed the great plain that stretches from the Atlantic to the Pacific, to kill or be killed ; those still earlier invaders that, parting on the great plateau of Central Asia, entered Europe, while the other half of the Aryan stock penetrated Hindostan ; that ceaseless flux of emigration from east to west,—were probably the fugitives from the accumulated consequences of the choice of this, the lot chosen by the improvident. But, unlike other animals, man often chooses another lot. He may limit his number : he may marry late, and have few children ; these courses are the prudential checks which lead to happiness.*

Let us preface any criticism of the doctrine by a remark perhaps not wholly irrelevant. On those who have not familiarised themselves with the literature and controversy which Malthus originated, it is impossible to impress any adequate sense of the fatalistic depression which this doctrine, misunderstood and misapplied, for a time produced—how the depressing conclusions drawn from it unnerved the hands and damped the hearts of philanthropists. Convinced of the impossibility of persuading the mass of people to take this doctrine as the guide of life, painfully impressed with the insignificant influence of isolated acts of self-restraint, and not perceiving considerations which cheered the prospect, they were filled with despair, and were driven to conclude that the path of progress turned out to be a blind alley, or terminated on the brink of a precipice. Raise wages ? Increase the comforts of the people ? Elevate a few ? Encourage emigration ? Of what avail ? The blind multitude will "people down" to wretchedness, and their last state will be more miserable than the first, for these futile efforts to diminish the misery of each will have succeeded in multiplying the victims and eternally disheartening well-wishers to the destitute. The most precious virtue was ostracised. Charity, hitherto considered the flower of the virtues, peculiarly favoured by courts of equity, and at times esteemed virtuous, even if the benefit of the recipient never crossed the giver's mind, was branded with odious names. A cloud of pessimism rested over the world. A conflict raged in tender minds between their feelings and the dictates of their understanding. And if mistakes were committed by those that acknowledged the truth of Malthus's teaching and were disposed to understand it, what gross caricatures were circulated by his enemies ! It was not merely stupid and insignificant men that wronged him. Thinkers like Mr. Sadler do not deserve even the immortality of infamy; it is

---

* " Prudential," and many of the other terms employed by Malthus, are infelicitous and inadequate. To illustrate this, I may refer to M. Le Fort's argument (*Revue des deux Mondes*, May 1867), that the vast standing army of France, necessitating much celibacy, has caused the population of that country to stand still.

needless to crucify the dead, and the author of the *Law of Population* was never in a literary sense alive. But when we find the lofty-minded Shelley, wont to accept the truth by whatever hands offered, avowing that he would prefer to go to hell with Plato than to heaven with Malthus, Coleridge vending incendiary nonsense about that "essential lie in morals," Malthusianism, and Southey raving in prose and verse as if Mr. Malthus were a kidnapper, the spectacle ought to be kept uncovered, if only to show what little security for soundness of judgment mere literary talents furnish, how genius is a capacity for perversion quite as much as a capacity for arriving at truth. Malthusianism was considered a form of devil-worship. Some said it must be false, seeing it impeached the beneficence of God. It was preached against as unscriptural from half the pulpits of the land. Byron gibed at Malthus's private life. Not that a little unfavourable criticism was not excusable. His disciples carried their master's doctrines to an outrageous length, and philosophers of the nineteenth century were found to speak of celibacy in language which would have been in place in the mouth of St. Jerome, and to propound as ridiculous schemes for obtaining it as ever occurred to the early Christians. One writer, for example, wished to kill off superfluous children by carbonic acid. Several recommended abortion. Fourier would have us all eat too much; in plethora lay safety.

Then Mr. Malthus's opponents could call attention to a few points in regard to which Mr. Malthus was manifestly wrong, or at all events ambiguous. Malthus spoke of population increasing at a geometrical rate, and the means of subsistence at an arithmetical rate. This was a random assertion; this relation is not always maintained; but the truth of Mr. Malthus's theory does not hang by this assertion. Again, it was affirmed that the theory turned upon a verbal fallacy, and originated in the employment of the word "tendency," first in a technical sense, and in subsequently transferring all the propositions which may be predicated of tendency of population thus understood to the popular sense, to the great alarm of the undistinguishing: the sun, it was said, tends in a technical sense to fly off into space, and so does man to outstrip his supply of food; but the latter contingency is as little to be dreaded or dreamt of as the former. This criticism, however, was not so well founded. The earth is impelled at every point in its orbit to fly off at a tangent, and is prevented by the centripetal force drawing towards the sun. Man possesses the power to fill the earth with his like; true, he rarely exerts that power, but he sometimes does; and Malthus's Essay is a reasoned catalogue of the forces, corresponding to the centripetal force, which induce him to limit his numbers. With better reason, it may be objected that Malthus employs the words "tendency" and "tend" in one sense when he speaks of men, and in a second sense when he speaks of their food. Consisting of numerous animals and vegetables whose powers of multiplication often exceed that which imagination can conceive, man's food tends, when circumstances favour the full exercise of its ability to multiply, to increase faster than man possibly could. There are few animals used by man for food that could not multiply more rapidly than he could under the most favourable circumstances. The propensity and power upon which Malthus bases his opinion are not peculiar to man. When he had doubled his numbers, the means of subsistence would have multiplied beyond the limits of conception. Only by giving to the term "tend" in one case the sense of "tend if unrestrained," and the sense of "tend if restrained" on the other, can it be true that population tends to increase at a faster rate than the means of subsistence do. As a matter of fact the case is the other way. Nay, on further examination, we shall find that the formula is not perfectly true without another improvement. Let a few families land in a desert island well wooded, to live in Swiss Family fashion; let them bring with them a few rabbits, pigs, goats, and other prolific animals, and within twenty years these families may have doubled their numbers; but within the same period these animals may have been multiplied thousands of times, and at a geometrical rate, notwithstanding that many have been killed to feed their importers. Still, only allow time to elapse, and, if the area occupied be not extended, the population will begin to outstrip the supplies of food.

Certainly there is no escape from the conclusion that man is shut up to some form of abstinence or famine and disease, except through a resort to emigration or through improvements in agriculture; and, as the latter device is limited, or at least as it is doubtful to what extent it can be employed, it may be put out of consideration as too dubious to be counted upon; so that it would seem that the only certain neutralising agency, apart from the prudential or positive checks, or abstinence in some form, is emigration. A fault of most of Mr. Malthus's disciples has been to under-estimate the power of the last. Somewhat blind to the endless tracts of prairie yet untouched by spade or plough, the virgin forests that wait to be cut down, to laugh with harvests, the marshes and stripes of shore to be reclaimed, and the arid expanses that will be fertilised as soon as they are irrigated by canals or the planting of trees, to the consequent increase of the humidity of the climate, they see in imagination the earth crowded like the Calcutta Black Hole—one vast opera crush. But gift each nation with the habits of industry that have drained Lake Haarlem, and that are not appalled at the project of draining the Zuyder Zee, people each square mile of Europe with 440 inhabitants, as Belgium, naturally barren, is peopled, and Europe alone might sustain nearly 320,000,000 souls. According to Sir John Herschel, the earth contains about 48,000,000 to 51,000,000 squares miles of dry land, and if we exclude one-fourth as totally unfit for cultivation —though in speaking of the far future it is rash to pronounce any part doomed to sterility—there remain some 39,000,000 square miles, which, at the rate of 440 inhabitants to the square mile, would support a population of 17,160,000,000. Put beside this the present paltry figure, and the possible development is seen to be enormous. Is it not in truth a presumptuous estimate of the importance of man to suppose that his dwelling-place is in danger of becoming too contracted? As if Africa, with its 9,000,000 square miles, Asia with its 12,000,000, had not been but scratched here and there ; as if the noxious fecundity, the crushing and disheartening luxuriance of vegetation and animal life in the tropics, along the banks of the Amazon and Niger, might not be made the slave of man's wants ! The valley of the Mississippi alone might feed the whole human race. And when the banks of the Vistula shall in far distant years be so densely peopled that Dantzic shall send no more corn to England ; when Odessa, become the capital of a crowded province, shall receive instead of sending forth corn ships ; when the United States, either by reason of the density of their population, doubled every twenty-five years, or the foolish and fatal " scourging " of the land, shall consume all their own corn ; then India, fertilised by the restoration of the irrigation · works of its old masters, and the formation of new works, may

be opened to the European world by roads, and railways, and
canals, and the time may have arrived for the fulfilment of the
antedated prophecy of Lord Dalhousie, that India would yet become a great grain producing and exporting country.   Figure to
yourself an earth peopled and cultivated as the neighbourhood
of Ghent or Bruges ; we dwell in a garden, and solitude is a forgotten idea ; in that day when man shall anxiously stretch his
hands to right and left for food, he need not stretch them in
vain, for the sea as well as the earth is capable of being cultivated, and of being utilised as a vast repertory of food.   To
cultivate the sea, to sow in it with certainty, is an idea of
yesterday.   Its fruits are yet only a few oyster-beds.   Pisci-
culture in rivers is meagre.   But what far-reaching consequences may be contained in the idea !   The epithet of the
" barren" sea, the epithet which Homer gave to it, and which
subsequent poets have repeated, may yet be falsified.
    One cannot study Malthus without being struck by the fact
that the pressure of population was felt when the earth had not
a quarter of its present inhabitants, and when, by his own ad-
mission, it was not over-peopled.   And if distribution was then
chiefly at fault, may not all errors now and for ages to come be
the same ?   The very appalling instances which he and his followers cite of the ravages of famine in ages when the earth was
unquestionably not too populous, are partial reassurances.   The
tendency in human nature to be most feared is not at present
its tendency to multiply excessively ; by compulsion or lethargy
we have been *adscripti glebæ* ; it is men's tendency to huddle
together and rarely to emigrate, and often to rot in the place in
which Providence has planted them.   " The plant man," says
Alfieri—and the epithet is admirable, for men cling with plant-
like tenacity to the spot in which they are born, and will turn
it into a warren rather than abandon it.   How few nations
have ever migrated in large numbers !   In modern times, only
the English, Irish, Germans, and Chinese.   It is a pity economists did not turn their batteries of abuse against those who
hindered emigration under the pretext of patriotism.   Laws
have been directed against emigration.   Frederick William I.
of Prussia prohibited it in set terms ; it was death for a Prussian to quit his country, or to help another to do so.   Against
this monstrous injunction Mirabeau protested, but to no purpose.
Was not every Prussian a soldier, and was not passing the

frontiers deserting one's colours? Happily these times are passing away; morality, that once could not go beyond a valley, and take in more than a race, has long since forded seas, and is not arrested at differences of colour; we have done, let us hope, with that patriotism which would detain a man to feed on herring and potatoes in Sutherlandshire, when buckwheat, bacon, and tea, waited him in Kentucky. In truth, we are now at the verge of an oscillation to an opposite extreme, and there are among us, as Rousseau says, people who love the Tartars in order to excuse themselves loving their neighbours.

Of course, it is true that men cannot advantageously emigrate without capital, and that the numerous attempts to do so have been lamentable failures. "Industry is limited by capital;" and virgin soil, requiring only to be tickled with a hoe to laugh with a harvest, will be a curse instead of a blessing if those who own it do not possess the wherewithal to till it; the chief crops will be fevers; and that fecundity which, if tamed, would have brought them plenty, will be the instrument of the emigrants' ruin. But recollect that the amount of capital in society is not fixed; that all, or almost all, that is expended in producing luxuries at home might be expended in producing necessities abroad, and that the wheat and corn consumed by race-horses at Melton Mowbray might have fed cart-horses in Wisconsin.

We must qualify one of the deductions frequently made from the theory. When Malthus told mankind that a duty lay upon it to restrict its numbers, he specified a duty which does not come home to every class. Rather the contrary is the duty of some classes of society. Though we may find fault with particular social arrangements, on the whole it must be granted that the men who do climb to the top, or who get into the middle ranks of society, are Nature's noblemen—the flower of the race. It seems to be pretty nearly proved that this class does not keep up its numbers. They marry, as a rule, late. Their children are few. More than the usual postponement of marriage among these people is precisely—pardon the apparently coarse comparison in consideration of our speaking on a subject the curse of which has been people not speaking plainly—as if all the exceptionally good animals were killed for food, and only those of an inferior quality allowed to breed. It may be conjectured that we are on the eve of discovering some laws which will modify materially the conclusions to be drawn from Malthus's theory. Already tentative theories are being formulated, and some of them are supported by a considerable amount of evidence. No doubt there is an eagerness to catch at every appearance of such laws, and to magnify every petty group of events that are favourable to one's case. The desire to emancipate the flesh is so strong, the resistance to such a harsh formula so universal and vigorous, that a certain suspicion is the proper mood in which to approach these laws. The most improvident of people are those who are always calling in the interposition of Providence ; there are always people prone to imagine that the universe was constructed with cunning arrangements for suffering man's passions to run on unreined, and who construe the beneficence of the Creator as a *carte blanche* for unlimited license. The late Mr. Sadler, a man of this last mood, laid it down that population increased at a rate inversely as its density. Lord Macaulay, reviewing this sham science in the *Edinburgh Review*, proved that, if Mr. Sadler was correct, there must be ladies in the backwoods of America each with 1,762,500 children, and that 200 children must be quite a common family for Westmoreland ladies—throwing the old woman who lived in a shoe entirely into the shade. Still there are on the carpet speculations gravely to be considered. They are of two kinds. One set of investigators tell us of the existence of physical checks, other than death, to the growth of population. Another set tell us of the existence of other passions which are certain to appear in due time, and which, without making any severe calls upon prudence, will always save mankind from the horrible consequences which Malthus predicted. Let us look at a few of the theories broached. In the first place, Mr. Doubleday, in his *True Law of Population*, arrives by a laborious, if not exhaustive, series of investigations, at the conclusion that, as nourishment increases, population decreases, and that, instead of population expanding pretty much as food grows more plentiful and better, the reverse is nearer to the truth. " The great general law, then," says the late Mr. Doubleday, summing up the results to which his investigations had conducted him, and which tallied with those of Fourier, " which, as it seems, really regulates the increase or decrease both of vegetable and animal life, is this, that whenever a *species* or *genus* is *endangered*, a corresponding effort is invariably made by nature for its preservation and continuance, by an increase of fecundity or fertility ; and that this especially takes place whenever such danger arises from a diminution of proper nourishment or food, so that consequently the state of depletion, or the deplethoric state, is favourable to fertility; and that, on the other hand, the plethoric state, or state of repletion, is unfavourable to fertility, in the ratio of the intensity of each state." Hence Mr. Doubleday concludes that increase or decrease, upon the whole, depends upon the proportion which the poor, the middle classes, and the rich, bear to each other. This theory was propounded in opposition to the "monstrous theory," "the disgusting and truly absurd assumptions" of Malthus ; and it may be urged, if not as an objection to the truth of "the true law," that it does not collide with Malthus's law, and does not insure men against the necessity of curbing their lusts. Moreover, Mr. Doubleday gives plausibility to his theory by omitting mention of a vast number of facts that point in an entirely different direction to that indicated by the facts which he quotes ; and he does not recollect that the diet which is meagre in a northern clime is luxurious in the tropics. Mr. Carey thinks that the intellectual labour incidental to civilised life diminishes the fertility of mankind. This may be ; but it may be observed, with regard to this theory as well as Mr. Doubleday's, that they are both compatible with a high rate of increase of population unless prudence and self-restraint be employed, seeing the rapidity of the growth of population depends less upon the number of births than upon the number who live. Accepting Mr. Doubleday's own theory, it would be quite possible that the rate of increase in a state of depletion would be slow if the infant mortality was great, and in a state of repletion population might wax amain if few children died. On the other hand, taking Mr. Cary's theory to be correct, it would be possible for a highly civilised and cultivated people to multiply far faster than a rude uncultivated people, if the rate of infant mortality was so low among the former as to redress the inequality in the rate of births. And it must be borne in mind that the very same circumstances which, according to these writers, insure few births insure few deaths.*

One alteration in Malthus's teaching it is possible to make without employing any doubtful hypothesis. So long as population is exceedingly sparse—so long as the country is peopled

* See Mr. Herbert Spencer's *First Principles*, vol. ii.

very thinly—until, in fact, society exists, the means of subsistence are scanty; and why? Not because population is too numerous, but because it is too small, because functions cannot be divided—because division and co-operation of labour cannot be employed. Until this term is reached it is prudence to increase the population. Bastiat partly saw that this was the case; he quoted it to his contemporaries as a ground for cheering them; he did not also mention that this ground of comfort was limited.

Malthus's law looks less alarming if we consider that it can be inverted, and that we can with equal propriety affirm that there is a constant tendency in the means of subsistence to increase faster than population; and, imitating Malthus, we might go on to assert that the disappearance of mankind, owing to reluctance to marry, was prevented only by certain checks, consisting chiefly of certain propensities. The sole reason why Malthus's way of looking at the matter is preferable to that here suggested is, that the tendency of which he speaks has hitherto usually been more dangerous than the opposite tendency. Nay, in old civilisations these primitive propensities are coerced or checked by passions of artificial origin; the latter, that for a time feebly thwarted the former, by and by became their formidable competitors, and, it may be, finally dominate over passions supreme in the rude and poor. These secondary passions play a larger and larger part in the world's history; in time they become the protagonists in the drama. Various forms of self-indulgence, vicious, if at all vicious, only in excess, become enlisted against the tendency to increase population. Vanity, ambition, desire for wealth, eagerness to get on, selfishness in many forms, the knowledge that about one woman in 188 dies in childbirth, for such are Dr. Farr's figures, are some of the influences that may be ranged on the other side. It is assuredly true of certain classes that these passions act with as much constancy and strength as the primitive sexual passion they combat; they have become a second nature. What is true of these classes may become more or less true of all, seeing these are passions the roots of which are in all men. Moral these agencies are, in so far as they prevent the too great growth of population; moral they are not if that implies self-denial. Further, it need not be pointed out that the very propensities dreaded by Malthus are frequently indulged in without any augmentation of population.

Malthus dilated on the evils of the quantity of population ; perhaps an *alter* Malthus will yet worthily speak of the physical quality of population, the proper corollary of his thesis. The regulations everywhere adopted touching intermarriage are rudimentary laws conceived in this spirit ; and the influence of what is now acknowledged to be a fact of some moment will one day doubtless be accurately measured.

Mr. Galton, commenting on the indiscriminate precept to postpone the period of marriage, says it is "calculated to bring utter ruin upon the breed of any country where the doctrine prevailed." And as to the race at large, are the Caucasian races to leave the world to less gifted races, and are the most gifted portions of the Caucasian races to leave it to the least worthy, whose fertility is often very high? To act on this principle would be to abandon what Darwin has shown to be the chief ameliorating agency in the case of other animals ; and so-called prudence would dictate the extirpation of the best specimens of the race. Tait's laws, that "fecundity at various ages is proportional to the number of years a woman's age is under fifty," and that fertility, or the number of children actually born to a woman, is proportional to the square of the number of years she is under fifty, may not be demonstrated ; but they rest on enough of evidence to make us aware of the advantage inferior races have, marrying as they do much farther below fifty than their superiors.

CHAPTER XXIII.

INTEREST AND PROFIT.

IN a few of the previous chapters, Wages and the chief cognate questions have been considered. The other half of the distribution of wealth and exchange will have been almost disposed of when Profits and Interest, the wages of abstinence, the fee derived from lending, or the advantages derived from using Capital, are considered. What Capital is, we may recal : it is wealth of any kind set aside to produce new wealth; it is wealth which is saved though not hoarded. And being the fruit of abstinence, capital can continue to be created only when the saver receives a certain advantage therefrom—that is a certain profit. According to the character of the Government, the security of property, the certainty as to the future, and the national character, this profit will vary. A Dutchman, prudent by temperament, and engaged in no very speculative business, may be content with 2 or 3 per cent ; in very brisk times an American may look for 30, or may demand 50, or even more. In times and countries of insecurity, or in trades which are full of perils, profits must be, of course, heightened. The prudent trader always insists that his profits shall contain an adequate remuneration for saving, insurance for losses, and wages for himself, or, as the French say, undertaker's profits. All these elements are lumped together in the gross profits ; but the first only constitutes the profits of the economist—the wages or remuneration of abstinence. And with this as the sense attached to " profits," we may affirm that in all businesses they tend to equality, for if any one capitalist be earning exceptional profits, by and by other capitalists will probably embark in his business, until they drag down profits to the level elsewhere. Not that the net profits at any given moment are the same in all trades ; far from it. The proposition laid down is, that—excluding from consideration, on the one hand, those who, by charters, patents, brevets, bounties, legal guarantees, and protective duties, or any artificial or natural monopoly, obtain as monopolists or favoured individuals exorbitant profits, and, on the other hand, the very large number of people who conduct their businesses in a manner that leads straight to bankruptcy, and who earn less than the average rate, and eliminating the allowance made for insurance and the rewards of peculiar skill, which are really wages— profits in the same country tend by competition to be equalised.

It follows from the creation of capital requiring abstinence and self-denial that it will be lent to none without a return. This return is interest. And as nobody will give away that which he possesses for less than that which others obtain for the hire of articles of wealth produced by similar amounts of labour, and for equal exertion of self-denial, it is most natural that there should be one rate of interest. This varying rate is quoted every day in the loan market. Loans are now to be had at 2½ per cent, now 3, now 5, sometimes 10. Interest, pure and simple, it may be observed, is as rare as profits pure and simple; it is scarcely exhibited save in the loans to Governments of proved solvency and good faith. In the rate of interest so called there is almost always an element of insurance.

Some have said that interest depends on the contemporary rate of profits, and profits on wages (in both not the gross amount, but the proportion). And, no doubt, this is faithfully descriptive of a large mass of what may be called primitive financial phenomena. But there are in practice important checks to this tendency; and as a country grows in years, and as it accumulates a mass of obligations, the influence of this law becomes less and less. Vast public debts, yielding dividends calculated according to the rate of interest and the security of some former period, influence the rate of interest, and prevent it from falling quite so far as the current rate of profits would sometimes warrant. So do vast amounts of railway debentures, and other debts contracted at former periods when loans were negotiated on different terms. Reciprocally, and of course still more evidently, the rate of interest affects the prices of security; the general law, subject to certain temporary influences, being that they rise in price as interest falls, and *vice versa*. The consequence is, that loans contracted as far back as Pitt's time now faintly affect the English money market. Accordingly, the variations of consols register the fluctuations in the price of money, and tend to rise when money is cheap, and *vice versa*. Thus, in 1852, when the bank rate of discount was on an average 2 per cent, consols were quoted 102, the highest figure ever attained in this century. To the statement that interest depends on the current rate of profits, other limitations must be set. The period for which a loan is made influences the rate of interest or discount. A short loan on the security of consols will not be made on the same terms as those on which a three months' bill is discounted, and the latter will not be discounted at the same rate as a six months' bill. Here *Qui solvit tardius solvit minus* holds. The probabilities as to the rate of profit until the *echéance* of the obligation and the degrees of risk enter into account; and we often witness a striking divergence between the rate of discount and the hire of capital for permanent investments. Still, these qualifications made, it may be said generally that interest depends on the rate of profits. True, the loan market is generally spoken of as the money market, and interest is said to depend on the amount of disposable money. If gold were meant by this term, the theory would be wrong; the amount of gold in the bank is no index of the rate of interest on discount; and to corroborate this statement, it may be mentioned that in 1866, with the latter rising to 10 per cent, the bank possessed more gold than in 1867 when the rate fell to 2 per cent, and that the rate of interest in Australia and California during the gold fever was very high. What is really meant by money is gold and all its equivalents. When the amount of deposits augments, when much purchasing power lies unused, when the reserves of the Bank of England and the Joint-stock Banks are increased, interest falls; in opposite circumstances it rises. The influx of bullion, to which the mercantile world attaches so much importance, is instrumental in producing the former result only if it can be made use of in augmenting the supply of loans. No doubt, in a crisis, the amount of the Bank reserve in gold and notes, and the demand for their accommodation, are the sole determinants; then it is gold or notes which people want to have. In normal times, however, the rate of interest will vary with the quantity of available advances in the shape of gold, notes of all sorts, bills of exchange, and all the equivalents of money, which are what borrowers want. It must not, however, be assumed that these determine the rate of interest. Their amount is itself determined by the quantity of capital which can be offered for sale, and it in turn by the rate of profit. In order to clear up this question, one of the most rarely understood portions of Political Economy, the difference between the trade in money and that in capital must be borne in mind. In the case of the former —which is the usual staple of short loans—the actual amount of coin is the immediate determinant; in the case of the latter an influx of gold may not affect the rate of interest. In fact, only when the supply leads to an augmentation of loanable capital, when it does not bring about a neutralising rise in prices, and when the consequence is that more corn, iron, etc., are offered for sale, will gold produce a permanent reduction of the rate of interest. Hence we must take with caution the statements of those who regularly predict a fall in the rate of interest whenever gold accumulates. No doubt within limits they are right. But it is equally clear that in the long run a rise of prices would be the sole result of a large augmentation of the stock of gold ; and one cannot accept as well founded the notion that a depreciation of gold would produce a fall in the rate of interest. By depreciating consols, it might have even the opposite effect. Eventually interest depends, we repeat, on the amount of capital and the demand for it ; the former on the rate of profits ; and profits on wages or the cost of wages. Of course we speak here of the proportion which the capitalist's share bears to the whole produce, not of the gross amount of his profits. The latter depends upon the productiveness of labour.

It is an easy transition from this question to another of equal importance. Why, as a country is densely peopled—why, we may say, as society advances—do profits tend to fall ? Hume and Smith answered that competition caused the fall, that the competition of sellers of capital brought down the profits. This account is alleged to be incorrect, and Mr. Mill points out that a fall of price in all commodities would not lower profits. He alleges that profits are depressed mainly by the fact that as population grows in density the difficulty of obtaining food for the wage-receiving population is intensified, and that people are driven by this difficulty to cultivate soil of bad quality or unsuitable situation, which had, when the population was thin, made culture impolitic. The connection between these facts appears, if we consider that wheat and potatoes, and other commodities forming the staple of a workman's actual wages, tend to be

Y

obtained at an ever-increasing outlay of labour, and that to give a labourer even the mere necessaries of life tends to absorb an increasing proportion of the gross produce. At an expenditure in wages of 20 quarters, a farmer gains one year 400 quarters out of 600 quarters, the gross proceeds of the farm, the farmer obtaining 66⅔ per cent. A subsequent year he improves some acres of marsh or moorland, each acre of which may indeed be made to yield as much as the old land did, but at an additional expenditure of labour ; the gross profits procured may now be swelled by the improvements to 1000 quarters, but the wages-bill may show that 400 quarters have been expended in labour, and that while his net profits are 600 quarters, the rate of his profits may have fallen from 66⅔ per cent to 60 per cent. The decline might go on if the farmer annexed acres of diminishing fertility ; and if we mentally substitute for him a whole people confined to a limited territory, and obliged by the pressure of their multiplying wants to drain the marshes which before had nourished a few waterfowl, to dyke round the polders with vast and costly walls, to mix with marl the soil, to bind together shifting sand by sowing it with broom or the Alpine Pine, we shall follow the route by which old countries find their way to low profits. To this account, however, it may be objected, first, that if it were the diminishing returns of successive increments of labour which were the cause of the diminution of the rate of profits, the rate of wages rather than that of interest would tend to fall. Secondly, though it is true that if all articles fell in prices profits would not decline, this cannot be said if all articles but labour declined in value. And such would be the case if capital augmented at a much greater rate than labour. I am inclined to think that this, rather than the above, must be the true explanation of the actual fall of value in capital and interest, its hire, in several countries —countries in which surprising improvements in machinery and agriculture have retarded the realisation of the theory that successive applications of labour are attended by diminishing returns.

There are always considerable differences between the rates of interest in the different countries of Europe. These differences, so far as they are not rates of insurance, represent the various amounts of surplus capital. Thus, interest on the Amsterdam Bourse is generally considerably lower than interest elsewhere on the Continent. Why do these variations continue? The cost of transmission of coin is of course one cause of the differences, so far as they are due to scarcity or abundance of metals; and how effectual it may be may be seen by the following passage which I quote from Mr. Goschen : "The interest being taken at a percentage calculated per annum, and the probable profit having, when an operation in three months' bills is contemplated, to be divided by four, whereas the percentage of expense has to be totally borne by the one transaction, a very slight expense becomes a great impediment. If the cost is only $\frac{1}{2}$ per cent, there must be a profit of 2 per cent per annum in the rate of interest, or $\frac{1}{2}$ per cent on the three months, before any advantage commences; and thus, supposing that Paris capitalists calculated that they may send their gold over to England for $\frac{1}{2}$ per cent expense, and chance their being so favoured by the exchanges as to be able to draw it back without any cost at all, there must nevertheless be an excess of more than 2 per cent in the London rate of interest, over that in Paris, before the operation of sending gold over from France, merely for the sake of the higher interest, will pay." So far as the differences in the rate of interest are due to the scarcity or want of capital, in the economical history of the particular country we must seek the cause.

Interest has frequently been condemned as immoral and pronounced unlawful. Every one is aware that the Jews were forbidden to charge interest for loans to each other. Aristotle thought interest unnatural : money was naturally barren; why should it beget anything? The Fathers combated the practice. Calvin's defence of it sounded strange to men who had heard Luther's invectives against interest. Popes and Councils thundered against it, and Dante peoples a round of the *Inferno* with usurious sinners. Sometimes acknowledging the injustice of their prohibitions, and observing the facility with which their prohibitions were evaded, legislators permitted the taking of interest, and prohibited usury—*i.e.*, a high rate of interest. Bentham was the first adequately to expose the absurdity and injuriousness of such restrictions, and to show that they wounded those whom they were intended to benefit. His arguments are unanswerable. The Legislature in 1854 repealed the usury laws—though the equity courts have sometimes been disposed to partially re-enact them. But in assenting to the reasons why the charging of an usurious rate of interest should not be made a perfect obligation, people have forgotten that it may still remain an imperfect obligation. Of course, the penalties menacing those who exceeded the legal interest did the borrower no good, but much harm, for the high rate of interest generally arose from the bad security ; and as the law stepped in with the effect of making the security more insecure, the borrower, thanks to the law that would favour him, was unable to borrow at all, or was able to do so only clandestinely, and at an enormous rate, sufficient to repay the usurer for breaking the law and running the risk of exposure and punishment. Again, if the legal rate were fixed too low the available capital might be carried away, and the people who were most in need of loans, and who in their extremities would willingly have offered a higher percentage, may be unable to procure advances, and may be thereby ruined. This has frequently happened. We do not often hear now-a-days of undisguised proposals for fixing the rate of interest, but in a slightly disguised form they are not uncommon. Thus, there are projects for fixing the rate of discount, or naming a maximum rate. To be successful, this plan would require to be prefaced by measures for fixing the amount of capital and the demand for it.

CHAPTER XXIV.

RENT.

RENT, in one sense, may be considered a form of interest. The landowner gets profit from his land when he tills it himself, interest when he lets it to others. The awkwardness of this phraseology partly arises from our usually employing the terms "rent" and "hire" in the case of fixed capital, and interest in the case of circulating capital. Some, however, will think that it is not language only that is offended by this conjunction of interest and rent, for English Economists have devoted great pains towards elucidating a law of rent, to which they attach much importance, and which places land in a distinct category. This theory professes to tell how rent arose, and what are its laws. Postulating that the earth is limited in amount and varying in value, according to the quality of the soil and the situation, they have said that at first, and so long as population was sparse and the soil of the first quality abundant, men paid no rent; that new necessities forced them to cultivate land of the second quality, which then paid no rent; and that the occupiers of the first, who enjoyed an instrument of exceptional power, an advantage measured by the difference in value between the produce of it and of soil of the second quality, were asked to pay a rent equal in value to this advantage. This course, it is said, goes on as more wheat becomes necessary : one century the sunny slopes or fat carses are cultivated ; another century the plough is driven along the bleak hill-side ; and there is always, according to this theory, one kind of soil under cultivation which is too poor to pay rent; the difference between its produce and that of other soils measuring their rents. This theory would be most valuable if it were the abbreviation of the history of agriculture in the past and the plan of its course for the future, and were it actually true that the path of cultivation

ran uniformly from the poor soils to the fertile.   But the course·
is often not so.   The backwoodsman first goes to inferior soils;
it is late, when the woods are cleared and the climate is purified,
that he tills the fertile old river-beds.   The Italian peasant
of the Maremna skulks down furtively to the rich poisonous
plains.   If we widen the signification of the term fertility, so
that it includes every convenience which can affect the value of
land, the theory may indeed be historically true, but it dwindles
down into the vague and uninstructive assertion that the passage from one piece of land to another has been pretty much as
people thought fit.   The theory, considered as a statement of
the actual history of agriculture, therefore, contradicts our knowledge, or does not add to it.

Let us look next at its value as a statement of present facts.
The substance of the theory is, that there is always some land
which does not pay rent, inasmuch as it yields only the ordinary
profits of capital, and that the rent of superior soils is equal
to the difference between their produce and that of the worst
land under cultivation.   Examining this theory more closely,
one is in the first place disagreeably impressed by its loose and
shifting character.   Rent, it is said, is measured by the difference in fertility between the soils which do, and the soil which
does not, yield more than the ordinary profits of capital.   This
assertion is clear ; but, not being true, it is next changed into
the assertion that rent is equal to the difference in fertility or
accessibility of the soils which do, and the soil which does not,
yield more than the ordinary profits of capital.   This is not the
only modification : besides variations in fertility and degrees of
proximity to markets, the enunciators of this theory introduce a
number of indefinite elements, such as healthiness of situation,
etc., that affect the value of land ; and when they have introduced all these elements, they proceed to make the theory still
more uncertain by informing their readers that rent arises not
solely from differences in soil, but that it proceeds also from
" the inequality in the returns to the capitals successively
expended on the same soils."   Such a theory, so shifting, and
presenting so many sides, almost defies attack, though at the
same time its indefiniteness rouses one to the suspicion that
it may be useless.

It is freely owned that the theory does not explain all that is
known by the name of rent.   It does not hold good of the rents

paid by the ryots of India. There rent resembles a land-tax. They are not exposed to competition. Their rents do not necessarily vary with the fertility of the soil. "By conquest, the earth became the property of the holy Parasa Rama; by gift, the property of the Sage Casyapa, and was committed by him to Cshatriyas (the military caste) for the sake of protection." So say the Hindoo laws; and, as conquerors, the owners of the land were able to exact what rent they thought fit. In the case of the ryots of Persia and Turkey, as well as of India, rent is in truth of the nature of a land-tax; and though custom has created a species of tenant-right, limiting in practice the landlords' exactions, they are, in theory at least, unlimited. Even in practice there have been too often no other limits to the rapacity of rulers than starvation on the one hand, and the fear of revolt on the other. Nor does Ricardo's theory hold good of labour rents or métayer rents, which are fixed by arbitrary custom. It does not hold of rent in countries like Ireland, in which tilling the soil is the only occupation open to the mass of the people, whose necessities may compel them to submit to whatever rent the landlord is pleased to exact. It does not hold of countries in which there is no commerce offering an outlet to capital which does not find in agriculture fair profits. Perhaps it is too much to demand that Ricardo's theory of rent should cover these numerous cases. But what we have a right to expect, and the test which it is lawful to apply, is, that, supposing a state of general competition, and land a marketable article, bought and sold as ordinary goods and chattels, the theory should accurately fit the actual facts. Does the theory satisfy this test? I think not.

Ricardo stated that rent was the sum paid for the use of the " original and indestructible powers of the soil." And if rent be such, then in no old country of the world—not even in Great Britain, the only country where there exist landlords and farmers in abundance—is there much of such a thing as rent, for the natural and inherent properties of the soil have long ago been destroyed, or, if they have not been destroyed, they are not economically useful. Except in the most rudimentary form, agriculture cannot long subsist without a careful renewal of the properties of the soil. The farmer must renew his soil as well as his seed. Land may be worked out like a lead or coal mine. Why did the traveller, in Virginia or the Carolinas,

long before the Civil War, stumble every now and then on
ruined buildings and deserted fields? Why have declines in
the annual yield of some of the Northern States been observ-
able? Why has Sicily, once the granary of Rome, with its
meadows producing unexampled returns, sunk into a miserable
country, one-third of it barren, or exporting a little olive oil?
Why is Palestine, once a land flowing with milk and honey,
barren and thinly peopled, the veritable antithesis of that which
it is painted by the prophets? Why, to take a still more
striking instance of decadence in wealth, have the banks of the
Euphrates, which once may have been as fertile as the banks of
the Thames, been transformed into baked and parched plains.
One agency alone did not accomplish all these changes; repeated
misgovernment shared in the work of desolation; conquests did
so too. But though misgovernment and conquest may have
exercised a blighting influence, the present barrenness is principally attributable to the so-called original and indestructible
properties of the soil being peculiarly transient, to agriculture
being long possible only if the properties of the soil are
perpetually replaced by manure or other devices. The slave
planter of Virginia wore out his soil, bought a plantation
elsewhere, and migrated. The Sicilian at last drained the
fertility of his milch cow, as Michelet calls the island.
When the cisterns that crowned, or the terrace walls that
girdled, the hills of Palestine fell into ruins, vegetation was
parched by the heat of summer, and the soil swept away
by the unfertilising rains of winter. The canals that in-
tersected and watered the banks of the Euphrates were
suffered to fill up, and a goodly region became "a wilderness,
a dry land, and a desert." These are the consequences of
trusting to "the original and indestructible powers of the soil."
Liebig, the first to draw attention to the vastness of the operations of this spoliation system, shows how often farming has
been conducted on this principle, and always with the result of
bringing on sterility. In the best farmed countries, in which
rent forms an important element of the national wealth, rent is
for the most part the return for capital actually expended on
the soil.

It is said that rent arises from the difference of soils in their
fertility or their proximity to the markets, or in the difference
of returns in the capitals. Of course, it is very obvious that

rent might be exacted if the land were of uniform fertility, provided farmers, consuming their own produce, had their markets
at their doors. There being in this instance no difference in
cost of production, surplus value could not arise, yet rent
in respect of a monopoly might. Should the whole land be
required to feed the population, it might be neither true that
there was any piece of land not paying rent, nor that rent
originated in the difference of soils. In such circumstances,
every morsel of land might yield a rent simply in virtue of
appropriation. Take now the alternative propositions, that rent
originates in the difference of returns to capital on the same soil,
and that there is, as Mr. Mill says, "always some agricultural
capital which pays no rent, because it returns nothing beyond
the ordinary rate of profit :" neither are these propositions
faultless. " The same amount of demand and the same price
which enable this least productive portion of capital barely to
replace itself with the ordinary profit, enable every other portion
to yield a surplus proportioned to the advantage it possesses.
And this surplus it is which competition enables the landlord to
appropriate. The rent of all land is measured by the excess of
the return to the whole capital employed on it above what is
necessary to replace the capital with the ordinary rate of profit ;
or, in other words, above what is necessary to replace the
ordinary rate of profit." Mr. Mill's argument perhaps proceeds
on the tacit assumption that the farmer is the improver, and that
the work of draining and manuring the soil is executed by him.
Let us assume that the owner spends the capital. It may not
be true, and is not true, that all rent is the return on capital
actually expended on the soil. An island in the English Channel,
on which nobody had expended a farthing, would yield rent ;
and Bastiat and Carey, who resolve rent into the proceeds of
capital, are mistaken. But it certainly is true that in some instances rent is neither more nor less than the return on capital.
There might be whole districts in which this is the case, and in
these instances would the landowner give the use of any portion of his capital for nothing ? Certainly not ; and if he would
not, it cannot be said that there is always some land or agricultural capital not paying rent. Certainly it cannot be said
that rent in such circumstances necessarily arose from the inequality of the returns to capital expended on the same soil.
The simple fact that the area at command was limited, and that

a price must be paid for appropriation or monopoly, would account for the existence of rent.

Ricardo's theory of rent, if complete and accurate, should accord with the rents of any given agricultural district, provided the land is freely exposed to competition, and bidders are to be found ; does it accurately comply with the following facts ? Lake Haarlem, a lake fifteen miles long by seven wide, was drained by the Dutch Government in 1858, and 42,000 acres, which had previously been absolutely worthless, was sold for £661,000. Suppose the State, instead of selling the land, had rented it : Would there, at all events need there, be one portion of this land not paying rent ? Would the theory correspond to the state of matters in a country the whole soil of which was reclaimed from the sea ?

If it be then true, that in a country whose farmers actively compete for the land, there may, in the first place, be rent without any difference in fertility or accessibility, and there may be no land under cultivation not paying rent ; and, secondly, that all agricultural capital may pay rent,—it follows that Ricardo's theory of rent does not bear a close examination in regard to all points ; it does not meet all conceivable circumstances in a state of perfect competition, and it is therefore not a complete theory.

" Rent does not enter into price "—this proposition is apt to excite astonishment, and Mr. Buckle has spoken of it as inconceivable by one who has not seen it demonstrated. The demonstration is simple. Were there no rent—that is, no sum paid for "the natural and inherent properties of the soil"— did farmers sit free, were they in fact landowners—agricultural produce would not fall in price ; the owners of the superior soils would pocket the landlord's together with the farmer's profits ; nobody but the farmers would be a whit the better. At the same time, this startling proposition does not hold good of articles produced on a limited area, where practically the conditions of production are the same. There rent, or the price of appropriation, does enter into price. Secondly, as corn is grown to an enormous extent in countries where confessedly farming is not conducted in accordance with Ricardo's theory, where farmers are content to go without profits as measured by an English standard, and where the theory entirely fails to apply, rent may enter into the price of corn ; and, considering that the exports of Dantzic and Odessa permanently rule the market, perhaps rent does, as a matter of fact, enter into the price of corn. Nay, one may go further, and say, generally, of agricultural produce in England, that its price is regulated by that of produce, into the value of which rent does enter as an element. Rent, we may say generally, may be regarded as the price paid for the use of the various natural agents of production. In the conditions supposed by Mr. Ricardo, his account of it will generally hold good. But these conditions, Political Economists ought frankly to recognise, are rarely realised.

CHAPTER XXV.

TAXATION.

THE second part of distribution is concerned with distribution in virtue of force. Excluding mere violence or rapine, as now reduced to comparative insignificance, this division includes the whole field of taxation, and all such distribution as originates in legal compulsion. Into the phenomena of exchange economists have attempted to introduce unity, by the supposition of a condition of universal and unchecked competition ; but it has been felt that, with respect to taxation, the only way to introduce order into the multitudinous and multifarious facts is, by stating the rules which would guide an enlightened statesman, and noting the deviations from them—in fact, by assuming a perfect system of taxation, and regarding Political Economy as a form of Deontology. In defiance of their plans and arbitrary limitation of the field of distribution, almost all Economists have treated of taxation, and in this manner.

Of the growth of taxation there are everywhere signs. Montesquieu's observation, that taxes increase in proportion as freedom flourishes, is no flashy antithesis. Nor is the saying dishonourable to that state. The general expenses of society augment, chiefly or largely, because, with status destroyed, and contract universal, the number of helpless waifs to be cared for by the State, the tutor of those who cannot contract to their advantage, augments also ; because a species of socialism or equity inevitably arises ; and the number of things which it is everybody's interest to do, and most people's inclination to shirk, multiplying, the general expenses or taxes tend to increase also. Moreover, round the primitive idea of simple protection clothe themselves the ideas of the diffusion of health, knowledge, and assistance, as part of the duties of the State ; and even while fancying that they are clinging to the old idea of the province of the State, people have drifted far away, to a much more exigent doctrine.

It has perhaps been assumed too˙ hastily by English Economists that to provide for these general expenses, raising most of the revenue of a country by taxes is a necessity, and that doing so by means of monopolies or trading pursuits is a barbarous mode. I think I am pretty nearly right in saying that the common doctrine in this country is, that these last devices will by and by be completely extruded from the practices of civilised nations; and English financiers are apt to sneer at the practices of foreign governments in this respect. Why this certainty? Must these devices be necessarily inexpedient, and must Cameral Science, which on the Continent is held to include the management of State domains, mean only the administration of taxes? So far from this being true, it may be maintained that these devices will retain a place in the most enlightened financial systems. However well contrived, a fiscal system must produce grievances; its complete conformity with abstract justice is impossible. Force, always presumptively wrong, should be the last resort. The raising of a revenue by means of taxes or the employment of force is *prima facie* bad. It is, moreover, the setting apart from the work of production of a certain portion of the population; and, in an economical point of view, therefore, presumptively not to be preferred to a mode of raising the revenue by which no portion of the working population will be withdrawn from its avocations. There are, indeed, fiscal reasons for not letting a Government raise its whole revenue by engaging in profitable trades. It is generally agreed that we should not always let the Government provide means by its doing that which somebody must do, instead of by doing that which need not be done at all, chiefly for these reasons : because Governments, acting by rules, and not animated by the zeal that comes of self-interest, are pretty sure to fail whenever enterprise, suppleness, and plasticity of action, are demanded ; and partly because it may be as great a hardship to forcibly exclude private individuals from any field of enterprise as to forcibly raise money. But these reasons, sound as against the intrusion of Governments into complicated concerns, and partly sound as against their excluding others from any field of industry, do not apply to simple concerns, especially such as must, in the nature of things, be monopolies. Of these there are not a few, and probably they are multiplying. Landowning would seem to be among them, and the absorption of the " unearned increment" would seem fair enough ; the owning of railways, and canals, and harbours, and the working of ferries, may be so too ; the postal service ranks almost necessarily among such monopolies. As these, by their very nature, by the size of the capital required to carry them on, and the temptation to amalgamate, tend to become monopolies, there is not always a decisive reason, supposing another system has not been allowed to grow up, why the State should not be the monopolists. There is in truth a strong reason why it should be so, if the monopoly of the State saves its subjects from heavy burdens of taxation. How much more taxes, for example, would have to be wrung from the people of India if private individuals, and not the State, were the landowners? Our Government is onerous as it is ; it would be intolerable by India if we drew a revenue of fifty millions chiefly from customs and an income-tax. How many onerous dues we should have been saved had our crown lands not been lavishly gifted away, and had the· power of restraint been applied earlier than the time of Queen Anne ! Even when concerns do not of necessity become absolute monopolies, there is much to be said for the State either occupying the whole field or entering into competition with private individuals, provided the work can satisfactorily be executed by Governments. One may assert more. Granting that the work were executed not so well as by private persons, the advantage of being spared taxation would weigh for much, and would occasionally counterbalance the evil. Some occupations requiring joint action, and yielding profits very slowly, such as the administration of forests, might be conducted most economically by the State. And granting that an occupation is of a complicated nature, it is to be observed that the collection of many taxes—for example, those on spirits—is as complicated as most businesses are. The case for what Mr. Mill calls " authoritative interference " must be strong before it should be resorted to ; but when this stretch of authority is not fully justified, it may be justifiable and advisable to organise Government establishments, such as banks, alongside private establishments. Those who object that this course would augment at once the duties and inefficiency of Government, may be reminded that the number of taxes would thereby be reduced, and the State relieved of other duties. Those, again, who object that thus State interference would be dangerously expanded, must demonstrate—and the task would be difficult—that owning the postal service or railways pierces deeper into personal relations than the collecting of an income-tax or the enforcing of the Stamp Acts. So far, then, from the raising of revenue by such means being a barbarous mode, nothing more proper ; and a revenue without taxes, a State without an army of tax-gatherers, need not be everywhere an impracticable idea. Far, too, from being certainly greatly ahead of Continental countries in our fiscal system, we are perhaps behind not a few of them, notwithstanding the superiority of our customs, chiefly because we do not draw a large portion of an enormous revenue from inevitable monopolies or trades which can be conducted by the State. Had we been as wise and frugal as Prussia or Belgium, the Chancellor of the Exchequer might have suffered tea to be untaxed, owing to the abundant revenue obtained from the rent of crown and other lands ; from a con-siderable aliquot part of rents ; from railways—which could not have been managed more expensively than they have been by private companies ; or from docks and mines. Had the English Government done in India, where fully one-half of the revenue is obtained from the land, what it has done in England, the retention of the former must have become financially impos-sible. In every old country there grow up of necessity certain monopolies, and it would seem that the fitting course is for the State to make itself, if possible, the monopolist, since monopoly there must be. By such an arrangement the least possible disturbance of industry is effected, consistently with procuring a revenue. These are, so to speak, *natural* sources of revenue. They, moreover, are opportunely called into existence, just as the necessity for taxation grows. And yet of these natural sources of revenue this country has been singularly negligent. More, perhaps, than other States, it has allowed the profits of these necessary monopolies to be absorbed by private persons. Insular ignorance of the financial systems of foreign countries, and too much attention to the superiority of our customs, have made us forget that it is we who have to learn, and that the country of Peel and Cobden cannot claim predominance in wisdom over others with respect to taxation.

All Governments raise taxes ; they consequently all distribute wealth. What is the exact amount of money raised and distri-buted thereby it is impossible to say. The King of Dahomey publishes no budget ; most of the Sovereigns of Asia and Africa take what they can. Even in regard to Europe, it is hard to know the sum annually raised by taxation, for the budgets of the various nations are so varied in character that only a rude approximation is possible. Some of the budgets mix up the local and imperial taxes; in our budget the latter only appear. Budgets, moreover, do not admit of a comparison until they are closely analysed and sifted, for all States, to a certain extent, and some to a very large extent, obtain a revenue by trading— by availing themselves of some monopoly, or by performing some services. Thus, we obtain a revenue from the postal monopoly; the Prussians from tobacco; the Indian Government from the sale of opium; while part of the Belgian Government's revenue proceeds comes from State railways. Further, one ought to exclude such taxes as are paid by Government servants. These circumstances render it difficult to calculate the precise amount raised by taxation; but let us only reflect that this country alone raises annually some £100,000,000 by imperial and local taxes, and the reflection will fill us with an impressive sense of the magnitude of this agency. In modern times, taxes have with few exceptions been paid in money. To receive them in kind or in services was a barbarous practice, tolerable only when coin was scarce and barter common. The practice lingered, however, even in England, down to a very recent period, in the shape of an obligation binding on all occupiers to give four days' labour in the year to keep the roads in repair; and the Scotch Parliament, in 1696, ordered all persons engaged in husbandry to contribute six days' labour annually for the repair of the roads. Some old people in Scotland doubtless still remember turning out with their horses and carts, after or before harvest, to mend the country cross-roads. This duty, the equivalent in Scotch history of the famous or infamous *corvée* of France, and like it detested and injurious to agriculture, was subsequently commuted into an annual payment; hence the "commutation roads." The duty to serve in the militia, formerly incumbent on every man in this country, was the *corvée* in another form. To this day it exists in certain Continental countries in the form of an obligation on the part of every man to serve a certain number of years in the army.

The inconveniences of receiving contributions in kind or in service must have been early felt. How could a State wage war abroad and maintain a standing army of mercenaries, if the revenue consisted of perishables, or the obligation of subjects to turn out for a defined time? The holders of his land might serve their Prince for a few weeks at home; each man might be his own commissariat department for that period; but money, gold and silver, were needed to maintain an army in the field in a foreign land; and in measuring out censure of those sovereigns who clung to the so-called mercantile system, it should enter into our consideration how far this alleged confusion may not have been really a preference of money to other kinds of wealth, as more suitable for the purposes of war—how far the conduct of these sovereigns was not irrational, though not worthy of praise or imitation.

Adam Smith drew up a set of rules for the levying of taxes, and these rules are so often referred to and are so widely accepted, that we may here quote them. They are in substance as follow :— *First,* " The subjects of every State ought to contribute to the support of the Government as nearly as possible in proportion to their respective abilities : that is, in proportion to the revenues they respectively enjoy under the protection of the State." *Secondly,* " The tax which each individual ought to pay ought to be certain and not arbitrary." *Thirdly,* " Every tax ought to be levied at the time or in the manner in which it is most likely to be convenient for the contributor to pay it." *Fourthly,* " Every tax ought to be so contrived as both to take out and keep out of the pockets of the people as little as possible over and above what it brings into the public treasury of the State ;" and a tax will sin against this rule if it requires numerous collectors, if it checks the development of a branch of industry for which a country is suited, if it is accompanied by ruinous penalties and forfeitures, if it is levied on the raw materials of manufactures, and if it subjects the people to the frequent visits and the odious examinations of tax-gatherers. To these four rules may be appended a fifth, to the effect that taxation should as far as possible fall on luxuries that are injurious in moderation or excess. Since all taxes must lessen or impede some sort of expenditure, it is well that they should fall as much as possible on hurtful expenditure ; taxes should as much as possible perform the office of sumptuary laws, rooting out or checking the growth of consumption which is wasteful and morally injurious ; and it is on this ground that the present high duty on spirits is partly to be justified.

z

These four rules, which economists have rarely failed to quote and discuss, are striking proofs that those who say that Political Economy does not concern itself at all with *ought*, speak hastily. They show that here, with one consensus, economists have treated of the *right* mode of distribution. Smith's rules certainly are not the complete code of taxation. For example, one might supplement them by the above fifth rule, to the effect that taxation should as far as possible fall on luxuries, especially those that are commonly abused. Since all taxation must lessen some species of expenditure, it is well that taxes should fall as much as possible on hurtful expenditure, thus giving us a *natural* revenue. Of Sismondi's rules, the third partly answers to the above fifth rule : " taxation being the price paid for enjoyments, he who enjoys nothing ought to be asked to pay nothing ; taxes ought therefore never to take any portion of a revenue . that is necessary for the life of the contributor."

The first of Adam Smith's rules has probably gained acceptance from its being peculiarly liable to be misunderstood or read at pleasure; and, indeed, if taken literally, or as he interprets it, it is of doubtful justice. It would be intolerable that if one man paid 10 per cent on his income everybody else should pay the same, and that if the farmer with £600 a year pays £60, his labourer with £15 a year shall pay £1 : 10s. ; for this most inequitable equality would mean starvation for the latter ; it would be to demand of the farmer a trifle, of the latter his life. Equality is here not always equity. Nor can the equality of which Adam Smith speaks signify equal exactions from all possessing the same income ; the man who obtains £2000 a year from land, the fee-simple of which he owns, is far better able to bear taxation than the physician or merchant earning the same amount, but obliged by common prudence to lay aside a considerable portion as provision for his old age when his income will cease, and, it may be, for his widow and children in case of premature death. This equality cannot necessarily mean that every one should pay the same sums. In fact, there are two problems to be settled before its true significance can be imparted to this canon. In the first place, What is the nature of the bond of citizenship? Ought ability not to be considered in exacting taxes any more than the shopkeeper varies his rates according to the means of his customers? Or ought we to regard the State as designed to effect the utmost good to all its members? Rightly or wrongly, all fiscal systems have, with more or less consistency, recognised the latter principle, or, at all events, have disobeyed the former, and have generally taken as their ideals some form of socialism limited by the mainten- ance of the family. With few exceptions they have attempted to proportion the tax to the ability of the subject. In the second place, one has to consider by what practicable machinery one can effect this end, cr how one can extort from each equal sacrifices. Of course the perfect attainment of this ideal is an impossibility, like squaring the circle. Not to mention that assessments must be founded on perpetually varying data, the circumstances of each contributor are so different, and the payment of the same sum is so different a sacrifice to each, that every taxpayer would require a separate system, amended at short intervals, before perfect jus- tice was done. Manipulate taxes, graduate them ever so accu- rately, taxes will press too heavily on some points, too lightly on others ; too much will be taken from the widow's cruise ; too little from the miser's hoards ; and the course of financial re- form resembles the approximations of the mathematician—they approach the ideal of justice, yet never attain to it.

It was once a favourite belief that the best mode of approxi- mating to this standard of perfection was to levy a multitude of taxes. Whenever, therefore, financiers saw, or fancied they saw, an exemption from just burdens, they clapped on a tax. Whenever the subject disclosed his possession of money, the fisc descended on him. Now one wicket of escape was shut up, now another. If you did not consume taxed articles, the State has- tened to tax that which you did consume. This may be illus- trated from the history of customs duties. In pursuit of the above policy our tariff was swollen to monstrous dimensions by taxes, many of which, yielding little revenue, were retained in order to hinder escape from others more remunerative. In the middle of the fifteenth century the tariff contained 1630 articles. Huskisson, then President of the Board of Trade, began in 1823 a contrary movement. During his term of office he swept away a number of small taxes. Sir Robert Peel continued Huskisson's labours ; and the tariff, which in 1845 had con- tained 1163 articles, was gutted by Mr. Gladstone of all but some forty, all of which yielded an insignificant revenue, with the exception of tea, tobacco, sugar, coffee, spirits, and wine. Mr. Lowe has gone a step farther in the reaction against what

American financiers term "the diffused system," by removing the Corn-duty, which Sir Robert Peel left in 1846. Not that there was a process of reduction uninterruptedly going on ; on the contrary, Sir Robert Peel's reforms, in changing *ad valorem* duties into specific duties, increased the varieties. The propriety of the above policy has been challenged by Lord Overstone, Sir George Cornewall Lewis, and Mr. M'Culloch ; and we have seen the United States, urged by persons with similar views, at the close of the civil war, resort to a tariff including upwards of 2000 articles. The last of these authorities has denounced the removal of so many duties and the concentration of the taxes as rash and dangerous, a grand mistake, a blot on the financial reforms of the century. And certainly there is considerable weight in certain of his arguments. The man who eschews tea, coffee, sugar, tobacco, and spirits, now escapes indirect taxation ; he could hardly have done so when the tariff comprehended hundreds of articles. Those who do consume these articles pay enormously : for they must suffer since others escape. Were we only to levy custom dues at large ports, permitting vessels entering small ports to land their cargoes duty free, we should do as we now do to those who do not consume the few articles subject to duty. There is such a thing as a pernicious simplicity in taxation : the simplest, and perhaps the most unjust, mode of raising taxation, would be to extract it all from one man, if that were possible ; the existence of few imposts make manipulation of taxation difficult ; and the question is, whether Huskisson, Peel, and Gladstone, in applying the pruning-knife vigorously, have not lopped numerous branches which were of service. It is needless to deny that some of these removals did create and increase inequality, for the fact that indirect taxation then fell on the consumers of any one of hundreds of articles, while it now falls on the consumer of some half-dozen articles, suffices to prove this much. Shall we, then, retrace our steps, and undo the memorable work of these financiers ? It would be useless, we fear, were it possible ; and the reason why it would be useless to replace once more these duties reveals one of the obstacles to the attainment of ideal justice in regard to finance. Put out of consideration the absurdity, the crudity, the hurtfulness, of many of these taxes, falling on raw materials and the necessaries of life, and it will be found that a vast number of the remainder yielded next to nothing. In 1853 there were 123 custom taxes, the repeal of which involved a loss to the revenue of only £53,000. Such taxes involved much vexation and cost in their collection, and the country could not afford to endeavour to be just at such a price. At the same time, now that it is becoming hardened into a principle that no taxes ought to be reimposed, the paucity of our taxes may be a matter of grave import. Let us mention another attempt to solve the insoluble problem of perfect justice in taxation. The Physiocrats, and in more recent times Dr. Chalmers, suggested that the entire revenue of a country ought to be raised by a single tax imposed on rent. This suggestion might be admirable in a country where the expenditure was covered by the rent. But in this country the former considerably surpasses the latter. Nor would it be possible to transfer a portion of the burden to others than landlords. At the same time, a total or partial substitution of the State for landed proprietors would in such countries be greatly preferable to systematic interference with all affairs of life. Others have proposed to find the perfect *impôt unique* in the imposition of a certain percentage of capital; M. Emile de Girardin would make it a tax of one per cent. Now, not to speak of the practical difficulties in assessment, the so-called unique tax on capital would really be a group of taxes.

Taxes may be classified in many ways. To take the most fundamental economical classification, they may be divided into taxes on wages, profits, and rent. Taxes on successions or legacies, however, fall neither on profits, nor wages, nor rent. In another point of view, taxes may be said to fall on what is capital and what is not capital. They are direct or indirect, according as the person who pays the sum to the Exchequer does or does not indemnify himself, and shift the tax to another or others. Some taxes fall on income, others on expenditure; some on luxuries, others on necessaries. Some, to refer to more accidental distinctions, are imperial, and others local. Perhaps the most vital of those distinctions, in an economical point of view, is that drawn between taxes which do, and taxes which do not, fall on capital. Taxes which really strike capital, of course paralyse production. They dry up the sources of industry. There is generally, however, difficulty in deciding whether any particular tax affects capital, capital itself not being a physically determined quantity; and this truth is often

forgotten. Witness Ricardo and Mr. Dudley Baxter regarding
the duty, averaging 2½ per cent, laid on successions and legacies
as a tax on capital, and condemning it as such. This condemnation proceeds on the inadmissible supposition that every farthing which is received as a legacy is devoted to productive expenditure—a proposition which is utterly incredible. " If,"
says Ricardo, " a legacy of £1000 be subject to a tax of £100,
the legatee considers his legacy as only £900, and feels no particular motive to save the £100 of duty from his expenditure ;
whereas, had he received the £1000 and been required to pay
the £100 by means of a tax on income, on wine, on horses, or
on servants, he would probably have diminished, or rather not
increased his expenditure by that sum, and the capital of the
country would have been unimpaired." This " probably" is
doubtful. For all that appears on the surface of the supposition, the legatee would act alike in both cases. As to raising
the equivalent by an income-tax, if it took away £100 of every
£1000, it would be pronounced intolerable. Every man would
be fully aware that he was, in any event, £900 richer, and
taste would decide whether the sum was given for a picture, or
wines, or lodged in a bank, or invested in business. Besides, so
long as the produce of these taxes is employed in clearing off the
National debt, and helping to remove taxes from other capital,
the legacy and succession duties are defensible. In truth, it
is not so much the nature of a tax as the degree of it that determines whether it shall affect capital ; and perhaps the only taxes
which, whether high or low, certainly strike it, are those on raw
materials and instruments of manufacture. Not only are these
taxes hurtful to industry, inasmuch as they may hinder production, but they are bad, inasmuch as they sin against Adam
Smith's fourth maxim, and inasmuch as they take more out of
the pockets of the taxpayer than they bring to the State, the
nominal contributor recouping himself with interest.

According to another system of classification, taxes are divided
into taxes on wages, on profits, and on rent. A tax on wages,
it is usually alleged, is wholly a tax on profits, seeing it causes
a general rise of wages : this doctrine is true of a tax falling
on the wages of all labourers earning barely enough to support
them and their children ; it is rarely true of most kinds of
wages and salaries, a tax upon which falls on the wage-receivers,
though occasionally, perhaps after a considerable lapse of

time, they transfer it to their employers. Taxes falling on all profits diminish them, and they are not transferred to the community. Taxes falling on rent fall solely on the landlord, the State becoming a co-proprietor. At the same time, this holds good of economic rent technically so called ; such of the tax as falls on capital expended by the landlord upon his estate falls, or tends to fall, on the consumers. In this country imperial taxation on land is comparatively unimportant, much of it having been redeemed in consequence of the facilities which Pitt afforded for redemption, and of the assessments adopted by him being those of 1692.

A large portion of the local rates, however, nominally fall on land. though their precise incidence is a question of much doubt. From Ricardo's theory it is logically deducible that such rates are borne by the landowner. But we saw reason to doubt whether that theory was an accurate expression of the facts of the case. Ricardo is conducted to that conclusion by the assumption that as a farmer receives neither more nor less than the ordinary rate of profits, any extraordinary taxation must be a deduction from rent. But, in the first place, there is reason to believe that but for the expenditure in rates, certain portions of land would not have been cultivated, or cultivated so well. These rates may be capital expended on improvements. Secondly, they may be only a necessary aid to wages in order to keep the labourers in working condition. Thirdly, augmentations of rates, unforeseen when a lease was made, fall on the farmer. In these circumstances the incidence of rates is not upon the landlord. It was stated that a natural system of taxation was partially provided by the monopolies which grow up in each State ; that is, that revenue could thus be obtained with small outlay of force and little irritation. With somewhat less degree of truth it may be said that taxes on successions, bequests, legacies, form a group of natural imposts. Resorting to any of these, the State takes unearned profits, so to speak ; and it gives less pain and inflicts less injury to take away a portion of that which we owe to others than what we ourselves have won. In a special sense we owe legacies and bequests to law ; the rights of inheriting and bequeathing are unquestionably creations of Government ; and with special justice Cæsar may ask a portion of those things for which we are specially indebted to Cæsar. That which we have laboured for and made

our own by our sweat, we resign to another with deep reluctance; the taxgather is peculiarly abhorrent when he dips his
hand in the store of our own earnings; the turbulent are ready
to resist him, and the unscrupulous to defraud him when he
comes on this errand. But when he takes a portion of that which
other hands have produced, and when he takes little from those
who fairly expected much, it is with less natural reluctance that
we receive him, and our exasperation is less bitter because less
just. The State, as the insurer of the transmission of property,
and bound to raise a revenue with the least possible irritation, is
therefore peculiarly justified and interested in raising a revenue
by means of duties on the probates of wills, disposing of personal
property, letters of administration, and successions of property
to heirs, and legacies. So far from there being good grounds for
abolishing or curtailing these taxes, there are sound reasons
for extending them—not indeed to the verge of communism
or with the view of equalising fortunes, but so far as is compatible with the preservation of the saving tendencies. When
a person dies, rich and childless, without having executed a
will, his property sometimes goes to enrich a remote relation
whose face he may never have seen, of whose very name he
may be ignorant. The heir may be a stranger who has built no
expectations upon the heritage, and who consequently would not
be injured if the property passed to another. The rich man
may have contracted—and his distant relationship and absence
of intimacy all but guarantee that he has contracted—no obligations towards this stranger. If the deceased thought that
his distant relation could justly claim anything of him, he had
but to signify so in his testament, and his wishes would be
complied with. But when the heir-at-law is very remote, when
there is no will, and when the deceased has created no reasonable expectations, it does not appear why the property should
not escheat to the Crown; why the State's necessities, always
great, should not partially be relieved by property which only
an accident would send to the stranger; why other taxes, evils,
though perhaps necessary evils, should not be mitigated by a tax
marked by the peculiar merit of injuring nobody. Bentham
proposed that the law of escheat should be so extended that all
vacant successions should be appropriated to public purposes on
the failure of relations within the degrees known as prohibited.
But this measure would probably shock opinion too much. The

great plea in favour of his proposal is, that it would not cause disappointment—a plea likely to be perfectly true in the case of a second or third cousin, but not in the case of a first cousin. Escheating in the latter case would cause that hardship which depends upon the disappointment of expectations ; and if the reply were, in Bentham's words, that these expectations were founded on the known dispensations of the law, changing as these dispensations change, it may be asked whether, if the law were to announce that a younger brother should not succeed to the property of a childless elder brother, there would not be bitter disappointment. Manifestly there is a limit to this power of law to mould expectations, at all events until the lapse of many years. What has very frequently happened people will look for, and count a hardship to miss ; and on this ground it is doubtful whether escheating should come into operation immediately outside the forbidden pale. But no real hardship would be inflicted if considerable limitation was put, for example, to the rule that inheritances descend to the issue of the last purchaser *in infinitum*. Those who may object to such a measure in any shape as revolutionary may be reminded that the law of escheat is well known to the Constitution, and that at present the principle contended for is recognised, inasmuch as the succession-duty so far increases in proportion to the remoteness of the relationship of the heir ; the great defect being that the law, carrying pedantically out a theory, fails to recognise that there are degrees of propinquity which confer no titles, and which it would be no hardship to disregard, and that it never in any case takes more than 10 per cent. Of late these taxes on the transmission of property from the dead to the living have been stripped of several anomalies. Previous to 1853 they were imposed only on the probates of wills disposing of personal property, letters of administration granted when the owners of personal property died intestate, and legacies of personal estate. Real property, or more accurately freehold estates, escaped ; so also did personalty settled under a trust. But in 1853, with the approbation of most lovers of justice, though not with the approbation of all landed proprietors, Mr. Gladstone imposed a duty on successions to real property and legacies of real property, and thus a blot which Pitt attempted without success to expunge was removed. Settled personalty too was included. Notwithstanding this and other improvements, there are several yet to be made. Besides providing that the property, real and personal, of persons dying intestate should escheat to the Crown in the event of there being no heir, presumptively led to regulate his expenditure by expectations prompted by the deceased, it is to be hoped that some Chancellor of the Exchequer will yet do what Mr. Gladstone intended to do—levy some equivalent of succession-duty on corporate property. All property transmitted from one generation to another having been thus subjected to taxation, it would be perhaps proper to alter in some respects the rates, and to raise them when the relationship was pretty remote and the value of the property considerable, above 10 per cent, and to impose a smaller rate on small estates. The distinction between realty and personalty, with separate legal incidents attached to either, rapidly becoming of gross inconvenience, has here been made a pretext for gross inequalities. It seems needless to assume that every owner of land is a life annuitant, to be taxed accordingly. Those who are not annuitants ought to be treated precisely as they would be treated supposing they succeeded to personal property of equal value. The utmost consideration for the fact that real property is liable to peculiar burdens, and to the argument that it ought therefore to be treated with particular leniency, ought not to go further than deducting these charges from the value of the property transmitted ; and, indeed, this might be neglected so long as probate-duty is exigible, without due regard to the deceased's debts. Mr. Ricardo contrasts such taxes with taxes on revenue. The contrast is somewhat false—whether gross or net revenue is meant. All capital comes out of gross revenue, though all revenue is not turned into capital.

Another important economical distinction is that between taxes on operations and those on commodities. As an instance of the former we may cite stamps on deeds conveying property ; the latter are illustrated by the tea and spirit duties. The latter, as a rule, and unless the commodity is a constituent of the necessaries of life, or itself an instrument of production, ought to be preferred to the former, since these operations are largely undertaken to produce commodities, and to impede them by taxes is to dry up the source of wealth. The former, as Ricardo justly observes, " prevent the national capital from being distributed in the way most beneficial to the community." Under the head of taxes on operations may be included those imposed upon individual transactions, and those imposed on particular professions. The former consist for the most part of stamps, the other of licenses or *patente* taxes. Speaking with special reference to the fiscal system of this country, it may be affirmed that the former are, with few exceptions, liable to serious objections. Their number is excessive. They have generally been imposed solely with a view to produce the utmost without much regard to the means, and the consequence is that some of the most useful operations are saddled with duties, and that the revenue is fed by unnatural sources. Not a deed or instrument escapes ; at almost every step in the conduct of his affairs the merchant or the landlord pays toll ; and even if the actual expense is small, the trouble and perplexity as to the right stamp are serious. Now, imposts on necessary operations do not appear a whit less condemnable than imposts on necessary commodities, a species of tax generally abandoned, and the former are at all tolerable only because they are usually small, not because they are sound in principle. Speaking still with reference to the fiscal system of this country, many of the licenses are marked by fatally bad features. Who ought to pay licenses to practise a profession ? At first thought " Everybody," or " Nobody," would be the answer. But further reflection will probably convince one that the holders of privileges of the nature of a monopoly may fairly be called upon to submit to the payment of licenses, and this consideration may justify the existence, if not the amount, of the license duty exigible from members of certain professions. Again, it may be said that the sellers of articles of luxury ought to be taxed on the understanding that they will recoup themselves, and that the consumers of luxuries may reasonably be expected to be in a position to bear an unusual amount of taxation ; and this consideration may justify the license required, say of retailers of beer, though it scarcely justifies the virtual taxing of such articles twice over. But to compel auctioneers and appraisers to take out licenses is to impose taxes at random —it is to act on the principle of getting a revenue somehow. Justice, too, would require that in such cases as licenses were imposed the sum should be proportioned to the extent of the business, as is done with our beer licenses and the French *patente*, and not to put the small trader at a ruinous disadvantage in comparison with the large trader. If we add that a good many of these duties are costly to collect, the necessity for revision and expurgation is manifest. Let us here observe, in further illustration of the fourth maxim, that the impolicy of taxes levied in the early stages of production, or taxes on raw produce, as compared with those levied near the time of consumption, has always been alluded to by economists. Taxes on raw produce take more from the taxpayer than they bring to the Treasury. Thus, wherever wool is struck with a custom duty, as is the case in the United States, the purchaser of woollens must pay not only the tax but the interest upon it that has accrued from the time when they were imported.

A bitter controversy has, time out of mind, raged between the advocates of direct and indirect taxation ; and here and abroad many keep up an active agitation for the repeal of the latter, and the substitution of the former. They denounce indirect taxes as more expensive in collection than direct taxation ; while the direct taxes are alleged to be collected at a charge of 1½ per cent, the customs and excise duties, it is said by some, cost 10 per cent. Indirect taxes are charged with taking more out of the pocket of the taxpayer than they give to the Exchequer, since the importer of a dutiable article must pay interest on the duty between the payment of it and the selling of the article : thus a pound of tea naturally costing 1s. 5d., and struck by a duty of 100 per cent, must be sold at such a price as will compensate the seller for the risk and interest on the capital thus advanced, and must be sold again by every successive person into whose hands it comes, with a correspondingly extraordinary profit. Again, indirect excise taxes impede manufactures : with an excise officer, jealous of each change in the processes as probably concealing an attempt at fraud, watching over him, and obliged to conform to fixed hours and instruments, and employ prescribed locks and keys, the manufacturer of exciseable articles must produce dearly, and of necessity he rarely improves his processes. Sometimes taxing an ingredient prevents the manufacture of some article ; e.g. transparent soap. Then it is alleged customs do in a small degree what prohibitive duties did in a great degree. Customs inflict the same injuries at seaports which the confessedly bad *octrois* do to the inland trade of France. Moreover, they foster smuggling, and in time lawlessness and immorality. Indirect taxation, moreover, admits of exemptions of the worst kind, seeing the man who goes without tea, coffee, sugar, or tobacco, will pay nothing, though if he be likely childless and unmarried, he is peculiarly capable of paying. To this charge the champions of indirect taxation are apt to append the contradictory remark that indirect taxation falls on the necessaries or at least the secondaries of life, and, consequently, mulcts everybody. There are a number of miscellaneous and subsidiary objections taken to indirect taxation, the gist of them being the strong temptation to fraud which it creates, and the cover which the indirect mode of taxation affords for raising unnecessarily large revenue. Those who hold these views have a considerable controversial advantage in their usually not showing the direct taxes which they would substitute for the existing indirect. And as these taxes vary much in justice, it is difficult to point out blemishes in direct taxation equal to those pointed out in indirect. It is clear that, if financiers persist in this course, they will possess a peculiar advantage over other controversialists, who criticise that which they have not seen, and the description of which they must take on trust. There are, however, almost conclusive reasons why, if the merits of direct and indirect taxation are to be usefully discussed, the advocates of the latter should table a definite plan. Not a little doubt prevails as to the proper definition of an indirect tax, and as to what taxes are direct and what the opposite. How then is it to be known what the friends of direct taxation want, until they specify the taxes which they would substitute? Mr. Dudley Baxter has recently drawn attention to the divergency of opinion as to what constitutes a direct tax. Adam Smith understood thereby a tax on income; M'Culloch, a tax taken directly from income or property; Mr. Mill, a tax " demanded from the very person who it is intended or desired should pay it." To what important consequences these differences of opinion lead is manifest from the following extract from a letter by Mr. Baxter :—

" Property Tax and Rates.—Adam Smith and M'Culloch say, direct; Mr. Mill would say, one-third or one-half direct, two-thirds or one-half indirect.

" Successions.—Adam Smith and Mr. Mill say, direct ; M'Culloch indirect.

" Stamps.—Adam Smith, direct; M'Culloch, indirect ; Mr. Mill, part direct, part indirect.

"Licenses.—The same.

"Servants, horses, etc.—Adam Smith and M'Culloch, indirect ; Mr. Mill, direct.

"The only two classes on which all are agreed are the *Customs*, and the duties on internal productions, which constitute the mass of our *Excise*, these by general consent being indirect.

"This anarchy is not confined to English economists, but prevails quite as widely on the Continent. Take, for example, M. Maurice Block and M. Passy. M. Block, in his great work, *L'Europe Politique et Sociale*, classes taxes on the annual value of real and personal property and on servants and horses as direct, and all the rest as indirect. M. Passy, in the *Dictionnaire de l'Economie Politique*, ranks everything as direct except Customs and Excise.

"The difference may be illustrated in another manner, by taking the taxes and rates of the United Kingdom for 1867, amounting to about £84,000,000, and classifying them according to the above writers. The results are :—

"M. Passy.—Direct, £44,500,000 ; indirect, £39,500,000.

"Adam Smith.—Direct, £41,000,000 ; indirect, £43,000,000.

"M. Block.—Direct, £31,000,000 ; indirect, £53,000,000.

"M'Culloch.—Direct, £28,000,000 ; indirect, £56,000,000.

"Mr. Mill is not easy to sum up, but his total amounts would probably not differ very much from those of Mr. M'Culloch. Thus the results vary between wide ranges, from the direct taxes being 53 per cent, and the indirect 47 per cent according to M. Passy, to the direct being 33 per cent and the indirect 67 per cent according to Mr. M'Culloch." *

In view of these discrepancies it would be rash to affirm what is the general idea attached to a direct tax ; but probably most would consider it a tax paid to the officers of the State by the actual contributor without the intervention of a third party.† Yet in this point of view even the income-tax, the favourite of the foes of indirect taxation, cannot be pronounced uniformly a

---

* I may mention that these statements rather underrate than exaggerate the confusion that prevails on this head. In the revenue returns of the Dutch Government in *The Statesman's Year-Book*, customs are excluded from the indirect taxes. According to M. Villiaumé, "les principaux impôts directs sont établis sur les personnes, *l'exercise des professions*, la terre, les maisons, les transmissions à titre gratuit, celles à titre onéreux le timbre." Proudhon appears to think all our indirect taxes really direct.

† "Our direct taxes are whatever is collected from house to house by government officers, whether *avoidable* or *unavoidable*."—Newman's *Lectures on Political Economy*, p. 215.

direct tax. A good deal of the produce of it is not paid directly by the real contributors : the Bank of England, for example, pays the fundholders' income-tax, just as the tobacco manufacturers pay the tobacco-tax of smokers ; and the owners of real property pay income-tax through the occupiers. Nothing is more confidently affirmed than that customs must by their nature be always indirect taxes ; their incidence must, it is affirmed, be always on the consumers. Now, in the first place, it is to be observed that the assertion that customs are paid by consumers properly expresses a tendency occasionally counteracted. If the Chancellor of the Exchequer reduces the sugar-duties and declines to allow a drawback on stock that has paid the old duty, the holders of such stock, and not the consumers, may perhaps pay the duty. In the second place, this tendency may long be counteracted, provided there is imposed a tax which considerably raises the price and diminishes the demand; provided the reduction in profit be not considerable, and provided the quantity of fixed capital be great, the tendency may be very long counteracted, and during the whole time the tax is in operation it may be wholly or partly direct. In the third place, it may be possible to impose custom duties which will permanently be paid, either wholly or partly, not by the consumers but by the importers or producers. Assume that we draw our stock of sugar from a country engaged in the growth of sugar, and capable of selling it with profit to us some shillings cheaper than any other country can ; the former will of course sell the sugar to us at a price slightly below what would attract other competitors. Impose a duty of some shillings a cwt., without altogether destroying the peculiar advantage of the trade ; while we will pay no dearer for our sugar, the importers will pay the tax at the expense of their profits. If we add to these considerations the difficulty of ascertaining the actual incidence of many such taxes, distrust of sharp contrasts between direct and indirect taxes will be inspired.

The second reason why a definite scheme of direct taxation should be tabled, why Mr. Cobden's advice to keep agitating on the advantages of direct taxation in the abstract, leaving it to a future time, and to the Huskissons, Peels, and Gladstones of subsequent years to carry the principle into effect, is unsatisfactory, is, that few doubt that in the abstract direct taxation is preferable to indirect, and that, apart from the above natural taxes, if it were not for practical and insuperable difficulties, almost every farthing of the revenue ought to be so raised. The just criterion of taxation is to demand equal sacrifices of all ; and if it were known, in the first place, by an infallible, or even by an extraneous and tolerably accurate, standard, what were the means of every one, and the burdens thereon ; and secondly, if it were possible to collect direct taxes from the very poorest without exciting a revolt or incurring such expenses as would make the collection not worth the while, a direct tax—an income-tax—striking all incomes, from those of the millionaires to those of the meanest day-labourers, or a pro- perty-tax striking the substance of the highèst and the lowest, would be the proper mode of raising almost the whole revenue of the country ; and, retaining a few State monopolies, our tariffs might be burnt, and our army of excisemen discharged, if these two conditions could be realised. But these conditions are never fully realised ; insuperable difficulties intervene in the applica- tion of direct taxation. Except in the case of fundholders, or landowners whose rent-roll is accessible, or the public servants, whose salaries can be ascertained with certainty, it is difficult to know men's means ; in the case of a direct tax, the taxpayer must to a considerable degree assess himself ; and is he likely always to assess himself fairly ? Is it not too probable that he will commit fraud, or dupe himself by casuistical reasons into rating himself under the true figure ? Mr. Gladstone, not disposed to pass harsh judgments on his fellow-mortals, has declared that the Income-tax can never be permanently satisfactory, involving as it does self-assessment, which covers grievous frauds on the revenue, and fosters immorality. Basing their calculations on a comparison between income-tax returns and claims to compensation, the Inland Revenue Commissioners calculate that 40 per cent of the persons taxed to schedule D "understated their income to such an extent that a true return would give an addition of 130 per cent." And in shutting the door against these evils, we are pretty sure to give admittance to others : give the Commissioners an arbi- trary power of assessing, such as they now to some extent pos- sess, and you increase the harshness of the tax without wholly mitigating its injustice. A general property-tax labours under the same disadvantage. Such a tax was levied by the Roman Emperors under the name of the *tributum*, levied on all property, lands, or personalty; and the tax led to endless fraud. The second difficulty hindering the universal application of direct taxation is the difficulty of collecting direct taxes from the poor. What heart-burnings and discontent if the tax-gatherer knocked at every door and demanded dues from a day labourer! What trouble and expenditure of time and money, what vexatious litigation, what numerous arrestments of wages! Would not the poor resist? Should we not see outbreaks resembling those which poll-taxes have produced? Would not the machinery of collection consume almost everything? But why trust to conjectures? Experience with respect to the house-tax and local taxes proves that it would be impossible to levy direct taxes from the very poor. Either the poorest occupants must be left untaxed at all, which is the case with the imperial house-tax (it does not go below houses renting for £20), or the taxes paid by the very poor must be paid indirectly.

These considerations, perhaps, prove that the abolition of indirect taxes, and the substitution of an income-tax, would come sooner or later to the total exemption of the poor from taxation of any kind. Now, the same remark may be extended to other direct taxes. All the advocates of indirect taxation may not contemplate this as the end of their exertions; but it is this for which, consciously or unconsciously, they labour. Now, though justice requires that the rich should sacrifice more than the poor, and that they should sacrifice in proportion to their power of making sacrifices, it is not just that any who possess more than the bare necessaries of life should go wholly untaxed, if any mode of taxing them cheaply and easily can be devised. Take whatever view of society you please, and you will find such an obligation involved. If we should be taxed in accordance with the protection we receive, and if taxes are the price paid for it, the very poorest, not a pauper and not in imminent danger of becoming so, should contribute his mite to the Exchequer — cheerfully too, seeing he perhaps owes more to Government than the wealthy and powerful man, who might protect himself. There is no man that is not benefited by property being secured, justice administered, crime repressed, and invasion repelled; and consequently there is no man except those ·possessing only the bare necessaries of life, and therefore incapable of bearing taxation, that is not bound to give some-

2 A

thing. The privileges of riches carry with them the penalties
of sacrifice ; but that the opulent should pay all, and the poor
should pay nothing, as would very probably be the case under a
system of direct taxation, is not to be tolerated.

The friends of direct taxation say that the cost of its collection would be small in comparison with that of collecting indirect
taxes, and in proof of this assertion they put side by side the
large percentage expended in collecting the customs and excise,
and the small percentage expended in collecting the Income-tax
and the legacy and succession duties. The inference, however,
drawn from this comparison may be disputed. Abolish customs
and excise duties, and, in the event of the national expenditure
not being cut down, the alternatives are a fiscal system unjust,
or one quite as expensive as that which was abolished. Levy
the revenue from a few only, and the cost of collection will be
small, while the injustice committed will be immense. It
would be a very cheap way of collecting a revenue, and would
be in substance the same as the proposal under discussion, to
confiscate the property of the wealthiest men in the country,
and to put their goods up to auction. It would be cheaper
still, and not a whit more unjust, were it possible, to compel
one man to pay everything. Choose the other alternative,
agree to give something for the sake of justice, and the cost of
collecting direct dues will probably be raised to the cost of collecting indirect dues.*

As to the remark that indirect taxation is objectionable because money may thereby be extracted from the people without
their being painfully aware of it, this is true only to a limited
state in a country where education is general, and politics are
keenly discussed ; with the revenue returns published weekly in
our newspapers, it is scarcely true at all of this country; and so
far as it is true, this characteristic of indirect taxation may be
ranked as a merit, or at all events as an evil not unmixed with
good. In all shapes, taxation is an evil, necessary, perhaps, but
still a real evil ; and besides repealing all possible taxes and
lightening the burdens of a people as much as possible, finan-

* " We find that the cost of collecting the direct taxes in France, where
the fact of the great majority of the people being proprietors renders the
task peculiarly easy, is 3¾ per cent—*precisely the same rate as that of our
own customs duties.*"—Mr. Rathbone Greg's *Political Problems*, 297.

ciers must deliberate over the possible modes of collection, and choose the most agreeable to the people, for it is not money alone that measures the vexatiousness of a tax : the irritation and sense of rancour it excites must be set to its discredit. " Taxation," says Mr. Rathbone Greg, concentrating in a pithy observation some remarks originally made by Bentham, " must of necessity be a painful operation ; it is simple cruelty and folly not to perform it under the influence of chloroform." The requisite chloroform is a system of indirect taxation. As at present constituted, our system of direct taxation possesses several other advantages, of which not the least is its permitting people to contribute whatever amount at whatever time they please. The collection of a tax would be theoretically perfect as regards the payer if he could spread the payment of it over any period he chose, if he could pay such instalments as he desired, if his instalments were always accepted at the time he was best able to pay, and if he need not pay at all in the event of his poverty being great ; and these conditions are all but realised by our indirect taxes. They thus harmonise with Adam Smith's third rule. The advantage of being able to spread the payment of indirect taxes over a considerable period is, of course, to be the more prized now that the direct taxes must be paid pretty much in a lump. Constituted as they now are, they take nothing from the man who must be content with the bare necessaries of life ; and he is the only man that deserves exemption. If they lean on the poor with greater proportionate weight than on the rich, they are the only taxes that do so lean on them. As to the assertion that customs take much more from the people than they give to the Exchequer, this was true before bonded warehouses were so common as they now are ; but the charge has lost force and point, seeing the trader rarely pays duty on an article until he has actually sold it, or is on the eve of doing so. Warehouses are at his service, where he may store his goods until he thinks fit to sell or export.

On the whole, one may say that the propriety of direct or indirect taxes varies with the condition of the taxpayers. If they are poor, or if they consume luxuries, and are little engaged in trade, the resort to direct taxes is almost inevitable ; hence their uniform use in poverty-stricken States, such as Turkey, and in Continental countries peopled by peasant proprietors. And it will be generally a powerful Government that will resort principally to that direct mode of raising contributions; witness its employment in Oriental countries and mediæval countries. Augustus, compelled to respect the semblance of liberty, largely availed himself of direct imposts; while Constantine and his successors, habituated to obtain that which they sought, went straight to their ends when they wanted money.*

* See Gibbon's *Decline and Fall.*

CHAPTER XXVI.

TAXES—(*Continued*).

THERE has been not a little discussion as to the preference of an Income or Property tax. The difficulty of valuing the corpus of the property on which the possessor of an industrial income earns profits has, however, given the victory to the latter, and the so-called Property and Income Tax is better described as an Income-tax. It was first imposed by William Pitt in 1798. We were then in the midst of a terrible war with the French Republic. The old taxes had been stretched almost to the utmost degree of tension. Loan after loan had been contracted, until our enemies fondly fancied that we would be crushed beneath the burden of an enormous debt; and Pitt, beholding with alarm the fruits of his prodigal borrowing, desiring to introduce the new and wholesome policy of raising the expenditure or supplies of the year within the year, and determined to wage relentless war against a Power that was in his eyes incarnate anarchy and evil, trebled in 1797 the assessed taxes, or taxes on houses and windows. This measure disappointed his expectations. Though he had ingeniously taxed occupants on former returns, many eluded the tax, which fell much short of his estimates. Looking about him for a new financial vein to work, he struck upon the Income-tax; and though vigorously opposed in the House of Commons by Mr. Tierney, and in the House of Lords by many Peers, who expressed fears that it would fall chiefly on "ostensible possessions," an Income-tax of 10 per cent was adopted in 1799. In its first shape, it fell with full weight on incomes of £200 and upwards, striking incomes between £200 and £60 at inferior rates. From 1799 to 1815—throughout our long wrestle with the young Republic and the First Empire —it was continued in one shape or another, with a brief interval in 1802-3; and it annually brought to the Treasury sums rang-

ing from £6,000,000 to £15,000,000. When peace came, the
tax—avowedly a war-tax—was removed. But in 1842, Sir Robert
Peel reimposed it in the shape of a tax of sevenpence on the
pound on incomes of £150 and upwards, in order that he might
augment the diminishing revenue, and that he might be able to
strike from the tariff many vexatious duties. In 1854 it was
imposed to meet the expenses of the Russian war at the rate of
1s. 2d. on the pound on incomes of £150 and upwards. In one
shape or another it has since continued; it has been extended
to Ireland; and, adopted at first as a temporary expedient, it
will probably become a permanent feature of our fiscal system.

It is a mistake, or at all events misleading language, to speak
of the Income-tax as one tax; rather it is a collection of taxes
differing widely in character. It is a tax on salary, on the
profits of trade, on rent, and on the dividends of funds. We
say salary and not wages, because to collect Income-tax from
the poor, even if returns of their earnings were procurable,
would be out of the question. Suppose the tax-gatherer asked
a labourer what was his income. He would answer pretty
much as La Fontaine's cobbler answers a similar question—
"'What do you earn a-year?' 'A year! upon my word, sir,'
said the jolly cobbler, 'it is not my way to count in that
style; and I don't keep heaping up day after day; enough
that at last I get to the end of the year; each day brings its
bread.'" Were it possible, however, to obtain the information
by means of stamps on wages, and other ingenious devices,
and were it worth while to risk the odium which the collection
of sums from the poor would entail, it would be very unjust
and foolish to resort to a measure which would probably increase at once the poor-rates and the revenue. For these
reasons a portion of the community is wisely exempted from the
operation of the tax. At the same time, it is highly questionable whether £100 is the proper figure. It appears to be too
high. There is, moreover, a striking inconsistency in the theory
underlying the present arrangement. An income of £99 is
assumed to be incapable of bearing direct taxation, and yet he
who enjoys an income of £110 is taxed on £50, as if not
£100, but only incomes above £60, were capable of bearing
direct taxation.

New difficulties are encountered in applying the tax to
incomes of £100 and upwards, and these difficulties are so

serious and so hard to overcome, that, in the opinion of many
statesmen—in the opinion of Mr. Gladstone, among others—
the Income-tax cannot be permanent, and must be cast aside at
the first opportunity. It is the measure of a needy State, they
hold. The difficulties experienced in levying the tax are re-
vealed in two complaints, loud and frequent. The first may be
thus expressed :—Under the cover of pretended fairness to all,
gross unfairness is committed, and much partiality shown.
While one portion of the community is taxed on any sums
which it pleases to name, the other portion is taxed as the
State pleases. In other words, while some are permitted to
assess themselves loosely, others are rigidly assessed by public
officers. Consequently the tax, it is said, assumes the shape of
a twofold tax on honesty ; not only are the honest made to contribute a disproportionate share because the dishonest choose to
underrate their profits, but the latter render the tax less productive than was anticipated or than necessities demand, and
they may consequently load the truthful and scrupulous with
new burdens, imposed to bring to the Treasury the needful
money. The incomes of those coming under schedule A—landowners and owners of houses—are known, or at all events
may be known, pretty accurately; there are extraneous standards
to gauge the incomes of these men ; for them to defraud the
State to any great extent is impossible. But schedule B, which
comprehends farmers, affords room for escape ; and, indeed, the
manner in which farmers' incomes are assessed is a confession
that the tax is levied much at random. It is assumed quite
arbitrarily, and often very wrongly, that in England the farmer's profits amount to one-half of the rent of his farm, and in
Scotland to one-third. True, he may appeal to show that his
profits are really less than this, or are, in fact, none at all : that
is a security against his being overtaxed ; but there exists none
for his being undertaxed. Schedule B, it may be added, is in
altogether an anomalous state. There appears to be no reason
why farmers should not be treated as those assessed to schedule
D are. The incomes of those assessed to schedules C and
E are accurately known, inasmuch as they are paid by the
Government, the Income-tax being deducted beforehand. But
schedule D includes people whose incomes cannot be accurately
known, and can be guessed at only rudely ; and in dealing with
such people, the choice lies between permitting the trader or

professional man to contribute what he pleases, and to defraud the Exchequer if he chooses, or to tax him at random, running the risk of defrauding him. Again, it is objected that those who save and invest their savings are treated unfairly, being taxed twice over. Thus, if a man out of an income of £10,000 saves money which he expends in purchasing stock, he may be taxed on £10,000 *plus* the dividends of his stock. Though not applicable to simple hoarding, this objection is unanswerable so far as investments are concerned ; and perhaps the only reason why a change does not take place is, that it is difficult to obtain accurate information with respect to any other form of savings than insurance policies.

Such is the first difficulty encountered in carrying into operation the principle of an Income-tax : another difficulty, equally grave, arises when the former is surmounted ; for it is perceived that, even if it is known what is the money value of everybody's income, it will not be fair to load those possessing the same income with the same tax. Take sixpence in the pound from a man with no family—he scarcely feels the impost ; take it from the father of a large family—the impost may be onerous and serious. Recognising this fact, the law formerly allowed abatements to the fathers of a certain number of children. Again, for A, a shopkeeper or agent, whose business may cease to-morrow, and certainly will not be continued to the benefit of his representatives after his death, to pay £30 on an income of £500 is to bear a burden much heavier than that borne by B, who, with an income of £500 derived from land, pays £30 also. The former possesses only a terminable annuity, out of which he must provide for his old age and for his family ; the latter, possessing a perpetual annuity, is under no pressing obligation to save. The latter has secured an income for ever ; that of the former is a terminable annuity of uncertain duration ; and instead of viewing these two men as of equal substance, the owner of landed property yielding £500 of rent ought to be ranked with a trader or professional gentleman whose income is £500 *plus* such a sum as would purchase a perpetual annuity of £500. Accordingly, it is alleged that those coming under schedules B, D, and E—the recipients of terminable and sometimes precarious annuities—are still subjected to great hardships in comparison with those assessed under schedules A and C, whose annuities are certain and perpetual. It is, moreover,

doubtful whether the allowances made in favour of the industrial classes as to the average of profits on three years and the
deduction of insurance premiums redress the inequality.

In making his financial statement in 1853, Mr. Gladstone
endeavoured to defend the tax against the objection that precarious incomes are too heavily taxed in comparison with realised
property. Taking land as the typical source of realised income, and trade as that of precarious income, and premising
that the former was taxed on the gross proceeds, only unimportant deductions being allowed, he calculated that the
owners of land were assessed at 16 per cent above their net
incomes, and that a further deduction of one-fourth ought to be
made in consideration of the mortgages and settlements with
which land and houses are charged.   When all these deductions
were made, it would he found, he calculated, that of the two
classes of annuitants, one, possessed of interminable incomes, was
charged at the rate of 7d. a pound, and the other, possessing
terminable annuities, at the rate of 5¼d. ; and hence he concluded, that, without pushing into prominence the facility which
traders and professional men possessed, and sometimes used, to
accommodate their burdens to their shoulders by giving in false
returns, it was clear that the Income-tax did draw a line of distinction between the two classes of incomes.   But why should
all mortgages be subtracted, in order to arrive at the net incomes
of landowners ?   Such charges as were imposed on the land before the present owner came into possession, or such charges as
were contracted by him in order to improve his property, may
perhaps justly be deducted; he did not enjoy the benefit resulting
from the former charges ; and the latter were the capital, which
portion of his rent merely replaces.   But having excluded these
two kinds of expenditure, we have still a vast amount of mortgages and other charges contracted, in order to be devoted to
purposes wholly unconnected with the land, or even to purposes
of pure waste ; and to find net income, debts so contracted
should not be subtracted.   As well might one subtract the
amount of unpaid tailors' bills from the income of a Government clerk to ascertain his assessable substance.   On the whole,
perhaps, the tax does favour the possessors of realised property, though the above considerations help to prove that the
partiality is not so vast as agitators represent.   At the same
time, it would be wrong to speak of the inequality as existing

wholly between the different classes included under different schedules, for they exist as between people assessed under the same schedule. Thus, the owners of houses complain that no deductions are made from the rents in order to exclude the mere return of capital ; and the owners of mines consider it a hardship to be assessed pretty nearly as if their property was to last for ever.

Those who complain of the hardship of taxing terminable incomes at the same rate as permanent incomes, frequently encounter the following rejoinder :—" The boon you ask is already granted. To the former is in reality meted out treatment differing from that which is meted out to the latter. If the terminable annuity is taxed at the same rate as the interminable, the latter is taxed for ever, the former only so long as the annuitant enjoys it. An income of £500 a year, derived from trade, is taxed only for a limited period ; proceeding from land, the same income is taxed for all the generations to come." Though specious, this rejoinder is unsound, for two, if not more, reasons. The Income-tax has been regarded by, perhaps, most statesmen as a temporary expedient ; its duration has been short ; and imposed to satisfy a passing want : it has, when the purpose of the moment was served, been either abolished or reduced. Interminable annuities have not been interminably taxed. Therefore the rejoinder starts from a mistake. Moreover, even if interminable annuities were taxed perpetually, the holder of the terminable annuity would still be a sufferer. Out of his income he must provide, if he be a prudent man, not only the means of subsistence in old age, but the wherewithal to support his nearest dependants, and to leave them in comfort at death. And his savings, if profitably invested, will be subject to the tax. On the other hand, the income of the interminable annuitant lasts for ever, and during his tenure of it he has to divide it with none. He has fewer legitimate calls to satisfy. There is not, in fine, equality of sacrifice. Mr. Lowe has mooted another ingenious defence of the indifferent treatment of precarious and interminable, or " industrial " and " spontaneous " incomes. You do not, he says, draw any such distinction—nobody ever proposed to draw any such distinction —in the case of other taxes ; licenses and tea-duty are the same to all, no matter what be the source of the income ; and yet, if the rule that the owners of precarious annuities should fare more leniently than others be good for the Income-tax, it is good for all taxes. But, as regards most of these taxes, they are paid voluntarily; they, as a rule, fall only upon luxuries; and the fact that a person does render himself amenable to such taxes is presumption that he is in a position to bear the burden without inconvenience. The Income-tax, on the other hand, is taken by the strong hand from all. Moreover, Mr. Lowe's argument proves considerably too much, for, if the Income-tax should be levied like all other taxes, as his argument implies, we should have it levied on all persons, none being too poor to be taxed. And lastly, I presume that if it were in any way possible to make the indirect imposts fall with more equality than they now do— if we could devise any mode by which indirect taxes would be paid in exact proportion to the means of the payers—we should gladly avail ourselves of it.

To remove this hardship, it has been proposed to capitalise all incomes, to reduce them to the same denomination, and to tax them only when thus reduced. Mr. Hume, Dr. Farr, and not a few others, have advocated the separate capitalisation of each income by actuarial calculations. Such a mode of assessment might be theoretically correct, but the expense, and delay and disputes, incidental to this mode of assessment, not to mention the varying character of the tax, stamp it as impracticable; and the same may be said of the proposals of Mr. James Mill to allow deductions in the case of industrial and professional incomes equal in amount to sums which would yield a perpetual annuity equal to the reserved incomes.* Mr. John Stuart Mill would exempt all savings from taxation if it were possible to be correctly informed of their true amount; and, in the event of that being impossible, he would exempt one-fourth of terminable incomes, on the assumption that this is, on an average, the proportion which the possessors of such incomes ought to save, and that, if actual savings cannot be determined, the next best thing is to roughly calculate and exempt what people ought to save. The proposal made by his father and Mr. M'Culloch to deduct a sum such as would give for ever to a man's successors an income equal to what he reserves for himself, Mr. Mill rejects, inasmuch as a man is under no obligation to make so abundant provision

* Mr. Hubbard has spoken of the former as "a very complicated, intricate, and unpracticable series of individual arrangements."—*Evidence before Commission of* 1861.

for his descendants, who are entitled only to be put in the way
of earning their living.   His own proposal is a practical mode of
mitigating an evil not to be wholly removed, but it is pretty
obviously open to two objections.   If equality of sacrifice ought
to be the criterion, nothing short of Mr. M'Culloch's proposal
would satisfy the requirements of the case.   If, on the other
hand, equality of sacrifice is to be rejected as impracticable here,
and it be laid down that immunity should be extended to what
a person ought to save, it is clear that the proportion proposed
by Mr. Mill to be exempted would sometimes exceed the amount
which one is bound to leave to one's representatives.   To let
one-fourth of a millionaire banker's income be exempted from
the tax would be utterly unjustifiable on the ground that such
was the amount he ought to save ; and to be at all fair, the
privilege should be refused to incomes of a certain amount.   It
may be suggested that an approach to equity would be made by
a manipulation of the probate, legacy, and succession duties.
Let the proximate ascendants and descendants of the owners
of industrial incomes receive partial exemption as regards
the payment of these duties, and much of the hardships complained of will be removed.   Those assessed to schedule D
would enjoy some of that immunity to which necessary care for
their dependants entitles them.   They would thus be relieved
according as they had exercised that care.   They would have to
pay only on what had been their means.   Moreover, the change
would not be very strange, since there exist numerous classes of
exemptions from probate duty.   I make no apology for entering
pretty minutely into the subject of the Income-tax.   Adopted
in this country and the United States as a temporary expedient, and apologetically alluded to by every Chancellor of the
Exchequer, it will nevertheless probably remain a permanent
feature of the financial system of this country, and will, it is
likely, be imitated abroad.   It is conceivable even that, personal
property becoming liable to local rates, the Income-tax returns
will be made the basis of all local rates.   If such be the destiny
of the Income-tax, no pains in perfecting its plan can be wasted.

Even the fraud committed under cover of self-assessment is
not wholly insusceptible of correction.   Publish the returns; set
vanity against avarice, the generally strong desire not to be
thought poor against the desire to escape payment of one's
dues ; the returns may be far more accurate than they are.

Certain facts are calculated to make one think that the repugnance to publicity is apt to be exaggerated. Government officials do not complain that their incomes are known; comparatively few contributors avail themselves of the power to withhold the disclosure of their affairs from the district Commissioners, and to reserve them for special Commissioners. It is by means of publicity that the estimates under the Verghi or Turkish Income-tax are made nearly accurate; and the United States afford the spectacle of the publication of incomes. Of considerable merit, too, is the proposal that the rent of taxpayers' dwellings should, where there is reason to suspect fraud, be made the basis of assessment.

Without extenuating the amount and kind of immorality which schedule D begets*—and immorality is an inseparable concomitant of taxation in all shapes—it may be questioned whether the income-tax should be made temporary. Easy to collect and to graduate, it is, looked at from the Chancellor of the Exchequer's point of view, an admirable tax; the most manageable in the whole list. It has its place, too, in the fiscal system as a measure of justice. Without it some classes would escape their fair share of the national burdens. Repeal this tax, and the wealthy and upper stratum of the middle-class almost escape taxation; certainly they will not pay in proportion to their means; and the man with £2000 a year will contribute perhaps only a few shillings more than a neighbour whose income is £200. All taxes, and custom and excise duties in an eminent degree, tempt men to falsehood; and the income-tax is demoralising, chiefly because it has hitherto been very high. When low, it is doubtful whether very many would send in thoroughly false returns. But if it were the case that persons in trade obtained a great exemption by self-assessment, there soon would commence a movement that would in time partially deprive them of the benefit of the exemption; bad taxes tend to right themselves in the course of time; the profits of the trades that eluded the tax would be great, and would attract so many, that, by the force of competition, the profits of those under schedule D would tend to be reduced to the common level.

* The *New York Tribune* speaks of the Income-tax as calculated "to make us a nation of liars and oath-breakers. It remains a standing premium on fraud and falsehood."

A question frequently mooted and not yet settled is, Whether extraordinary sums, such as wars or other national emergencies demand, should be raised by taxes or loans? The most common and practical shape which the question takes is, Whether war expenditure should be raised by additional taxes or an increase of the existing taxes, or Whether a Government should resort to loans? Can we doubt what has been the general answer? Loans are so facile a resource,* it is so easy to persuade contemporaries that they are labouring for the benefit of posterity, which has no say in the matter, increases of present taxes are so unpopular, new taxes approximate so closely to impossibilities, and the prospect of a safe and good investment for capital when trade is dull, with the expectation of bonuses and other allurements, is so captivating to the money market, that it is no wonder financiers have lavishly borrowed; and these circumstances sufficiently explain why not an European State, great or small, is free from debt. Above all other nations we have been prodigal in this respect. When great emergencies first arose in this country, we ran madly into debt. At the beginning of his war with France, Pitt borrowed furiously. In this course he persevered until he grew alarmed at the work of his hand, and between 1793 and 1801 he added about 330,000,000 to the National Debt. In this century there has been a reluctance, ascribable to the effects of Pitt's policy, and the abstract arguments of Chalmers and Ricardo, to avail ourselves of loans; and in proof of the alteration in our conduct, it may be observed that much of the expense of the Crimean war, the last severe ordeal, was met by an Income-tax of 1s. 2d. and 1s. 4d. on the pound, and that a penny on the pound was added on the existing Income-tax to provide for the Abyssinian Expedition. Though numerous deviations may be quoted from this course— though Mr. Chase chose to raise the enormous expenses of the American civil war by vast loans, though such has been the course of France, and though Sir George Cornewall Lewis resorted to a loan during the Crimean war—the tide of opinion now sets in

* " Whatever the Government takes from the people for purposes of war is destroyed. If the amount is obtained by taxation, it is destroyed, and we are all poorer. If the amount is obtained by loans, it is still destroyed, and we are all poorer none the less. But if it is obtained by taxation, we all *know* that we are poorer to that extent. Whereas, if it is obtained by loans, we delude ourselves with the belief that we are as well off as ever."—*North American Review*, April 1869.

favour of raising the expenses of the year within the year. Not without reason ; many moral and financial considerations point this way. It is easy to delude ourselves that we are benefiting posterity, when we believe posterity will bear the burden, and this fatal delusion is the hotbed of wars. Declaring war seems no longer the solemn step which it really is, when it does not visibly bring all its hardships. Before Dr. Chalmers's time it had been customary for statesmen to speak of the expenditure of loans as not falling on the substance of the year, but as laid on the shoulders of posterity. He pointed out that loans, equally with taxes, were paid out of the wealth then in existence, and that the amount available for wages and for creating new wealth was lessened by war-loans as much as by war-taxes. But these arguments are not quite conclusive against the use of loans on certain occasions. For, in the first place, these loans need not, and in the case of the United States, for example, were not, entirely contributed out of the resources of the nation that expended them ; in spite of the stupid prejudice against European capitalists, Englishmen and Germans were included among the lenders to the Federal Government, and much of the money required by France in her great struggle came out of English pockets. Lending on these principles—a country where the rate of profits is 10 per cent, say, borrowing where the rate is 4—forms a kind of international insurance. Again, there is always among a rich and saving people a portion of capital which is ready to be sent abroad. Now Indian railways absorb it, now Canadian railways, now Atlantic telegraph companies. If the loans lick up this floating capital and nothing more, they need not subtract anything from the resources available for wages. A statesman must elect between loans and the taxes which he has at his command, and it may well be that he will prefer borrowing to making taxes really protective by their height. Further, a loan, when not forced, is a voluntary offering, and presumptively comes out of the means of those who have the superfluities of life, while taxes are the compulsory contributions of those who may not possess even the necessaries. The very ease with which loans are obtained —an argument against their constant use—justifies their use in emergencies. Loans, too, may come out of the luxuries of one country, and so spare the capital of another. Lastly, it is to be observed that there occur occasions when, taxes failing to satisfy expectations, or a particular emergency arising, it may be necessary or advisable to resort to short loans in the form of Exchequer bills or bonds. It would be difficult, perhaps, for her Majesty's Government to go on without Montague's invention. These considerations make it rash to pronounce war-loans wholly bad. We are not, however, without a rough guide as to the propriety of using loans and taxes in emergencies. If loans can be contracted without greatly raising the rate of interest, we may take it for a sign that they have not much diminished the productive resources of the country; if the rate remain what it was, we may conclude that the loan has drained only the superfluities of the country—what would have been sent abroad or consumed unproductively. At the same time, there is always one standing advantage in raising loans by taxes in preference to borrowing. When taxes are raised we are done with the expenditure for ever, but the burden of loans remains, necessitating a costly and permanent machinery of collection, abridging the power of resorting to taxes in difficulties, perhaps rendering a considerable portion of the people adverse to productive occupations, and, if the loan be heavy, and the coupons be owned largely by foreigners, furnishing demagogues with fuel for their designs. Loans expended productively are of course perfectly defensible; they may be fairly charged to capital. The only difficulty is to ascertain what forms of outlay are really productive; and that this difficulty may frequently be very great, as has already been observed, the discussions respecting our expenditure in India prove. Probably the practice of borrowing money for carrying on war will receive a check from the growth of a new doctrine with respect to our obligation to pay debts incurred for purposes which we disapprove. Repudiation has an ugly sound; but future generations may not be deterred by the word from declining to pay for wars which they disavow as grossly unjust. Of course, the contingency of another loan would be preventive of, or obstructive to, this course; but what if nations should come over to the opinion, supported by so many economists, that loans are in all circumstances bad?

Much importance cannot be attached to the theory that a debt is of considerable utility to a country. It stimulates industry by the creation of difficulties, says one. As if there were not enough of difficulties in the world without artificially hatching others! It affords a channel for conveniently investing funds in the hands of trustees, or for making provision for the future. As if there were no mortgages or leasehold securities ! Nor will it avail much to affirm with Macaulay that borrowing promotes the virtue of a nation, seeing it is impossible to borrow much without fulfilling former obligations. All the fidelity which is indispensable to the despotic borrower is fidelity in taxing his subjects. Over any practice, however bad, be it only old, there grows a crust of reasonableness, or an apparent coating of utility ; but that which conceals the injurious effects of the National Debt is still thin after nearly two centuries. In the event of a Government deciding to borrow, the question will arise whether the money ought to be obtained by means of terminable or interminable annuities. I name these two modes only, for the hypothecation of a special tax is now rare, at all events in European States. The tendency has of late, though with notable exceptions, been in favour of the former ; and the importance of pledging the nation to a reduction of the debt is such that no doubt terminable annuities would be preferable but for the fact that capitalists disposed to lend to Governments do, as a rule, like to purchase terminable annuities, constantly decreasing in value as they are. The trustees of charitable institutions, and almost all who wish to make financial arrangements with respect to a remote future, prefer .perpetual annuities, nearly constant in value. The conveniences due to a national debt, which have induced some to pronounce that burden a boon, consist for the most part of the facilities perpetual annuities afford for making settlements with certainty. And the indisposition to purchase terminable annuities, unless the interest is very high, has precluded Governments from largely employing a device which would have prevented the accumulation of gigantic debts. Of our debt only a small fraction is terminable. Yet it seems that the victory rests with the former, though there is no arithmetical gain by use of them, as has sometimes been supposed by eminent statesmen. Perpetuities created by any one generation may yet be as little tolerated as a perpetuity created by any one member now is ; and interminable annuities can scarcely exist if each generation claim the right of revision. There has indeed been exhibited by recent war financiers some disposition to prefer loans repayable at no distant period. Bonds, or *bons du trésor*, maturing in a certain number of years, and capable of being redeemed after

2 B

the expiry of a still shorter period, are resorted to notwithstanding the high interest required by subscribers, partly in the hope of being able to utilise the cheapness of money which often marks the close of a war. There is a further question cognate with this subject. Ought a Government to borrow at a comparatively low rate of interest and receive only a portion of the nominal principal, or ought it to offer a comparatively high rate of interest on condition of receiving the whole principal? Ought it, for example, to allot £100 of stock or rentes to every contributor of £75, or ought it to give £100 in stock to every contributor of £100, making the interest in the former case 3, in the latter 4 per cent? No universally applicable rule can be laid down with regard to this point. There may exist a fear of conversions necessary to be humoured. Some account, though certainly very small, ought to be taken of the ease of transmission. In order to make a loan acceptable, issuing at a nominal figure may be necessary. The chance of being paid off at par may have to be thrown in as a bait, and an appeal may have to be made to the speculative persons. But if the stock was borrowed pretty high, the possibility of conversion, on the stock rising to a premium, ought to be borne in mind. To refer to the chief operations in our financial history: In 1844, Mr. Goulburn, operating on £248,000,000, presented to stockholders the option of accepting a 3¼ per cent stock for a 3½, or of being paid the principal. In the same year Belgium converted its 5 per cent into 4½. It is found, if the financier chooses his time well, that few prefer to be paid off. Some, indeed, are under engagements forbidding their selling out; but, especially if a slight bonus is offered, conversion proves a highly efficacious instrument in the hands of a Government possessing a surplus, or with cheap money at its command, especially if the terms of the bargain admit of immediate paying off, if the stock operated on receives a high rate of interest, and if there are other kinds of stock receiving less.

CHAPTER XXVII.

COLLECTION OF TAXES.

NEXT in importance to the question of the incidence of taxation, and strangely neglected, is that of its collection. Two modes of collecting taxes have been practised. They have been farmed, or, as is now more common, they have been collected by officers of the Government. The latter is, indeed, the more common now-a-days, but there are notable examples of the former. The immensè revenue of the Roman Republic and Empire was farmed. A tax was put up to public auction, and knocked down to the highest bidder; and thereby wealthy capitalists found themselves disposers of the resources of vast countries. One company was privileged to suck Asia; the tithes of Sicily belonged to another; and a third drained Macedonia. As every student of history knows, of the eight chief taxes of France five were farmed previous to the French Revolution; and the discontent excited by the exactions of the farmers-general, as the contractors were designated, and the contrast between their enormous and suspicious wealth and the general poverty of those on whom they battened, were in no small degree causes of the Revolution, and of the bloody manner in which it was accomplished. The French people bitterly hated the farmers-general that had grown rich in their odious profession. Certainly not the least of the numerous reforms accomplished at the Revolution was the abolition of this mode of collection. Nor is the practice of farming unknown to this country. The Customs of England were for many years farmed. In the year 1329, the Bardi, a great Florentine family, rented them, paying £20 a-day. In 1400, they were let for £8000 a-year. Queen Elizabeth gave a lease of them to Sir Thomas Smith, Secretary of State, for rents varying from £14,000 to £15,000. But in 1671, the collection of Customs was entrusted to a Board of Commissioners; and, since that time, the only taxes openly farmed, with the exception of the hearth-tax, have been road-taxes. The change was for the better. The former mode of collecting taxes is apt to be at once dangerous and expensive. The farmer must obtain a profit out of the proceeds of the tax; that profit must be large, because there has generally been an odour of infamy about the "publican's" trade, and because it can be pursued only by those whose large capital, and the ability to furnish the large securities required, give them the position of monopolists; so that a tax collected by farmers would be sure to take much more from the people than it brought to the exchequer. It has been alleged, though probably with much exaggeration, that the farmers-general and treasurers of France netted between 1726 and 1776 money equal in value to £250,000,000. And expensiveness is only one, and not the worst, of the bad features of the system. Those who are familiar with the history of the reign of Louis XIV. and that of Louis XV., who recollect the animosity which the wealth of the farmers-general excited, and the cruelty with which the farmed taxes were exacted—those who know anything of the abuses perpetuated under cover of the "farming" of Turkish finance—will not entertain for a moment the idea that such a mode of collection would be tolerable if applied to many kinds of taxes. To enable the farmers to extort contributions, private persons must be gifted with extraordinary and dangerous powers, such as could not be tolerated by a free and high-spirited people. Taxation, a bitter pill with whatever comfits or bon-bons accompanied, would be immeasurably more detestable if it was imagined, rightly or wrongly, that private persons fattened on the earnings wrung from the people. And yet, seduced by a diseased conviction of the inefficiency of a Government to accomplish anything so well as private persons, there have been found persons to maintain that all taxes should be collected in this manner. As well might it be maintained that the Government should accept the tenders of private persons for the defence of the country or for administering justice.* In a

---

* These remarks apply chiefly to Occidental Europe, where a staff of fairly honest collectors can be obtained. In the case of Turkey, for example, they must be taken *cum grano*; there, the Government, I understand, has returned to the "iltizam" system, after attempting to collect the revenue without the intervention of middlemen.

certain sense, indeed, it is true that the indirect taxes are farmed. But this is inevitable, and it is a disadvantage only counterbalanced by the accompanying advantages.

Though this mode of gathering the revenue by open farming has fallen into general desuetude, and though it is abandoned in England almost wholly, we need not look far or long in order to detect clamant evils in respect to collection ; and when all obnoxious taxes will have been repealed, when the poor will contribute only their fair and light share, when no tax will enhance the prices of the necessities of life, or fall upon the raw materials of industry, a bold Chancellor of the Exchequer will find ready for his sickle a lusty crop of abuses to be cut down. Absorbed in the consideration of the incidence of taxes, economists have been unmindful of the paltry item of collection, and hence they have suffered to remain without a protest monstrous anomalies. Not that the field is untrodden. Yet how far short are we still of the ideal ! The ideally best machinery for bringing taxes into the Treasury, the machinery which the architect of a new State would create, and which consequently every statesman should aspiringly keep before him as the object of his imitation, so far as that may be possible, would be one board or department, with subdivisions, each charged with the collecting of a separate tax or group of taxes. By ,this unity of functions economy would be effected to the utmost in the expenses due to control ; and it is most probable that the savings would extend far beyond this point, for, leaving out of question the probable saving in buildings, it is consonant with experience that the public servants could thus be utilised to the utmost. Such is the ideally best mode—and " ideally best " here signifies cheapest. How does the mode of collecting taxes in this country conform to this ideal? Very indifferently. A host of departments, fortuitous concourse of functionaries, an agglomeration of historical accidents, are entrusted with the collection of our revenue ; and nowhere else is the national taste for revelling in anomalies, that instinct which says that whatever is crooked is probably right, and whatever is straight is certainly wrong, more strongly exhibited. To begin with imperial taxes, there are the two great departments of Customs and Inland Revenue totally distinct. Alongside these there is, or rather was some years ago, a distinct department of Stamps and Taxes ; and, though its board has been absorbed by that of the Inland Revenue, the officers of the Excise and the Stamps and Taxes have been kept radically distinct. If this course be defensible, if it be right and proper to keep up two distinct sets of officers, and to give higher wages to officers of the Stamps and Taxes, it is very strange that the Department of Taxes should not collect one farthing of its revenue, which is paid into the hands of the Collectors of Excise. The proposal to amalgamate the two great Departments of Customs and Excise is not new, and in 1862-3 a Parliamentary Committee inquired into the expediency of doing so. Though, as was natural, the change, which would have affected powerful vested interests, was opposed, many of the witnesses gave evidence, often reluctantly, which went all the other way, and showed that it was not impossible to amalgamate the two services with advantage.

These, however, do not complete the list of departments engaged in collecting the imperial taxes : a portion of the imperial taxes is collected by mere amateurs. The Land-tax and the Inhabited House-tax, together with the Income-tax, are collected by a machinery which, as Mr. Lowe has well said, has antiquity, and little else, to recommend it. We speak now of England : the machinery is different and less objectionable in Scotland ; in Scotland these taxes are, for the most part, collected by Government officers. But in the former, the Land-tax, as well as the Income-tax, is collected by a vast irregular army of amateurs ; and it is not unduly disparaging these men to affirm that they cannot execute their work so well as men specially trained for the purpose. Cases of gross scandal are not unknown. We have heard of a bootmaker, an Income-tax collector, being told by a needy taxpayer, in debt both to her Majesty and the bootmaker, that it was out of his power to satisfy both ; whereupon the tax-collector expressed his willingness not to press her Majesty's claim. Such a system opens facilities for fraud ; it to the utmost opens boundless facilities for negligence—more costly even than fraud. It is part of the scope of the ideal which we have indicated that the same board which should collect imperial taxes should also collect local taxes. The French assign the collection of some of the local taxes to the imperial officers ; some of the imperial taxes are collected in the United States by the local officers. It is probable we should have to follow the former mode. Clearly, at all events, there is no reason in the world why one functionary should collect the borough, another the county rate, and a third the poor-rate. There are good grounds why the expenditure of the last should not be regulated by a central board ; the ground of economy, the certainty of a central board being indifferently acquainted with local circumstances, and the likelihood of money being lavishly expended if it were not " earmarked," sufficiently establish the soundness of keeping up these distinctions. Would the poor-rates be what they now are if voted in Supply ? Of course not. At the same time, there is no reason, usage apart, why the two sets of taxes should be collected by entirely different functionaries ; and, indeed, economy, the chief plea for separating the expenditure, speaks strongly in favour of conjoining the collection. One functionary, or one set of functionaries, might with ease and advantage collect all the taxes in a particular parish, and might hand into the Imperial Exchequer the proceeds of the Imperial taxes, and into the local treasuries the proceeds of local imposts. The idea of collecting all the Imperial taxes by the same set of persons is not wholly new ; it has been proposed that the Customs and Inland Revenue should be formed into one department engaged solely in surveying, and that the revenue should be paid to the Post-Office. Nor is it wholly new to propose that all the local taxes should be collected by one set of functionaries. The junction of these two ideas will give what is wanted—one set of machinery employed for collecting all kinds of taxes. Of course, there is something strange and singular in the idea of Government officers collecting local taxes ; it offends so-called constitutional notions ; but the shock would be rapidly got over. The present practice is glaringly indefensible. To have often in each parish in Scotland a different set of collectors for the police taxes and those connected therewith, and another for the poor-rates, and to have alongside these the departments of Stamps and Taxes, and perhaps the Customs, each acting as if another did not exist, augurs something wrong.

Though the chief advantage of this consolidation would be the gain to the Government in regard to economy, and though it is to this—the clearest gain—that most importance should be attached, the change would be beneficial to the people ; and, not to speak of such trifling advantages as saving of time, it would open the way to a reform which, without it, is impossible. Clearly it is advantageous to people who must pay a considerable amount of taxes, local or imperial, to be permitted to spread their contributions over some time; it has always been a strong argument for indirect taxation that it affords this facility. The most convenient course would be permission or option to pay taxes by instalments—a course, however, which would be detrimental to the public services, seeing the cost of collection would be indefinitely increased. Previously, the people of England were permitted to pay assessed and income taxes quarterly. That was found not to be suitable, and Mr. Lowe has made the English, like the Scotch, pay once a year. Next in convenience to the taxpayers would be careful provisions that local taxes and imperial taxes should not be collected simultaneously, or in close proximity. It may be, as Mr. Lowe observed, that it is for the interests of Governments to be able to collect their revenues as quickly as possible. That may be, though it is not clear that, because wars may be over in seven days, because it is more and more necessary that Governments should be in a position at any unfixed time to avail themselves of their whole resources, it should, therefore, be advantageous to obtain as much as possible of the revenues at a fixed period, the beginning of the year. Be that as it may, this circumstance constitutes no reason why the local and imperial taxes should be collected, as they often are, in a lump, or why they should not be collected at such different times, if not in such morsels, as would be most convenient. However contemptible the matter may be to the wealthy, it is a very serious circumstance to the poor to be obliged to pay a vast number of taxes all in a heap; and in the eyes of true statesmen there is no real grievance too mean to be redressed, if it can be done without causing a greater. Now, it is vain to hope that these delicate considerations will be attended to so long as there are a vast number of disconnected functionaries intrusted with the collection. They will be heeded only when the collection of local and imperial taxes is united.

Economists and statesmen have been strangely indifferent to the amount and nature of local taxes. These have been neglected for the more showy and stirring theme of Customs. And yet local taxes constitute no despicable item, nor are they free from glaring faults. Nearly twenty millions sterling are altogether raised by these means in England alone. Surely these are figures big enough to satisfy the imagination, to kindle some spark of ardour, and to stimulate inquiry into the manner in which this vast sum is raised. The first glimpse into the theme is calculated to prompt an investigator to penetrate farther in the hope of discoveries, for he perceives principles at work totally antagonistic to those which control imperial taxation, and he seems to be confronted with the necessity of deciding that either local taxation or imperial taxation is totally wrong. He perceives that while imperial imposts are partially direct and partially indirect, in the proportion, say, of about 16 to 81, local taxes are, with scarcely an exception, direct. How reconcile this? the inquirer asks. Are not the imperial finances or the local finances radically false in principle? In the one case it was laid down that justice could be attained only by the imposing of indirect taxes, which affected incomes that would otherwise have escaped taxation; and, if this be so, it apparently follows by irresistible sequence, that local taxation, raised almost wholly by direct imposts, is unsound and unjust. The rich man, or the well-to-do, pays almost everything. Is this right?

Let us mention a few other peculiarities of local taxation. While imperial imposts press with almost equal weight on real and personal property, local imposts fall chiefly on the former. Perhaps the greater portion of the local taxes is borne by property falling under schedule A, which pays about one-third of the Income-tax; occupiers of land may indeed incidentally contribute, owing to an unexpected increase of rates, and the tenants of houses bear an accidental share; but ultimately most of the rates, when apparently paid by the occupier, are deducted from rents. This is one anomaly. Another is the fact that the means of the landlords are reckoned in one way, when they have to pay local taxes, and in some other way when they have to pay Income-tax: Why, to pass to another anomaly, should there be no uniformity in the allowances made in ascertaining net annual value? and why should the country rates be raised in accordance with one valuation and the poor-rates in accordance with another? Why should the landlord in Scotland pay directly one half of the rates, while the English landlord *directly* pays nothing? Why should the latter, who *indirectly* pays everything according to one theory, be without his share in the administration of the proceeds? And, ending this imperfect catalogue of anomalies, which might be indefinitely extended, I would ask what modern Government thinks of setting aside an imperial tax for a special purpose ? No European Government ever thinks of imposing a special tax, the proceeds of which are appropriated to raising soldiers. Why, then, should there be a different procedure in regard to local taxation ? Why should there be a special impost set aside for the relief of the poor, another for tolls, etc. ? Why should not these taxes be lumped together, instead of the proceeds of each being earmarked and legally applicable only to a group of purposes rigidly defined by law ?

A few considerations will help to explain, if not justify, the existence of some of these anomalies.

I do not pretend to be able to give reasons for all these anomalies ; some are indefensible ; but two circumstances lead one to conclude that much of the alleged injustice is more apparent than real. In the first place, to levy numerous indirect local taxes in the interior of a country would be to impede traffic and movement to an intolerable degree. We may submit to every ship coming from abroad being searched ; but that every cart or wheelbarrow should be ransacked, that each city should be a fortress, each gate guarded by a *douanier*, and every passing citizen a *suspect* —the idea is intolerable, and it passes the conception of Englishmen how the French have so long endured the *octrois* or local imposts levied at the gates of their cities. The Belgians have wisely commuted the *octrois;* a great service was done by the abolition of their equivalents in England. The French will perhaps follow these examples. The injuries which the *octrois* inflict on the industries of Paris are too evident to tempt copyists, or even to promise continuance. Moreover, while indirect taxes in the interior would almost of necessity fall on articles of food or raw materials of industry, to make Customs available for local expenditure it would be necessary to imitate the course pursued by the Swiss Confederation, which allots a portion of the proceeds of the Customs to each Canton. In partial justification of the weight with which local taxes press on real property may be mentioned the fact that some of the so-called local taxes are really perpetual rent-charges. A few of them have pressed upon real property for centuries, during which time the land has probably been repeatedly bought by purchasers, who took into account the rent-charges, and paid such a sum as would leave them a clear net income. The most extravagant results, it has been objected, flow from such a theory. Only give time enough, let real property pass through sufficient hands, and the State may appropriate almost every farthing of the landlord's rent without the landlord being taxed. This objection, however, forgets that it is only contended that exceptional taxes, not all taxes, on real property, tend to become rent-charges ; if, as is the case in France, there is, corresponding to the land-tax, a tax on personal property, or rather a poll-tax, the former, however long continued, will not sink into the nature of a rent-charge. Purchasers cannot in these circumstances deduct the tax from the purchase-money, seeing all other investments for their money will subject them to equal charges. But though rates may be of the nature of rent-charges, it is extremely desirable that these and their amount should once for all be ascertained. If the State has appropriated a certain portion of the soil, let the precise amount be determined, and do not keep suspended over the heads of landlords the alarming doctrine that the State has an indefinite mortgage on their estates. If it is true that landlords now possess advantages which counterbalance the hardship of paying more than the landless do to local rates, let the former be valued accurately, so that the special imposts may never exceed the worth of the peculiar favours. After the exceptional claims on the landlords are satisfied, it would be right, I submit, to revive the old doctrine that all kinds of property, personal as well as real, should be liable to local burdens ; and the Income-tax returns might serve as the basis for both local and imperial imposts. There are precedents to justify one in speaking of this as an old doctrine : the famous 43 of Elizabeth contemplated the rating of all kinds of property ; in Scotland the rates were levied on " means and substance." Of course difficulties confront one in applying the principle ; and Mr. Wells has ably argued that these are so serious that the New England States, abandoning the taxation of personalty, should draw all from realty. But so far as his objections are not objections to an Income-tax in every form, they are applicable only to a country like America, where each State controls its own finances. The outlines are clear. The reluctance to disclose one's income to parish officials is a difficulty no longer, if imperial and local taxes are collected by the same staffs. Parliament voting so much a pound, let the local authorities vote so much also ; the entire sum may be collected without any one but Government officials knowing each man's quota. No re-

semblance in all this—almost a *facsimile* of New England practices—to the common proposal to charge to the Consolidated
Fund a certain portion of the local burdens.   As to the difficulty
arising out of personal property with no particular venue, it would
be in harmony with present practices and justice if the owner
were rated to the place in which his business was conducted ;
personalis sequitur personam would generally be a sound rule ; if
he were a landholder, or lived on the proceeds of foreign investments, he might be permitted to choose the district to which he
desired to be rated—a choice which might be dangerous so long
as some parishes pay a few pence in the pound, and others a few
shillings, but innocuous when these anomalies are removed.
Obviously just, and supported in the main by the authority of
Sir George Cornewall Lewis, such a scheme will probably one
day take the place of the present confusion.

Why not assign all the local functions in one district to one
body ?   The rejoinder is—What proper local unit could we find
suitable at once for the administration of poor-rates, police-
rates, highway-rates, lighting-rates, improvement-rates, public
health and sewerage rates, etc. ?   Some political philosophers
would establish in their old positions the shire, the ward, and
hundred ; but these, together with the parish, are fast changing
into antiquarian divisions.   When communication was less
easy than it is, the parish was perhaps a good enough unit in
the then simplicity of local government ; but with communication facilitated as it is, the interests of remote persons closely
interwoven as they are, the settlement laws largely modified,
and the duties of local authorities multiplied, the parish ceases
to be a natural unit.   The best unit for purposes of the poor-
law may not suit the purposes of public health, and as each
unit must have its separate board, several bodies controlling
separate funds spring up in each district.   That this must be
always the condition of matters, that the abandonment of these
antiquated divisions, and the substitution of others conforming
to the distribution of population in the nineteenth century, is
impossible, and that there is no establishing a local board in
each district, voting and raising the entire local revenue, and
allotting it to the various local objects in such a manner as
may be thought fit, is a question which Mr. Goschen has made
practical, and in regard to which the admirable communal divisions of France may serve as models.

What imposts should be local is a question that raises the gigantic subject of centralisation. Without venturing to deal with the whole subject, it may be observed that it is rash to join in the common invectives against financial centralisation, because under it are disguised some of the very best tendencies of our time. Centralisation may mean growth of common interests, men becoming more and more a family, the rise of true socialism. It may mean that there are henceforth no purely local interests, the welfare of each district being of consequence to all the others. This popular ogre may mean absence of waste. It may mean that in political government, as in industrial government, the advantages of massing energies and of highly dividing labour are beginning to be appreciated at their true and high worth. And if it also has brought in its train evils that seem to stamp it as a curse, industrial history, the counterpart of political history, reminds us that centralisation may be noxious only because it comes prematurely. First, the individual unit must be a healthy political organism; then successively the family, parish, or county, must be knit together; and not until there is homogeneity among the parts should they be formed into a whole by a system of centralisation. Force it on—treat India financially as if it were uniform—and it is highly probable that the unity will have to be broken up. Our country, however, appears to have passed that stage. There appears, for example, to be reason for thinking that the Imperial Government would be warranted in procuring certain loans for local authorities at a lesser rate than they can ;* and it is also more than questionable whether the principle adopted in the Education Act, of assisting by an imperial grant districts, the rates of which rise above a certain figure, should not be applied to poor-law purposes.

* See *Westminster Review* for October 1870.

CHAPTER XXVIII.

PROTECTIONISM.

HITHERTO we have supposed taxes to be imposed for the purpose of obtaining a revenue; but one would carry away a very
erroneous, and quite an optimist, idea of what taxation is and
has been, if it were not understood that the obtaining of a
revenue has been but one of the objects, and often one of the
minor objects, of taxes. They have been, and still are, frequently imposed in order to "protect," as the phrase is, some
goods, and to prohibit or hinder the entrance of others. In
taxes, statesmen long supposed they had a helm by which they
could direct the course of the industries of a country at pleasure
—a mould in which national tastes could be shaped, a power
that could reverse the decrees of nature, and erect manufac-
tories which climate, soil, the inhabitants, and all their circumstances, repudiated. To write the history of Protectionism
would be to write the commercial history of many centuries and
many countries. Volumes might be filled with the subject.
The task is too big to be possible, and, perhaps, if accomplished,
it would greatly profit no one. But we may mention a few of
the chief points in this story, so as to impart some faint idea
of the part which Protectionism has played. To fix a date as
its beginning is almost impossible, for much of Protectionism is
the mature outcome of a spirit which is as old as man—one
thing with many names, which in commerce and trade takes
the forms of Protectionism, privileges of guilds and trades, etc.

  Protectionism is usually described in connection with the
Mercantile Theory. It is said that duties were imposed with
the double object of securing the home market to the home
producers, and of preventing the efflux and stimulating the
influx of gold. A preliminary question, however, is pertinent,
Was there ever a Mercantile Theory? With confidence all
economists answer "Yes." Most of them paint it as one of

the most baleful scourges that ever visited our race. They tell us that it deluged the earth with seas of blood, and spilt and wasted uncounted wealth ; and we are asked to believe that men will be poorer and more estranged for centuries to come by reason of this supreme and protracted exhibition of infatuation and folly. And when the ignorance of past ages would be contrasted with the enlightened present, and when we would flatter ourselves with a sense of superiority, there is no more common device of vanity than to speak of a time when the wise as well as the unlearned believed that gold and wealth were synonymous. And yet good reasons may be adduced for taking away this flattering unction from modern times, and for believing that the existence of the Mercantile Theory or System is a superstition that ought to be discarded. Of these reasons the following are the chief :— Undeniably no Mercantile Theory or System ever existed in the same sense that there existed a Ptolemaic system of astronomy. Rau, a great authority on the literature of the science, owns that nobody systematically expounded and advocated the theory. The astronomers of Alexandria openly avowed that the earth formed the centre of the universe ; at most, the fault of those who are called the adherents of the Mercantile System was occasionally to employ arguments and recommend practices perfectly justifiable only on the assumption that all wealth is comprised in the precious metals. Shown the premises from which they were unconsciously reasoning, they would have repudiated the premises, and perhaps recoiled from their conclusions. They may have allowed the true nature of wealth to slip out of memory, and may have spoken as if they knew of no other kind of wealth save gold and silver ; but these errors arose not so much from holding a wrong theory of wealth, as from holding no theory at all, or none firmly. Occasional loose expressions must not be made use of in order to pin down the statesmen of the sixteenth or seventeenth century to an outrageously absurd doctrine. We do not describe every one who in common parlance speaks of the sun moving round the earth as a believer in the Ptolemaic theory ; neither ought we to range among the believers in the Mercantile System every one who talked, in a semi-metaphysical and vague strain, of gold being all and all in commerce, especially if we know him to entertain convictions utterly inconsistent with such a theory. It corroborates this view to observe that the so-called Mercantile Theory was never applied to all kinds of trade. They who are said to have conducted international trade on this principle did not at home esteem gold of supreme importance. Mun, "the great apostle of the Mercantile System," has chiefly in view foreign trade; the title of his book, *Treasure by Foreign Trade*, reminds one of the fact.* Touching home trade they had rational ideas. Nor will it suffice to establish the existence of this pseudo-theory to prove that the Governments of the seventeenth and eighteenth centuries took many measures to increase the quantity of gold and silver. For if they punished with fines or death the exporter of coin, they were at infinite pains to increase the population; if they prohibited the egress of gold, they prohibited emigration also; if they encouraged the introduction of specie by premiums, there were premiums offered for the encouragement of population; and if there may be quoted stray statements favouring the Mercantile Theory, there are extant others, to the effect that the people, intelligent and virtuous minds and strong arms, form the only veritable wealth. Thus, during the time the Mercantile Theory is said to have flourished, there certainly existed, and was apparently equally diffused, at least one antagonistic theory. Nor is the manifest absurdity of the Mercantile Theory a light argument against its having ever been entertained. Where all may discover the truth, all are not likely to err; and every one possesses in his own experience ample means of refuting such a theory. They were not fools, these statesmen, so much derided by economists. How could they have been so blind to what is to us clear as noon-day? Adam Smith is right when he says, "It would be too ridiculous to go about seriously to prove that wealth does not consist in gold and silver, but in what money purchases, and is valuable for purchasing;" and the ridiculousness was at all times palpable.

---

* Mun, the alleged exponent of the Mercantile Theory, in his book, actually employs certain expressions which show that he had some dim idea of gold and silver not being the sum of wealth. He speaks of this realm being "exceeding rich by nature." He also distinctly guards himself against one fallacy of which he is accused: "Neither is it said that money is the life of trade, as if it could subsist without the same; for we know there was great trading by way of commutation or barter when there was little money stirring in the world." He also conceives the possibility of our growing wealthy "by an industrious increase of our own means."—*England's Treasure*, pages 24 and 15.

Moreover, there was never a time at which there were not witnesses testifying to the true nature of wealth. In Xenophon and Aristotle are to be found unexceptionable ideas with respect to money. In one of his dialogues Lucian exposes the folly of those who confounded gold with true wealth ; to Lucian, or to Solon, into whose mouth is put the sentiment, it appears that iron, out of which the sword is fabricated, is more really wealth than gold. And had not the last twenty centuries the fable of Midas to teach them impressively the limited value of gold ? It is also a suspicious circumstance that authors are at variance as to the age when the Mercantile Theory arose. Most of them select the seventeenth century ; but if the mere taking of measures to prevent or impede the egress of gold suffices to convict the contemporaries of Colbert of slavery to a puerile delusion, is not the selection arbitrary, seeing the Romans were not always indifferent to the efflux of gold ? Can all the modern censors of Colbert be esteemed guiltless of the fallacy they condemn so long as they cling to the Bank Act, designed to guard against the exportation of bullion ? In the face of these considerations it is perhaps our duty to conclude that the Mercantile System or Theory never existed. What did exist, and is not yet extinct, is a strong association between wealth and the common measure of it, producing loose expressions upon which moderns have fastened too tenaciously; a conviction that gold and silver were peculiarly advantageous possessions, since they were universally acceptable, and almost eternally durable ; and a theory, which such writers share in common with the great majority of men of business and economists, that if the supply of precious metal be abandoned to the ordinary action of commerce, the supply will not be sufficient or constant, as is the case with other commodities.

It was frequently the policy of a nation to obtain a large supply of gold and silver—a policy nowise resting on a belief that the only form of riches was gold.* Though the Mer-

* The words of Adam Smith are here pertinent : "Some of the best English writers upon commerce set out with observing, that the wealth of a country consists, not in its gold and silver only, but in its lands, houses, and consumable goods of different kinds. In the course of their reasonings, however, the lands, houses, and consumable goods seem to slip out of their memory ; and the strain of their argument frequently supposes that all wealth consists in gold and silver, and that to multiply these metals is the great object of national industry and commerce."

2 c

cantile Theory is a figment, the theory of the balance of trade
was actually credited.

Frequently laws were passed punishing heavily those who
exported gold. Still more frequently there were ingenious fiscal
contrivances, so that the quantity of gold imported should sur-
pass the quantity exported, or that " the balance of trade,"
should be in our favour. " Care was taken," said Lord Bacon,
an advocate of these measures, that " the exportation should
exceed in value the importation ; for then the balance of trade
must of necessity be returned in coin or bullion." " The ordinary means," says Mun, " to increase our wealth and treasure
is by foreign trade, wherein we must ever observe this rule : to
sell more to strangers yearly than we consume of theirs in
value." Bounties were given to those who exported certain
articles, and duties, often 100 or 200 per cent *ad valorem*,
were imposed on imports, with the view of diminishing them
and increasing the exports. Until recent times, Chancellors
of the Exchequer regularly congratulated the country on the
exports exceeding the imports. It was a subject for " Prosperity Robinson " to make merry over. The idea is exhibited
in the anxiety with which American financiers observe the inequality between their exports and imports. It is almost needless to say that this theory respecting the advantage of the
balance of trade was erroneous. The value of the exports and imports could not continue to be equal, for then the motive for
trading would have disappeared. The figures on which the believers in the balance of trade relied were, as a rule, delusive, since
the cost of articles *minus* the freight was compared with the
cost of articles *plus* the freight, and since, to refer to America,
the exports were valued in a depreciated currency and the imports in gold. Nor was the anxiety about the efflux of specie
well founded, though it was more reasonable when, international
commerce being limited and precarious, it *might be* unsafe to
trust to the ordinary cause of affairs for a regular supply of
bullion. It is a mistake to assume that when the imports
exceed the exports, an efflux of bullion must take place in
order to make good the deficiency ; but it is equally a mistake
to assume that the difference constitutes a clear gain, and is not
partly ascribable to the export of the coupons of State debts
and railway bonds. The difference, far from representing the
results of efficiency in industry, may represent wholly or very

largely indebtedness. Of course the above anxiety to obtain money was somewhat foolish—though not so foolish as it would at first sight appear at a time when, international commerce being limited and precarious, it was unsafe to trust to it for a regular supply of gold, as Mun says, " the great revenue of the king; the sinews of our wars; the terror of our enemies."

Before glancing at the deterrents to importation, and the encouragements to exportation, let us glance at the Navigation Laws. Long before their repeal they had become nuisances. But let us be just to those who framed these measures : absurd, hurtful, and intolerable, they were not so utterly absurd, hurtful, and intolerable when first established ; the Navigation Laws perhaps served a purpose. These laws were passed at different times by the English Parliament ; but the chief of them—the Act of Navigation—was passed in 1651, mainly with the view of crippling the commerce of the Dutch, then the carriers of the world. It was enacted that goods coming from Asia, Africa, or America, could be imported into England or Ireland only in English vessels, manned chiefly by Englishmen. As to European goods, they could be imported only in English vessels, or vessels belonging to the country where the goods were produced, or whence they were usually exported. This law, so altered in the reign of Charles II. as to permit the importation of all but certain " enumerated articles," and in 1821 and 1828 still further relaxed by Mr. Huskisson, substantially remained in force down to the end of 1849. The monopoly of the coasting trade, including the carrying of passengers as well as goods, still remained in the hands of the English, and was surrendered as late as 1854. It is an easy task to prove that these regulations were expensive. Foreigners, and the hated Dutch among them, could carry for us only if they happened to be in a position to carry cheaper than our own shipowners ; and to expel the Dutch from the field, and to forbid their ships to bring cargoes of any of the staples of commerce, was to deliberately prefer dearness to cheapness. Our colonies, also, from which foreign vessels were debarred, suffered pecuniarily, for the colonist was compelled to buy and sell through the channel of the mother-country, though it might be advantageous for him to deal directly with foreigners. Ostensibly, the British shipowner was enriched by these measures ; but the reality of his seeming advantages he denied. He complained of his

being forbidden to hire foreigners—the cheapest sailors—
and of his being enjoined to overman his ships. Moreover,
there was always a danger of other countries retaliating ; and
if he was secured the trade of his own country, he was in constant danger of being shut out elsewhere. Frankly owning
that these regulations entailed a sacrifice of money, their defenders, quoting Adam Smith, nevertheless maintained that the
Navigation Laws were necessary for the safety of a country like
ours, dependent on its fleet. These laws, they said, swelled our
mercantile marine ; a large seafaring population grew up under
their care ; and, when occasion arose for us to put forth our
whole strength, this country drew from its numerous sailors
skilled crews for men-of-war. Though on paper this theory
looked well, and though perhaps this consideration wisely
weighed with statesmen dreading the power of the Dutch,
the actual facts do not distinctly verify the theory ; for it is
dubious, to say the least, whether the Navigation Acts did
really add to the force of development inherent in our mercantile marine. Was the steady increase in our mercantile marine
anything more than the natural outcome of our situation ? Was
this nursery of seamen at all necessary if impressment had been
removed ? Certainly the answers to these questions were sufficiently dubious to have rightly made Adam Smith pause before
pronouncing the Act of Navigation " perhaps the wisest of all
the commercial regulations of England."

Dates must here to some extent be arbitrary. We know not
when or where Protectionism arose. Scattered specimens of the
policy are to be seen everywhere. Isolated Acts in the spirit of
it, fines and corporal punishments, menacing those who imported
certain articles, were wrung from Governments by the selfishness of some interested party, or were voluntarily adopted by
Princes who had set their hearts on acclimatising some branch
of foreign industry, and were often prepared to wade through
wastefulness and blood to attain their ends. The idea of Free-
trade could permeate only a few exceptional minds at a time
when countries were separated by antipathies wider than the
estranging sea. The possibility of trusting to a foreign country
for any staple of trade would scarcely be credited by men accustomed to see their country at any moment breaking off relations with the outer world. Patriotism meant hatred of
foreigners ; it was hardly possible to trade with them. Yet it

is just and curious to observe that there does not appear to have been in the fourteenth and fifteenth centuries the same readiness to blunder about Protectionism, and to hide the loss which it inflicted, as there was in later and more enlightened times. It was high State interests, considerations of a distant gain outweighing the present loss, that influenced Cecil to protect the farmer. It was left to a more refined age to discover that it was economical not to buy in the cheapest market. It is late before we see men protecting all round, and before imported merchandise is taxed excessively. Before the sixteenth century there was greater freedom of trade between countries than between provinces of the same country. France traded freely with Scotland : Picardy and Champagne were severed. M. Chevalier mentions the Chancellor de Birague, an Italian who came to France in the suite of Catherine de Medici, as among the first who proposed and caused the adoption of the Protectionist system. Of course, there had been previous instances. Charles V., for example, mulcted Venetian merchandise by a tax of twenty per cent. But the system was matured by Colbert, clerk to the Council of Finance under Louis XIV. Strange inconsistency in his labours ! A Free-trader at home, a Protectionist abroad ! An inconsistency, by the way, repeated by Napoleon I., who, while he threw down the fiscal barriers that separated France, Belgium, Holland, part of Germany, and Italy, endeavoured to cut off intercourse with England. An inconsistency in still later times exhibited by List, who, while labouring to establish commercial liberty between the various States of Germany, sought to girdle her with a ring of iron ! While at home Colbert laboured to break down the fiscal barriers which separated one province from another, he laboured to cut off the connection of France with foreign countries, by putting upon foreign goods duties that were designed to keep them out of the French market. Colbert's tariff, issued in 1664, was, if not the beginning of Protectionism, certainly its first master-stroke. On both sides of the Channel the measure was followed up by stricter and absurder regulations. M. Chevalier writes thus of the absurdities perpetrated in France :—

"In 1720, to protect textile fabrics, used chiefly for dresses, they were not contented with simply prohibiting the printed cloths of India, still known by the name of ' Indians ;' an edict pronounced the pain of death against those who should have the boldness to introduce them into French territory, under the pretext that they might bring the plague with them. Under the Convention, in 1793, a law made twenty years in irons the penalty of importing English goods : so strictly were laws of this kind interpreted at that period that an individual wearing an English quilted waistcoat could be sent to the galleys for twenty years. Finally, under the Directory, 10th Brumaire, Year V., a law was passed which prohibited generally all goods manufactured in England, which came nearly to the same as saying everything manufactured ; and as articles furnished by other nations might be of English production, the law extended the prohibition to the manufactures of the whole world."

Of course we retaliated. In 1692, an *ad valorem* duty of 25 per cent was imposed on all French goods, while goods of other countries were subjected to duties of about 5 per cent; in 1696, the rate was doubled ; and Adam Smith calculates that 75 per cent was usually the lowest duty on French goods. The heavy penalties attached to transgressions of the laws were indeed removed long ago, but, with the exception of a short period, these enactments remained down to 1860.

A word or two must be said of the protection of agriculture, in order to illustrate the evils of Protectionism. The illustrations might be taken from many countries, for the protection of agriculture has been common ; I take them from England. At various times the Legislature had encouraged the exportation of corn by means of bounties, and discouraged its importation by heavy duties. At other times the exportation was prohibited. For some years previous to 1733 the policy of the country had been to stimulate exportation by liberal bounties, and to hinder importation by heavy duties ; but in 1773 it was enacted that foreign wheat might be imported on paying a duty of 6d. a quarter whenever the home price rose to 48s. or upwards, and that exportation was to be forbidden and the bounty to be withdrawn when the price was 44s. or upwards. It is a sign that men are at fault when, in the pursuit of their object, they are obliged, by encountering endless difficulties, ceaselessly to alter their course. This sign was given to the English Parliament ; but, not heeding the sign, it staggered on from blunder to blunder. The Act of 1773 was rejected for another in 1791, which laid new trammels on importers. Yet neither the landowners nor the farmers were content; this Act was abolished for a sliding scale, by which corn was totally excluded when the home price fell below 66s., and it was permitted, with more or fewer restrictions, to enter when it rose above that price. In 1814, again further tinkering : the House of Commons saw that it was better to give no more bounties, and to permit men to export when they thought fit. This law lasted but a little time; in 1815, 1822, 1828, and 1842, new measures were passed, all of them endeavouring to reconcile the contradictory objects of conferring upon the landowners the benefits of a monopoly, and by some ingenious sliding scale taking the sting out of it. None of these measures were satisfactory to any of the parties interested ; a conviction began to dawn that cruel injustice was being perpetrated on the bulk of the people for the sake of imaginary benefits, and to the profit of the landlord ; famine coming to turn the wavering balance, in 1846 the fate of the Corn Laws was sealed ; and corn, subject to a duty of 1s. a quarter—since removed by Mr. Lowe—was free to be imported from 1849. If it were worth while to rummage industriously among the rubbish-heaps of legislative errors, one might collect from the history of France instances of absurdities equally gigantic. But let one suffice : it was decreed by the French Convention that to send abroad a sack of wheat was to commit an offence as heinous, and punishable in the same manner, as to murder its owner in cold blood.

American Protectionism is so notable a fact, and possesses so much present interest, that a few details regarding its rise may not be out of place. Protectionism is not exclusively a weed of monarchies ; on no soil has it grown more lustily than in America. The statesmen who founded the Republic were Protectionists at heart. Mr. Horace Greeley has dug up from the speeches and writings of Washington, Jefferson, Madison, and Alexander Hamilton, expressions which prove at least that they all thought much was to be done by " encouraging " home manufactures. Indeed, Hamilton presented a famous report to that effect to the House of Representatives in 1791 ; and Jefferson, retaliating upon the British and French Governments for the arbitrary Orders in Council and Decrees of Berlin and Milan of 1811, actually refused to admit the goods of either of these countries, thereby creating not merely protective but prohibitive duties in favour of American industries. Though the close of

the war saw the removal of this embargo, a protective system
of great stringency was re-established in 1828, and remained in
force four years.   It was then altered by Clay's Compromise Act.
American Protectionism really dates from 1842, when, in spite
of the strenuous resistance of the Southern party, a protective
tariff was established.   It lasted until 1848.   In 1861 the
United States turned back to the old leaf, and since then Protectionism has kept the upper hand.

Profound study is not necessary in order to be convinced of
the weight of the numerous economical reasons which Free-trade
marshals on its side ; and if it has not gained the universal adhesion of mankind, it is partly because some have been interested in industries specially favoured, and would gladly sacrifice the welfare of the community to the lucre of a class, and
because others of a better stamp imagine that Free-trade is the
clutching at an immediate good to the peril of higher benefits
in the future.   How many would see the iniquity of a system
which was supposed to bring them riches, and which could not
be abolished except at their cost ?   A train of reasoning that
leads to the loss of a class is apt to be considered unsatisfactory
by its members.   But all who are ready to listen to the behests of truth, be what they may, may be convinced that Protectionism is always attended by a present pecuniary loss ; and
they only are formidable antagonists of Free-trade who openly
admit a present loss, and justify it by the promise of a future
gain.   Foreign trade and home trade are advantageous on the
same grounds ; and if it be economically hurtful to have free-
trade between France and England, it is hurtful to have free-
trade between Edinburgh and Glasgow, or, for that matter, to
have free-trade between one street and another.   Diogenes,
living in a tub, dependent on no man, is the model and only
consistent Protectionist.   As one man differs from another in
aptitude, rendering division of labour politic and profitable, so
countries and their inhabitants differ in their aptitudes ; and
varying climate, extent of unoccupied soil, and degrees of density
of population, give birth to a territorial division of labour.   It
is not economical for every one to be one's own tailor ; neither
is it economical for every country to be its own grower of wine
while Spain and France can produce better.   The American
who gets cotton goods from the protected mills at Lowell, when
he might, by relaxing his tariff, ship these goods from England

at a considerable reduction, suffers a loss only a few shades removed from that of the man who attempts to become jack-of-all-trades. For, observe, as it is good to follow one trade even were there no physical or mental impossibility to the discharge of others, provided the trade chosen be the one for which there is most aptitude, so it behoves nations—communities of men to each of whom this rule should be a guide of life—to cultivate those pursuits for which they possess especial aptitudes within themselves or in their country, and to neglect for those even many pursuits to the cultivation of which nature has set up no insuperable barriers. That Protectionism is always attended by a present loss is a fact that swims on the surface. In vain Mr. Horace Greeley would elude this fact. For why are heavy duties resorted to, except to prevent too great cheapness and plenty? He may say that Free-trade produces only nominal cheapness; but if this be so, why should it be necessary to exclude from the foreign market consumers who want real, not nominal cheapness? Looking only at the present, one may say that to give us dear corn, dear silks, dear ribbons, etc.; to make that which supports or adorns life hard to obtain; to turn plenty into scarceness, is the protectionist policy. Protection to the producer signifies immediate injury to the consumer. It promises to the former, because it exacts of the latter, high prices; and too frequently Protectionism is nothing more respectable than one of those big blustering appellatives, in the shelter of which men take what is not their own. A reservation, however, must be appended. Customs duties sometimes fall on the importer, not on the consumer; and if this were a common occurrence, it might seriously impair the doctrine that protective duties are the taxing of the home consumer for the sake of the home producer. But this incidence is confined to the following rare circumstances: If the sole market, open to the importer of the staple goods of one country, is the country imposing the duties; secondly, if the other market open to him was so distant or otherwise disadvantageous that it would be preferable to pay the tax; or, thirdly, if the only available place for procuring commodities of vital moment to the importing country was the country imposing the duty. Wherever the profits are such as to admit of a diminution without falling below the usual rate, it may be possible for a country to tax the foreigner. Need we say that of course retaliation would be possible? It is obvious that if we export little and yet import much, the gain is ours ; the fact evinces the efficiency of our labour. On the other hand, the fault of the adversaries of Reciprocity is, in assuming that the exports of each year must pay for the imports, and in regarding the former as of no consequence, forgetting that they are in the long run the measure of the former.

Though we do not hear in this country undiluted Protectionism, the form of it called Reciprocity has appeared, and is being actively propagated. We are told by pamphleteers and public speakers that "reciprocal Free-trade" is a good thing ; that we should by all means open our ports freely to countries that do the same by us ; but that to admit the goods of countries with protective or prohibitive tariffs, duty free, or subject to duties which do not equal those imposed abroad, is to commit a mistake, and to sacrifice our real interest in unqualified obedience to a theory which is of limited application. This phase of Protectionism, hailed as a startling discovery, is not by any means novel. When Sir Robert Peel introduced in 1842 his famous Budget which removed many of the minor custom duties, Colonel Torrens, a well-known economical writer of the time, published *Letters on the Budget*, in which it was laboriously contended that we were sacrificing ourselves to a misunderstood theory.

It is very easy to prove that Protectionism is always attended by a present loss. All attempts to conceal this are delusions. Americans may point to the enormous manufactures reared at Lowell and Lawrence, under the wing of Protection, and may say—"See what Protectionism has done for us." They may tell Free-traders that these manufactures, fostered by heavy duties, are so many new markets to agriculture, and they may quote price-lists to show how farmers in the neighbourhood of these towns have been blessed with high prices. They may repeat strings of figures to confound Free-traders with the enormous development of the produce of iron. A dispassionate observer, nevertheless, perceives that these protected industries involve a national loss ; these industries can be economical only if the foreign iron and cotton goods can be sold more cheaply than —or as cheaply as—iron and cotton goods exported. But it is clear that goods made in the United States cannot be so sold ; for if they could, there would then be no need of Protection. Any man who can count his fingers must perceive that if the

English ironmasters' products can be kept out of the American market, and that market can be monopolised by the Americans only by imposing a heavy tax on the goods of the former, the farmers, and manufacturers, and railway companies, who use iron, are fined heavily; and that all these glowing statistics in degree represent schemes as opposed in principle to present gain as the rearing of oranges in Spitzbergen. So far all is simple; and most intelligent Americans and Australians freely own that for the present at least they pay dearly for Protective tariffs. To take but one witness, Sir Charles Dilke bears testimony to the readiness of Americans to admit this much; and any one who has conversed with intelligent Americans in regard to this subject will be able to corroborate him. For the first time, the Protectionist case deserves to be reasoned about, and to merit a respectful consideration, when it is frankly owned that a loss is incurred for the present, in order to obtain future pecuniary rewards, or present moral benefits. Let us hear what the American Protectionists have to say on this head. Their apology runs thus:—Nothing more common than to see industries which were once alien to a country acclimatised, and become its staple industries. Witness England, one of the staple industries of which at this day is wool. Edward III. was the first to introduce it; and before his time, as Fuller says—"The English were ignorant of that art, as knowing no more what to do with their wool than the sheep that wear it, as to any artificial curious drapery." Now, why should not the stimulus of Protection by and by acclimatise industries with us that are for the time being rather unsuited to our circumstances, and by and by give us, for example, iron as cheap as that made in Staffordshire, seeing both coal and ore are to be obtained in abundance in our States? Moreover, economy is not the sole test of what is the best policy for a country; safety must be considered; the contingency of war, and the inconvenience of being suddenly cut off from European markets, should be ever taken into account. For in what position would America be if, trusting to England for all iron goods, she found herself at war with England? So long as war is a possibility, it will be well to have one's markets within one's territories. It is not good, the Americans go on to say, to dwell in a country where there are few manufacturing cities; an important element of national life is absent; diversity of pursuits is good; intellectual culture is encouraged; and, in order to create this diversity and promote culture, we consent to suffer some loss. To the aid of these considerations come others. Corn consumed at home brings manure to the soil, supplying it with the salts which were taken from it ; incessant exportation of corn to Europe would be wasteful in the highest degree ; already the Eastern States begin to show traces of this exhaustion, for, next to England, they are the largest buyers of guano.

This view, not logically fallacious, deserves more respectful consideration than it has received at the hands of those who think it sufficient to employ the arms of Mr. Cobden, and who will not condescend to suit their weapons to their enemies ; and it is pretty certain that the indifference of Americans to the remonstrances of Europeans is somewhat due to the persistency of the latter in believing the Americans are fools enough to conceive that Protectionism is not accompanied by a loss, when they take to a manufacture with respect to which they have no advantages, and abandon agriculture, with respect to which they have some ninety per cent of advantage. Their plea may be unsubstantial ; it is not illogical. At the same time, every country, and the United States especially, severed from Europe by 3000 miles, possesses a natural protection for its manufactures in the cost of freight and the natural preference of countrymen, it may be friends, to foreigners ; home industries have patents, so to speak ; and if this natural protection does not suffice to create manufactures, it may be assumed that they are not wanted. Admit that ironworks and cotton-mills should be established, and that the people at large should be taxed for their support : a tariff is not the best, but probably the worst, mode of conferring State aid ; and it would be better for Congress to vote annually some million dollars to be presented to the manufacturers of Lowell and Lawrence and Pittsburg. It would then be known what Protectionism costs ; now that is but vaguely known and lightly considered. The manufacturers would receive openly their subsidies, which now they receive in an underhand manner, and every year the question would come before the nation whether Protectionism was worth millions. This system would be cheaper, too, for there would be no rise in the price of the home and foreign product. American ships then would not be deprived as they now are of return cargoes. A bounty given directly is sure to be ultimately more economical than one indirectly subtracted from the pockets of the people, for in the one case the subsidy, coming out of taxes, presumptively comes from wealth which would have been expended unproductively; in the other case the subsidy, coming out of capital, will diminish it and what it produces. President Grant showed good sense in expressing—in a Message to Congress on the decline of American commerce—a preference for direct subsidies. And if it be deemed right to foster certain industries for the future well-being of the community, it is just that the cost should not, as now, fall upon certain members, but should be paid out of the general taxes which, in a civilised country, are the contributions of all members.

When Proudhon challenges the expediency of Free-trade, on the ground that if the balance of trade be habitually in favour of one nation and against another, the latter will be gradually emptied of precious metals, and will, in course of time, alienate much of its patrimony to strangers, he does not deny that the economical advantages lie with Free-trade; but he believes that it is not always good to weaken nationality, or suffer Englishmen to own the soil of France. Can we, who until the other day did not permit a foreigner to own land unless by means of a subterfuge, say the basis of his argument was palpably absurd? Has it in all ages been admitted by statesmen to be good policy to allow the foreigner to acquire real property without let or hindrance? When Proudhon, reminding us that labour alone should be paid for, points out that advantages of soil, not extra labour, are often the causes of superiority of industry, and that the *douane* has been established with a view to intercept the amount not due to labour, I indeed doubt whether he does not enlist the principle of nationality whereever it serves his case, and dismisses it when it does not. I question too whether the *douane* does not compensate the wrong person. When Proudhon adds that Protectionism is a principle similar to, or rather the correlative of, the guarantee of labour—the obligation to prefer indigenous produce, on condition that indigenous labour is preferred—we may fear that he is approving of a dangerous compact; but one looks in vain in the works of most English economists for sufficient proof that the fear is incorrect. They simply tell us that Protectionism is expensive to a nation. That is but part of the question. It still remains to be determined whether Protectionism may not occa-

sionally be of service in apprenticing a nation, so to speak, to
some industry at first uncongenial, but subsequently proving
suitable to it ; whether it is always safe to trust to foreigners
for a supply of commodities that may be of vital consequence
in war ; whether a mixture of city life, the concomitant of
manufactures, may not be so precious as to counterbalance some
present loss ; whether the collapse of a large class or interest
living by a precarious home industry is always outweighed by
cheapness, sometimes distributed in imperceptible portions to
consumers ; and, lastly, whether the decline in production, due
to an adoption of Protection, may not sometimes be followed
by a better system of distribution ? If I may be permitted to
give an opinion on these questions, I should say that all European countries, and the United States, have outgrown the
necessities of Protectionism.

CHAPTER XXIX.

PATENTS.

TAXES are not the only ways in which Governments distribute wealth. Laws relating to property, its judicial adjudication, the transmission of property, patents, and copyrights, and bankruptcy, that are expressive of the will of the State, and are put in operation by it, are important agencies in the same work; and some of these I shall now briefly consider, beginning with patents. Patents are selected because they are the type of a *quasi* property.

Whatever be one's opinion with regard to the propriety of patents, it does not admit of reasonable doubt that a broad distinction must be drawn between the essence of a patent and property. And if any one be alarmed at this doctrine, we remind him that the laws of every country, and those of this country included, draw the distinction. The laws of every country permit the man who has built a house to retain it throughout life, and to transmit it to his descendants: the inventor of a new mode of building houses is not permitted to monopolise it for ever; he may not be permitted to enjoy it all his life, far less to transmit it to his descendants, for in this country the monopoly must expire in fourteen years, and, unless new arrangements are entered into, it expires in seven years. In some countries the monopoly is never granted. When one has built a house, it is not necessary to pay the Government fees in order to be permitted to let the house and draw the rent: everywhere, and in England especially, where the rights of property are jealously guarded, high fees must be paid to the Government in order to obtain patents. They are viewed by the law as a contract between the Crown and a subject; the former grants a certain privilege for which the latter pays. Further, property has been in all ages, theoretically at least, respected, and those who pillaged owned that they did wrong. Since the reign of James I. patents have been granted sparingly. The Statute of Monopolies only permitted them as exceptional measures. During the reign of James I. four patents a year were granted; during the next reign the rate was about six a year; none were granted during the Commonwealth; and they have become exceedingly numerous only within this century. Indeed, it is since 1852, when new facilities for obtaining them were given, that the number has become considerable. Further, while no king, not the most despotic, has claimed the right to seize his subjects' property when it seemed good to him, the Secretary of State for War is by law entitled to monopolise all improvements and inventions affecting warlike instruments. Again, it is not necessary for the builder of a house to prove that it is a special boon to his fellows before he be permitted to inhabit it to the exclusion of others : patents were originally granted to those only who had invented something plainly beneficial, and such is still the theory, though since 1852 little observed. According to Sir Edward Coke (quoted by Mr. Macfie in his volume on patents), "there must be urgent necessity and evident utility" before a patent can be granted. And this distinction, drawn by law in these bold lines, equity approves. Patents ought not to be property, if for no other reason than that while two persons cannot make the same material thing, two persons may invent, and sometimes have invented, the same device or combination of devices ; and that, while consequently it is only just to give to the man who has made a house the exclusive use of it, it is not at all obvious that the person who has discovered a process of making houses should forbid all generations to come to avail themselves of that mode without his leave. If you fashioned with your own hands-a pair of cart-wheels, it is implied in this that no other person made these identical wheels. But that you thought of applying wheels for purposes of draught, does not at all exclude the possibility of scores of other persons having come upon the same idea independently of you. To speak of an invention as one's own, and to conclude therefrom that one ought to monopolise the process or discovery, is to commit a transparent fallacy; it is to confound similar things with the same things ; a thing called by the same name with the thing itself. A patent may be granted to a person who introduces an unknown art into this country; and hence it might happen that a person who did not invent a particular thing might be privileged to prohibit others who did invent it, previously or subsequently to the introduction, from availing themselves of their own labours. Surely equity draws here between the rights of property and patents a clear distinction. At bottom there is this distinction :—The former, when actually present, sanction the appropriation of what was created or discovered by the appropriator or his representatives ; the latter control the labour of other people, and appropriate processes which may have been discovered independently. This circumstance alone obliges us to put the two in different categories. Nor is the difference a piece of worthless refinement. Independent invention of the same machine or process is of frequent occurrence. Whoever is familiar with the history of science cannot but recall hosts of instances in which it was difficult to determine who was the discoverer— instances in which a great truth, like some comet, burst simultaneously on the view of observers in different countries. For almost every scientific discovery a French, a German, and an English claimant are in the field. In truth the same problem had been set to thousands ; several found the answer. If there should be but one living claimant, industry is pretty sure to disinter the germs of the discovery in the past. In the case of a still greater number of discoveries, it is impossible to say who was the discoverer, seeing many contributed hints. Was it Talbot, or Daguerre, or Niepce, that first discovered photography ? Can one dogmatise about the first man to apply electricity to telegraphy ? These inventions did not issue, like Minerva from the brain of Jove, complete in all their parts. Stone after stone was added by various hands. After all the simplest inventions have been made, many of the rest are the slow elaborations of numerous brains. Inventors, like playwrights, often work *en collaboration*. The inventor is generally the last link in a long chain. As Proudhon remarks, what is given is not a *brevet d'invention*, but a *brevet de première occupation*. Moreover, re-discoveries are constantly being made. Many of the inventions covered by existing patents are really old. Mr. Woodcroft, Superintendent of Specifications, and an unexceptionable witness, states that there are " patents which are but old inventions, as old as the hills." Lastly, I would observe that while it is usually for the general interest that some one

should be the exclusive owner of a piece of land, seeing he is
pretty sure to make the best use of it, the same cannot be said
of the exclusive possession of a process ; such exclusive possession is likely to deprive mankind of much of the benefit of
the invention.   There exists, then, a clear and broad distinction
between rights of property and patents ; and when people maintain that the patentee's rights should be of the same unlimited
nature as those of the builder of a house, they lay down that
which equity and law alike repudiate.

   Why, then, are patents granted at all ?   For two reasons.
Simultaneous or independent discoveries of the same machine
are, after all, not so universal.   The merit sometimes belongs to
one man ; and it is disheartening to him to see his thoughts
stolen.   He gave half his life to investigating how to card
wool.   He sat up late and rose early.   He neglected his
family and his business for his darling pursuit.   Health and
money went.   The joiner and machine-maker swallowed everything.   How cruel, then, that when the dream of the enthusiast's
life is realised, the long-pondered idea embodied, an undeserving
intruder should embezzle the benefits !   Could it be expected—
and we come now to the second reason—that, if this were
the prospect before inventors, they would scorn delight and live
laborious days to attain their far-distant goals ?   Seeing before
him no prospect of return, wanting a powerful stimulus, would
not the inventor roll his talents up in a napkin ?   His lot, which
is at present proverbially bad, would then be so unrequited and
uncertain that he would listen to his friends' remonstrances,
would be warned by their sneers, and, repressing the prolific
thoughts with which his breast teemed, he would labour no
more at a thankless task.   There might then be no Arkwright
or Watt.   The former might remain a humble barber, and the
latter might mend spectacles.   Or, if it happened that the men
who were in travail with thoughts that were to revolutionise
industry, brought them forth, finding in the consciousness of
having effected a service to mankind a sufficient reward, and
content with fame as their guerdon, would those who have
within them the germs of small inventions bringing no fame, be
content to labour without reward ?   Paper-making, gunpowder,
printing, the mariner's compass, the telescope, were invented
without the stimulus of patents.   Supposing we continued to
have the correlatives of these discoveries, which confer fame

enough to satisfy, would we have patent hooks-and-eyes, matches, capsules for bottles, and all the little articles that make life smooth ? It is doubtful, to say the least. Where is the man that would, out of pure love to humanity, give us a new button ? He who reclaims a moor receives a perpetual *brevet ;* should not he who invents a plough receive at least a temporary *brevet ?*

Few will dissent from the conclusion that inventors do deserve and need some substantial reward, and that, if patents were abolished, a substitute would be necessary in order to stimulate ingenuity and to quench the sense of injustice which every man would feel who saw others enriched by the work of his brain. It is not, however, so clear that the patentee is at present rewarded in the manner in which he ought to be ; and to the law, as it stands, several objections may be justly taken.

In the first place, it may be alleged that the law is unfair and one-sided. It scatters rewards in certain favoured furrows. Suppose A (a physician) discovers a medicine or regimen peculiarly valuable in the case of cholera—a discovery which does for it and kindred ailments what vaccination does for small-pox. B, on the other hand, discovers a machine for making nails or tacks. The former, who has conferred a benefit on the human race certainly as considerable as that conferred by B, possesses no legal right to obtain one farthing of reward ; it is left to chance to determine whether he shall be rewarded at all ; whereas the latter is put in the way of obtaining a fortune. The former cannot monopolise his improvement, and may not get a reward : the latter can monopolise his labours, and the law does all it can to get him a reward. And it is not only mechanical inventors that are partially treated as compared with other discoverers ; rewards are allotted to a particular class of mechanical inventors. We are accustomed to say that the chief merit of a machine is the principle of it. Yet it is this, the crowning glory of genius to discover, which cannot be patented. Thus the law grants to certain discoverers favours which it does not grant to others equally meritorious. Is there a foundation in justice for this difference of treatment ?

The law, thus unfair as between inventors of vendible articles and the inventors of others which are not vendible, is also unfair as between different inventors of vendible articles. As the

law stands, with £50 to be paid to secure the rights for seven
years, and £100 to be paid to secure it for other seven, the ingenious poor man labours under a considerable disadvantage.
And this disadvantage is considerably increased by the fact that
the law is so complicated, the patentee so liable to go wrong,
that an agent, who must of course be fee'd, is all but necessary.
This is not all : if the inventor is poor, the privilege for which
he has paid thus dearly may be barren. Such is the ambiguity
inherent in the law of patents, that in English Courts, accustomed
to protracted cases, disputed patents occupy a longer time than
any other. Mr. Grove observes, " things have arrived at a dead-
lock. The Courts now really cannot try these cases." It is,
therefore, in the power only of an inventor that is rich, or that
has the command of money, to wrench his invention from the
grasp of a rich and unscrupulous manufacturer who would
usurp it. The law being obscure from its very nature, the ver-
dicts are necessarily uncertain also ; and only those who are
rich enough not to be seriously inconvenienced by being de-
feated will dare to put their claims to the test. If there is
the slightest plausibility in the case of his opponent, the real
inventor, if he be poor and prudent, will hesitate to embark in
a hazardous lawsuit, but will rather acquiesce in robbery, glad
if he induce the robber to come to a compromise, and to forego
a little of the plunder. On the other hand, if the infringers of
the patent be poor, prosecution may not be worth while, and,
as in the case of Sir David Brewster's kaleidoscope, the inventor may see his rights frittered away. Further, the law
often gives the reward to a man who by no means deserves it,
or who certainly does not deserve the whole reward. We do
not speak now of injustice as between the inventors of vendible
articles and of the discoverers of truths ; that is considerable ;
but this injustice is shown in the treatment of the man who
finishes a machine and the man who has all but finished it. A
man has occupied many years in contriving a type-distributing
machine. The main idea is realised, but there are certain imperfections ; the machine does not work satisfactorily ; and he
is turning over in his mind how to surmount this the last and
trivial obstacle to success, when another man, borrowing the
main idea—say of a travelling bar seizing certain notches in the
types—slavishly copies the design in all the details, but manages
to overcome the slight defect which the other had not overcome,

or which he may have mentally overcome, though he has not embodied it. ˏThis borrower—this robber, to be plain—gets everything ; the real benefactor, who in equity and morality is entitled to almost everything, will be, by an English Court of law, declared entitled to nothing. Worse may happen in certain circumstances ; the real inventor, " the true and first inventor," to quote the legal words, may receive nothing, while the first person who gave publicity to the invention is handsomely rewarded. Such, it is said, was the fate of the inventor of the achromatic telescope. " It is the last step that counts." Yes ; but this maxim, which is a rule of conventionality, should be repudiated in a court of law, ˏwhere rules of justice alone should be administered.

A patentee can put what price upon his machines he pleases ; and though generally he chooses to sell licenses at a pretty low price in order to extend the demand, sometimes he does not. He is a monopolist ; and we know what are the sins of monopolists. He may choose to do a quiet business. He may be interested in the machine not being used at all ; and, instructed and paid by some one whose trade would be affected, he may claim a royalty practically prohibitive. At any rate, here is the fact that machines are rendered more expensive than they need be, that the number of their owners is fewer than need be, that their capital is greater than need be, and that the wealth of the country is thus diminished in divers needless ways. If, in the face of all this, it still be repeated that the loss incurred by adhering to the present mode is trivial, we may surely shake the most rooted incredulity when we draw attention to the countries which have discarded patent laws altogether, and which are enabled to utilise to the utmost all foreign and home inventions. Switzerland, our growing commercial rival in cotton and ribbons, is one of the countries which have put aside patents ; and with truth it has been remarked, that though the patent laws of foreign countries are for the most part modelled on ours, they exhibit greater solicitude for the public interest.

Admitting, then, that the inventor should be rewarded in some way, and that the way in which he is now rewarded is objectionable, how remedy the chief faults and observe the principle ? Several ways suggest themselves, and one is this :— Out of the patent fees, amounting annually to upwards of

£70,000, might be formed a prize fund, to be distributed among inventors in sums varying from £10,000 to £10, according to merit. This plan—though sanctioned by some legislation which permits the Judicial Committee of the Privy Council to extend the duration of patents—is mentioned only to be rejected. The power which it would put into the hands of one department, or, as in practice it might prove, into the hands of one person, would be enormous, and would be liable to be abused to further private fancies. The facilities for jobbery would be endless. Moreover, the most enlightened department could have no better guide in distributing these prizes than the estimation of what was likely to be advantageous; and with no better guide to merit than this fallible one, the most original, the most meritorious inventors, might fare very badly; for it is of the nature of the inventions of a Watt, a Crompton, or a Howe, to excite incredulity, and perhaps years pass before their services are discerned in all their length and breadth. It is ridiculous to suppose that a number of chemists, far less the Attorney-General, could judge accurately of the worth of inventions submitted to them. This would involve an industrial censorship. Under this artificial system, mediocre men would gather goodly sheaves, while there would be little for the man of genius to glean. Perhaps we may ultimately have to revert to such a system, but it should be adopted only as a last resort. A second proposal, deserving consideration, inasmuch as it was submitted by a Royal Commission of which Lord Stanley was chairman, is that the patentee should continue to draw his profits in the present manner—that is, by licensing others to use his invention—but that, in order to prevent the use of a very powerful invention being obstructed, it should be open to the Crown to buy up any invention, with or without the consent of the patentee. This is made in partial deference to the reasoning we have given above; and, together with a power to compel inventors to sell licenses to the public, it ought perhaps to form a feature in any future improvements in patent-laws. Yet more seems to be wanted; and the following seems to be the direction which reforms ought to take :—Let any one who thinks he has discovered a serviceable machine lodge provisional specifications as at present, and let small registration fees be charged, though, in the event of this change, they ought to be considerably less than they now are. So far all would be in *principle* as it now is; the first difference would be, that every other person would be at liberty to make machines so specified, without let or hindrance of the inventor, and would be entitled to use it for a defined and considerable time—say for two years—without payment. But after this time expired, it would be in the patentee's power to ask for a royalty, the amount of which it would be for a court of law to decide, from every one who used it, and which might be calculated on the principle that the frequency with which the invention was employed was the test of its utility. The Patent Office would thus be a purely record office, the archives of which would be the only admissible evidence to prove the inventor's right. What would be the advantages of this course? Not a few. In the first place, it would be out of the power of any one to obstruct the full use of a machine that happened to be useful by exacting too high a royalty; and that would be much. Secondly, it would be more in the power of a manufacturer to experiment fully with an invention, to test its capabilities, and, if it did not suit, to abandon it. Men would not, as now, have to " pay £3000 for a year's right to use a new process which proved unworkable, and have to pay a *solatium* of £1000 a year for leave to discontinue it." Thirdly, as the royalty would not be paid until the machine or process had done service, and until it had repaid itself wholly or partially, the price of it would be lessened; and if the employers of it were not increased, at all events the necessary capital of those that did employ it would be diminished. Further, by leaving it to a court of law to assess the amount of royalty, we should preserve the idea that patents are an exceptional favour given for the benefit of industry—" not *ex debito justitiæ*, but an act of royal favour." Fifthly, if the invention had not been extensively employed, the court would have almost conclusive proof that the invention did not deserve to be protected. By demanding proof of extensive use the court would be able to confer most of the advantages of what, in the enormous multiplication of patents, may become necessary, another Statute of Monopoly. If this system were found to fail, it is probable that the removal of patents would be the better course.

Between copyright and patents the law draws a distinction very justly. Copyright lasts at least forty-two years, and may last longer. No two men ever wrote the same book; two men have independently made the same inventions. No one is ever in doubt as to the authorship of a certain book, unless indeed the authorship has been purposely concealed, or all evidence has been lost ; in the case of inventions, as we have seen, there are frequently doubts. Moreover, while the Copyright Act only guards against textual or all but textual reproduction of a book, or portions of it, while the knowledge and the ideas contained in the book are free to be reproduced in a multitude of shapes, it is precisely this knowledge which it is the object of a patent to monopolise. So great a difference exists between the two, that copyright approaches closely to, if it does not actually coincide with, property in general ; and it has been questioned whether the man who gains by a successful operation on the Exchange is a whit better entitled to transmit his property to his descendants than the author of a book. Why should one man live to-day in affluence because his grandfather was a successful stockbroker, while the lineal descendant, say, of a Shakspeare, a Milton, a Fielding, or a Scott, may starve, while publishers obtain fortunes by printing the works of these men ? The only reason of much weight I am able to conceive is, that the artist usually does not labour in order to enrich his descendants, and that, consequently, the extension of his rights would do little to stimulate or improve his labours. Literary production has flourished without property ; other kinds of production have not.

For certain of the existing regulations with respect to patents and copyrights it is impossible to find a sufficient reason. Why should the inventor of a machine obtain a patent only for fourteen years, unless the Crown, on the advice of the Judicial Committee of the Privy Council, extend the period, and the painter of a picture keep the copyright for a period which *might* be sixty years ? Why, again, should a patentee be obliged to pay £150, while the latter pays nothing to speak of ? Why should the patentee who sells his rights obtain no further benefit, while the rights revert to the author after the expiration of twenty-eight years ? These differences do not correspond to differences in subject-matter.

CHAPTER XXX.

CHARITY.

WE now arrive at the third part of Distribution. The former divisions were distribution by exchange and distribution in virtue of superiority. The third part, called Donative Distribution, treats of the voluntary distribution of wealth without an equivalent. Into this domain it is difficult to introduce order ; at first sight all appears caprice ; laws completely accurate cannot be evolved ; and to formulate hypothetical laws at all approaching to the truth is impossible. Yet the chaos may be partially reduced to order : even if it could not be reduced, we should be bound not to ignore it. Political Economy must take cognisance of all the modes of distribution that intervene between the conferring of value and the destruction or consumption of it ; and it is no more permissible to leave out of account a large domain of facts on the ground that they are tangled and confused, than it is for a geographer to omit a mountain peak because its height is not known. Yet even here we can do almost as much to introduce order as the natural historian does ; we can number the families that come under this species, though we cannot do so accurately, indeed, seeing services which formerly fell under the head of Exchange are being transferred to Donative Distribution, and *vice versa*. We can do more : pursuing that course which has served to introduce order into taxation, we can occasionally apply a standard of what is proper, and note the deviations in practice from it.

Undoubtedly, the chief part here has been played by kinship. That which we call in the lower animals instinct, and in man natural affection, which prompts the dog to suckle its young, and men and women to rear, and support, and educate, and lavish wealth upon, their children, exhibits the strength of kinship in the highest degree. There is, and has been, no more important agency than this in the distribution of wealth. Assuredly it was once among the most important agencies, when the relations of kinship and the family bond were understood to include more than they now do. We saw that communal property was among the oldest ways of holding property. A correlative fact to this is the sense of common origin among the members of the commune, or clan, or gens. The common name of the clan frequently shows this sense, and still more plainly it is shown in the comprehensiveness of their notions of kinship. It has been pointed out by M. Dareste that wherever property is held in common, the communal owners believe that they have sprung from a common stock ; and each person may observe for himself how, as collective property disappears, as run rigg is abandoned, as it ceases to be the custom to divide the common land at stated intervals, the degrees of affinity which are recognised, and which are regarded as involving the responsibility of support, are narrowed. The chief of the Clan Keppoch, or of the sept Butler, looked after the wellbeing of every clansman or septman as of a relation. The clansman was understood to be some far-off relative of the chief, entitled to support in need.

Wealth devoted to religion, to the erection of temples and churches, to the performance of sacrifices, ceremonials, and services, and to the support of ministers, priests, and other religious officials, falls to be considered here. This forms no insignificant domain. The economical effects of religions are vast. Take into account the character of not a few of the religions that are, or have been, prevalent. Mark how they regarded their deities, framed in their own likeness, as big ruffians, to be appeased by lavish gifts, by costly sacrifices and libations. Pass in mental review all that we know from history of the costliness of the superstitions of antiquity ; the temples on which the art of antiquity was expended, and in which the treasure of kings and states was hoarded, the costly sacrifices, the offerings, the apparatus for augury and omens. Add to this the fact that there is no satisfactory evidence of any tribe being wholly devoid of some arrangements for worship, necessarily involving expense, while we possess abundant evidence of tribes which neither buy nor sell. Everywhere savages, in some rude, coarse fashion, try to appease the unknown powers which they believe encompass them. They, children in their understandings, and mere animals in their instincts, give to the gods their own earthy appetites. Their gods or demons are to be appeased by huge bonbons, by ample largesses of the sweatmeats and good things of the country. Re-enter the circle of European life, and observe how the Church, when it emerged from persecution, and when it had gained possession of the seats of authority, drew to itself the wealth of the world. Penitent kings and nobles, dying men, souls sick of the turmoil of the world, and longing for repose—that *ennui* of the middle ages—superstitious fear and love for mankind, laid their contributions on the altar. By the vices and virtues of primitive times the Church profited. It acquired goodly lands. The revenues of monasteries equalled those of States. The Church swallowed up the communal lands. The very mendicant orders were wealthy, and men that had taken vows of poverty administered thousands of pounds. The Reformation and the confiscation of the monasteries shook some fruit from the boughs. They are now all but stripped by needy States. More and more are churches coming to be dependent upon voluntary contributions. With large differences of opinion in regard to religious truth, with no appearance of many of these differences disappearing, with a growing respect for them, it is becoming daily more and more dubious to thinkers of all shades whether a certain portion of public property should be set aside for the support and propagation of doctrines that are by no means believed by the whole public. As this feeling grows, churches will be more and more compelled to trust to the free offerings of their adherents ; and as these free offerings are liable to fluctuate, and especially as they are not always forthcoming in the localities in which they are most wanted, it will be necessary for churches to frame schemes of sustentation. The all-embracing genius of Dr. Chalmers may be said to have found what may be called Ecclesiastical Economy. The happy combination of the Sustentation Fund with the congregational funds, exhibited by the Free Church of Scotland, is an example which others may have to imitate.

All money given in charity falls to be considered here ; and vistas, truly immense, open up when this word is mentioned. This domain is boundless. To keep alive the sick, and the aged, and the indigent, we have to-day Poor-laws. Nature's poor-law is starvation. The wounded stag is left by its mates to perish. The sick or weak die off in youth in the struggle for existence. If the infirm and the sick are not exposed, as they were in the chief States of Greece, if infanticide is not practised and recommended, as it was by Aristotle, it is too probable that the fate of the poor is slavery. It is the second form of poor relief. Pauperism does not arise in the present circumstances so much from abundance as from the inferior quality of population. It is found where the population is by no means dense, and where real wages are high.* It is due to the fact that humanity forbids us to kill off the weak, or to suffer them to die. Such is probably the only efficacious mode of immediately dealing with pauperism ; and in declining to employ it society has declared that it prefers to endure the inconveniences of pauperism to witnessing any of its members starve. He that does not or cannot work shall not eat, is the only law that can effectually secure the world from non-valeurs; and this law having been abrogated, we must expect to find every system of poor relief accompanied with more or less evils, and a state of equilibrium wanting. A poor-law and no abuses are contradictions. One fault of our poor-law now and in past times is that it has not frankly committed itself to either principle. Giving rations inadequate to keep men in working condition, or indulging in insults and petty annoyances, only brutalises the pauper, and renders his redemption impossible.† And thus one law is often in the latest form marked by the cruelty of the natural law of starvation without its efficacy.

When slavery and exposure ceased to prevent the growth of pauperism, there arose organisations for the relief of paupers, and these were of a public or ecclesiastical nature. We shall glance at a few specimens of both kinds of organisation. In the ancient world, with population sparse and each man in tribal relationship, with the natural law of selection freely working, it was impossible for pauperism to spring up, unless in large towns. That which we understand by pauperism —a vast and dense collection of the permanently destitute —perhaps arose first in Rome, whither flocked escaped slaves and all the waifs of a world. A rude poor-law was

---

* "There is a real pauper and vagrant class in New York and Philadelphia, although unlimited supplies of land are to be had, on the lowest possible terms, in the neighbouring Western States. How astonishing still is the pauperism in Australia, with mutton at 1½d. a pound, and miners' wages at £2 : 5s. and upwards a week !"—*Sir C. Trevelyan.*

† See a striking passage in Combe's *Moral Philosophy.*

framed by the Emperors. During the Republic, it had not been uncommon to distribute corn at reduced prices. This liberality was by and by petrified into a custom; and as Rome increased in influence corn was distributed gratis to all citizens; the distribution became systematic; a time had arrived when dense poverty was a permanent fact; pauperism existed; and the right to assistance was recognised. It is to be observed, however, that assistance was not given to the poor throughout the empire. Only a few cities, where there were vast collections of poor, copied the example of Rome. In Antioch and Alexandria there were paupers; there were few outside the great towns. It was the Church that first extended relief across the whole face of Europe. Every monastery was, theoretically at least, the guardian of the poor. 'Poverty was no crime, all charity was virtuous. The beggar knocked as freely at the door of the monastery as at that of a casual ward. The immense domains of the Church were, in a sense, the patrimony of the poor. In a certain rude fashion the Church discharged its duty; and, unless when famine came, the poor were fed. The confiscation of the immense possessions of the monasteries, comprising more than a third part of the real property of the kingdom, was, therefore, a severe blow to the poor in England. The relief given by parishes was at first but a sorry substitute.

Before Henry VIII. confiscated the possessions of the monasteries, the Legislature had passed not a few laws regarding the poor. It is frequently assumed that these and the earlier English Poor-laws were dictated by a spirit of charity; but close examination of these laws does not confirm this natural assumption and surmise. The ugly truth appears to be that some of them were intended to diminish, instead of increasing, the resources of the labourers — to hurt, not help them. Strange as it may appear, certain portions of the English Poor-law apparently originated in attempts to impoverish the poor; and for some time efforts, with scarcely an alloy of charity, were made to render the labourer more helpless. Serfage, or prædial slavery, which had arisen out of pure slavery, and, in some rare cases, by voluntary abnegation of liberty, having passed away in England, employers paid with reluctance the wages which freemen demanded; and when the great famine in the middle of the fourteenth century had thinned the ranks of labour, wages and this reluctance increased. Various attempts, therefore, beginning with the Statute of Labourers, were made by Parliaments of employers to fix the rate of wages, and to pen up labourers in their native parishes. So cruel were these statutes, so well contrived to keep men poor, that they give plausibility to the assertion that the English pauper is an artificial production, the miserable work of guilty laws. How could there not be stagnant pools of pauperism created, when the natural flow of labour towards a common level was arrested, and when poverty was dammed up by barriers or penalties? A statute passed in the reign of Henry VIII. provided for the relief of the poor; the previous statutes had spoken only of restrictions. The famous forty-third of Elizabeth directed the parishes to relieve the blind, the lame, and the impotent, and to provide work for those out of it. It is to be observed that alongside this Act were others which gave the Justices of the Peace power to fix the rate of wages, and to confine the poor to their parishes by means of heavy penalties. The Justices of the Peace did not always exercise this power, which had fallen into desuetude long before the Acts had been repealed. In 1662 a change in the Settlement-laws took place; and, harsh as the new measure was, it was a considerable relaxation. The poor were not to be strictly confined to their parishes; they were permitted to migrate; but whenever the overseers thought that a stranger was likely to become chargeable to the parish, they could remove him. It was not until the end of last century that the removal of all but those actually chargeable was forbidden. In 1722 the workhouse system was begun. Those that received parochial relief might be compelled to reside in the workhouses. Towards the end of the century it became customary to supplement wages by rates, with the view of supplying the labourer with a minimum rate of wages. No device more fatal to the working classes could have been chosen. Wages were paid in rates. Nothing could have been more ruinous than the administration of the English Poor-law at the end of last century and the beginning of this. We told the peasant that the more he introduced to his lot—then a lot of misery and heavily-taxed bread—the better he deserved of his country. Pitt spoke of giving him a cow provided he were in want. We told him on no account to curb his passions. The wages of thoughtlessness and imprudence, Nature had said, were sufferings heavy and grievous; but the squire, and the rector, and the farmer, said that Nature was wrong, and that the wages of thoughtlessness and imprudence were regular wages, paid by the parish in hard money. " We want soldiers," said one; " We want cheap labour," said another; "Are not the Scripture's commands ' Multiply and replenish the earth?' " asked a third. The fruits of this teaching and the English Poor-law ripened terribly. Natural laws avenged themselves on the poor and on the rich. As Mr. Charles Knight truly observes in describing that time, the dream of Pharaoh, that " seven lean and ill-favoured kine did eat up seven fat kine ; and when they had eaten them up, it could not be known that they had eaten them, but they were still ill-favoured as at the beginning," was all but realised under the old Poor-law.

CHAPTER XXXI.

PAUPERISM—(*Continued*).

PARISHES sent in petitions, the burden of which was that "the annual value of lands, mines, and houses in this parish is not sufficient to maintain the numerous and increasing poor, even if the same were free of rent." Here was one parish, which sixty years ago had not contained a single pauper, so overrun by paupers that the entire land, with the exception of sixteen acres, was abandoned as unprofitable, the rates having absorbed the rent. These times are not far distant: they are but one remove from us; and yet, turning over their records, we seem to be contemplating a state of society separated from ours by centuries. Antipathy of the poor towards the rich as such, the antipathy of the rich towards the poor because they were poor, machine-breaking, and burning of ricks in order to cheapen bread and vex farmers—all this common, betokened a state of disaffection and anarchy of which we can form with great difficulty an adequate conception. From 1812 to 1832 it is probable that "Merry England" contained within it as much misery as ever was contained within the same space. We are ready to speak of a country being in danger of being "ruined." It is a frequent phrase, and generally it is much too big for the occasion. People are prone to say that such and such a thing "saved" the country, and generally this phrase is the exaggeration of rhetoricians who employ the grandest words on all occasions. Yet for once these phrases were truthful; in sober truth, this country was in danger of being "ruined" by pauperism, and the Act of 1834 may be said to have "saved" it from anarchy.

In August 1834, the Poor-Law Amendment Act was passed. By it a Central Board was appointed, with large powers. The main change effected in virtue of this Act was the residence in the workhouses or poorhouses which might be required of all persons in receipt of parochial relief. Pauperism was to be made more manifestly a disagreeable lot. The natural stimulus to extricate oneself from dependence on others was to be replaced. The diet of the poorhouse was to be plain, so that idleness and dependence should have no dainty flesh-pots. All the little luxuries which the poorest day-labourer can procure for himself were to be removed; and all means short of cruelty were to be taken to remind the pauper that the sooner he earned a livelihood for himself the better for him. It cannot be the right of one who owes his life to the bounty of others, who has failed to earn a livelihood, who is a pensioner on the resources of the world, without perhaps having added to these resources one handful, to bring into the world children whose fate will too probably be very wretched, and who will certainly have to be maintained throughout youth by strangers; and, therefore, the sexes were separated, the men being put in one department and the women in another. This arrangement has been pronounced cruel, and piteous pictures have been painted of the wife torn from the arms of her husband, and all because they were poor. This is sad, no doubt : if the world was constructed otherwise than it is, if food increased just as population increased, the wife and husband would be suffered to remain together. But, the world being as it is, poverty being dependent on population, how much sadder to see children enter life almost predestined to know nothing of the sweets of competency, and to drink the bitterness of want and poverty, and to inhale from their earliest days the degrading associations of the poorhouse ! Surely the lot of these children is not to be forgotten ; and the State that gives the pauper bread and shelter may ask as the price of its beneficence that he shall not multiply. The man that exists by the favour and at the expense of others possesses no claims to more than a bare subsistence. It is much if he receives the necessaries of life. This Act instituted numerous other improvements. It is true that the evils appear to be reviving ; but there is good reason to believe that under the old poor-law they would have become ere this intolerable.

In Scotland, previous to 1845, the relief of the poor had been left to private benevolence, or to a very irregular system of public charity. True, ever since the year 1579, there had been power to levy assessments. Power was given " to taxe

and stent the haill inhabitants within the parochin, according to
the estimation of their substance, without exception of personnes,
to sik ouklie charge and contribution as sall be thocht expedient
and sufficient to sustaine the saidis puir peopill." But as the
exercise of this power was not compulsory, many parishes in
Scotland, especially in the Highlands, continued to raise no
rates.   In 1845, a new system was introduced, which reproduced some of the principles of the English Poor-law.   A Board
of Supervision was established to "inquire into the management
of the poor in every parish or burgh in Scotland."   The chief
difference in the administration of the Scotch Poor-law is, that
the able-bodied are not entitled to relief, and that out-door relief,
instead of being somewhat rare as in England, is a common mode
of dispensing it in Scotland.   In Scotland, however, there is a
growing tendency to employ the workhouse test.   Other points
of difference are, the fact that all parishes in Scotland are not
compelled to assess themselves, and that the ecclesiastical origin
of poor relief is still attested in the anomalous right of the kirk-
sessions to elect members to the Parochial Board.

In France there is no Poor-law, as we understand it ; and
private charity, aided by assessments and subventions, attends
to the relief of the poor.   Take the city of Paris ; the following
is the manner in which the money for the relief of the poor is
raised :—

The budget of Paris charities for 1862 shows an expenditure of
£1,001,184 : 8 : 6, including £99,349 for breadstuffs, £57,053 : 12s.
for wine, £69,068 : 16s. for meat, and £66,800 for other kinds of food.
Indigent children cost £94,300 : 15s. ; and out-door relief amounted to
£130,809 : 1 : 8.   This is a large sum spent annually on the relief of
the poor and the gratuitous treatment of the sick.   It is raised in
various ways.   In the first place, the property belonging to the hospi-
tals and the poor produces an income of £102,795 : 17s.   Then the admissions to the theatre are taxed to the poor to the extent of £64,000.
The poor take a percentage of the profits arising from the sale of graves
in the cemeteries—for 1862 this percentage produced £7800.   The Central Bakery produced £76,800.   There are also small items ; the entire
sum being made up by a municipal subvention for ordinary expenses of
£361,829.

We subjoin another passage from Mr. Jerrold's *Children of
Lutetia*, as explanatory of the mode of relieving the poor :—

I grant that they have no poor-laws framed on our model ; but he who says that there is no poor-law in Paris, for instance, speaks in his ignorance. Is not every public amusement taxed for the poor ? and are not the markets, as I have shown, compelled to yield something of their profits for the necessitous ? In twenty different ways laws, and customs which are as strong as laws, tax all classes of the well-to-do for the benefit of the poor. Every Bureau of Benevolence has its own particular plan for laying its population under contribution. Even from the ration of the soldier there is a spoonful for the hungry. No poor-law in France ! In Paris, at least, I know there are a hundred poor-laws ; many of them, I can vouch for it, being most excellent, because least felt by those who are just removed beyond the operations of charity. Every man, woman, and child, is directly appealed to on behalf of the poor.

These facts will help to put the reader in a position to judge of the best mode of relieving the poor. And a question which meets us at the threshold of this inquiry is, whether the relief of the poor should be left to the care of private charity, or whether it should be taken up by the State as a public duty. Many persons dispose of this question very summarily, with the remark that as no man has a right to be supported by others, as charity is a merit, not a duty, it follows, or rather is therein involved, that nobody ought to be compelled to be charitable. Charity is a favour, they say, and for the State to impose charity as a duty is to overstep its province. Now, in this favourite position, occupied by Dr. Chalmers, Faucher, Bastiat, and Spencer, lurk several fallacies. According to popular classification, actions that are good are divided into two kinds—those which it is a duty to perform, and those which it is meritorious to perform. So far this is proper ; but it is fallaciously assumed that actions which are ranged under the one category in certain circumstances, may not be properly ranged under the other in different circumstances, and that actions bearing a common name are for ever relegated into one or other of these categories. Let us explain. These actions agree in the circumstance that they both conduce to the general happiness. All moralists, whether they hold that this is *the* criterion of the morality of actions, or that it is *a* criterion of morality, or that it is a theoretical criterion which cannot be employed in practice, will assent to this. Look now, in this light, at the difference between duties and meritorious actions. It would be desirable to see both kinds of actions carried out, but if we must choose, it would be most desirable to see the former carried out. The existence of society would necessarily be imperilled if men were permitted to murder ; the existence of society need not be imperilled if men gave nothing to the lame and the impotent. The first reason, then, why law inculcates preservation of life as a duty, and does not always inculcate charity, is, that the former is generally of more consequence than the latter. Again, every command or law is so far an evil : it involves an outlay of force ; to carry out the law, punishment and pain must be inflicted, and unless something is to be gained by the infliction of pain, it is, of course, an unwarrantable evil. To cut off a man's leg is an evil to be justified only by his suffering from disease ; to order a man to be thrown into jail is also an evil, defensible only in the event of some advantage being gained. Not only is every law an evil, and indefensible unless it accomplishes some benefit, but the pain inflicted must never counterbalance the advantage to be gained by it. Now, this is a second reason why charity is generally left optional ; in enforcing charity it is reasonable to suppose that we should inflict evil out of proportion to the good we should effect. Thirdly, it is not always easy to distinguish those cases in which persons acting out of charity will produce injurious results from those in which they will do good. It is easy to see that the respecting of every man's property is good ; but it is not easy to ascertain with accuracy in what cases charity ought to be given. To give each man his life is good ; to give alms to every man that is in want may not be good, but may sometimes be ruinous. This is a third reason why charity is not always enforced. But it may sometimes happen that these circumstances are absent. It may be, in the first place, that poverty has grown to such a pitch that the existence of society, or at all events social order, is imperilled ; and we have but to recall the state of matters which existed in this country in the first quarter of this century, in order to perceive times when this danger menaced us. It may be, in the second place—and if ravenous mobs clamoured for bread it would be the case—that the penal consequences necessary in order to extort money for charitable purposes would be immensely counterbalanced by the benefits that would be produced. Thirdly, the distress may be so general, the necessity for relief so clear, that it cannot be a matter of doubt that the giving of charity would benefit, not deteriorate, those that received it. When these circumstances are present, the State may as reasonably enact laws for this purpose of raising poor-rates as it enacts them to protect men. Even Dr. Chalmers admitted that a great many kinds of distress ought to be alleviated by public charity. When the Irish famine raged, was not the Government justified in giving several millions to relieve the starving multitudes? And the supporters of the Poor-laws maintain that existing circumstances correspond to those stated here; that the poor cannot be left in destitution without danger to society; that the irritation which the compulsory payment of poor-rates causes is immensely outweighed by the boon which they confer; and that there are hundreds of thousands who are really in need. To put the matter in another light :—Our duties are of two kinds, perfect and imperfect obligations—*i.e.*, those which force may be employed in order to carry out, and the contrary. Usually charity falls within the latter class, but sometimes it does not. When the reasons against employing force are absent, when it would be dangerous to leave distress unrelieved, when the penalties indispensable to a poor-law would be atoned for by a clear gain, when there are persons who unmistakably deserve relief, charity becomes a perfect obligation. An ignoring of this, it appears to me, is one of the weak points in the arguments of Dr. Chalmers, Herbert Spencer, Bastiat, Léon Faucher, and many others, who declare that money for the relief of the poor ought not to be raised by force.

I pass to a second fallacy involved in their positions. Most of these economists say that the State cannot concern itself with aught but the protection of its subjects. Whenever it oversteps this, it goes out of its province; it becomes an oppressor; it quits its own territory, and invades that of the private individual, says the plausible but somewhat shallow Bastiat, when it concerns itself with the relief of the poor. Here is not one fallacy, but several. Even were it true that the State should only protect, it may be pursuing this legitimate path when it forces everybody well off to help those that are badly off. It may thus save the community from crimes that would be sure to be committed by reckless hordes of poor. It may even save the community from an insurrection, the rallying cries of which would be, " War to the castles, peace to the cottages," " Bread or lead," " Bread or blood "—an insurrection of starvation ; and Bacon has told us, and each one may guess, that a revolt of the belly is the worst of all revolts. Bowing, then, to this arbitrary circumscription of the province of Government, we may, nevertheless, hold that a poor-law may be defensible. But this theory is wrong ; and to most minds it will be a sufficient refutation of it, that no Government has confined itself to preserving peace. He who says that all men have erred in a problem which all have tried, must produce arguments of demonstration or credentials of inspiration. Bastiat may be addressed in his own words, used in another connection. " When a man has got the length of saying to his fellows— ' From the days of Adam to our time the human race have been upon a wrong course ; and if only a little confidence is placed in me, I shall soon bring them back to the right way again.' . . . When a man sets out in this style, it is much if he is believed by five or six adepts ; but between that and being believed by one thousand millions of men the distance is great indeed." Precisely ; and these words should have been taken to heart by Bastiat himself. Strange, indeed, would it be if the province of all Governments, whether a thorough despotism or a pure democracy, were the same. Strange if intervals of times and differences of situation made no radical difference in the province of Governments.

Sir Henry Maine, in his book on *Ancient Law*, has illustrated the prevalence in ethical and legal speculations of belief in a social contract which at some unknown day in the depths of antiquity was formed, and by which society arose. Men met together one fine morning, and agreed to live in society. This agreement has been called the Social Contract. Of course, this contract is a pure fiction, a philosophical romance. No record of such an agreement exists, and the faint glimmer of light which ancient law throws on the early conditions of mankind shows them existing in families, not, as the Social Contract necessarily supposed, a number of loose units. This notion, once openly employed by political philosophers of all sorts—by Hobbes, Locke, Grotius, Rousseau, and, with certain modifications, by Hume, for example—to explain the origin of society, still lurks in the minds of many, and is, I doubt not, the father of the prevalent conception of the limits of Government. If rude savages met together in order to form a Government, what could their object be but to surrender to Government those functions which all Governments agree in attempting to perform ? To protect is the only thing which Governments can necessarily do better than private persons; and as this advantage was the only one which the fictitious human units could be expected to count upon obtaining from forming a society, the unconscious believers in the Social Contract conclude that men entered society in order to obtain this, and that to attempt to do more is a breach of trust on the part of the directors of society. Hume roundly says that men entered society for the sake of protection : the people, " voluntarily, for the sake of peace and order, abandoned their native liberty." This theory, false historically, is ethically wrong. The province of Government is the doing of what it can do better than private persons; and as no two Governments are alike, as the only one quality in which they agree—the possession of power—involves no similarity as to how much that power can accomplish or how much it can accomplish well, as the relation of subjects to rulers in regard to intelligence and morality varies widely, as no Government continues to possess exactly the same power and the same ability to wield it for the public interest, it follows that the province of no two Governments, or of the same Government at two different periods, is exactly the same. A common objection to relief by the State is, that it demoralises men by severing from idleness the penalties which nature has attached to it. State relief, it is said, declares that even if a man labour not he shall live. But this argument, if good for anything, is good against private benevolence ; for, if private benevolence is efficient, none, not even the idle, are suffered to starve. True, men will become less provident if their existence is assured; but if private benevolence wounds prudence less than public charity, it is because under a system of the former character men are more liable to suffer want. Again, it is objected, that if there were no relief the labourer would be equally well off, seeing wages would rise to such a point as would enable him to support himself in old age, in sickness, and when work failed. This is to credit the labourer with the prudential habits of the capitalist, and to suppose every ploughman ordering his life as a great shipping company orders its affairs. As a matter of fact, nine out of ten will forget old age, and assume that work will always be plentiful, and their health always good. " Necessary " wages may mean to them sufficient to procure necessaries in ordinary times. When hardship comes, they may be found penniless.

Are we to say that pauperism is an inevitable and inseparable accompaniment of civilised society? Must the problem of misery never find a solution? Cannot those who, when physical difficulties are to be overcome, justly hold the most sanguine language, contrive to put every person in the way of obtaining his own living? Are the alternatives starving and pampering? The answer commonly given to these questions is desponding. Men are here pessimists. They are disposed to say that it is as inevitable that there should be paupers as that there should be blind and lame. Like captives who have tried to break their bonds and have been baffled, they succumb in despondency and chagrin. And yet is this despondency justified? Some considerations seem to make us doubt whether it is. Draw a circle round those whose bodily ailments or imperfections, physical or mental, prevent them from earning their bread. This is the fixed quantity which it falls to charity, public or private, to tend. These " incurables" are few. Except in the case of insanity, these malformations are not increasing, and, as we become better acquainted with the laws which regulate the growth of human monstrosities, we may hope to foresee and prevent them to some extent. The rest, and the great majority of paupers, are the victims of no disease or malformation inevitably incapacitating them for work. The bulk of the men can handle a spade in some fashion, and the women can nurse a child or scour a room. This is so far encouraging. And lazy, awkward, " feckless," to use an expressive Scotch word, as they are, it will probably be possible to conceive circumstances in which any one of these men, neither imbeciles nor invalids, could earn a comfortable livelihood. Let a vast series of strikes take place among unskilled labourers ; let emigration drain away the farmer's hands ; let the supply of labour be diminished by these or other means ; let there be an enormous expansion in the demand for labour ; and the majority of the present dependants on the bounty of society would become the providers of themselves. Not a few who are now frozen in lethargy through idleness would be thawed into activity by the hope of a considerable wage. Except those whose vagabond propensities were deeply implanted by years of residence in casual wards and workhouses, high wages would stimulate to activity the vast body of paupers. The able-bodied person who is a pauper, because of the pleasures that compete for ascendency over him idleness proves the strongest, would perhaps move his sluggish limbs and brain if shown that pleasures far transcending that of doing nothing were at his beck. At present these paupers are *non-valeurs*. They are, economically considered, in the same position as lands of indifferent quality skirting the margin of some settlement. These lands lie barren until the growth of population, with the consequent necessity of widening the food-supplying area, confers upon them value, and forces the community to resort to soil that before yielded nothing for man. Then, that which brought its owner nothing, brings him a rent. So, when a demand for labour extends, faculties which were worth nothing to their owner bring him wages.

Not only can we conceive of times and situations in which the bulk of the existing paupers would be absorbed by industry, but we can recall times and situations in which they would have been absorbed. And this much may be admitted without pandering to nonsense about the gloriousness of past times ; on the contrary, it is a corollary from progress. The standard of a good workman has been raised, and is being raised. The industrial "passmen" might have taken honours a century ago. Man ceasing to be employed as a motive power, sheer strength does not suffice. Intelligence is exacted of the private when his weapons and manœuvres are complicated. If one is to rise above the sorriest drudgery and work of the most unremunerative kind, education must be added to native talents. Enough of wages to stimulate men to work and to buy pleasures that overpower those of idleness can be obtained only by those who have been well trained ; and thus the pauper, of necessity ill-trained, does not feel the very spur which he most needs. At the same time, we attribute more significance to the rise in the moral standard required of the workman as industry progresses, and is organised. The workman forms a part of a vast organism : he is a wheel, or the tooth of a wheel, belonging to a vast machine ; and if that wheel or tooth snap, or do not move smoothly, a vast machine works inefficiently, and is perhaps by and by brought to a stand. The modern artisan must, therefore, conform to numerous regulations ; he must come and go as a master decrees ; he must not fail to appear when he is wanted, for his absence may be a loss to many besides himself ; he is enlisted in a regular army, and must abandon the license of a guerrillist. All different when each man worked in his own workshop : then he was answerable to no man for his time, and he could lay aside his tools in a mood of idleness, and loll in the tavern until his purse was empty and his credit gone. A man with vagabond instincts might work when work itself was a species of vagabondage. How different now ! Enter the first factory ; mark the demeanour of the hands, the activity, unremitting attention that is exacted of all during the hours of work on pain of expulsion ; observe how those who at home are quarrelsome and talkative, and fitful and eccentric, here school themselves and put aside their weaknesses. Turn from this picture of discipline to Hogarth's picture of the idle apprentice ; will not one say that no caricaturist who desired to strike effectively at vice would paint an apprentice at his loom, with a pot of beer before him, and sunk in sluggish sleep ? While deploring the wasteful habits of workmen, employers who have ample experience will bear testimony to an improvement in the habits of their workmen, and will acknowledge that permanent or protracted intoxication is rarer than it once was. The very vices which employers denounce are but the drawbacks to gains vastly outweighing them. Employers complain that workmen are less easily satisfied than they once were : this discontent, which the workmen call self-respect, indicates the presence of qualities that are valuable. It indicates that the workman has begun to think for himself : he is no longer a mere machine ; he is on the way to being a good citizen, though perhaps he travels at a slow pace, and stops to dispute with his fellow-travellers.

Here, then, we arrive at another cheering conclusion.* It is not retrogression or degradation, absolute as well as relative, that is to be deplored ; it is the fact that a portion of the race has been stationary, and has squatted in content, while the rest of mankind has been on the march. And consolation does not stop here : will any visitor to the houses of those who recruit pauperism, as he breathes the enervating and brutalising atmosphere laden with vice or at best stupidity, hears the coarse language

---

* " L'humanité dans sa marche est une colonne de soldats, qui, partis du même pas et au même instant aux battements mesurés du tambour, perdent peu à peu leurs intervalles. Tout avance ; mais la distance de la tête à la queue s'allonge sans cesse ; et c'est un effet necessaire du mouvement qu'il y ait des trainards et des égarés."—*Proudhon.*

which forms the daily bread of the inmates, marks the ignorance devoid of all curiosity save that of pruriency, dare to
vaunt that, had he been exposed to these noxious influences, he
would have been an industrious citizen, able and eager to provide for himself? Will he not rather confess that circumstances, which he did not control, and for which he has no merit,
made him respectable and respected? Will it not strike him
that his excellences as well as their vices are to a great extent
felicitous accidents?

Looking at the State systems of charity, as administered in
England and Scotland, even with an eye not disposed to exaggerate failings, we cannot fail to observe some defects, and one
of them is this : We labour to relieve paupers with considerable
success ; but we do little to obviate the necessity of relieving
them. State charity comes to the aid of those who have fallen,
and of those only. It forbears to put forth a hand to support the
man that is tottering; when he lies prostrate on the ground, everything is at his service.* Now, what should we say of the sani-
tary arrangement of a city, in which men may fling filth into the
streets, and in which all that is done is to remove the filth
when the streets become almost impassable? Would it not be
better to stay the evil at the fountainhead?—to bar the flood
when it is a brook, not when it is a resistless river? Private
charity is open to the same criticism. Thus we have Magdalene
Asylums in abundance ; but how few asylums to save girls and
women from being Magdalenes ! Horne Tooke speaks of a poor
friendless girl who asked to be admitted to a Magdalene Asylum,
and who was told she could not, seeing she was pure. By and
by she returned—and was admitted. Unfortunately, the case
is still not an impossibility ; and it will continue to be so, so
long as want of foresight or pedantic adhesion to routine
forbids the establishment of societies designed to prevent
the necessity of people sinking into want and degradation.
Charity is not organised—this is the second fault. A game
of cross purposes is assiduously played by the State and
private charities ; private societies pull to pieces the work of
the State, devoting what energies they can spare to the task of

---

* " The damning fault of the Poor-law is, that it does not even profess to
improve the condition of the poor, so as to offer a prospect, however distant, of extinguishing pauperism, or reducing it to a minimum."—Sir
Charles Trevelyan's *Articles on London Pauperism.*

pulling against each other. Charity distributed by the State is tolerable at all, and does not produce monstrous consequences—does not make industry deserted—because to the doles are attached certain disagreeable penalties—because dependence is made disagreeable to all those who can extricate themselves from it. But what avails this harsh and healthy teaching if, in the next street, is a house where relief is dispensed without inquiry?—if birth in a certain parish, or attendance at church, constitutes a title to so many loaves a-year or so many shillings a-week? State benevolence, however well administered, tends to blunt the sting of dependence; between them State charity and private charity tend to break it. Not only do the State and the private charities checkmate each other, but private charities exist alongside each other, jealously ignoring each other, and sometimes zealously labouring to undo the work of each other. And it is possible for a cunning knave to obtain a moderate competence by sponging upon several institutions. Private charity, it seems to us, would be in its fit place were it the complement of public charity; each private charity would do its duty were it the complement of all the others. And as State machinery, necessarily made to discharge duties in the gross, and incapable of bending itself to humour each case, is not well adapted to remedy pauperism, private benefactors ought to retire from the field occupied by the State, and labour to raise those that have fallen, and to save others who are on the road to ruin. There private benevolence would find a broad domain, which it might till with unmixed good. So great is the need of a due separation of the provinces of the two charities, that it is a matter for question whether the French are not right in declaring all charitable bequests invalid unless they are approved of by the State. Happily in London and several other towns there begins to be evinced a sincere desire to organise the different private charities, and to demarcate their province from that of the State charities.

Of the various remedial measures, the most popular, though not the most efficacious, is emigration. To remove paupers, or men being in danger of becoming so, would be a superficial remedy, unless they were removed in vast numbers. To remove a few paupers fails to effect much good. It is but plucking a weed here and there in an overrun field; the seed of the jungle that is left quickly effaces your work. Apart from emigration on a large scale, it is to "the might of little means" we must trust. And among those little means judicious loans should perhaps count. Here we should take a hint from France. And when we say "judicious," this is only to indicate a much larger principle, that it is not so much money or money's worth in articles, as painstaking observation, a readiness to sacrifice time, and, generally speaking, a disposition to care for the poor, that are needed. It may be well to mention that this principle has been tried in Paris and New York with marked success. The Edinburgh Association for the Relief of the Poor is a successful experiment in this direction.

A third defect is the absence of classification of the inmates of workhouses and poorhouses. Apart from the division of the two sexes, and the sick and the infirm, there is often little or no classification. A workhouse is a jumble of unfortunates, corrupting or incommoding each other.

A fourth is the remnant of the laws of settlement. These laws originated in a desire to pen up the poor within certain limits, and the effects were to reduce them to a state of dependence if not villenage. Though modified in a great degree, they still arrest the natural tide of emigration. As residence is required in order to give a settlement in a parish, men hesitate to remove even when they could immeasurably better their condition. These laws breed pauperism in another way; with settlement laws in existence, the landowner is tempted to refuse houses to labourers in order that they may not acquire settlement. In England, previous to the passing of the Union Chargeability Act, this was carried to a most mischievous excess. A systematic attempt was made to clear parishes, and to drive the poor (quoting the words of a Royal Commission) "into dwellings more fitted for brutes than for human beings." The time for the utter abolition of these laws, condemned as far back as 1847 by a Select Committee of the House of Commons, as "productive of hardship to the poor, and injurious to the working-classes, by impeding the free circulation of labour," and "injurious to employers," and "injurious to ratepayers," has come. But would not, it will be asked, the abolition of these laws create great inequalities in the distribution of the burdens? Would not the towns be overtaxed? In considering these questions it must be borne in mind that the burdens are at present irregularly distributed, and that the evil has not to be created : it exists. The laws of settlement do not remove, perhaps do not alleviate, this inequality. But if it did happen that the poor congregated in particular localities, to the detriment of the ratepayers therein, it does not appear impossible to find a remedy, and arrangements such as the following would probably succeed :—Let there be levied in each union or parish an ordinary rate to be devoted to the relief of the poor therein, and a much smaller and extraordinary rate—say one-fourth of the former—which would pass into the hands of the Poor-law Board or the Board of Supervision, to be dealt with by these Boards. When the rates had risen to a certain sum, to be fixed by the Boards, the parish or union might receive a grant out of this supplemental fund. In this way the burdens would be more equally distributed, and, at the same time, the ratepayers' interest in keeping down the rates would not be, or would be only inappreciably, diminished.

Lastly, the great poor-law of England is not to be found in her statute-book but in her schools, and it consists less of penalties than the diffusion of innocent amusements and the increase of the general health ; and only when we possess a healthy population will pauperism cease. When all defects in our institutions are blotted out by the hand of the law or private intelligence, and when public and private charities are all that could be desired — the helpmates of each other, preventing misery as well as alleviating it, and permitting population to flow freely and to find its level—the poor will be long with us, unless they co-operate. For consider the fact which must be faced. When a manufacturer has on his hands goods that will not sell, what does it behove him to do ? To contract his stock, to cease to produce, or to take it elsewhere. Well, in this England and Scotland, be it sadly and firmly said, the stock of men of inferior endowments is too large. If these inferior human goods are to be sold, if they are to receive wages that will keep them in comfort, they must contract the supply. It is in their power to do so. It is in their power, therefore, to better their condition.

INDEX.

———

Printed by R. CLARK, *Edinburgh.*

88 PRINCES STREET,
Edinburgh, June 1875.

EDMONSTON & DOUGLAS'
LIST OF WORKS.

——o0o——

The Culture and Discipline of the Mind, and other Essays.
By JOHN ABERCROMBIE, M.D. New Edition. Fcap. 8vo, cloth, 3s. 6d.

Wanderings of a Naturalist in India,
The Western Himalayas, and Cashmere. By DR. A. L. ADAMS of the 22d Regiment. 8vo, with Illustrations, price 10s. 6d.
"The author need be under no apprehension of wearying his readers. . . He prominently combines the sportsman with the naturalist."—*Sporting Review.*

Notes of a Naturalist in the Nile Valley and Malta.
By ANDREW LEITH ADAMS. Author of ' Wanderings of a Naturalist in India.' Crown 8vo, with Illustrations, price 15s.
"Most attractively instructive to the general reader."—*Bell's Messenger.*

The Orkneyinga Saga.
Edited, with Notes and Introduction, by JOSEPH ANDERSON, Keeper of the National Museum of the Antiquaries of Scotland. 1 vol. demy 8vo. Price 10s. 6d.
"Will supply a desideratum in our early historical literature that has long been felt. '
"No labour seems to have been spared that was required to make the Saga interesting and intelligible to the ordinary student of history."—*Scotsman.*

Alexandra Feodorowna, late Empress of Russia.
By A. TH. VON GRIMM, translated by LADY WALLACE. 2 vols. 8vo, with Portraits, price 21s.
"Contains an amount of information concerning Russian affairs and Russian society."—*Morning Post.*

Always in the Way.
By the author of 'The Tommiebeg Shootings.' 12mo, price 1s. 6d.

The Malformations, Diseases, and Injuries of the Fingers
and Toes, and their Surgical Treatment. By THOMAS ANNANDALE, F.R.C.S. 8vo, with Illustrations, price 10s. 6d.

Odal Rights and Feudal Wrongs.
A Memorial for Orkney. By DAVID BALFOUR of Balfour and Trenaby. 8vo, price 6s.

Sermons by the late James Bannerman, D.D., Professor of Apologetics and Pastoral Theology, New College, Edinburgh. In 1 vol., extra fcap. 8vo, price 5s.

The Life, Character, and Writings of Benjamin Bell, F.R.C.S.E., F.R.S.E., author of a 'System of Surgery,' and other Works. By his Grandson, BENJAMIN BELL, F.R.C.S.E. Fcap. 8vo, price 3s. 6d.

On the Action of Mercury.
By Professor J. H. BENNETT. Second Edition. 8vo, cloth, price 4s.

The Holy Grail. An Inquiry into the Origin and Signifi- cation of the Romances of the San Greäl. By Dr. F. G. BERGMANN. Fcap. 8vo, price 1s. 6d.

"Contains, in a short space, a carefully-expressed account of the romances of chivalry, which compose what has been called the Epic cycle of the San Greäl."— *Athenæum.*

Bible Readings. Fcap. 8vo, price 2s.

"The Author of these Readings has realised the worth of the Bible through her own experience and through the experience of the humble women whom she has tried to educate ; her homage to it is indicated in every page by the freedom and courage with which she avails herself of its illuminations, by her confidence that when God speaks, we can hear and know his voice."—*Spectator.*

Homer and the Iliad.
In Three Parts. By JOHN STUART BLACKIE, Professor of Greek in the University of Edinburgh. 4 vols. demy 8vo, price 42s.

By the same Author.

On Self-Culture : Intellectual, Physical, and Moral.
A *Vade-Mecum* for Young Men and Students. Sixth edition. Fcap. 8vo, price 2s. 6d.

"Every parent should put it into the hands of his son."—*Scotsman.*

"Students in all countries would do well to take as their *vade-mecum* a little book on self-culture by the eminent Professor of Greek in the University of Edinburgh."—*Medical Press and Circular.*

"An invaluable manual to be put into the hands of students and young men." —*Era.*

"Written in that lucid and nervous prose of which he is a master.—*Spectator.*

Four Phases of Morals : Socrates, Aristotle, Christianity, and Utilitarianism. Lectures delivered before the Royal Institution, London. Fcap. 8vo, second edition, price 5s.

Musa Burschicosa.
A Book of Songs for Students and University Men. Fcap. 8vo, price 2s. 6d.

War Songs of the Germans.
Fcap. 8vo, price 2s. 6d. cloth ; 2s. paper.

Political Tracts.
No. 1. GOVERNMENT. No. 2. EDUCATION. Price 1s. each.

On Greek Pronunciation.
Demy 8vo, 3s. 6d.

On Beauty.
Crown 8vo, cloth, 8s. 6d.

Lyrical Poems.
Crown 8vo, cloth, 7s. 6d.

The New Picture Book. Recreative Instruction.
Pictorial Lessons on Form, Comparison, and Number, for Children under Seven Years of Age. With Explanations by NICHOLAS BOHNY. Fifth Edition. 36 oblong folio coloured Illustrations. Price 7s. 6d.

Daily Meditations by Rev. G. Bowen of Bombay.
With introductory notice by Rev. W. HANNA, D.D., author of 'The Last Day of our Lord's Passion.' Second Edition, small 4to, cloth, price 5s. ; or French morocco, red edges, price 7s. 6d.

"Among such books we shall scarcely find another which exhibits the same freshness and vividness of idea, the same fervour of faith, the same intensity of devotion. . . . I count it a privilege to introduce in this country a book so fitted to attract and to benefit."—*Extract from Preface.*

"These meditations are the production of a missionary whose mental history is very remarkable. . . . His conversion to a religious life is undoubtedly one of the most remarkable on record. They are all distinguished by a tone of true piety, and are wholly free from a sectarian or controversial bias."—*Morning Post.*

The Home Life of Sir David Brewster.
By his daughter, Mrs. GORDON. 2d Edition. Crown 8vo, price 6s.

"With his own countrymen it is sure of a welcome, and to the *savants* of Europe, and of the New World, it will have a real and special interest of its own." —*Pall Mall Gazette.*

France under Richelieu and Colbert.
By J. H. BRIDGES, M.B. Small 8vo, price 8s. 6d.

Works by John Brown, M.D., F.R.S.E.
JOHN LEECH, and other papers. Crown 8vo. *In the press.*

LOCKE AND SYDENHAM. Extra fcap. 8vo, price 7s. 6d.

HORÆ SUBSECIVÆ. Eighth Edition. Extra fcap. 8vo, price 7s. 6d.

LETTER TO THE REV. JOHN CAIRNS, D.D. Second Edition, crown 8vo, sewed, 2s.

ARTHUR H. HALLAM ; Extracted from 'Horæ Subsecivæ.' Fcap. sewed, 2s. ; cloth, 2s. 6d.

RAB AND HIS FRIENDS ; Extracted from 'Horæ Subsecivæ.' Forty-ninth thousand. Fcap. sewed, 6d.

RAB AND HIS FRIENDS. Cheap Illustrated Edition. Square 18mo ; ornamental wrapper, 1s.

RAB AND HIS FRIENDS. With Illustrations by Sir George Harvey, R.S.A., Sir J. Noel Paton, R.S.A., and J. B. New Edition, demy quarto, cloth, price 6s.

MARJORIE FLEMING : A Sketch. Fifteenth thousand. Fcap. sewed, 6d.

OUR DOGS ; Extracted from 'Horæ Subsecivæ.' Nineteenth thousand. Fcap. sewed, 6d.

"WITH BRAINS, SIR ;" Extracted from 'Horæ Subsecivæ.' Fcap. sewed, 6d.

MINCHMOOR. Fcap. sewed, 6d.

JEEMS THE DOORKEEPER : A Lay Sermon. Price 6d.

THE ENTERKIN. Price 6d.

Memoirs of John Brown, D.D.

By the REV. J. CAIRNS, D.D., Berwick, with Supplementary Chapter by his Son, JOHN BROWN, M.D. Fcap. 8vo, cloth, 9s. 6d.

Select Hymns for Church and Home.

By R. BROWN-BORTHWICK. 18mo, price 2s. 6d.

The Life of Gideon.

By REV. JOHN BRUCE, D.D., Free St. Andrew's Church, Edinburgh. 1 vol. fcap. 8vo, price 5s.

"We commend this able and admirable volume to the cordial acceptance of our readers."—*Daily Review.*

Business.

By a Merchant. 1 vol. fcap. 8vo, price 7s. 6d.

"A masterpiece of gorgeous writing, and altogether he deserves the name of the 'Poet-Laureate of Trade.'"—*Dundee Advertiser.*

"This little book, if it is not unfair to suggest such a comparison, belongs to the same class as 'Burton's Anatomy of Melancholy.'"—*Saturday Review.*

On Teaching, its Ends and Means.

By HENRY CALDERWOOD, LL.D., Professor of Moral Philosophy in the University of Edinburgh. Second Edition, fcap. 8vo, price 2s. 6d.

"A reliable guide for teachers."—*Courant.*

"Eminently sensible and suggestive."—*Scotsman.*

By the Loch and River Side.

Forty Graphic Illustrations by a New Hand. Oblong folio, handsomely bound, 21s.

My Indian Journal,

Containing descriptions of the principal Field Sports of India, with Notes on the Natural History and Habits of the Wild Animals of the Country. By COLONEL WALTER CAMPBELL, author of 'The Old Forest Ranger.' 8vo, with Illustrations, price 16s.

Popular Tales of the West Highlands,

Orally Collected, with a translation by J. F. CAMPBELL. 4 vols. extra fcap. cloth, 32s.

Inaugural Address at Edinburgh,

April 2, 1866, by THOMAS CARLYLE, on being Installed as Rector of the University there. Price 1s.

Carswell's Gaelic Prayer Book.

The Book of Common Prayer, commonly called John Knox's Liturgy. Translated into Gaelic, A.D. 1567, by Mr. JOHN CARSWELL, Bishop of the Isles. Edited, with an English Translation, by THOMAS M'LAUCHLAN, LL.D., Translator of the Book of the Dean of Lismore. 4to, *half Roxburghe.* Price 30s.

On the Constitution of Papal Conclaves.

By W. C. CARTWRIGHT, M.P. Fcap. 8vo, price 6s. 6d.

"A book which will, we believe, charm careful students of history, while it will dissipate much of the ignorance which in this country surrounds the subject."—*Spectator.*

Gustave Bergenroth. A Memorial Sketch.

By W. C. CARTWRIGHT, M.P. Author of 'The Constitution of Papal Conclaves.' Crown 8vo, price 7s. 6d.

" To those who knew this accomplished student, Mr. Cartwright's enthusiastic memoir will be very welcome."—*Standard.*

Life and Works of Rev. Thomas Chalmers, D.D., LL.D.

MEMOIRS OF THE REV. THOMAS CHALMERS. By REV. W. HANNA, D.D., LL.D. Cheap Edition, 2 vols., crown 8vo, cloth, 12s.

Daily Scripture Readings. Cheap Edition, 2 vols., crown 8vo, 10s. ASTRONOMICAL DISCOURSES, 1s. COMMERCIAL DISCOURSES, 1s. SELECT WORKS, in 12 vols., crown 8vo, cloth, per vol., 6s.

Lectures on the Romans, 2 vols. Sermons, 2 vols. Natural Theology, Lectures on Butler's Analogy, etc., 1 vol. Christian Evidences, Lectures on Paley's Evidences, etc., 1 vol. Institutes of Theology, 2 vols. Political Economy ; with Cognate Essays, 1 vol. Polity of a Nation, 1 vol. Church and College Establishments, 1 vol. Moral Philosophy, Introductory Essays, Index, etc., 1 vol.

Characteristics of Old Church Architecture, etc.,

In the Mainland and Western Islands of Scotland. 4to, with Illustrations, price 25s.

Dainty Dishes.

Receipts collected by LADY HARRIETT ST. CLAIR. New Edition, with many new Receipts. Crown 8vo. Price 5s.

" Well worth buying, especially by that class of persons who, though their incomes are small, enjoy out-of-the-way and recherché delicacies."—*Times.*

Journal of Henry Cockburn, being a Continuation of the

"Memorials of his Time," 1831-1854. By HENRY COCKBURN, one of the Judges of the Court of Session in Scotland. 2 vols. 8vo, price 21s.

" It would be impossible to get too much of Henry Cockburn. . . . It is to be dreaded we have now got all that he has left us. . .". The result is a work which, if specially delightful and valuable as a contribution to Scotch history, is also an important, though in some respects special or detached, addition to English literature."—*Scotsman.*

Archibald Constable and his Literary Correspondents: a

Memorial. By his Son, THOMAS CONSTABLE. 3 vols. 8vo, price 36s., with Portrait.

" The cream of a generation of interesting men and women now gone from among us—these are the subjects of this important memoir." – *Saturday Review.*

"These three volumes are decidedly additions to our knowledge of that great and brilliant epoch in the history of letters to which they refer."—*Standard.*

" He (Mr. Constable) was a genius in the publishing world. . . . . The creator of the Scottish publishing trade."—*Times.*

"These three volumes are of a singular and lasting interest."—*Nonconformist.*

" The third volume (Sir Walter Scott) of this elaborate and interesting history is almost an independent work."—*Athenæum.*

" We heartily commend this book to the notice of all readers."—*Guardian.*

Wild Men and Wild Beasts—Adventures in Camp and
Jungle. By LIEUT.-COLONEL GORDON CUMMING. With Illustrations by Lieut.-
Col. BAIGRIE and others. Second edition. Demy 4to, price 24s.
　　Also, a Cheaper Edition, with *Lithographic* Illustrations. 8vo, price 12s.

The Church of Scotland: her Position and Prospects.
By REV. J. E. CUMMING, D.D. Crown 8vo, price 3s.

Notes on the Natural History of the Strait of Magellan
and West Coast of Patagonia, made during the voyage of H.M.S. 'Nassau' in the
years 1866, 1867, 1868, and 1869. By ROBERT O. CUNNINGHAM, M.D., F.R.S.,
Naturalist to the Expedition. With Maps and numerous Illustrations. 8vo, price 15s.
　　"There is a good deal of interesting and novel information in the present
volume, and we can recommend it especially to those whose tastes lie in that
direction."—*Standard.*

Gisli the Outlaw.
From the Icelandic. By G. W. DASENT, D.C.L. Small 4to, with Illustrations,
price 7s. 6d.

The Story of Burnt Njal;
Or, Life in Iceland at the end of the Tenth Century. From the Icelandic of the
Njals Saga. By GEORGE WEBBE DASENT, D.C.L. 2 vols. 8vo, with Map and
Plans, price 28s.

Plates and Notes relating to some Special Features in Struc-
tures called Pyramids. By ST. JOHN VINCENT DAY, C.E., F.R.SS.A. Royal
folio, price 28s.

By the same Author.

Papers on the Great Pyramid. 8vo, price 4s.

Some Evidence as to the very early Use of Iron. 8vo, sewed,
price 2s. 6d.

On a Remarkable Stone in the Great Pyramid. Price 3s.

The Law of Railways applicable to Scotland, with an
Appendix of Statutes and Forms. By FRANCIS DEAS, M.A., LL.B., Advocate.
1 vol. Royal 8vo, price 38s.
　　"Probably the best book on Railway Law to be found at this moment within
the three kingdoms."—*Courant.*
　　"Indeed, for fulness, clearness, and explicitness of information, we could not
name a better; and for accuracy of thinking, for exhaustive treatment, and articu-
late arrangement of all materials appropriate to its subject, and for precision, ele-
gance, and flexibility of literary style, we doubt if it has many equals."—*Scotsman.*

· The Amazon.
An Art Novel. By!FRANZ DINGELSTEDT. Fcap. 8vo, price 2s.
　　"It belongs to a class of novels of which *Wilhelm Meister* is chief—the *art* novel."
—*North British Review.*

Manual of Chemical Analysis.
By W. DITTMAR, Professor of Chemistry in the Andersonian University, Glasgow.
1 vol. fcap. 8vo. [In the Press.

The Large Game and Natural History of South and South-
East Africa. From the Journals of The Hon. WILLIAM HENRY DRUMMOND.
8vo, Illustrated, price 21s.

"The freshest and most interesting sporting book that has appeared for many
a day; freshest in subject and in treatment, most interesting in the novelty of its
scenes and the greatness of its adventures, is the Hon. W. H. Drummond's Large
Game of the South and South-East Africa."—The Scotsman.

Memoir of Thomas Drummond, R.E., F.R.A.S., Under-Secre-
tary to the Lord-Lieutenant of Ireland, 1835 to 1840. By JOHN F. M'LENNAN,
Advocate. 8vo, price 15s.

"A clear, compact, and well-written memoir of the best friend England ever
gave to Ireland."—Examiner.

Political Survey.
By MOUNTSTUART E. GRANT DUFF, Member for the Elgin District of Burghs;
Author of 'Studies in European Politics,' 'A Glance over Europe,' &c. &c. 8vo,
price 7s. 6d.

By the same Author.

Elgin Speeches. 8vo, cloth, price 8s. 6d.

A Glance over Europe. Price 1s.

Address as Rector at the University of Aberdeen. Price 1s.

East India Financial Statement, 1869. Price 1s.

Remarks on the Present Political Situation. Price 1s.

Expedit—Laboremus. Price 1s.

Veterinary Medicines; their Actions and Uses.
By FINLAY DUN. Fourth Edition, revised and enlarged. 8vo, price 12s.

Social Life in Former Days;
Chiefly in the Province of Moray. Illustrated by letters and family papers. By
E. DUNBAR DUNBAR, late Captain 21st Fusiliers. 2 vols. demy 8vo, price
19s. 6d.

The late Rev. John Duncan, LL.D., in the Pulpit and at the
Communion Table. With a Biographical Supplement. Edited by DAVID BROWN,
D.D., author of "The Life of John Duncan, D.D." Crown 8vo, price 7s. 6d.

Deep-Sea Soundings. Colloquia Peripatetica.
By the late JOHN DUNCAN, LL.D., Professor of Hebrew in the New College,
Edinburgh; being Conversations in Philosophy, Theology, and Religion. Edited
by REV. W. KNIGHT, Dundee. Fourth Edition. 1 vol. fcap. 8vo. Price 3s. 6d.

"Since these lectures were published there has appeared an exceedingly
interesting volume, entitled 'Colloquia Peripatetica,' by the late John Duncan,
LL.D., Professor of Hebrew in the New College, Edinburgh. These Colloquies are
reported by the Rev. William Knight, who seems to be admirably adapted for the
task he has undertaken. His friend must have been a man of rare originality,

varied culture, great vigour in expressing thoughts, which were worthy to be expressed and remembered. . . . . . The reader who shall give himself the benefit and gratification of studying this short volume (it will suggest more to him than many of ten times its size) will find that I have not been bribed to speak well of it by any praise which Dr. Duncan has bestowed on me. The only excuse for alluding to it is, that it contains the severest censure on my writings which they have ever incurred, though they have not been so unfortunate as to escape censure. . . . . Against any ordinary criticism, even a writer who is naturally thin-skinned becomes by degrees tolerably hardened. One proceeding from a man of such learning and worth as Dr. Duncan I have thought it a duty to notice." — *Extract from Preface to 'The Conscience.' By the late Professor F. D. Maurice. Second Edition,* 1872.

Recollections of the late John Duncan, LL.D., Professor of

Hebrew and Oriental Languages, New College, Edinburgh. By the REV. A. MOODY STUART. Extra fcap. 8vo, 3s. 6d.

"Mr. Moody Stuart had rare opportunities of knowing Dr. Duncan."—*Manchester Guardian.*

Edmonston and Douglas' Juvenile Library.

Square 18mo, with Illustrations. 1s. each.

DICK AND I.	NELLY RIVERS' GREAT RICHES.
LITTLE TALES FOR TINY TOTS.	STORIES TOLD IN THE WOOD.
BIRDS' NEST STORIES.	NEW NIGHT-CAPS.
THE CHARITY BAZAAR.	LITTLE TRIX, OR GRANDMAMMA'S LESSONS.

A Memoir of the Right Honourable Hugh Elliot,

By his Granddaughter, the COUNTESS of MINTO. 8vo, price 12s.

"Lady Minto produced a valuable memoir when she printed the substance o the work before us for private circulation in 1862. It now, in its completed shape, presents a full-length and striking portrait of a remarkable member of a remarkable race."—*Quarterly Review.*

The Spiritual Order, and other Papers selected from the MSS.

of the late THOMAS ERSKINE of Linlathen. Crown 8vo, cloth, price 5s.

"It will for a few have a value which others will not the least understand. But all must recognise in it the utterance of a spirit profoundly penetrated with the sense of brotherhood, and with the claims of common humanity."—*Spectator.*

"Very deserving of study."—*Times.*

By the same Author.

The Unconditional Freeness of the Gospel.

New Edition revised. Crown 8vo. Price 3s. 6d.

An Essay on Faith. Fourth Edition, 12mo, 3s.

Good Little Hearts.

By AUNT FANNY. Author of the 'Night-Cap Series.' 4 vols., fancy covers, 1s. each; or cloth extra, 1s. 6d. each.

Charity Bazaar.	Nelly Rivers' Great Riches.
Birds' Nest Stories.	Stories Told in the Wood.

First Fruits and Shed Leaves. 1 vol. fcap. 8vo, price 5s.

" The author seems to possess many of the qualities which go to make a poet. He has much lyrical power. The prose essay is one of the best parts of the book." —*Graphic.*

" He (the author) touches the solemn and the tragic as he touches the tender and the true, with a fine vigour, in which strength and gentleness are fitly joined." —*Scotsman.*

L'Histoire d'Angleterre. Par M. LAMÉ FLEURY. 18mo, cloth, 2s. 6d.

L'Histoire de France. Par M. LAMÉ FLEURY. New Edition, corrected to 1873. 18mo, cloth, 2s. 6d.

Christianity viewed in some of its Leading Aspects.
By REV. A. L. R. FOOTE, Author of 'Incidents in the Life of our Saviour.' Fcap. cloth, 3s.

Autobiography of Mrs. Fletcher (of Edinburgh), with Letters
and other Family Memorials. Edited by her daughter. Crown 8vo, price 7s. 6d.

" This is a delightful book. It contains an illustrative record of a singularly noble, true, pure, prolonged, and happy life. The story is recounted with a candour, vivacity, and grace which are very charming."—*Daily Review.*

Kalendars of Scottish Saints, with Personal Notices of those
of Alba, etc. By ALEXANDER PENROSE FORBES, D.C.L., Bishop of Brechin. 1 vol. 4to. Price £3 : 3s. A few copies for sale on large paper, price £5 : 15 : 6.

" A truly valuable contribution to the archæology of Scotland."—*Guardian.*

" We must not forget to thank the author for the great amount of information he has put together, and for the labour he has bestowed on a work which can never be remunerative."—*Saturday Review.*

" His laborious and very interesting work on the early Saints of Alba, Laudonia, and Strathclyde."—*Quarterly Review.*

The Deepening of the Spiritual Life.
By A. P. FORBES, D.C.L., Bishop of Brechin. Fifth edition. 18mo, cloth, price 1s. 6d.; or paper covers, 1s. ; calf, red edges, 3s. 6d.

Frost and Fire;
Natural Engines, Tool-Marks, and Chips, with Sketches drawn at Home and Abroad by a Traveller. Re-issue, containing an additional Chapter. 2 vols. 8vo, with Maps and numerous Illustrations on Wood, price 21s.

" A very Turner among books, in the originality and delicious freshness of its style, and the truth and delicacy of the descriptive portions. For some four-and-twenty years he has traversed half our northern hemisphere by the least frequented paths ; and everywhere, with artistic and philosophic eye, has found something to describe—here in tiny trout-stream or fleecy cloud, there in lava-flow or ocean current, or in the works of nature's giant sculptor—ice."—*Reader.*

The Cat's Pilgrimage.
By J. A. FROUDE, M.A., late Fellow of Exeter College, Oxford. With 7 full page Illustrations by Mrs. BLACKBURN (J. B.) 4to, price 6s.

Gifts for Men. By X. H.

1. The Gift of Repentance.
2. The Gift of the Yoke.

3. The Gift of the Holy Ghost.
4. The Promise to the Elect.

Crown 8vo, price 6s.

" There is hardly a living theologian who might not be proud to claim many of her thoughts as his own."—*Glasgow Herald.*

Glimpses of Life in Victoria.

By a Resident. 8vo, with Illustrations, price 12s.

"Out of sight the best book about Australia that has come into our hands."— *British Quarterly.*

The Gospel in Isaiah : being an Exposition of the 55th and

56th Chapters of the Book of his Prophecies. By JOHN GEMMEL, M.A., Fairlie. Ex. fcap. 8vo, price 5s.

Arthurian Localities : their Historical Origin, Chief Country,

and Fingalian Relations, with a Map of Arthurian Scotland. By JOHN G. S. STUART GLENNIE, M.A. 8vo, price 7s. 6d.   :

Works by Margaret Maria Gordon (née Brewster).

WORKERS. Fourth thousand. Fcap. 8vo, limp cloth, 1s.

WORK ; or, Plenty to do and How to do it. Thirty-fifth thousand. Fcap. 8vo, cloth, 2s. 6d.

LITTLE MILLIE AND HER FOUR PLACES. Cheap Edition. Fifty-fifth thousand. Limp cloth, 1s.

SUNBEAMS IN THE COTTAGE ; or, What Women may do. A narrative chiefly addressed to the Working Classes. Cheap Edition. Forty-fourth thousand. Limp cloth, 1s.

PREVENTION ; or, An Appeal to Economy and Common-Sense. 8vo, 6d.

THE WORD AND THE WORLD. Twelfth edition. Price 2d.

LEAVES OF HEALING FOR THE SICK AND SORROWFUL. Fcap. 4to, cloth, 3s. 6d. Cheap Edition, limp cloth, 2s.

THE MOTHERLESS BOY ; with an Illustration by J. NOEL PATON, R.S.A. Cheap Edition, limp cloth, 1s.

"Alike in manner and matter calculated to attract youthful attention, and to attract it by the best of all means—sympathy."—*Scotsman.*

' Christopher North ;'

A Memoir of John Wilson, late Professor of Moral Philosophy in the University of Edinburgh. Compiled from Family Papers and other sources, by his daughter, MRS. GORDON. Third Thousand. 2 vols. crown 8vo, price 24s., with Portrait, and graphic Illustrations.

' Mystifications.'

By Miss STIRLING GRAHAM. Fourth Edition. Edited by JOHN BROWN, M.D. With Portrait of ' Lady Pitlyal.' Fcap. 8vo, price 3s. 6d.

Scenes from the Life of Jesus.

By SAMUEL GREG. Second Edition, enlarged. Ex. fcap. 8vo, price 3s. 6d.

"One of the few theological works which can be heartily commended to all classes."—*Inverness Courier.* ·

Arboriculture ; or, A Practical Treatise on Raising and ·

Managing Forest Trees, and on the Profitable Extension of the Woods and Forests of Great Britain. By JOHN GRIGOR, The Nurseries, Forres. 8vo, price 10s. 6d.

"He is a writer whose authorship has this weighty recommendation, that he can support his theories by facts, and can point to lands, worth less than a shilling an acre when he found them, now covered with ornamental plantations, and yielding through them a revenue equal to that of the finest corn-land in the country. . . . His book has interest both for the adept and the novice, for the large proprietor and him that has but a nook or corner to plant out."—*Saturday Review.*

" Mr. Grigor's practical information on all points on which an intending planter is interested is particularly good. . . . We have placed it on our shelves as a first-class book of reference on all points relating to Arboriculture ; and we strongly recommend others to do the same."—*Farmer.*

An Ecclesiastical History of Scotland,

From the Introduction of Christianity to the Present Time. By GEORGE GRUB, A.M. 4 vols. 8vo, 42s.

The Laws of Trade-Unions in England and Scotland.

By WILLIAM GUTHRIE, Advocate. 8vo, price 3s. 6d.

"Should be in the hands of every Trade Union officer in the kingdom."—GEORGE HOWELL, *Secretary of Parliamentary Committee on Trade Unions.*

Chronicle of Gudrun ;

A Story of the North Sea. From the mediæval German. By EMMA LETHER-BROW. With frontispiece by Sir J. NOEL PATON, R.S.A. New Edition, price 5s.

Notes on the Early History of the Royal Scottish Academy.

By Sir GEORGE HARVEY, Kt., P.R.S.A. Second Edition. 8vo, price 3s. 6d.

The Resurrection of the Dead.

By WILLIAM HANNA, D.D., LL.D., author of 'The Last Day of our Lord's Passion,' etc. 1 vol. fcap. 8vo, price 3s. 6d.

The Life of our Lord.

By the REV. WILLIAM HANNA, D.D., LL.D. 6 vols., handsomely bound in cloth extra, gilt edges, price 30s.

Separate vols., cloth extra, gilt edges, price 5s. each.

1. THE EARLIER YEARS OF OUR LORD. 8th Thousand.
2. THE MINISTRY IN GALILEE. Third Edition.
3. THE CLOSE OF THE MINISTRY. 6th Thousand.
4. THE PASSION WEEK. 5th Thousand.
5. THE LAST DAY OF OUR LORD'S PASSION. 47th Thousand.
6. THE FORTY DAYS AFTER THE RESURRECTION. 9th Thousand.

The Guidman of Inglismill, and The Fairy Bride.

. Legends of the North. With Glossary, etc. 4to, price 2s. 6d.

Heavenly Love and Earthly Echoes.

By a Glasgow Merchant. 7th Edition. 18mo, price 1s. 6d.

" Fitted to be useful and heart-stirring to all who are in earnest in religion. We hope and believe it will reach many more editions."—*Christian Work.*

Herminius.

A Romance. By I. E. S. Fcap. 8vo, price 6s.

Historians of Scotland.

Price to Non-Subscribers, 15*s. per volume.* An Annual Payment of £1 will entitle the Subscriber to Two annual volumes.

1st Issue.	} FORDUN'S SCOTICHRONICON. Vol. I. WYNTOUN'S CHRONICLE. Vol. I.
2d Issue.	} WYNTOUN'S CHRONICLE. Vol. II. FORDUN'S SCOTICHRONICON. Vol. II.
3d Issue.	} LIVES OF ST. NINIAN AND ST. KENTIGERN. LIFE OF SAINT COLUMBA.

" Mr. Skene has laid students of Scottish history under a further obligation by his careful and scholarlike edition of Fordun's work."—*Quarterly Review.*

** Detailed Lists of the forthcoming Volumes on application.

If the Gospel Narratives are Mythical, what then?

Crown 8vo, price 3s. 6d.

" This is a striking little essay . . . thoughtful and subtle. It is an attempt to show that something like the philosophy of the Christian Gospel would be forced upon us by the facts of our spiritual nature."—*Spectator.*

Lectures on Scotch Legal Antiquities.

By COSMO INNES, F.S.A., author of ' Scotland in the Middle Ages.'

Contents:—I. Introductory. II. Charters. III. Parliament. IV. The Old Church. V. Old Forms of Law. VI. Rural Occupations. VII. Student's Guide Books. VIII. Appendix. In 1 vol. demy 8vo, price 10s. 6d.

By the same Author.

Sketches of Early Scotch History. 8vo, price 16s.

Concerning some Scotch Surnames. Small 4to, cloth antique, 5s.

Instructive Picture-Books.

Folio, 7s. 6d. each.

" These Volumes are among the most instructive Picture-books we have seen, and we know of none better calculated to excite and gratify the appetite of the young for the knowledge of nature."—*Times.*

I.

The Instructive Picture Book. A few Attractive Lessons from the Natural History of Animals. By ADAM WHITE, late Assistant, Zoological Department, British Museum. With 54 folio coloured Plates. Eighth Edition, containing many new Illustrations by Mrs. BLACKBURN, J. STEWART, GOURLAY STEELL, and others.

II.

The Instructive Picture Book. Lessons from the Vegetable World. By the Author of ' The Heir of Redclyffe,' ' The Herb of the Field,' etc. New Edition, with 64 Plates.

III.

The Instructive Picture Book. The Geographical Distribution of Animals, in a Series of Pictures for the use of Schools and Families. By the late Dr. GREVILLE. With descriptive letterpress. New Edition, with 60 Plates.

IV.

Pictures of Animal and Vegetable Life in all Lands. 48 Folio Plates.

V.

Recreative Instruction. Pictorial Lessons on Form, Comparison, and number, for Children under 7 years of age, with explanations. By NICHOLAS BOHNY. Fifth edition. 26 Oblong folio Plates, price 7s. 6d.

The History of Scottish Poetry,

From the Middle Ages to the Close of the Seventeenth Century. By the late DAVID IRVING, LL.D. Edited by JOHN AITKEN CARLYLE, M.D. With a Memoir and Glossary. Demy 8vo, 16s.

Johnny Gibb of Gushetneuk, in the Parish of Pyketillim :

with Glimpses of the Parish Politics about A.D. 1843. Third Edition, with a Glossary. 12mo, ornamental boards, price 2s. ; or cloth, price, 2s. 6d.

"It is a grand addition to our pure Scottish dialect ; . . . . it is not merely a capital specimen of genuine Scottish northern *dialect ;* but it is a capital specimen of pawky characteristic Scottish humour. It is full of good hard Scottish dry fun." —*Dean Ramsay.*

Sermons by the Rev. John Ker, D.D., Glasgow.

Tenth Edition. Crown 8vo, price 6s.

"This is a very remarkable volume of sermons. We have not seen a volume of sermons for many a day which will so thoroughly repay both purchase and perusal and re-perusal. And not the least merit of these sermons is, that they are eminently suggestive."—*Contemporary Review.*

"The sermons before us are indeed of no common order ; among a host of competitors they occupy a high class—we were about to say the highest class— whether viewed in point of composition, or thought, or treatment."—*British and Foreign Evangelical Review.*

Studies for Sunday Evening; or, Readings in Holy Writ.

By LORD KINLOCH. New edition, in 2 vols. fcap. 8vo, price 9s.

By the same Author.

Faith's Jewels.

Presented in Verse, with other devout Verses. Ex. fcap. 8vo, price 5s.

The Circle of Christian Doctrine ;

A Handbook of Faith, framed out of a Layman's experience. Third and Cheaper Edition. Fcap. 8vo, 2s. 6d.

Time's Treasure ;

Or, Devout Thoughts for every Day of the Year. Expressed in verse. Fourth and Cheaper Edition. Fcap. 8vo, price 3s. 6d.

Devout Moments. Price 6d. Hymns to Christ. Fcap. 8vo, price 3s. 6d.

A History of Scotland, chiefly in its Ecclesiastical Aspect,

from the Introduction of Christianity till the Fall of the Old Hierarchy. For the Use of Schools. By M. G. J. KINLOCH. Edited by the BISHOP OF BRECHIN. 18mo, price 2s. 6d.

"Miss Kinloch must have worked hard, and as in a labour of love, to accumulate all the ecclesiastical lore she displays."—*Scotsman.*

Lindores Abbey, and the Burgh of Newburgh: their His-
tory and Annals.   By ALEXANDER LAING, F.S.A. Scot.   1 vol. small 4to.
With Illustrations.   [*Nearly ready.*

The Philosophy of Ethics:
An Analytical Essay.   By SIMON S. LAURIE, A.M.   Demy 8vo, price 6s.

Notes, Expository and Critical, on certain British Theories
of Morals.   By SIMON S. LAURIE.   8vo, price 6s.

The Reform of the Church of Scotland
In Worship, Government, and Doctrine.   By ROBERT LEE, D.D., late Professor
of Biblical Criticism in the University of Edinburgh, and Minister of Greyfriars.
Part I. Worship.   Second Edition, fcap. 8vo, price 3s.

Letters from Jamaica: 'The Land of Streams and Woods.'
Fcap. 8vo, price 4s. 6d.
   " Nowhere else that we know can you get a better idea of the outward aspect of
things in Jamaica."—*Scotsman.*
   " A very entertaining and well-written book."—*Graphic.*
   " Letters from Jamaica certainly do not sin on the side of ' speaking an infinite
deal of nothing.'   They contrive to convey in a little space, and in a pleasant form,
much information about a place and people of unusual interest." — *Pall Mall
Gazette.*

Life among My Ain Folk.
By the Author of " Johnny Gibb of Gushetneuk."   12mo, ornamental boards,
price 2s. ; cloth, 2s. 6d.
   " We find it difficult to express the warm feelings of admiration with which we
have read the present volume."—*Aberdeen Journal.*
   " Here is a rich treat of description, character, humour, and broad fun."—*Non-
conformist.*
   " Done with a skilful and loving hand."—*Daily Review.*

Life in Normandy ;
Sketches of French Fishing, Farming, Cooking, Natural History, and Politics,
drawn from Nature.   By an ENGLISH RESIDENT.   Third Edition, crown 8vo,
cloth, ex. gilt, price 4s. 6d.

A Memoir of Lady Anna Mackenzie,
Countess of Balcarres, and afterwards of Argyle, 1621-1706.   By ALEXANDER
LORD LINDSAY (Earl of Crawford).   Fcap. 8vo, price 3s. 6d.
   " All who love the byways of history should read this life of a loyal Covenanter."
—*Atlas.*

Lismore, Book of the Dean of.
Specimens of Ancient Gaelic Poetry, collected between the years 1512 and 1520,
by the REV. JAMES M'GREGOR, Dean of Lismore—illustrative of the Language
and Literature of the Scottish Highlands prior to the Sixteenth Century.   Edited,
with a Translation and Notes, by the Rev. THOMAS M'LAUCHLAN, LL.D.   The Introduction and additional Notes by WILLIAM F. SKENE, LL.D.   8vo, price 12s.

Literary Relics of the late A. S. Logan, Advocate, Sheriff
of Forfarshire.   Extra fcap. 8vo, price 3s. 6d.

Little Ella and the Fire-King,

And other Fairy Tales. By M. W., with Illustrations by HENRY WARREN. Second Edition. 16mo, cloth, 3s. 6d. Cloth extra, gilt edges, 4s.

Little Tales for Tiny Tots.

With 6 Illustrations by WARWICK BROOKES. Square 18mo, price 1s.

Little Trix; or, Grandmamma's Lessons.

Square 18mo. Price 1s.

A Survey of Political Economy.

By JAMES MACDONELL, M.A. Ex. fcap. 8vo, price 6s.

"The author has succeeded in producing a book which is almost as easy reading as a three-volume novel."—*Athenæum.*

"Of its class it is one of the best we have seen ; and had we to choose for a beginner among the crowd of manuals and introductions to the study, there is much which would induce us to recommend the present volume."—*Spectator.*

"Mr Macdonell's book, entitled 'A Survey of Political Economy,' establishes him as a writer of authority on economical subjects."—MR. NEWMARCH.

Ten Years North of the Orange River.

A Story of Everyday Life and Work among the South African Tribes, from 1859 to 1869. By JOHN MACKENZIE, of the London Missionary Society. With Map and Illustrations. 1 vol. crown 8vo, cloth, extra gilt, price 4s. 6d.

Nugæ Canoræ Medicæ.

By DOUGLAS MACLAGAN, Professor of Medical Jurisprudence in the University of Edinburgh. A new edition, enlarged, with Illustrations by THOMAS FAED, R.A. ; WILLIAM DOUGLAS, R.S.A. ; JAMES ARCHER, R.S.A. ; JOHN BALLANTYNE, R.S.A., etc. In 1 vol. 4to, price 7s. 6d.

DEDICATED BY PERMISSION TO THE QUEEN,

The Hill Forts, Stone Circles, and other Structural Remains

of Ancient Scotland. With Plans and Illustrations by C. Maclagan, Lady Associate of the Society of Antiquaries of Scotland. 1 vol. folio, price 31s. 6d.

"We need not enlarge on the few inconsequential speculations which rigid archæologists may find in the present volume. We desire rather to commend it to their careful study, fully assured that not only they, but also the general reader, will be edified by its perusal."—*Scotsman.*

Memorials of the Life and Ministry of Charles Calder

Mackintosh, D.D., of Tain and Dunoon. Edited, with a Sketch of the Religious History of the Northern Highlands of Scotland, by the Rev. WILLIAM TAYLOR, M.A. With Portrait. Second Edition, extra fcap. 8vo, price 4s. 6d.

Macvicar's (J. G., D.D.)

THE PHILOSOPHY OF THE BEAUTIFUL; price 6s. 6d. FIRST LINES OF SCIENCE SIMPLIFIED; price 5s.

Mary Stuart and the Casket Letters.

By J. F. N., with an Introduction by HENRY GLASSFORD BELL. Ex. fcap. 8vo, price 4s. 6d.

Max Havalaar;

Or, The Coffee Auctions of the Dutch Trading Company. By MULTATULI ; translated from the original MS. by Baron Nahuys. With Maps, price 14s.

Why the Shoe Pinches.

A contribution to Applied Anatomy. By HERMANN MEYER, M.D., Professor of Anatomy in the University of Zurich. Price 6d.

The Estuary of the Forth and adjoining Districts viewed

Geologically. By DAVID MILNE HOME of Wedderburn. 8vo, cloth, with Map and Plans, price 5s.

The Herring :

Its Natural History and National Importance. By JOHN M. MITCHELL. With Six Illustrations, 8vo, price 12s.

The Insane in Private Dwellings.

By ARTHUR MITCHELL, A.M., M.D., Commissioner in Lunacy for Scotland, etc. 8vo, price 4s. 6d.

Creeds and Churches.

By the REV. SIR HENRY WELLWOOD MONCREIFF, Bart., D.D. Demy 8vo, price 3s. 6d.

Ancient Pillar-Stones of Scotland :

Their Significance and Bearing on Ethnology. By GEORGE MOORE, M.D. 8vo, price 6s. 6d.

Political Sketches of the State of Europe—from 1814-1867.

Containing Ernest Count Münster's Despatches to the Prince Regent from the Congress of Vienna and of Paris. By GEORGE HERBERT, Count Münster. Demy 8vo, price 9s.

Biographical Annals of the Parish of Colinton.

By THOMAS MURRAY, LL.D. Crown 8vo, price 3s. 6d.

History Rescued, in Answer to 'History Vindicated,' being

a recapitulation of 'The Case for the Crown,' and the Reviewers Reviewed, *in re* the Wigtown Martyrs. By MARK NAPIER. 8vo, price 5s.

The Natural or the Supernatural.

By a Layman. Fcap. 8vo, cloth, price 2s. 6d.

Nightcaps :

A Series of Juvenile Books. By "AUNT FANNY." 4 vols. square 16mo, cloth. 2s. each volume.

1. Little Nightcaps.	3. New Nightcaps.
2. Big Nightcaps.	4. Old Nightcaps.

" Six pretty little books of choice fiction. The only objection we can make to the quality and fashion of Aunt Fanny's Nightcaps is, that some of their joyous notions are more calculated to keep infantile wearers awake all night than to dispose them to slumber. As nightcaps for the daytime, however, they are, one and all, excellent."—*Athenæum.*

NEW NIGHTCAPS. New and cheaper Edition, Fancy Cover, price 1s.

ODDS AND ENDS—*Price 6d. Each.*

Vol. I., in Cloth, price 4s. 6d., containing Nos. 1-10.
Vol. II.,   Do.   do.   Nos. 11-19. '

1. Sketches of Highland Character.	2. Convicts. 3. Wayside Thoughts.
4. The Enterkin.	5. Wayside Thoughts—Part 2.
6. Penitentiaries and Reformatories.	7. Notes from Paris.
8. Essays by an Old Man.	9. Wayside Thoughts—Part 3.
10. The Influence of the Reformation.	11. The Cattle Plague.
12. Rough Night's Quarters.	13. On the Education of Children.
14. The Stormontfield Experiments.	15. A Tract for the Times.
16. Spain in 1866.	17. The Highland Shepherd.
18. Correlation of Forces.	19. 'Bibliomania.'
20. A Tract on Twigs.	21. Notes on Old Edinburgh.
22. Gold-Diggings in Sutherland.	23. Post-Office Telegraphs.

Poems.

By DOROTHEA MARIA OGILVY, of Clova. Second Edition, crown 8vo, price 4s. paper ; 5s. cloth ; 5s. 6d. cloth gilt.

Willie Wabster's Wooing and Wedding.

By DOROTHEA MARIA OGILVY, of Clova. Second Edition, with Glossary. 12mo, price 1s. 6d.

The Orkneyinga Saga.

Edited, with Notes and Introduction, by JOSEPH ANDERSON, Keeper of the National Museum of the Antiquaries of Scotland. With numerous Illustrations. Price 10s. 6d.

"No labour seems to have been spared that was required to make the Saga interesting and intelligible to the ordinary student of history."—*Scotsman.*

Man : Where, Whence, and Whither ?

Being a glance at Man in his Natural-History Relations. By DAVID PAGE, LL.D. Fcap. 8vo, price 3s. 6d.

Kidnapping in the South Seas.

Being a Narrative of a Three Months' Cruise of H. M. Ship 'Rosario.' By CAPTAIN GEORGE PALMER, R.N., F.R.G.S. 8vo, illustrated, 10s. 6d.

France : Two Lectures.

By M. PREVOST-PARADOL, of the French Academy. 8vo, price 2s. 6d.

"Should be carefully studied by every one who wishes to know anything about contemporary French History."—*Daily Review.*

Suggestions on Academical Organisation,

With Special Reference to Oxford. By MARK PATTISON, B.D., Rector of Lincoln College, Oxford. Crown 8vo, price 7s. 6d.

Practical Water-Farming.

By WM. PEARD, M.D., LL.D. 1 vol. fcap. 8vo, price 5s. ¡

Prince Perindo's Wish.

A Fairy Romance for Youths and Maidens. Crown 8vo, illustrated, price 3s. 6d.

Popular Genealogists;
Or, The Art of Pedigree-making.   Crown 8vo, price 4s.

The Pyramid and the Bible:
The rectitude of the one in accordance with the truth of the other.   By a CLERGY-
MAN.   Ex. fcap. 8vo, price 3s. 6d.

Quixstar.
By the Author of 'Blindpits.'   A Novel, in 3 vols.   Crown 8vo, price 31s. 6d.
   " 'Quixstar' is what George Eliot would call 'a study of provincial life,' and
an exceedingly well-executed and well-rendered study it is."—*Literary World.*
   "Undoubtedly Quixstar is not a book to be swept away with the mere novels of
the season."—*Graphic.*

A Critical History of the Christian Doctrine of Justification
and Reconciliation.   By ALBRECHT RITSCHL, Professor Ordinarius of Theology
in the University of Göttingen.   Translated from the German, with the Author's
sanction, by JOHN S. BLACK, M.A.   8vo, cloth, price 12s.
   "An exceedingly valuable contribution to theological literature.   The history
begins no earlier than the Middle Ages ; since he considers that in earlier times,
while the theory of a price paid to Satan was current, there was no real theology
on the subject.   A more thorough historical study of the doctrine of the Atone-
ment, and a correct understanding and appreciation of the various forms it has
assumed in different schools, are very much needed in this country."—*British and
Foreign Evangelical Review.*

Reminiscences of the 'Pen' Folk.
By one who knew them.   4to, price 2s. 6d.

Reminiscences of Scottish Life and Character.
By E. B. RAMSAY, M.A., LL.D., F.R.S.E., Dean of Edinburgh.   Library Edition,
in demy 8vo, with Portrait by James Faed, price 10s. 6d.
   ⁎ The original Edition in 2 vols., with Introductions, price 12s., is still
on sale.
   "That venerable Dean, who is an absolute impersonation of the 'reminiscences'
of all the Scottish Churches, who in his largeness of heart embraces them all,
and in his steadfast friendship, his generous championship of forgotten truths and
of unpopular causes, proves himself to be in every sense the inheritor of the noble
Scottish name which he so worthily bears."—*Dean Stanley's Lectures on the Church
of Scotland.*

Dean Ramsay's Reminiscences of Scottish Life and Charac-
ter.   The Twenty-third Edition, containing the Author's latest Corrections and
Additions.   With a Memorial Sketch of the Life of Dean Ramsay, by COSMO
INNES.   1 vol. ex. fcap. 8vo, price 6s.
   "This exquisite miniature biography gives to that unique volume a greatly en-
hanced value and attractiveness."—*Daily Review.*

Dean Ramsay's Reminiscences.
85th Thousand, fcap. 8vo, boards, price 2s. ; cloth extra, 2s. 6d.
   "The Dean of Edinburgh has here produced a book for railway reading of the
very first class.   The persons (and they are many) who can only under such circumstances devote ten minutes of attention to any page, without the certainty of a
dizzy or stupid headache, in every page of this volume will find some poignant
anecdote or trait which will last them a good half-hour for after-laughter : one of
the pleasantest of human sensations."—*Athenæum.*

Recess Studies.
Edited by SIR ALEXANDER GRANT, Bart., LL.D.   8vo, price 12s.

Rockbourne.

A Tale. By MARION ELIZA WEIR, author of 'Mabel's Experience,' 'Patience to Work and Patience to Wait,' etc. Ex. fcap. 8vo, cloth, extra gilt, 5s.

"A tale of a very noticeable character."—*Nonconformist.*

"Admirably fitted to be placed in the hands of young people, and may be read with profit by their elders."—*Daily Review.*

A Tale of Ages.

Being a Description of some of the Geological and Historical changes which have occurred in the neighbourhood of Edinburgh. By RALPH RICHARDSON, Hon. Secretary of the Edinburgh Geological Society. Demy 8vo, price 6s.

The One Church on Earth. How it is manifested, and what

are the Terms of Communion with it. By REV. JOHN ROBERTSON, A.M., Arbroath. Extra fcap. 8vo, price 3s. 6d.

Historical Essays in connection with the Land and the

Church, etc. By E. WILLIAM ROBERTSON, Author of 'Scotland under her Early Kings.' In 1 vol. 8vo, price 10s. 6d.

Scotland under her Early Kings.

A History of the Kingdom to the close of the 13th century. By E. WILLIAM ROBERTSON. In 2 vols. 8vo, cloth, 36s.

"Mr. Robertson's labours are of that valuable kind where an intelligent and thorough sifting of original authorities is brought to bear upon a portion of history handed over hitherto, in a pre-eminent degree, to a specially mendacious set of Mediæval Chroniclers, and (not so long ago) to a specially polemical and uncritical class of modern Historians. He belongs to the school of Innes and Skene, and Joseph Robertson, and has established a fair right to be classed with the Reeves and Todds of Irish historical antiquarianism, and the Sharpes, and Kembles, and Hardys in England."—*Guardian.*

Doctor Antonio.

A Tale. By JOHN RUFFINI. Cheap Edition, crown 8vo, boards, 2s.

The Salmon ;

Its History, Position, and Prospects. By ALEX. RUSSEL. 8vo, price 7s. 6d.

A Handbook of the History of Philosophy.

By DR. ALBERT SCHWEGLER. Fifth Edjtion. Translated and Annotated by J. HUTCHISON STIRLING, LL.D., Author of the 'Secret of Hegel.' Crown 8vo, price 6s.

"Schwegler's is the best possible handbook of the history of philosophy, and there could not possibly be a better translator of it than Dr. Stirling."—*Westminster Review.*

"The Germans are fortunate, in consequence of their philosophical criticism, in the production of better and better text-books, among which may be mentioned *Schwegler's History of Philosophy.*"—*Professor Rosenkranz of Konigsberg in Journal of Speculative Philosophy.*

Seven Years of a Life.

A Story. 1 vol. crown 8vo, price 7s. 6d.

The Scottish Poor-Laws : Examination of their Policy,

History, and Practical Action. By SCOTUS. 8vo, price 7s. 6d.

" This book is a magazine of interesting facts and acute observations upon this vitally important subject."—*Scotsman.*

Gossip about Letters and Letter-Writers.

By GEORGE SETON, Advocate, M.A. Oxon., F.S.A. Scot. Fcap. 8vo, price 2s. 6d.

" A very agreeable little *brochure*, which anybody may dip into with satisfaction to while away idle hours." —*Echo.*

' Cakes, Leeks, Puddings, and Potatoes.'

A Lecture on the Nationalities of the United Kingdom. By GEORGE SETON, Advocate, M.A. Oxon., etc. Second Edition. Fcap. 8vo, sewed, price 6d.

Culture and Religion.

By J. C. SHAIRP, Principal of the United College of St. Salvator and St. Leonard, St. Andrews. Fourth Edition, fcap. 8vo, price 3s. 6d.

" A wise book, and, unlike a great many other wise books, has that carefully-shaded thought and expression which fits Professor Shairp to speak for Culture no less than for Religion."—*Spectator.*

John Keble :

An Essay on the Author of the ' Christian Year.' By J. C. SHAIRP, Principal of the United College of St. Salvator and St. Leonard, St. Andrews. Fcap. 8vo, price 3s.

Studies in Poetry and Philosophy.

By J. C. SHAIRP, Principal of the United College of St. Salvator and St. Leonard, St. Andrews. Second Edition, 1 vol. fcap. 8vo, price 6s.

A Memoir of the late Sir James Y. Simpson, Bart. M.D.

By JOHN DUNS, D.D., Professor of Natural Science, New College, Edinburgh. Demy 8vo. With Portrait. Price 14s.

"One of the most charming, instructive, and useful biographies extant."—*Courant.*

" Will be much read and admired."—*Edinburgh Medical Journal.*

Archæological Essays by the late Sir James Y. Simpson,

Bart., M.D., D.C.L. Edited by JOHN STUART, LL.D., Secretary of the Society of Antiquaries of Scotland, Author of 'The Sculptured Stones of Scotland,' etc. etc. 2 vols. sm. 4to, half Roxburghe, price £2 : 2s.

The Four Ancient Books of Wales,

Containing the Cymric Poems attributed to the Bards of the Sixth Century. By WILLIAM F. SKENE. With Maps and Facsimiles. 2 vols. 8vo, price 36s.

"Mr. Skene's book will, as a matter of course and necessity, find its place on the tables of all Celtic antiquarians and scholars."—*Archæologia Cambrensis.*

The Coronation Stone.

By WILLIAM F. SKENE. Small 4to. With Illustrations in Photography and Zincography. Price 6s.

Fordun's Chronicle of the Scottish Nation.

With English Translation. Edited, with Introduction and Notes, by WILLIAM F. SKENE. 2 vols. 8vo, price 30s.

"Mr. Skene has laid students of Scottish history under a further obligation by his careful and scholarlike edition of Fordun's work."—*Quarterly Review, July* 1873.

Sketches of Highland Character. ("But the queys was goot.")

With Seven Full-Page Illustrations by W. RALSTON. Engraved by WILLIAM BALLINGALL and J. D. COOPER. 1 vol. 4to, price 6s.

"The engravings are excellent."—*Standard.*

"Mr. W. Ralston has here the proper subject, and is simply delicious both in drawing and character, and we certainly say with him and the author 'The Queys is Goot.'"—*Nonconformist.*

"Nothing can be happier or truer to nature than the artist's representations. The whole story is indeed excellent, and thus illustrated forms a bit of real life and nationality preserved for all time."—*Inverness Courier.*

Sketches of Highland Character. Cheap Illustrated Edition, small 4to,
sewed, price 1s.

The Sermon on the Mount.

By the REV. WALTER C. SMITH, Author of 'The Bishop's Walk, and other Poems, by Orwell,' and 'Hymns of Christ and Christian Life.' Crown 8vo, price 6s.

Disinfectants and Disinfection.

By DR. ROBERT ANGUS SMITH. 8vo, price 5s.

" By common consent Dr. Angus Smith has become the first authority in Europe on the subject of Disinfectants.—*Chemical News.*

Life and Work at the Great Pyramid.

With a Discussion of the Facts Ascertained. By C. PIAZZI SMYTH, F.R.SS.L. and E., Astronomer-Royal for Scotland. 3 vols. demy 8vo, price 56s.

An Equal-Surface Projection for Maps of the World, and

its Application to certain Anthropological Questions. By C. PIAZZI SMYTH, F.R.SS.L. & E., Astronomer-Royal for Scotland. 8vo, price 3s.

Britain's Art Paradise ; or, Notes on some Pictures in the

Royal Academy, 1871. By the EARL of SOUTHESK. 8vo, sewed, price 1s.

Saskatchewan and the Rocky Mountains.

Diary and Narrative of Travel, Sport, and Adventure, during a Journey through part of the Hudson's Bay Company's Territories, in 1859 and 1860. By the EARL OF SOUTHESK, K.T., F.R.G.S. 1 vol. demy 8vo, with Illustrations on wood by WHYMPER, price 18s.

Sir Walter Scott as a Poet.

By GILBERT MALCOLM SPROAT. 8vo, cloth, price 2s. 6d.

Ruined Castles, Monuments of Former Men, in the Vicinity

of Banff. By JAMES SPENCE. Crown 8vo, price 5s.

"In gleaning out and collecting into a book all that has survived and is at the same time worth preserving in their history, accompanied by succinct and pleasantly-written descriptions and pen-and-ink sketches of their present condition, Mr. Spence has done some service to his county."—*Scotsman.*

Scottish Liturgies of the Reign of James VI., from MSS. in

the British Museum and Advocates' Library. Edited, with an Introduction and Notes, by the Rev. GEO. W. SPROTT, B.A. Extra fcap. 8vo, cloth, price 4s. 6d.

"The title of this book will be enough to make many pass it by as of mere denominational interest. It is, on the contrary, one of national importance, and ought to be carefully studied by all who, through any line of descent, connect themselves with early Scotch Protestantism."—*Courant.*

Memoir of Sir James Dalrymple, First Viscount Stair,

President of the Court of Session in Scotland, and Author of 'The Institutions of the Law of Scotland.' A Study in the History of Scotland and Scotch Law during the Seventeenth Century. By Æ. J. G. MACKAY, Advocate. 8vo, price 12s.

History Vindicated in the Case of the Wigtown Martyrs.

By the Rev. ARCHIBALD STEWART. Second Edition. 8vo, price 3s. 6d.

Dugald Stewart's Collected Works.

Edited by Sir WILLIAM HAMILTON, Bart. 10 vols. 8vo, cloth, each 12s.

Vol. I.—Dissertation. Vols. II. III. and IV.—Elements of the Philosophy of the Human Mind. Vol. V.—Philosophical Essays. Vols. VI. and VII.— Philosophy of the Active and Moral Powers of Man. Vols. VIII. and IX.— Lectures on Political Economy. Vol. X.—Biographical Memoirs of Adam Smith, LL.D., William Robertson, D.D., and Thomas Reid, D.D. ; to which is prefixed a Memoir of Dugald Stewart, with Selections from his Correspondence, by John Veitch, M.A. Supplementary Vol.—Translations of the Passages in Foreign Languages contained in the Collected Works ; with General Index.

The Procession of Pope Clement VII. and the Emperor

Charles V., after the Emperor's Coronation at Bologna, on the 24th February 1530, designed and engraved by NICOLAS HOGENBERG, and now reproduced in facsimile. With an Historical Introduction by Sir WILLIAM STIRLING-MAXWELL, Bart., M.P. In one vol. large folio.

Jerrold, Tennyson, Macaulay, and other Critical Essays.

By JAMES HUTCHISON STIRLING, LL.D., Author of 'The Secret of Hegel.' 1 vol. fcap. 8vo, price 5s.

"Dr. Stirling's opinions are entitled to be heard, and carry great weight with them. He is a lucid and agreeable writer, a profound metaphysician, and by his able translations from the German has proved his grasp of mind and wide acquaintance with philosophical speculation."—*Examiner.*

Songs of the Seasons.

By THOMAS TOD STODDART, Author of 'The Angler's Companion.' Crown 8vo, price 6s.

Christ the Consoler;

Or, Scriptures, Hymns, and Prayers, for Times of Trouble and Sorrow. Selected and arranged by the REV. ROBERT HERBERT STORY, D.D., Minister of Roseneath. Fcap. 8vo, price 3s. 6d.

A Lost Chapter in the History of Mary Queen of Scots Re-

covered, with portrait of Countess of Bothwell, and facsimile of Dispensation. By JOHN STUART, LL.D., Author of 'Sculptured Stones of Scotland.' Fcap. 4to, price 12s. 6d.

"This is an indubitable instance of meritorious treasure trove."—*Scotsman.*

Memoir of James Syme, late Professor of Clinical Surgery in

the University of Edinburgh. By ROBERT PATERSON, M.D., President of the College of Physicians, Edinburgh. With Portrait. 1 vol. crown 8vo, price 7s. 6d.

Works by the late Professor Syme.

OBSERVATIONS IN CLINICAL SURGERY. Second Edition. 8vo, price 8s. 6d.
STRICTURE OF THE URETHRA, AND FISTULA IN PERINEO. 8vo, price 4s. 6d.
TREATISE ON THE EXCISION OF DISEASED JOINTS. 8vo, price 5s.
ON DISEASES OF THE RECTUM. 8vo, price 4s. 6d.
EXCISION OF THE SCAPULA. 8vo, price 2s. 6d.

The History of English Literature.

THE STANDARD EDITION. By H. TAINE, D.C.L. Translated by HENRY VAN LAUN. New and carefully Revised Edition. In 4 vols. small demy 8vo, price 7s. 6d. each ; also kept in half-calf, half-morocco, and full tree-calf bindings, suitable for Presentation and School Prizes.

"The most interesting and the most philosophical history that has been written of English literature."—*Globe.*

"Will take its place in the very foremost rank of works on the literature of England."—*Spectator.*

"Deserves a conspicuous place in every library filled with the immortal works of which it narrates the history."—*Daily News.*

"An excellent text-book for the use of students ; very much superior to any of those now in use at our schools and colleges."—*Examiner.*

Thermodynamics.

By P. G. TAIT, Professor of Natural Philosophy in the University of Edinburgh. New and enlarged edition. [*In preparation.*

Sales Attici :

Or, The Maxims, Witty and Wise, of Athenian Tragic Drama. By D'ARCY WENT-WORTH THOMPSON, Professor of Greek in Queen's College, Galway. Fcap. 8vo. price 9s.

Two Little Rabbits, or the Sad Story of Whitetail.

By G. A. DALRYMPLE. With 8 Illustrations. Square 18mo, price 1s.

Hand-Book of the Education (Scotland) Act, 1872.

Containing—I. A digest of the Act, with subjects grouped for the convenience of School Boards. II. Copy of the Act, with Explanatory Notes. III. The Incorporated Acts, Industrial Schools' Act, etc., and Index.   By JAMES TOD, Advocate.   Fifth Edition.   Crown 8vo, price 5s.

"A valuable and trustworthy guide."—*Courant.*

"The most thorough and most useful companion to the Act."—*Daily Review.*

Travels by Umbra. 8vo, price 10s. 6d.

Hotch-Pot.
By UMBRA.   An Old Dish with New Materials.   Fcap. 8vo, price 3s. 6d.

The Merchant's Sermon and other Stories.
By L. B. WALFORD.   18mo, price 1s. 6d.

"A volume of very modest appearance which deserves more than the brief notice for which we can find space.   The four tales it contains are all pleasant and spirited little stories.   The last of these, 'Polly Spanker's Green Feather,' is really admirable."—*Spectator.*

A History of the Battle of Bannockburn, fought A.D. 1314.
With Map and Armorial Bearings, and Notices of the principal Warriors who engaged in that Conflict.   By ROBERT WHITE, Author of 'A History of the Battle of Otterburn.'   1 vol. 8vo, price 12s.

Dante's—The Inferno.
Translated line for line by W. P. WILKIE, Advocate.   Fcap. 8vo, price 5s.

Researches on Colour-Blindness.
With a Supplement on the danger attending the present system of Railway and Marine Coloured Signals.   By the late GEORGE WILSON, M.D.   8vo, 5s.

Wordsworth's Tour in Scotland in 1803, in company with
his SISTER and S. T. COLERIDGE; being the JOURNAL of MISS WORDSWORTH, now for the first time made public.   Edited by PRINCIPAL SHAIRP, LL.D. Second Edition, 1 vol., crown 8vo, price 9s.

"If there were no other record of her than those brief extracts from her Journal during the Highland Tour, which stand at the head of several of her brother's poems, these alone would prove her possessed of a large portion of his genius. Larger extracts from them occur in the poet's biography and in the edition of the Poems of 1857, and often they seem nearly as good as the poems they introduce. Might not that wonderful Journal even yet be given entire, or nearly so, to the world?"—*North British Review.*

An Historical Sketch of the French Bar, from its Origin to
the Present Day.   By ARCHIBALD YOUNG, Advocate.   Demy 8vo, price 7s. 6d.

"A useful contribution to our knowledge of the leading French politicians of the present day."—*Saturday Review.*

Notes on the Scotch Salmon Fishery Acts of 1862 and 1868.
With Suggestions for their Improvement.   By ARCHIBALD YOUNG, Advocate Commissioner of Scotch Salmon Fisheries, &c. &c.   8vo, price 1s. 6d.

www.ingramcontent.com/pod-product-compliance
Lightning Source LLC
Chambersburg PA
CBHW031822270326
41932CB00008B/516